Frenemies

Why do Americans have such animosity for people who identify with the opposing political party? Jaime E. Settle argues that in the context of increasing partisan polarization among American political elites, the way we communicate on Facebook uniquely facilitates psychological polarization among the American public. *Frenemies* introduces the END Framework of social media interaction. END refers to a subset of content that circulates in a social media ecosystem: a personalized, quantified blend of politically informative "expression," "news," and "discussion" seamlessly interwoven into a wider variety of socially informative content. Scrolling through the News Feed triggers a cascade of processes that result in negative attitudes about those who disagree with us politically. The inherent features of Facebook, paired with the norms of how people use the site, heighten awareness of political identity, bias the inferences people make about others' political views, and foster stereotyped evaluations of the political out-group.

JAIME E. SETTLE is an Associate Professor of Government, director of the SNaPP Lab, and co-director of the Social Science Research Methods Center at the College of William & Mary. She studies the American public's day-to-day experience with politics. Settle has published in *Nature*, the *American Journal of Political Science*, and has been supported by the National Science Foundation.

Frenemies

How Social Media Polarizes America

JAIME E. SETTLE
College of William & Mary

CAMBRIDGE
UNIVERSITY PRESS

CAMBRIDGE
UNIVERSITY PRESS

University Printing House, Cambridge CB2 8BS, United Kingdom

One Liberty Plaza, 20th Floor, New York, NY 10006, USA

477 Williamstown Road, Port Melbourne, VIC 3207, Australia

314–321, 3rd Floor, Plot 3, Splendor Forum, Jasola District Centre, New Delhi – 110025, India

79 Anson Road, #06–04/06, Singapore 079906

Cambridge University Press is part of the University of Cambridge.

It furthers the University's mission by disseminating knowledge in the pursuit of education, learning, and research at the highest international levels of excellence.

www.cambridge.org
Information on this title: www.cambridge.org/9781108472531
DOI: 10.1017/9781108560573

First published 2018

Printed in the United States of America by Sheridan Books, Inc.

A catalogue record for this publication is available from the British Library.

Library of Congress Cataloging-in-Publication Data
NAMES: Settle, Jaime E., 1985– author.
TITLE: Frenemies : how social media polarizes America / Jaime Settle.
DESCRIPTION: Cambridge ; New York : Cambridge University Press, 2018. |
   Includes bibliographical references and index.
IDENTIFIERS: LCCN 2018013745 | ISBN 9781108472531 (hardback)
SUBJECTS: LCSH: Facebook (Firm) | Facebook (Electronic resource) | Social media–United
   States–History–21st century. | Polarization (Social sciences)–United States–History–21st
   century. | Right and left (Political science)–United States–History–21st century. | Ideology–United
   States–History–21st century. | BISAC: POLITICAL SCIENCE / Government / General.
CLASSIFICATION: LCC HM743.F33 S47 2018 | DDC 302.23/1–DC23
   LC record available at https://lccn.loc.gov/2018013745

ISBN 978-1-108-47253-1 Hardback

We are not enemies, but friends. We must not be enemies. Though passion may have strained it must not break our bonds of affection. The mystic chords of memory, stretching from every battlefield and patriot grave to every living heart and hearthstone all over this broad land, will yet swell the chorus of the Union, when again touched, as surely they will be, by the better angels of our nature.

Abraham Lincoln
First Inaugural Address
March 4, 1861

Contents

Figures

Tables

Acknowledgments

Three pivotal factors enabled this book to become a reality.

The initial motivation for writing the manuscript was a response to the wrath of a string of "Reviewer 2's." During the course of one of the most fruitful collaborations of my life – with the original UCSD Facebook gang of James Fowler, Robert Bond, Chris Fariss, Jason Jones, and Lorenzo Coviello – we received persistently negative reviews on a chapter of my dissertation that we submitted repeatedly for publication as a stand-alone article (Settle *et al.* 2016). Rightly so, the anonymous reviewers noted that politically relevant behaviors on Facebook were conceptually underdeveloped and that we could not make strong claims about what we were measuring when we analyzed, for example, the text of Facebook status updates. Therefore, any argument we made about the cause or consequence of particular behaviors on the site would be built on theoretically shaky ground.

My desire to address thoroughly this concern eventually transformed into a desire to write a book-length treatment of what it meant to be "political" on Facebook and what, in my view, is the most dire consequence of politically informative interactions: the psychological polarization of the American public. I'm indebted to my co-authors-turned-friends for the privilege of working with them on our earlier joint work, and I thank James Fowler for telling me back in 2013 to "just write the book already." Although no data from our collaboration with Facebook was used in this book, I am a better scholar for having had the experience of working in such an environment and for being pushed to think hard about problems at the edge of our current knowledge about American political behavior.

Second, the data collection for the book was feasible because of support from the National Science Foundation (SES-1423788). I am grateful to Brian Humes and the panel of anonymous reviewers who took a chance on a young scholar interested in the social underpinnings of interpersonal political interaction.

My interest in social media was only a small portion of the initial grant proposal, but it has turned into a fruitful one. My professional trajectory was altered fundamentally because of the support and I hope that the contribution from this book (and the additional research funded by the grant) merits the investment in my scholarship.

The final turning point that made the book a reality was the opportunity to spend two days with some of the best minds in the field, talking over the book's theoretical development and data collection. The College of William & Mary's Department of Government, Reves Center, and Arts & Sciences sponsored a book workshop for me in the fall of 2016 that I will cherish always as the intellectual highlight of my career thus far. My immense gratitude to Shanto Iyengar, Markus Prior, Anand Sokhey, and Stuart Soroka for sharing their critical and constructive assessments. My W&M colleagues Chris Howard, Ron Rapoport, Dan Maliniak, Jeremy Stoddard, and Joanna Schug were generous with their time and feedback, as well.

Writing a book was an all-consuming endeavor at times, and I want to take the opportunity to thank the many people who have encouraged me throughout this process.

I often feel like I've won the lottery with respect to supportive department colleagues. Paul Manna read my stream-of-consciousness proto-first draft and was willing to spend an afternoon discussing it with me. Chris Howard, characteristically, provided his dry wit and practical mentorship. Steve Hanson willingly gave of his time to talk with me about the book-writing process. John Lombardini pushed me to think deeply during an incredibly stimulating conversation about the role of rhetoric and humor in democratic culture. Mike Tierney and Ron Rapoport perpetually compete for the title of Head Cheerleader. Marcus Holmes was a step ahead of me busy with his own book manuscript, but let me gripe about my own for too many hours to count. I am also grateful to S. P. Harish, Marcus Holmes, Jeff Kaplow, John Lombardini, Dan Maliniak, Claire McKinney, Phil Roessler, and Maurits Van der Veen, for the many beers we shared during various incarnations of the junior faculty writing group.

I've been fortunate to present the research in this book to a wide variety of audiences outside of my department, and I am appreciative for the feedback provided by attendees at the University of Virginia American Politics Workshop (2014), Human Nature Group Retreat (2015), Human Nature Group Masters Retreat (2015 and 2016), University of Arizona School of Government and Public Policy Colloquium (2015), Conference on Experimental Approaches to the Study of Democratic Politics at Princeton's Center for the Study of Democratic Politics (2016), Political Psychology pre-conference at APSA (2016), and University of Pennsylvania American Politics Workshop (2017).

The students in my Social Network and Political Psychology (SNaPP) Lab have contributed along the way to both the idea and data generation in this book, and our collaboration wouldn't have been possible without the Social

Science Research Methods Center. Thanks in particular to Abby Newell, Aidan Fielding, Alexis Payne, Amanda Wong, Cort Enoksen, Dan Brown, Drew Engelhardt, Emily Draper, Emily Goldfein, Gracy Murray, Kim Sarro, Megan Carter-Stone, Meg Schwenzfeier, Michael Payne, Shannon Caietti, and Zarine Kharazian. Sahil Mehrotra deserves special thanks for the multitude of tasks, small and large, he took on to facilitate the execution of the research in this book. I ventured forth independently from Taylor Carlson, my research partner in crime the past few years. However, it is abundantly clear that this book would not exist without her. Thanks to her for always being willing to talk through ideas with me, for the seemingly endless number of HITs she managed on Mechanical Turk, and for her patience in the delay on our joint projects.

I am also grateful to the students in my political behavior, political psychology, and polarization courses in the 2014–2017 period, who generated countless interesting discussions about social media. Thanks also to the staff at the William & Mary Washington Office, who facilitated such phenomenal opportunities to connect with speakers and site visits to learn about the practice of social media in contemporary American politics.

I feel fortunate to also have been nurtured by many mentors along the way. Vin Arceneaux is a friend first and a mentor second, and I am exceptionally grateful to him in both capacities. Johanna Dunaway offered particularly helpful comments and feedback. Diana Mutz graciously offered her time and advice in talking about the process of book writing. Marc Hetherington offered encouragement and enthusiasm when I needed it most. I am also appreciative of the feedback of the anonymous reviewers of the manuscript whose input added the finishing touches on it. I first met with Robert Dreesen, my editor at Cambridge University Press, in the summer of 2014. His interest and enthusiasm in the possibility of the manuscript gave me confidence during the long process through which it became a reality.

One of the lessons learned when I conducted my very first independent research project back in college was that work and life are rarely simultaneously balanced. I am grateful to my family and friends who enabled me to work intensely even when that interfered with my non-work life. Thanks for being there waiting for me on the other side.

To my friends. Nicole Conner asked me just frequently enough about my "book baby" that I always wanted to have a decent update, and she makes sure I celebrate my professional accomplishments in style. Amy Oakes legitimized my feelings about the writing process by reminding me that it was okay if not every part was fun. May everyone be so lucky to have a friend-colleague like her. Helen Murphy asked me pointed questions that kept me accountable. Devesh Tiwari kept me grounded. Chris Dawes' friendship has been, and always will be, important to me and I thank him for cheering me on from afar during this process.

To my family. To my dad, Gene Settle, for telling me that he had "passed the baton" to me when he retired. If in my career I impact even a tiny fraction of the people he did over the course of his, I will have accomplished something. To my mom, Patty Settle, for never questioning my ability to achieve what I wanted and instilling in me the value of setting and meeting a deadline. My extended family has mastered the delicate art of asking questions about my progress without putting pressure on me, and I deeply appreciate their interest and encouragement. Finally, Marc and Linda Turner read the manuscript more closely than anyone else has, and possibly ever will. Thank you to them for pushing me to make my ideas clear and for intervening in my abuse of the semi-colon and split infinitive. All remaining errors are my own.

A Fundamental Change in Political Communication

October 15, 1994. Susan Lewis is doing what all politically interested and motivated citizens do in October of a contentious midterm election: everything possible to persuade the people she disagrees with to change their opinions and to encourage the people she agrees with to vote. Lately, she's been glued to CNN, grateful for the round-the-clock coverage that still seems like a novelty. She devours any information she can get her hands on and feels compelled to share her opinions with others. There is no way for Susan to easily contact everyone she knows, but she does her best. She'll sing the praises of her preferred candidate to anyone who will listen. It is too expensive to make long-distance phone calls to friends and family who live in more competitive congressional districts, but she mobilizes the people in her local community. Susan photocopies flyers with information about voter registration and posts them at her church and in the break room at work. She volunteers for the state party's phone bank and canvasses door-to-door in her community with a clipboard in hand.

Susan's sister, Janet, couldn't be more different in terms of her level of political engagement. Although Janet trusts Susan's opinions and typically agrees with her political views, she has always avoided politics, perhaps as a legacy of her sister's diatribes and rapt attention to the news of the day. For the most part, Janet is successful in her efforts to completely ignore political news and policy debates. She doesn't subscribe to a newspaper and has plenty of other channels to watch when the news comes on the television in the evening. Janet occasionally overhears her co-workers talking about the latest clash between the political parties, but it's easy enough to avoid the conversation. Her sister inevitably makes discussions at holiday meals awkward when she attacks the views of their uncle, but it only happens a couple of times a year. Her close friends seem similarly politically disinterested, perhaps part of the reason they originally became friends. Janet doesn't give much thought to what other people think about politics; not only does partisan identity seem unimportant or irrelevant, but Janet isn't even sure how she would learn that information, since it isn't visible in her interactions with them.

This depiction of political interaction is outdated. Interpersonal political communication has undergone major changes in the last twenty-five years. While traditional forms of interaction will always persist – face-to-face political conversation with colleagues, friends, and family is a staple of democratic citizenship – changing technologies have lowered the costs for certain behaviors, while rendering obsolete others.

While the details of their communication patterns are antiquated, the roles these characters play are still familiar. Most of us know a Susan, someone who cares deeply about politics. Political scientists call people like Susan *opinion leaders* or members of the *engaged public* (Abramowitz 2010), and in dozens of studies across multiple decades, we've found that people like Susan are in a minority. For some readers, those sufficiently politically engaged and old enough to remember the costs of political communication before the rise of the Internet and social media, Susan's efforts may inspire nostalgia. But the average American, reminiscing back to the pre-Internet era, can probably better relate to Janet. Most people, most of the time, don't think too much about politics (Converse 1964). While many Americans report that they have political discussions at least occasionally, the majority of people prefer to seek out entertainment over news, given the choice.

Technology in and of itself does not cause societal change (Starr 2005), but how people adopt and integrate technology has enormous implications for the ways in which we engage with one another. This can be readily observed in the domain of political interaction. Fictional Susan Lewis, circa 2018, has dozens of outlets to share her political views and persuade her social network, allowing her to reach more people, more quickly and dynamically than ever before. She follows candidates and elected officials on the social media site Facebook, and, paired with push notifications on her phone from her favorite news sites, she knows about current events almost instantaneously. She regularly posts links to important stories in her News Feed[1] and goads people into engaging in political discussions on Facebook by sharing funny political cartoons she stumbles across. In the last election, her presidential candidate's Facebook app used an algorithm to identify all the people in her social network who lived in competitive "battleground" states, and Susan was able to easily and personally reach out to them to remind them to vote.

The advent of social media, particularly the popular social networking site Facebook, has had a profound effect on the "Susans" of the world, but as the anecdote at the beginning of the chapter shows, Susan has always been politically engaged, even when it was very costly in terms of time and effort to do so.

While alterations to the media environment have made political communication *easier* for Susan, they've had a much more dramatic effect on Janet.

---

[1] The Facebook News Feed is introduced in Chapter 2, but, in brief, it serves as the home page of the Facebook site customized to each individual user based on the content circulating in their social network.

Social media has rendered changes to political communication that fundamentally alter the way the disengaged public experiences politics. Writing a vignette for Janet in the age of social media looks something like this:

October 15, 2018. Janet Lewis now knows more about the political opinions of her family, friends, and acquaintances than she ever has before, but not because she has sought out that information. When she scrolls through her Facebook News Feed – which she does every day in order to share pictures of her grandkids and keep tabs on what people from her past are doing – she inevitably encounters political content in the form of news stories, memes, and videos, with commentary written by her social connections accompanying it all. It seems in the months leading up to an election, she simply can't escape the onslaught. She's always felt this way about her sister, but now she's connected to at least a dozen people who post about politics all the time.

While her friends who post this content share views with which she tends to agree, a substantial minority post content that so obviously signals divergent political views that even Janet can recognize the disagreement, although she cares little and knows less about current political issues. This seems especially to be the case with those Facebook friends with whom she would never talk about politics in person, such as long-lost friends from high school, her grandson's piano teacher, and the other volunteers at the food bank. Based on what they post, she's begun to make associations about which kinds of people tend to believe what kinds of things. It seems as if there is a huge gulf between the members of the two political parties.

Janet has always avoided political conversations. But for the first time, she has a window into the conversations of groups of people with whom she disagrees strongly. They all seem to egg each other on, liking and writing encouraging comments on each other's posts, and posting information Janet thinks must be biased or factually incorrect based on what Susan posts. As a consequence of seeing this, Janet has become more judgmental about those people with whom she disagrees, and she assumes the worst about the people who appear to have such extreme opinions. She's never much cared for politicians, but she now has developed negative feelings for the people who believe what those politicians spout.

We would say that Janet has become *psychologically polarized*. She's not alone. Using a variety of different measures, political scientists have shown that a large and likely growing proportion of Americans have very negative attitudes toward people and candidates who identify with the opposing political party.

Susan would have been an opinion leader in any era of American politics. However, Facebook offers her an unprecedented platform to express her political opinions, disseminate political information, and draw others into political discussions. People like Susan create an atmosphere within the Facebook News Feed that has the potential to psychologically polarize people like Janet, those who don't know or care that much about politics. Susan has several hundred friends on Facebook who may see the political content she circulates, and the vast majority of them are like Janet, choosing not to actively engage with it. But Facebook users are not able to easily escape exposure to the content opinion leaders post. Because of the motivations most people have for using the site – to learn about the social lives of their friends and family – that exposure has consequences for the connections they make between people's political and social identities.

The findings of this book suggest that psychological polarization can result from the political communication environment on social media, for both the politically engaged and disengaged publics. While there are many reasons that Susan Lewis may be more polarized now than she was two decades ago, previous explanations cannot fully account for why people like Janet have become more negative about their fellow citizens. Exposure to political interactions on Facebook could play an important role in that process. The changes to the way in which opinion leaders interact with and influence those in their networks, and the result of exposure to the vitriolic ecosystem of political communication online, have facilitated Americans in forming derogatory judgments about people who disagree with them.

We begin with a puzzle that has consumed political scientists studying American politics for the past twenty years: political polarization. Scholars almost uniformly believe that political elites are more polarized today than they have been since the American Civil War, and there is ample empirical support documenting and explaining the rise of this phenomenon. There is less consensus about the extent to which the average American has developed more extreme political attitudes and opinions. But in the process of exploring the trajectory of policy preferences of the mass public, we discovered something else. Distinct from the extremity of the policy views Americans hold, they have developed stronger in-group preferences for their own political party alongside more negative effect for those across the aisle and they perceive more distance – socially and politically – between the two groups. How this psychological polarization has occurred is a question that remains an unresolved puzzle.

PSYCHOLOGICAL POLARIZATION

Scholars have written prolifically on the many facets of polarization that affect the American political system. Among political elites, polarization is characterized by the disappearance of moderates in Congress and the two parties pulling apart ideologically, whether measured by interest group ratings (Poole and Rosenthal 1984), scaled measures of roll call votes (Poole and Rosenthal 2001; Clinton *et al.* 2004; McCarty *et al.* 2006), or measures of party vote percentages and party unity scores (Bond and Fleisher 2000; Stonecash *et al.* 2003; Jacobson 2004). Although there have been eras of deep polarization in the country's history, the increase in polarization that has developed since 1970 has resulted in the most polarized Congress seen in modern times. There are few indications that this trend will reverse itself and many more signs of the existence of feedback mechanisms that may perpetuate polarization. Ideological moderates are less likely to run for Congress (Thomsen 2014) and elected officials are less likely to hear from their constituents who belong to the other political party (Broockman and Ryan 2016).

What is less apparent is the degree to which the mass public has become polarized. The most prominent debate – between Alan Abramowitz and Kyle Saunders on one side, and Morris Fiorina and Samuel Abrams and colleagues on the other – went in circles, largely because of disagreements in the definition and measurement of polarization (Saunders and Abramowitz 2004; Abramowitz and Saunders 2005, 2008; Abramowitz and Stone 2006; Fiorina and Abrams 2008; Abramowitz 2010; Abrams and Fiorina 2012; Fiorina 2013). At the core of this initial debate over mass polarization in the early 2000s was the question of whether Americans had become more extreme in their viewpoints or had simply sorted their partisanship with their ideological viewpoints, what Lelkes (2016) differentiates as ideological divergence and ideological consistency.[2] In the process of debating the evidence for these two forms of attitudinal polarization, scholars uncovered evidence for two coexisting phenomena that are more related to Americans' attitudes about their political identities and the relationship between groups in the political system.[3]

Leaving aside the question of whether Americans hold more extreme or sorted policy preferences, there is substantial evidence that they see large differences between the parties, develop political identities that overlap considerably with their social identities, and disparage the out-party. These *psychological* forms of polarization matter as much or more than the empirical reality of preference polarization for understanding the way in which Americans view themselves and view others in the political landscape.

Affective polarization can be conceptualized as partisans' increasingly negative feelings and negative trait attribution toward identifiers of the opposing party (Iyengar *et al.* 2012; Lelkes 2016). A contributory, but distinct, pattern is the rise of *perceived polarization*, or the extent to which the mass public identifies the political parties and their adherents to be polarized (Lelkes 2016). These perceptions have important influences on emotional evaluations of the parties (Levendusky and Malhotra 2016a) and on people's motivatation to exaggerate their perception of party difference for reasons related to identity affirmation (Bullock *et al.* 2015; Prior *et al.* 2015).

---

[2] Lelkes defines ideological divergence as "the degree to which the distribution of ideology has moved apart" and ideological consistency as consisting of "two components: sorting, or the degree to which ideology matches identity, and constraint, or the correlation between issue positions" (Lelkes 2016, p. 394).

[3] The study of psychological forms of polarization has almost primarily studied attitudes toward partisan groups. However, as we'll explore in Chapter 4, the symbolic aspect of ideology – our self-identification with an ideological group – has also become more salient over time. Thus, while the focus here will be on studying attitudes toward members of the opposing political party (out-partisans), analogous results could be hypothesized for attitudes toward members of the opposing ideological group.

Evidence is mounting for these two forms of psychological polarization. Feeling thermometer survey questions asked in the American National Election Study (ANES) over time demonstrate that while positive feelings toward one's own party have stayed consistently high, feelings toward the opposition party have dropped considerably in the last thirty years (Iyengar *et al.* 2012; Kimball *et al.* 2014). These ratings are closely tied to emotional evaluations: in 2012, almost half of partisans reported being afraid of and almost two-thirds reported being angry at the presidential candidate of the opposition party (Kimball *et al.* 2014). On average, the political parties are perceived to be about 20 percent farther apart on a broad set of issues than they are in reality (Levendusky and Malhotra 2016a).

Taken to the extreme, both of these forms of polarization suggest that partisans could perceive greater social distance between the parties in addition to recognizing greater policy difference. Perhaps disturbingly, but most relevant for the argument of this book, Americans do appear to have become more negative about each other. Large proportions of Americans would be "displeased" if their child married someone from another political party (Iyengar *et al.* 2012). Fewer than 15 percent of people view the out-party – including both candidates and voters – as possessing core moral traits (Miller and Conover 2015). Findings presented in this book reveal that majorities of people agree that voters of the out-party are ignorant, narrow minded, and ideologically driven.

Furthermore, there is evidence that partisan identity affects evaluations that have nothing to do with politics, and may even be involuntary, such as our evaluations of physical attractiveness (Klar and Krupnikov 2016; Nicholson *et al.* 2016), worthiness of academic scholarships (Iyengar and Westwood 2015), and job interview callbacks (Gift and Gift 2015). Even more distressing is that social norms appear to encourage people to overstate their antipathy toward the political out-group. Explicit measures of bias – asking people directly to self-report their attitudes – typically underestimate the extent of negative sentiment because of social desirability concerns. But when assessing partisan bias, explicit measures reveal as much or more bias than implicit measures designed to more subtly capture biased attitudes. This is the exact opposite of what we observe when we measure bias against different racial or religious groups (Lelkes 2016).

Collectively, this evidence demonstrates that with or without true movement to the ideological poles in the policy opinions of the average American, the contemporary political climate has activated Americans' political identities and affective orientations. Many Americans have processed the polarizing messages from political elites and the media in a way that alters their evaluations of the parties, candidates, and, most strikingly, their fellow citizens. The classic explanations about why Americans' policy opinions have moved to the poles cannot entirely account for the identity-based aspects of polarization. People translate their attitudes toward the abstract notion of the political parties to concrete feelings about Americans who do not share the same partisan identity.

How did this come to be? The answer to this question is of the utmost importance. These sentiments have implications for the trust Americans have in each other, our leaders, and our political institutions, as well as our perception of the legitimacy of our opponents' viewpoints.

There are a number of existing explanations for the rise of affective polarization. Americans' social identities have become increasingly aligned with their political identities, raising the stakes of partisan competition (Mason 2018). In a more polarized political environment, partisan cues become important drivers of opinion, especially out-party cues (Nicholson 2012), and the negativity of the modern campaign environment likely contributes to negative attitudes (Sood, Iyengar, and Dropp 2012). The fragmented and partisan media, including both cable news and Internet news, furthers this divisive messaging (Stroud 2010; Levendusky 2013; Garrett *et al.* 2014; Levendusky and Malhotra 2016b; Lelkes *et al.* 2017), and the homogeneity of people's social networks likely reinforces these other mechanisms of polarization (Parsons 2015).

The explanation on which I focus is one that encompasses many of the ideas proposed previously. Where do all of these factors intersect, creating a maelstrom of political interaction to which many Americans are exposed on a daily basis? On social media, especially the Facebook News Feed, the most ubiquitous forum for online interaction. The News Feed serves as the home page for each Facebook user's personally tailored experience on the site, delivering a distillation of the information posted and shared by the people and groups to whom a user is connected. The framework of social identity theory (Tajfel *et al.* 1971) predicts that – given social and political sorting in American society, the resultant political discussions within largely homogeneous social networks, and the unprecedented levels of exposure to partisan media and negative campaigning – the effects of intergroup interactions should be to reinforce in-group identity and foster the perception of difference between groups.

Most scholars have conceptualized social media as a new form of communication technology whereby media and political elites can transmit information directly to the interested public in a dynamic, interactive, social way. Others have focused on the receiving end of this relationship, studying why people click on and read particular types of political news. However, this theorizing has not extended to assess the way in which the change in technology has altered the way in which citizens communicate with each other about politics, and the consequences of that change.

This book is written to fill that void.[4] I argue that the defining characteristics of political communication on the Facebook News Feed are uniquely suited to

---

[4] The lack of consistently worded and regularly collected measures of the psychological forms of polarization prevents researchers from clearly establishing the growth in these attitudes over the past fifty years. I am similarly limited in my ability to argue that social media has caused a change over time in evaluations of out-partisans. Instead, we will evaluate the psychological *mechanisms* about how social media facilitates people in forming negative opinions.

facilitate psychological processes of polarization: identity formation and reinforcement, biased information processing, and social inference and judgment. The confluence of features and norms on Facebook affects the interactions people have with each other, creating a communication ecosystem that facilitates negative and stereotyped evaluations of the Americans with whom people disagree. We will more fully explore these ideas in Chapters 2 to 4 and test the arguments in Chapters 5 to 8. But we must first address a pressing question about the focus of the book. Why should we care about political interaction on Facebook specifically?

POLITICS ON SOCIAL MEDIA

The far-reaching impact of the Internet in revolutionizing the way in which people access political information has been thoroughly chronicled (Bimber 2001; Norris 2001; Jennings and Zeitner 2003; Kaye and Johnson 2004; Kenski and Stroud 2006). But the potential of the Internet in changing the way in which people interact with each other was not fully realized until the advent of Web 2.0, a series of technologies that facilitated social connections and interactivity between users. The term "social media" refers to an ever-changing and growing set of web-based interactive applications such as Facebook, Twitter, Instagram, Snapchat, YouTube, Tumblr, Flickr, Reddit, or Vine; any list constructed while writing this book will inevitably be incomplete or outdated by the time it is published.[5]

However, not all of these social media technologies are created equally in terms of their utility for political interaction. The Pew Internet and American Life Project has studied extensively the way in which Americans incorporate social media into their political communication. And while candidates, elected officials, and the media have adopted a wide variety of social media and social networking sites, there is one platform that stands above all others in terms of its general popularity among American adults and its ubiquity for political engagement: Facebook. More than three times as many Americans have Facebook accounts as have Twitter accounts; five times as many Americans get political news in a given week from Facebook compared to those who get political news on Twitter (Pew Research Center 2014b).

Why Study Facebook?

The effects of using any particular social media platform result from the combination of the features of the site, called affordances, and the norms that develop around the way in which users employ those affordances. In addition

---

[5] The more narrow term "social networking site" (SNS) refers to web-based applications with particular features, elaborated on in Chapter 2.

to its widespread adoption for political communication, the book's focus on one particular social media platform, Facebook, is justified in two primary ways. First, Facebook is the social media site with the highest concentration of affordances that could foster polarization. My argument is predicated on the way in which certain technological features foster particular psychological phenomena, and Facebook is an interesting test case because the confluence of these features permits interesting empirical tests of their interaction and reinforcement. Political communication on Facebook is conceptually related to more traditional forms of political behavior, but the ways in which the behaviors are different are pivotal to understanding the polarizing aspects of Facebook interaction. Identifying and describing these patterns within the Facebook ecosystem provides a baseline for future scholarship testing the scope conditions of the argument. This future research can build on the present findings by extending the work into different social media platforms containing different configurations of these key affordances – platforms that may not yet exist.

Second, Facebook has cornered enough of the market on social media communication in early twenty-first-century America that it merits scholarly attention. In this sense, Facebook is a unique social phenomenon worthy of study, even if the behavioral patterns detected on the site cannot be generalized to other forms of social media. As we'll see in the next chapter, Facebook has become so integrated in the daily lives of the majority of Americans that the consequences of these interactions are important in their own right.

The Origins of Facebook

Mark Zuckerberg founded Facebook in 2004 while he was a student at Harvard University. The company's legendary and heavily disputed origin story was the basis for the 2010 movie *The Social Network*. The site grew rapidly, and since 2006 anyone age 13 or older can become a registered user of Facebook. Facebook's user base is unfathomably large. By mid-2016, the company reported that they had 1.65 billion users.

At the time of its initial public offering (IPO) in early 2012, Zuckerberg articulated a clear vision for the company. In a letter filed with the Securities and Exchange Commission (SEC) as part of the IPO, Zuckerberg wrote that Facebook "was built to accomplish a social mission – to make the world more open and connected ... At Facebook, we're inspired by technologies that have revolutionized how people spread and consume information."[6] The constantly evolving features on the site are explicitly designed to accomplish these aims.

The letter in the SEC filing articulates that "personal relationships are the fundamental unit of our society" and emphasizes the extent to which the site is

---

[6] The entirety of the Form S-1 Registration Statement is available on the Securities and Exchange Commission's website.

designed to facilitate interpersonal communication. The company's primary aims are to enhance social connectivity among the mass public, but it aspires to do so with the goal of building a service to "give people the power to share and help them … transform many of our core institutions and industries." From early in its development, Facebook incorporated features that fostered communication about one of the most prominent societal institutions: politics. It was not long after the company's expansion beyond college campuses that candidates, elected officials, and opinion leaders alike adopted the site for political purposes. In addition to the "Political Affiliation" aspect of the profile page, every new iteration of the site – the introduction of the News Feed in 2006, the "like" button in 2009, and the "groups" feature in 2010 – was embraced quickly by those looking to capitalize on social connectivity to alter the operations of our political institutions.

Other sources have documented the rapidly growing use of social media by politicians (Golbeck *et al.* 2010; Lassen and Brown 2010; Gainous and Wagner 2013; Glassman *et al.* 2013; Davis *et al.* 2016; Evans and Clark 2016; Jungherr 2016; Kreiss 2016). In 2006, 32 percent of US Senate candidates and 13 percent of US House candidates had profiles on Facebook (Gulati and Williams 2013); by 2011, 90 percent of representatives and senators were registered with the site. Every major news network has an active presence on the site. News sites that arose in the Web 1.0 era of blogs and niche news have readily taken to Facebook to expand their readership. Beyond these traditional players in the political communication environment, social media in particular has spawned the development of organizations that appear to be devoted primarily to generating and circulating content to the users who like their Facebook page.

In the next chapter, I characterize the aspects of the Facebook platform that contain the affordances and functionalities that are most crucial to facilitating Americans in forming negative judgments about their fellow citizens based on their political opinions. The argument is about the way in which the mass public interacts with each other; however, it is important not to lose sight of the fact that political elites, mass media, and political advocacy organizations are key players in generating the content that opinion leaders help circulate to the wider public.

Who Uses Facebook?

Previous research about political behavior on social media has largely focused on people who are active participants in creating and circulating political content, the minority of Facebook users like Susan in the vignette opening this chapter. While these individuals are critical in fostering a potentially polarizing information environment, this book focuses more on the audience: people who are "listening" and are exposed to political content, in most cases unintention-ally. The book's findings should thus be applicable to the population of American Facebook users, not just the most politically active among them. While this

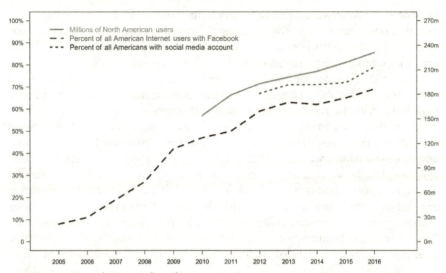

FIGURE 1.1 Growth in social media usage in America, 2005–2016
The lightest gray line shows the growth in the number of daily active users, in millions, of the Facebook site in North America (Canada and the United States) using data from Statista. The two dashed lines show the growth in the percentage of Americans who report that they have a social media account, and the percentage of Internet users who say they have a Facebook account, using data from Pew.

population is different in some ways from the American public at large, it is not subject to the same kinds of selection biases that structure the composition of the group of people most likely to encounter political information in other ways, such as by reading a daily newspaper or watching cable television.

As of mid-2016, 79 percent of all Internet-using American adults report using at least one social networking site (Greenwood *et al.* 2016). While Pew's data includes usage of a range of sites – including Twitter, Google Plus, Linked In, and Pinterest – in each of the surveys on which these data are based, the overwhelmingly most ubiquitous site is Facebook (Pew Research Center 2014b). Only 24 percent of Pew's panel reports using Google Plus, and only 22 percent reports using Twitter. Statista reports that in 2016, there were 191.3 million Americans with Facebook accounts and only 66 million Americans with Twitter accounts. Figure 1.1 above reports the total percentage of Americans who have an account on a social networking site over time.

I build on the time series data Pew has generated about the growing use of Facebook with data from two original surveys[7] conducted in the spring of 2016 to assess the extent to which Facebook usage has permeated the daily

---

[7] These two surveys, the Political Discussion Survey and the END Framework Survey, are introduced later in the chapter.

lives of most Americans. The first survey included both Facebook users and non-Facebook users. The second survey followed up with the Facebook users and asked respondents both how frequently they logged into the site as well as how many times a day they scrolled through their News Feeds.[8]

In a series of regression models shown in online Appendix C, the strongest correlates of whether a person has a Facebook account are age and gender. Consistent with the results found by Pew and others, women are more likely to have Facebook accounts, to spend time on Facebook, and to scroll through their News Feed more regularly. Age is inversely associated with Facebook account ownership and usage, although sizable proportions of Americans of all ages use Facebook regularly. Income is negatively associated with whether someone reports having a Facebook account, but neither race nor education are. While race is not associated with the decision to maintain a Facebook account, there is suggestive evidence that white Americans scroll through their News Feeds less frequently than do non-white Americans. Neither education level nor income is correlated with the frequency of Facebook usage or News Feed scrolling.

More consequential for an assessment of the potentially polarizing consequences of using social media are selection effects related to political characteristics. Partisan strength and political interest are correlated with whether someone has a Facebook account. But even supermajorities of political independents (70.5 percent) and the politically uninterested (70.7 percent) report that they have Facebook accounts compared to about 80 percent of the most partisan and most interested Americans. Ideological strength, past voting history, and political knowledge are not associated with opening a Facebook account.

While this might indicate a slight selection effect into who creates Facebook accounts,[9] none of these political variables is associated with the frequency or intensity with which someone uses Facebook. The factors that typically explain what kinds of people are most politically engaged are not the factors that best explain regular Facebook usage or News Feed scrolling, suggesting few selection biases shaping the composition of people who are active on the site on a daily basis. The only variables that are associated with heightened Facebook usage are those related to news engagement: whether people report that the

---

[8] I limited the survey to only those people who reported they had a Facebook account, and I assessed people's responses to the question, "How frequently do you spend time on Facebook?" For those respondents who reported that they did most days or every day, I followed up with the question, "On a typical day when you use Facebook, how many times a day do you scroll through your News Feed, either on a mobile device (like a phone or tablet) or a computer?"

[9] Of course, it could also be the case that using Facebook makes people more partisan and interested in politics. While increased partisan attachment is a prediction consistent with my expectations for the consequences of generating political content and receiving social feedback on it (Chapter 7), the people most likely to generate political content are already the most partisan. The surveys were not designed to assess the direction of causality in this highly endogenous relationship.

Internet is their main source for news as well as the frequency with which people seek out news. Thus, the traditional correlates of political engagement and political information seeking – interest in politics, political knowledge, partisan strength, partisan leaning, or past voting behavior – are not associated with the frequency or intensity of a person's daily exposure to the Facebook News Feed.

The survey was not exhaustive of every contribution to the decision to use Facebook, and there are almost certainly differences between people that are correlated with creating and using a Facebook account. But in terms of explaining what kinds of people "opt in" to regular usage of Facebook and repeated exposure to the News Feed, these results show that a broader swath of Americans than just the politically engaged public use Facebook. Unlike the findings of Arceneaux and Johnson (2013), who show that systematically different kinds of people are exposed to cable news programming, a similar pattern does not emerge for exposure to Facebook more broadly. As we'll see in Chapter 5, there are important differences between those users who post political content and those who do not, but a very large majority of the American public is exposed to political content on Facebook in the course of their normal usage of the site.

Although some may argue that focusing on the hallmark characteristics of a single communication platform limits the generalizability of the argument and findings of this book, I disagree. A majority of Americans spend time on Facebook on a daily basis, and among those who do, the majority scrolls through their News Feed at least once a day. While not perfectly representative of the American public at large, a far larger group of Americans – with far fewer systematic biases shaping its composition – report being regularly engaged with their News Feed than report watching cable news or reading a newspaper regularly. And when they do, they cannot avoid encountering political content.

Political Engagement on Facebook

The Pew Internet and American Life Project has conducted the most thorough tracking of the growth of social media for political purposes, largely focused on the role of social media as a source for political information or a way to communicate about politics with others.

Large minorities of people report that they use social media in some capacity for political engagement, but few users report regular and sustained usage for these purposes. In other words, a much greater proportion of people report seeking or encountering political content on Facebook than report creating or circulating it. Most people don't generate political content frequently – only 14 percent report that some, most, or all of the content they generate is about politics. Yet, a substantial proportion have generated content at some point, ranging from the 28 percent of users who have posted stories or articles to the

47 percent who have liked content other users have posted, with other forms of engagement falling somewhere in between.

Pew's finding about the proportion of Facebook users who use the site for news (66 percent) translates to an estimate that 44 percent of the overall American adult population uses Facebook to get news (Gottfried and Shearer 2016). That figure is equivalent to or greater than the proportion of Americans who report using cable news, local news, or newspapers to access information,[10] but the intensity of exposure appears to be higher on Facebook. In my survey, on average, people report seeing political information half the time they scroll through their News Feeds, even when they are not looking explicitly to find it. This high rate of exposure to political content might not matter if people see political information and communication on social media, but don't pay any attention. However, Pew reports that of those users who report that they see political posts, 52 percent report paying some or a lot of attention, a figure that jumps to between 60 and 70 percent for the most ideologically consistent users in the sample (Pew Research Center 2014b).

Novel Behavior, Novel Questions

To date, political scientists have tested hypotheses about the antecedents and consequences of political engagement on social media within the framework used to study traditional political behaviors. There is a large body of literature trying to explain online engagement with factors such as political interest, efficacy, and knowledge and to disentangle the causal relationship between online and offline political behavior. Researchers have assessed exposure to political information primarily from a news-seeking and agenda-setting framework, applying the theories of selective exposure to study which information on social media users are most likely to click and the consequences of doing so on learning and issue salience.

This accumulated knowledge is useful, but it misses a fundamental point about Facebook. *People use the site to stay connected to and learn about*

---

[10] Data from the American National Election Study (ANES) reveal that in 2012, 76 percent of Americans had watched television programs about the campaigns, but the question wording does not include anything about the frequency of exposure to television programs. Pew's report finds that 49 percent of respondents say they got news from local TV (Pew Research Center 2014b) and between 37 and 44 percent for different cable news channels. In a different study using data from Nielson, the Pew Research Center reports that 38 percent of American adults watch some cable news during the month (Mitchell *et al.* 2013). Similarly, the ANES reports that in 2008, 68 percent of Americans who read a daily newspaper in the past week had "read about the campaign in any newspaper." However, only 38 percent of Americans report that they regularly read a daily newspaper (Heimlich 2012). These statistics suggest that a greater proportion of Americans are regularly encountering news on social media. Finally, considerably more Facebook users (62 percent) than Twitter users (40 percnet) report that they have seen news on the site (Pew Research Center 2014b).

other people. The functionalities of the site are optimized for social engagement more generally, subsuming its use for political purposes, and these aspects of the site should inform our conceptualization and measurement of political engagement on Facebook. For most people, most of the time, exposure to political information is largely incidental and occurs in a context in which they are actively seeking social information about their connections.

Thus, we should reorient our focus on the consequences of posting and encountering political content on Facebook by deriving hypotheses based on more accurate assumptions about how and why people actually use the site. I propose the *END Framework* for the study of social media political interaction. END refers to the characteristics of a subset of content that circulates in a social media ecosystem like the Facebook News Feed: a personalized, quantified blend of politically informative *expression, news,* and *discussion* that is seamlessly interwoven in a single interface with non-political content. Creating and consuming content are novel and distinct political behaviors, albeit ones that fuse together characteristics of more traditional behaviors. Differences in the content itself, the context in which interactions occur, and the composition of the people who interact with each other produce unique expectations about the consequences of regularly using the News Feed for politically relevant outcomes.

Reframing our study of political interaction on Facebook by considering it first and foremost a *social* behavior highlights the importance of particular avenues of inquiry. Instead of focusing solely on consequences for offline political behavior or downstream policy attitudinal changes, we should think about consequences more directly related to the site's primary function: expressing identity and learning about the lives of other people. I consider the most important of these potential social consequences to be the notion of psychological polarization. How is it that regular usage of the Facebook News Feed could facilitate the formation of negative attitudes toward people who hold different political views than our own?

First, Facebook fosters the ready availability of signals about others' political preferences. As we will see, people are able to glean cues about the partisan identities of other users even from information that is not overtly political. Thus, the volume of information that is *politically informative* is much larger than the volume of information that is explicitly political. Because users engage with the site for the purposes of social inference, they are highly attuned to recognizing indications of how other people think and behave. Frequent usage of Facebook gives users increased practice in their social inference skills, bolstering their confidence in their abilities to map the socio-political terrain of their social network.

Second, social identity theory suggests that once group identity is recognized and made salient, intergroup interactions should lead to polarized evaluations differentiating the in-group from the out-group. Thus, the very same affordances on Facebook that are designed to bring people together – the ability to share content within the site from all corners of the Internet, the functionalities to like and comment on other people's posts, and the quantification of this social feedback – can actually push people farther apart. Facebook users watch each other navigate a complex and polarizing information environment and have a window into the not-so-deliberative processes through which others acquire information and form their opinions. Within the broader context of twenty-first-century American political polarization, the identity-reinforcing aspects of Facebook serve to bolster assessments of the political in-group at the expense of denigration of the out-group.

DATA AND METHODOLOGY

The analysis in this book is primarily focused on Facebook users, but it is useful to compare those who use Facebook to those who don't for two main reasons: (1) to test for any politically relevant selection effects into site usage; and (2) to test the key argument of the book – that Facebook users are more psychologically polarized than are non-Facebook users. To do this, on a large survey (n=3,030) dubbed the *Political Discussion Survey*, I included a number of demographic, social, and political variables in addition to a survey question about whether the respondent had a Facebook account. As we saw above, it turns out that selection into regular Facebook use is largely unrelated to the factors that drive political behavior. On the same survey, respondents answered three batteries of questions related to psychological polarization. Later in the book, these questions will allow us to assess whether Facebook users are more polarized than are non-Facebook users (hint: they are).

The respondents in this initial survey who indicated that they had Facebook accounts were re-contacted several weeks later to participate in a follow-up study that focused on their Facebook behavior. Throughout the book, this study is referred to as the *END Framework Survey*.[11] Respondents reported on their Facebook usage behaviors, the information to which they were exposed on the site, and additional facets of polarization. The full survey is available in the online appendices. As part of the END Framework Survey, I included the *Social Connections Battery*. Modeled after a technique used by scholars of political discussion, this component of the survey allows us a window into Facebook users' assessments of their most politically prolific Facebook contacts. By coding the nature of the offline relationship between these contacts and the survey respondents, we get traction on the role of social distance in the judgment process of Facebook ties.

All of the studies described above are observational, aimed at characterizing patterns among a set of Facebook users sampled to mirror the composition of the American public. To assess the mechanisms that could have created these patterns, we use different types of studies.

[11] Both surveys were fielded by Survey Sampling International, the Political Discussion Survey in mid-April 2016 (primarily for the purposes of another research project) and the END Framework Survey in late April 2016.

The *Inference Studies* are a set of three studies conducted in February to April 2016 that are a type of classification task. Respondents were randomly assigned to assess between six and ten stimuli that were formatted to look like typical Facebook content. After each stimulus, they answered a set of questions about the user who supposedly posted the content to Facebook. At the end of the study, respondents answered a set of questions about their own Facebook usage. These studies feature prominently in Chapters 5 to 8 and form the core of the argument that Facebook users not only recognize the partisan identity of other users based on what they post, but also that they evaluate and judge members of their out-group in a manner consistent with the processes suggested by social identity theory.

In the fall of 2016 in the weeks leading up the presidential election, I conducted two additional studies in conjunction with one another. The first of these, the *Accuracy Study*, is an extension of the approach used in the inference studies. However, instead of using publicly available content for the study stimuli, I had a group of subjects (the "posters") generate political Facebook content and answer a set of questions about their partisanship, ideology, and levels of political knowledge. A different sample (described momentarily) then assessed those users based on the content they generated in an identical framework to the inference studies. This permits a test of the accuracy of the judges' perception compared to the reality of the posters' traits.

The second additional study, the *Generation Experiment*, was an experiment conducted on a student sample. In the pre-survey, subjects first generated a piece of political content. Next, they completed the inference task where they were the "judges" in the Accuracy Study described above, except they were told they were evaluating content by other study participants. Then, before the subjects arrived in the lab for the second portion of the study, we formatted the content they'd generated to look like a Facebook post and randomly assigned them to receive high or low levels of social feedback on it. When they returned for the lab portion of the study, they received their "post" with the feedback that they were led to believe (temporarily, at least) had been generated by other study participants.

Appendix A includes an elaboration of all of these studies, as well as descriptive statistics of all the samples used. While the observational studies were conducted on subjects that can be described as approximating a nationally representative sample, the samples used in the other studies are decidedly convenience samples. A full consideration of the implications of this choice is in Appendix B.

OUTLINE OF THE BOOK

In the chapters that follow, I build on the key points introduced in this chapter to offer compelling evidence that engaging with politically informative content on the Facebook News Feed has facilitated the processes that result in psychological polarization.

In the next chapter, we'll take a step back and more fully consider the contemporary role of social media in the day-to-day lives of most Americans. We will explore how Facebook has affected other forms of social behavior to provide the background context necessary to appreciate why the END framework predicts particular consequences of News Feed engagement on attitudes toward other people. The chapter highlights six distinguishing features of the content on Facebook that contribute to social inference and the formation of affective attitudes, features that play a pivotal role in the studies later in the book. In Chapter 3, we'll formalize the definition of News Feed political engagement – generation and consumption of politically informative content – at the intersection of political expression, information seeking, and discussion. In addition to articulating the key distinctions of the online manifestations of these behaviors, we'll develop the theoretical groundwork about how to apply existing theories of political information processing and interpersonal interaction to these novel forms of behavior.

In Chapter 4, I fully outline the END Framework of communication, theorizing how generating and consuming politically informative News Feed content contributes to psychological polarization. After more thoroughly exploring what we know about these forms of polarization, we'll consider how the defining characteristics of News Feed interaction facilitate distinct processes that contribute to the way in which people draw political inferences and make judgments about their social connections on the site. This theoretical chapter sets up the foundation for the empirical results in the second half of the book.

We will then turn to a puzzle that has emerged from previous research on social media. How is it possible that although most people report that they don't post very much about politics, supermajorities of Facebook users report they have learned the political views of the people they are socially connected to on the site? Chapter 5 provides the first half of the answer: while a small minority of users generate explicitly political content that is partisan and opinionated, a much larger volume of content is implicitly political. Furthermore, there is a broad and varied definition of what kind of content is considered to be "political." Certain topics are almost universally recognized as pertaining to politics, but a wider set of content can be considered politicized.

In Chapter 6, we'll expand upon these notions to focus on informative signaling and inference on the News Feed. Facebook users – regardless of their level of political sophistication – are able to make inferences about the political inclinations of users who post political, as well as politicized and seemingly apolitical, content to the News Feed. The ability to infer underpins the assertion that the Facebook News Feed fosters people's recognition of social and identity differences that align with political views. Inference forms the foundation for social evaluation and judgment, an important step in psychological polarization.

Chapter 7 reveals the extent of the cognitive biases that shape Facebook users' inferences about others on the site. Our focus will be on three particular phenomena: the out-group homogeneity effect, perceived polarization, and the false consensus effect. Despite the fact that most Americans have moderate ideological opinions, Americans believe that there are vast differences between the two parties and their adherents. People attribute extreme and overly consistent ideological views to anonymous others based on the content of what they post, and they think the friends of people they disagree with are more extreme than their own friends. These perceptions of extremity are strongest among those who use Facebook most frequently. Additionally, the informational cues prolific on Facebook content facilitate biased estimates about the size of the political in-group, and generating political content reinforces users' political identities when they receive social feedback from their network.

Social identity theory suggests that identity recognition and biased inference should go hand-in-hand with negative assessments of the out-group. In Chapter 8, we'll explore the social evaluation and judgment that result from the way in which people process politically informative News Feed content. Users are considerably more negative about their friends with whom they disagree, judging harshly their knowledge levels and the credibility of the sources they use. These social inferences extend beyond the people to whom we are directly connected. People who generate and consume the most political content on Facebook hold the strongest negative stereotypes about Facebook users and members of the out-party more generally.

The final chapter of the book condenses its central arguments: the defining aspects of engagement with News Feed content – the behaviors at the intersection of political expression, information seeking, and political discussion on social media – are uniquely suited to foster the development and perpetuation of psychological polarization. We'll consider the normative implications of these findings and whether changes to the affordances and norms on the site could reverse the trajectory on which we find ourselves.

Facebook in Context: Theorizing Interaction on Twenty-First-Century Social Media

Asserting the novelty of the consequences of people's use of an emerging technology risks overlooking analogous effects of the technology's forerunners used in earlier eras. The study of the effects of social media interactions seems especially ripe for this shortsightedness. As Robert Darnton writes in the introduction to *Poetry and the Police*:

Now that most people spend most of their time exchanging information – whether texting, twittering, uploading, downloading, encoding, decoding, or simply talking on the telephone – communication has become the most important activity of modern life ... The marvels of communication technology in the present have produced a false consciousness about the past – even a sense that communication has no history, or had nothing of importance to consider before the days of television and the Internet.

Darnton 2011, p. 1.

Tom Standage's book *Writing on the Wall: Social Media – The First Two Thousand Years* makes this point even more explicitly. He explores the idea that the era of broadcast media is actually the historical anomaly among the long trajectory of eras featuring media forms with characteristics that resemble aspects of digital social media. Similarly unfounded in its novelty is the idea that the polarized, fractured state of today's media environment is historically unprecedented. American newspapers in the eighteenth and nineteenth centuries were incredibly partisan and vitriolic (McGerr 1986; Schudson 1998; Hamilton 2004; Starr 2005).

Our myopia is not only oriented toward the past. In a similar way, our failure of imagination to envision the near constant evolution of the technological environment means that any study too rooted in the particular idiosyncrasies of a single media platform risks irrelevance as new platforms and ways of engaging become "the next big thing." While historians urge us to keep one eye on the past, media technology scholars implore us to keep one eye on the future. Facebook is the predominant forum for online social networking in America at this moment in time, but there is no reason to assume that it always will be. Before the rise of Facebook, SixDegrees.com, Friendster, and MySpace all rose and fell as the primary sites for networked online interaction. Nor is Facebook currently the largest social networking site in every country across the globe: hundreds of millions of people in China use microblogging sites such as Sina Weibo or social networking sites such as QZone, for example.

The limitation of a book studying the effects of interaction on Facebook that does not deeply consider the generalizability of the features of the site is premature obsolescence. The value of a study of the consequences of engaging on a particular social media platform is derived from understanding what features and functions of the site cause the effects we observe. In what ways are contemporary forms of social media similar to the social communication of eras past? What essential components of online social networks transcend platform specificity and are likely to cause similar effects in technologies we can't yet imagine?

Before proceeding with the story line unpacking the relationship between Facebook use and psychological polarization, in this chapter I take a step back and consider the impact of social media on American society more broadly and within the context of historical communication technologies that were equally innovative or disruptive in eras past. In broadening our focus, albeit temporarily, we can explore the way in which Facebook has affected other forms of social behavior to appreciate why we might expect certain consequences on political behavior. Facebook is an interesting and rich case study because of the effects of its unique convergence of affordances and norms on human interaction. A detailed description of how people engage with one another on Facebook is crucial context for building a theory to understand the consequence of the political and politicized forms of these interactions.

SOCIAL MEDIA CULTURE IN THE EARLY TWENTY-FIRST CENTURY

Standage notes that "the desire to be connected to one's distant friends, using whatever technology is available, is timeless" (2013, p. 246). It is not the underlying concept of social media that is novel. As Standage clearly demonstrates, humans have a long and variegated history with many of the features that we consider hallmarks of the digital media age: the bidirectional creation of what qualifies as news; the fusion of objective news information with social commentary; the concepts of webs or networks of social communication; and the use of media technology to coordinate opinion and reveal consensus. Social media in the twenty-first century has parallels to social media in other eras of history, but what is unique is its reach and penetration: people spend enormous amounts of time on platforms that connect more than a billion people to each other in real time. The ideas below only scratch the surface of the possible themes that could be explored, but they are pertinent ones for studying inter-personal political communication in the United States – the scope of this book.

Social Media Is Interwoven into Our Lives

In its first quarter report to stockholders in May 2016, Facebook CEO Mark Zuckerberg reported that on average across the world, users spend 50 minutes a day on the Facebook, Instagram, and Messenger platforms combined.[1] Com-Score finds that among American users, one out of every five minutes spent online is on a social networking site, with Facebook far outpacing all other platforms. While the average American user spends slightly less time – only 35 minutes a day according to statistics generated by comScore – because most of the site's users engage every day, the average user spends over 900 min-utes a month on the site.[2] As pointed out in a *New York Times* column, time spent on Facebook equates to one-sixteenth of the average user's waking hours in a day.[3]

Time spent on Facebook exceeds time spent on any other leisure activity except watching television, according to the Bureau of Labor Statistics time use surveys.[4] In fact, "checking Facebook" is an activity that has become so pervasive in our daily routines that it has sparked a self-help culture advocating for decreased usage of the site. A Google search of "Facebook detox" reveals literally thousands of articles and recommendations about how and why one should unplug. Scholars have even studied how "problematic Facebook use" can interfere with other aspects of a person's life (Koc and Gulyagci 2013; Lee-Won, Herzog, and Park 2015).

Physiologically, it appears that using Facebook induces a "core flow state" characterized by high positive valence and high arousal (Mauri *et al.* 2011).[5] What is it that people find so engaging on social media? How, in the span of just barely a decade, has social media engagement become such a prominent

---

[1] Facebook acquired Instagram in April 2012 for 1 billion dollars. Messenger is a free instant messaging service that integrates with the Facebook platform. It was originally part of the Facebook platform, but was spun off into a separate application in 2014. The company typically reports combined usage statistics for these three facets of its platform.

[2] Younger users – those aged 18 to 34 – actually spend over 1,000 minutes a month on the site. Users over the age of 35 spend over 900 minutes on average. See Andrew Hutchinson, "New comScore Traffic Report Underlines the Strength of Facebook, Rise of Snapchat." Social Media Today (March 31, 2016).

[3] James Stewart, "Facebook Has 50 Minutes of Your Time Each Day. It Wants More." *The New York Times* (May 5, 2016).

[4] ibid.

[5] Mauri *et al.* (2011) attempt to use physiological measurement to capture Csikszentmihalyi's (1975) concept of "flow," distinguished by intense enjoyment and engagement and present when "the challenge provided by the activity is high enough but the skills of the person can still cope with the situation" (p. 724).

part of the average American's daily life? What features of the technology – affordances, in the parlance of communication scholars (Gibson 1977; Norman 1999; Sundar and Limperos 2013) – make the site so compelling?

Standage points to the fact that humans are social in nature: the benefits of the ability to process social information appear linked to the growth of primate brains. The maintenance of social groups and the management of social status within them is built on the exchange of information about other people. Media technology – beginning with the emergence of writing and most recently with the emergence of online social networking sites – "enables literate humans to extend this exchange of information across time and space to include people who are not physically present" (Standage 2013, p. 8). Thus, the gratification we receive from connecting with others using social networking sites can be considered as part of a long evolution of our social brain.

Whether or not an evolutionary psychology story can be applied to our modern usage of social media is somewhat beside the point for most people who have thought deeply about the role of social media in contemporary culture. Dozens of books have been published chronicling the growing role of social media in every facet of our lives. Even narrowing the scope to focus just on the effects of social networking sites on our sense of self or our relationships with others, the literature is voluminous. Social psychologists have considered the role of narcissism and other personality traits on social media behavior and have debated technology's effects on social exclusion, conformity, and self-concept. Clinical psychologists express concern over cyber-bullying and harassment. Sociologists have grappled with the notion of "selfie culture." Millennials are certainly not the first generation to worry about having regrets, but perhaps they are the first to have an acronym to describe it: FOMO, or "fear of missing out." As part of the larger development of "on demand culture," social media may shorten people's attention spans and reduce incentives for meaningful social connection.

This last point is the subject of much deliberation. Some scholars argue that social media has undermined the foundations of face-to-face interpersonal communication (Powers 2010; Turkle 2011). Others retort that despite serious concerns about the role of social media in society more generally, it has actually deepened the way in which we connect with our family, our friends, and our communities (Tufecki 2012), facilitated certain forms of social capital (Hampton 2011), and lowered the costs of cooperation and collective action (Shirky 2008). These debates remain unresolved and only time will reveal the widest-reaching implications of the integration of social media into our lives.

Social Media and the Information Environment

In addition to the changes that social media has rendered to the expression of our self-identities and the maintenance of our interpersonal relationships, there is a large and growing literature evaluating the effects of Internet technologies broadly and social media sites specifically in disrupting the way we acquire and distribute information. Henry Jenkins argues that media convergence, or "the flow of content across multiple media platforms, the cooperation between multiple media industries, and the migratory behavior of media audiences who will go almost anywhere in search of the kinds of entertainment experiences they want" (2006, p. 2) is not a technological process, but rather "… a cultural shift as consumers are encouraged to seek out new information and make connections among dispersed media content" (2006, p. 3).

Standage (2013) contends, however, that we should be more circumspect in our assessment. Discussing the distinction drawn between digital technologies ("new media") and old technologies ("mass media"), he argues that the era of broadcast media in the late nineteenth and twentieth centuries was the aberration to the norm. He continues:

Look back before 1833 to the centuries before the era of old media began, however – to what could be termed the era of "really old" media – and the media environment, based on distribution of information from person to person social networks, has many similarities with today's world. In many respects twenty-first-century Internet media has more in common with seventeenth-century pamphlets or eighteenth-century coffee-houses than with nineteenth-century newspapers or twentieth-century radio and television. Standage (2013), p. 240.

Even conceding Standage's point, today's information environment represents a radical departure from the environment that preceded it before the rise of the Internet.

The social consumption of information, a point I elaborate on in the next chapter, has reshaped the production and distribution of content on old media. Disruption is certainly part of the story. Print newspaper circulation has dropped markedly. Magazine subscriptions have declined as blogs, Pinterest, and Facebook have displaced monthly or weekly publications as sources for entertainment news, celebrity gossip, and home-decorating advice.

Norm change is another important piece of the puzzle. The clearest example of this may be the rise of "clickbait," writing headlines intentionally designed to catch viewers' attention, even if not entirely accurate about the content of the story.[6] The functionalities that several social media sites provide to third-party websites to allow users to distribute content in some instances directly violates particular journalistic norms. Even subtle changes in affordances affect the way in which information is produced: in the early era in which Facebook was promoting a "like" button compared to a "share" button on third-party websites, the feature favored the inclusion of emotion in news stories, inducing discomfort for many traditional news producers.[7]

---

[6] Bryan Gardiner, "You'll Be Outraged at How Easy It Was to Get You to Click on This Headline." *Wired* (December 18, 2015).

[7] Joshua Benton, "'Like,' 'Share,' and 'Recommend': How the Warring Verbs of Social Media Will Influence the News' Future." NiemanLab (February 28, 2011).

Social media has changed not only content, but also how people are encouraged to consume traditional media. Television producers now encourage multitasking, the use of Twitter on a "second screen" such as a mobile phone, for example. Incorporating a hashtag into a show or its marketing increases mentions of the show by 20 percent,[8] and marketing research suggests that using Twitter while watching a show is associated with higher recall of advertising.[9]

A Convergence of Affordances

The term "social media" does not necessarily imply that a platform is built upon a networked group of users, and the definition incorporates a wide variety of web-based applications in which users can interact without establishing formalized connections to one another. Although colloquially people refer to Facebook and Twitter as "social media," scholars often distinguish these platforms as "social network sites" (or SNS for short). While both social media and SNS facilitate asynchronous and geographically unbound interactions, what differentiates social networking sites from social media more broadly is that SNS "allow individuals to (1) construct a public or semi-public profile within a bounded system, (2) articulate a list of other users with whom they share a connection, and (3) view and traverse their list of connections and those made by others within the system" (Boyd and Ellison 2007, p. 211).[10] On top of these base components, each site develops additional affordances designed to facilitate the unique niche the site fills. For example, Facebook and Twitter incorporate "microblogging," the ability to easily communicate small bits of text or visual content.

Each site can be thought of as the result of its affordances paired with the culture that arises around the way in which users employ those affordances. In the chapters that follow, I describe why the convergence of affordances on Facebook make it particularly well suited to foster psychological polarization. Here, I focus on the concepts underpinning the key affordances of Facebook to better understand how they structure the interactions between users on the site more generally.

---

[8] Mathew Ingram, "TV Engagement Secrets from Twitter, Everyone's Favorite Second Screen." *Fortune* (September 21, 2015).

[9] Heather O'Shea, "New Research: TV Viewers Who Engage on Twitter Have Higher Rates of Ad Recall." Twitter (March 18, 2016).

[10] Users interested in the history and development of social network sites are encouraged to consult Boyd and Ellison's foundational, very accessible introduction to the concept. In this book, I will use the term "social media," because as I discuss in Chapter 9, some of the affordances driving psychological polarization also tend to appear on social media platforms that would not be considered social networking sites by a strict definition.

Profiles and the Depiction of Self

For as long as humans have had technologies to record themselves, we have sought to document the details of our lives, trivial and monumental alike. People have always scrapbooked, sometimes collectively, as in the example of the "commonplace books" of sixteenth-century England (Standage 2013, ch. 4). Kodak's introduction of personal cameras in the late nineteenth century was revolutionary, in part because of the social construction of the act of taking a photograph (Bourdieu 1965) and the impacts the technology had on our sense of self and our social relationships (Gye 2007). The desire to share these memories with others who were absent at their creation is not a new phenomenon either. In an earlier era, friends and families were subject to slide shows and VHS home videos of family vacations projected in the living room. The introduction of digital cameras further altered our behavior,[11] and digital photography led to the rise of quasi-professionally produced photobooks as well as websites designed specifically for sharing photos.

Because of the capabilities of mobile devices that take increasingly higher quality pictures and videos, social media takes the written, visual, and auditory record of our lives to an entirely different level.[12] But on some sites, the presentation of self takes a backseat to other goals. For instance, very little information is required to create a Twitter account, and a user's profile on Twitter has considerably fewer options for personalization. A person's identity on Twitter is much less important than the content they disseminate. Likewise, Pinterest is a social media platform driven almost entirely by shared appreciation for content with little functionality built in to develop a profile highlighting one's self identity, apart from the content one has helped disseminate.

Facebook seeks to be a network where people connect their authentic selves to others, unlike other sites that permit users to adopt pseudonyms or screen names to conceal their true identities. It is actually a violation of Facebook's terms of service for an individual to have more than one account, and the site states that "we ask everyone to use the same name on Facebook that they use in everyday life."[13] When people attach content to their profiles, they do so with the intention of communicating about their actual lives.

Facebook is almost unparalleled in its ability to facilitate people in crafting a record of their lives: pictures of themselves, witticisms about the minutiae of their day, inspirational quotes that have meaning to them, videos of funny things their pets do, or important milestones their children reach, just to name a handful of examples. The Facebook medium is in large part optimized to facilitate this "digital commonplace book." The company regularly promotes

---

[11] Tom de Castella, "Five Ways the Digital Camera Changed Us." BBC News (February 28, 2012).

[12] Many different platforms are entirely built on the capability to communicate in non-written forms, such as Instagram, Vine, SnapChat, and other sites, and as technology evolves, we can expect social media to maximize the latest available features.

[13] "Names on Facebook," available at www.facebook.com/help/958948540830352.

new features designed to help people relive these moments, showing users a post on the anniversary of the date they originally created it, and creating "year in review" videos to string together the moments people shared on the site. Popular trends include "Wayback Wednesdays" and "Throwback Thursdays" (signified by the hashtags #wbw and #tbt respectively) where people will post older photos or content as reminders of past events.

Such high-resolution documentation of our lives in real time speaks directly to how we manage our presentation of self. Erving Goffman, the eminent sociologist, emphasized the extent to which we attempt to influence the impressions others make of us by scripting our performance in interpersonal interactions to fit the social conventions demanded by the nature of a situation, our ascribed role in it, and the audience with whom we're interacting (1959). Different contexts call for different presentations of self. However, technology has radically altered our ability to keep our separate roles distinct: "by bringing many different types of people to the same 'place,' electronic media have fostered a blurring of many formerly distinct social roles" (Meyrowitz 1986, p. 6). Meyrowitz actually wrote this in reference to the emergence of television and radio, but his words seem even more apt to a description of social media. In fact, one of the areas of SNS scholarship that has grown most rapidly relates to the way in which individuals construct and manage their self-identities (Carpenter 2012; Bareket-Bojmel *et al.* 2016; Halpern *et al.* 2016; Shin *et al.* 2017).

The Meaning of Connection

On LinkedIn and Instagram, we "connect." On Twitter and Pinterest, we "follow." On SnapChat, we "add." Each of these sites uses a unique parlance, but the general principle is the same: users formalize connections to other users of the site, either in a unidirectional way – where the connection is formed based solely on the initiation by one user, such as on Twitter – or in a bidirectional way – such as on LinkedIn, where users must acknowledge and accept the connection request. Each platform has different norms about who initiates these connections, what sort of offline relationship is necessary, if any, to merit a connection, and what the unspoken rules are for accepting connection requests.

On Facebook, we "friend," a bidirectional action requiring a "friend request" by one user and a "confirmation" by the second. What does it mean to establish a connection with another user on the Facebook site? At the core of Facebook, and the feature for which it was originally developed, is the idea of accelerating social connection between individuals. In a small study conducted by Pew in conjunction with Facebook, they found that as of 2012, Facebook users averaged seven new friends a month, and 80 percent of friend requests that were made were accepted (Hampton *et al.* 2012). Most of the time, but not always, we connect to people whom we've met face-to-face or to whom we have some connection outside of the site.

Dunbar's social brain hypothesis, also known as "Dunbar's Number" (1998), suggests that there is a limit of 150 people with whom a person can maintain a stable social relationship, based on the cognitive capacity needed to recognize and remember others. But half of Facebook users have more than 200 friends in their network (Smith 2014b), and younger users often have considerably more than that. Thus, what can we say about the notion of Facebook "friendship"? A single label applies to all of our connections on the site, whether we are connecting with a parent, a significant other, a best friend, a long-lost friend from high school, a colleague from work, or someone we casually met at a party.

In the world of Facebook, all friends are equal, but some Facebook friends are more equal than others.[14] The average Facebook user clearly cannot maintain meaningful social relationships with the entirety of their network on the site, even in the absence of the time restrictions that would make the upkeep of that many face-to-face relationships impossible. Dunbar himself argues that people identify a core network on Facebook that is about the same size as their face-to-face network (Dunbar 2016), and studies show that we are more likely to communicate on a regular basis with the people to whom we are closely connected in the offline world (Jones *et al.* 2013). Most people make a distinction between their "strong ties" and their "weak ties," even though there is no way to formally designate the ties in this manner.[15]

Our strong ties and weak ties don't function in the same way, and our weak ties neither provide the social support that our strong ties do nor influence us in the same way (Bond *et al.* 2012). But these relationships matter in the aggregate (Gee *et al.* 2017). Gladwell argues:

The platforms of social media are built around weak ties. Twitter is a way of following (or being followed by) people you may never have met. Facebook is a tool for efficiently managing your acquaintances, for keeping up with the people you would not otherwise be able to stay in touch with. That's why you can have a thousand "friends" on Facebook, as you never could in real life. This is in many ways a wonderful thing. There is strength in weak ties, as the sociologist Mark Granovetter has observed. Our acquaintances – not our friends – are our greatest source of new ideas and information. The Internet lets us exploit the power of these kinds of distant connections with marvelous efficiency.[16]

---

[14] The word "equal" here could be replaced by any number of others: influential, important, supportive.

[15] There is a functionality to identify contacts as members of one's family, although it is not a particularly prominent feature and is only visible to another user if they navigate through to a sub-menu on the profile page. Facebook automatically creates "Close Friends" and "Acquaintances" lists which users can populate, but these distinctions are not visible to others. A user can create other designations for lists of friends, but these categorizations are not accessible to others.

[16] Malcolm Gladwell, "Small Change: Why the Revolution Will Not Be Tweeted." *The New Yorker* (October 4, 2010).

However, Gladwell goes on to note that many evangelists for the potential of social media to revolutionize social change don't understand the distinction between the nature of friendship, online and off. We shouldn't expect identical influences from the hundreds of weak ties we have compared to the dozen or so close friends that most people have on the site (Dunbar 2016).

A Digital Soapbox

Various social media technologies in the past have served to connect people who are only weakly connected to one another. The coffee houses of seventeenth-century London were designed to be open to all in an effort to help cross class and privilege boundaries; in other work, Standage elaborates on the network between operators who passed messages up and down telegraph lines, building friendships even in the absence of having ever met in person (Standage 1998).

What is different in our contemporary era is the sheer number of people that a social media user can reach. Social media facilitates the phenomenon of nearly universal authorship (Pelli and Bigelow 2009), defined as the ability of a person to publish text that can be read by 100 or more people. Book authorship grew tenfold each century between 1400 and 2000, but since then, if including new media platforms, authorship has grown nearly tenfold every *year*. Moreover, the audience on social media is densely interconnected. While there are historical examples of large weak-tie networks, it is unprecedented in human history to have one-sixth of all humans on earth able to connect with one another via the click of a button. Facebook data scientists report that on average there are only three and a half "degrees of separation" between any two users on Facebook anywhere in the world.[17]

The Quantification of Our Lives

Social media sites develop affordances based on the balance between the importance of relatively static user content versus dynamic interaction between users. On sites where information about the user's identity is most important, such as LinkedIn, most of the functionality of the site is built around the profile, and there are fewer features for users to interact with one another in a way visible to others. Conversely, where the emphasis is on dynamic interaction or constantly changing information, such as Twitter, more features are designed for users to interact, both privately and publicly.

Facebook sits somewhere in the middle of this spectrum, and, as a result of highly cultivated digital identities plus an emphasis on social connection, the company has designed dozens of affordances for the interaction between the two. Many of these affordances are concentrated on the News Feed and are constantly evolving to further facilitate the balance between identity

---

[17] See https://research.fb.com/three-and-a-half-degrees-of-separation/.

maintenance and user interaction. Apart from the features that have been added over the years for commercialization purposes, the vast majority of the new features of the site are aimed at optimizing the way in which users give feedback on the content posted by other people. This feedback is then quantified – in the form of counts of the number of reactions, comments, and shares – and incorporated instantly and seamlessly into the display of the original content in all other users' feeds.

As a consequence, many Facebook users only post content they expect will elicit social feedback from others, and keep track of how "popular" particular posts are. Work in sociology and social psychology suggests that the desire to manage one's presentation of self and seek feedback from others is a powerful force. While there is ample academic work on this topic, it also has permeated the public consciousness. For example, Thomas Goetz, executive editor of *Wired Magazine*, writes a fascinating article about the extent to which "feedback loops," created when people are given information about their actions in real time, can actually change a wide variety of human behaviors. This is perhaps best exemplified by artist Benjamin Grosser's Facebook Demetricator, a web browser extension that removes all metrics from the Facebook interface.[18] Although he does not explicitly test the effect of removing all signs of quantification, he thoughtfully reasons through the implications of a dozen different details on the site that serve to fulfill our "desire for more."[19]

Our ability to quantify the amount of support for our expressions of identity has some positive impact, such as the ability to increase our levels of social capital (Lee *et al.* 2014), but entails significant mental health concerns as well. Of particular worry is the effect this reinforcing cycle of identity management and quantified feedback has on teenagers, who have developed their own norms that are not always visible to adults (Boyd 2014). A report from the Centers for Disease Control documenting the uptick in suicide rates among young teenagers led some to speculate that the pervasiveness of social media in the lives of children may be a contributing factor.[20]

Trending, Virality, and a Platform for Building Consensus

Martin Luther's *95 Theses* went viral, as did Thomas Payne's *Common Sense*. As a primitive way of measuring public opinion, Louis XV consulted with the chief of the Paris police, the comte de Maurepas, who had compiled volumes of satirical songs and poems about palace intrigue that were being circulated

---

[18] More information is available at http://bengrosser.com/projects/facebook-demetricator/.

[19] Interestingly, but somewhat tangentially, is the commercialization aspects of quantification: individual social media users aren't the only ones interested in the record of their lives. In the aggregate, the data we produce is exceptionally valuable to companies looking to profit from strategic marketing.

[20] Sabrina Tavernise, "Young Adolescents as Likely to Die from Suicide as from Traffic Accidents." *The New York Times* (November 3, 2016).

among the public. People have always used social media to try to assess what others believe and to reveal consensus opinion. There are even historical analogues to the notion that knowing something is popular begets further interest in the topic. In the eighteenth century, British subjects living in the American colonies, finding a pamphlet sold out at the news-stand, would infer that the idea had wide acceptance, increasing the likelihood that they themselves would ascribe to the ideas espoused in the pamphlet. These and many other examples from Standage's book (2013) make clear that people don't need the Internet to rapidly spread ideas and assess what other people think.

However, the penetration of social media sites generally puts these processes on steroids. Almost every platform has its own version – retweets on Twitter, upvotes on Reddit – but Facebook appears to be the site on which quantification and network interconnectedness have been fully maximized to accelerate contagion. Many different things go viral on Facebook: online quizzes, scientific findings and quack medicine, news about celebrity births and deaths, and mobile device video recordings of all manner of things. Computer scientists seek to understand how the underlying network structure facilitates the diffusion of particular ideas or trends, while marketers care more about finding the "secret sauce" that attracts people to particular kinds of content in the first place.

Facebook further facilitates the idea of virality in its "Trending Topics" feature, a box alongside the News Feed featuring a collection of stories circulating on the site that are drawing the most attention from users at any given point in time. Facebook states that "trending helps you discover interesting and relevant topics being discussed on Facebook that may not appear in your News Feed."[21] But the process through which "interesting and relevant" are identified and curated has been one of the most controversial features on the site, and the company has rebooted this tool several times. Initially, the chief criticism was that the editors in charge of the feature suppressed or enhanced certain topics because of political motives. Perhaps as a result of this criticism, in late August 2016, Facebook laid off the editorial team that had previously monitored the feature and replaced them with engineers whose instructions were to be more metric-based.[22] However, this change contributed to the charge that the feature further spread factually incorrect information, "fake news" about the candidates in the 2016 presidential election.[23] Continued changes to this feature are likely.

[21] "What is Trending?" available at www.facebook.com/help/1401671260054622.
[22] Caitlin Dewey, "Facebook Has Repeatedly Trended Fake News Since Firing Its Human Editors." *Washington Post* (October 12, 2016).
[23] While Facebook acknowledged the problem of fake news on the site, the company believes the problem has been overstated. See Scott Stump, "Sheryl Sandberg on Facebook and Fake News: 'We Don't Think It Swayed the Election,'" NBC Today Show (December 8, 2016).

THE NEWS FEED ECOSYSTEM

Social media has clearly been integrated into the daily lives of most Americans, and Facebook reigns supreme above all of its competitors in terms of market share and user engagement. The combination of the features described above – an emphasis on presenting and quantifying interactions between users based on their expressions of self – fosters particular communication patterns. In the first chapter of the book, we addressed the origins of the site and its rapid growth in its first decade. Here, I describe the user experience on the site, with the goal of providing the terminology and concepts needed to make the argument about the consequence of Facebook communication on our attitudes toward each other.

Every social media site is intentionally designed with a format to facilitate the behaviors its creators seek to cultivate. In its early days, Facebook desired to make the site more interactive to encourage users to communicate with one another within the site's interface instead of using it in ways analogous to its predecessors, like MySpace or Friendster. The affordance designed to accomplish this aim, and the most prominent feature of the Facebook site between 2006 and the time of publication of this book, is the News Feed.[24] Introduced in September 2006, the News Feed dramatically changed the way in which people used the site. In a Facebook post he made on the tenth anniversary of the feature's introduction, Mark Zuckerberg wrote:

At the beginning of Facebook, there was no News Feed. For more than two years, Facebook was just a collection of profiles. You could visit a friend's page to look up some basic details about them, but there was no way to see updates from all your friends or be sure they saw yours. With News Feed, all of a sudden you could share with all your friends at once. And you could see what was happening with all your friends in one place. News Feed was the first real social feed. It was such a fundamental idea that now, 10 years later, every major social app has its own equivalent of News Feed . . . News Feed has been one of the big bets we've made in the past 10 years that has shaped our community and the whole Internet the most.[25]

Prior to its introduction, when a user logged into the site, they would land on their own profile page. To see content posted by others, a user had to manually

---

[24] It appears that several companies have converged on the idea of a scrolling feature of new content on the main landing page of the site; Twitter's stream and Facebook's News Feed are the most prominent examples, although even some news sites have taken to the format. Much of this convergence appears to be driven by the fact that users spend more time on a site when information is presented in this fashion. For example, *Slate* reports that in randomized controlled testing in advance of its switch from a traditional home page to a scrolling landing page, the average visitor spent 9 percent more time on the site. If this format is more engaging to people, it may also drive site growth. The number of unique visitors to Facebook's site was essentially flat in the months leading up the introduction of the News Feed, but in the month following the introduction, page views increased 40 percent over the preceding month (Baron 2008, p. 86).

[25] Mark Zuckerberg (September 5, 2016), available at www.facebook.com/zuck/posts/10103084921703971.

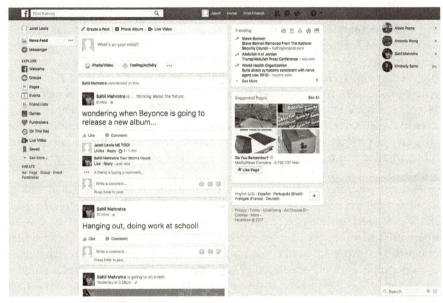

FIGURE 2.1 The home page for the Facebook website

navigate to their profile pages. Content creation on Facebook was largely limited to "writing" on one's own "wall" or writing on the "wall" of a friend, and to share pictures, users had to create "albums." In practice, although uploading pictures became quite popular, most people did not write on their own wall. Interactions between users took a backseat to the cultivation of online identity.

This shift – from profile management to user interaction about the content they generate – defines the experience of using Facebook.[26] The affordance incentivizes interaction, moving away from a home page featuring relatively static profile information to a dynamic and fully personalized page of the content posted by a user's friends. Now, the first thing users see when they log in is the content their friends have generated, not what they themselves have posted. To balance this shift, the News Feed was introduced simultaneously to the "status update," an input box that permanently appears at the top of the News Feed inviting users to post their own content to share with friends (see Figure 2.1). Thus, from the moment of logging in, a user encounters both an invitation to create content and to engage with the content posted by her friends. The addition of the "like" button in February 2009 and the ability to

---

[26] This could change at any point in time, and it likely will! Future readers will thus be tasked with applying the characterization depicted here to the study of whatever affordances are currently available on whichever social networking site is most popular at the time (Dickey 2013; Olson 2013).

comment on other users' posts shifted the focus away from merely cultivating one's own online persona to providing feedback to other users on theirs.[27]

The News Feed centralizes the public and semi-public forms of interaction between users, and the confluence of the site's features and the behaviors and norms developed around them create what I label the News Feed *ecosystem*. Analogous to the biological definition of the term, each user's personalized News Feed is a community of interacting people and the environment in which they find themselves. The ecosystem is bounded by a user's connections on the site, and in practice is highly permeable to the entry of information based on what content is introduced by a user's friends and the pages and groups to which a user is connected.

Readers who are Facebook users at the time this book is published will be familiar with the ecosystem I describe and probably will have interacted with the News Feed in the past 24 hours. But a detailed description of how it operates is of value for everyone else. I begin by describing the content that comprises it before I describe what we know about the algorithm structuring the operation of the News Feed. I then describe the way in which content circulates in the News Feed ecosystem in order to build the foundation on which my framework of social media communication is built.

Characterizing News Feed Content

There are very specific behaviors defining how people engage with material on the News Feed. Users *generate* News Feed content when they post, react, share, or comment on content that can, as a result of their engagement, appear in the News Feeds of their social connections. Users *consume* this content when they scroll through their own News Feed and are exposed to the content produced by others. Importantly, they do not need to click on this content in order to see it and therefore potentially be influenced by it.

The volume of material generated by the processes described above is staggering. In a recent quarterly report, the company stated that it had 1.23 billion daily active users in December 2016.[28] That's over a billion people a day who can post, share, comment, or like content, suggesting that the total volume of material circulating should be counted in the billions, at minimum.

What does this content look like? It includes: links to web pages and blogs about every topic imaginable; articles from a wide variety of media sources,

---

[27] In late February 2016, Facebook introduced the concept of "reactions" to expand upon the "like" button it introduced in 2009. The goal was to allow for a more nuanced set of sentiments to be expressed. For more information on the process used to develop this feature, see Liz Stinson, "Facebook Reactions, the Totally Redesigned Like Button, Is Here." *Wired* (February 24, 2016).

[28] See https://investor.fb.com/investor-news/press-release-details/2017/Facebook-Reports-Fourth-Quarter-and-Full-Year-2016-Results/default.aspx.

ranging from traditional news outlets to sites created solely to produce viral content; visual content such as pictures, memes, or cartoons; videos; status updates; profile pictures; and the likes, shares, and comments on any of this original content.[29] The common element is the communication of information in a social context that invites response from other individuals in the social network. There is very little visual distinction between different types of content, and at least through 2017, no distinction indicating the quality of a third-party source that produced content. For readers completely unfamiliar with the Facebook News Feed environment, online Appendix A contains several examples of the kind of content that circulates.

An Algorithmic Distillation of Our Social Reality

Quick mental calculation will demonstrate that the News Feed cannot feasibly show every piece of content that every single friend of a user posts. The process by which Facebook decides which content to show users is incredibly opaque and results from a proprietary algorithm that is constantly evolving. As one journalist writes:

Every time you open Facebook, one of the world's most influential, controversial, and misunderstood algorithms springs into action. It scans and collects everything posted in the past week by each of your friends, everyone you follow, each group you belong to, and every Facebook page you've liked. For the average Facebook user, that's more than 1,500 posts. If you have several hundred friends, it could be as many as 10,000. Then, according to a closely guarded and constantly shifting formula, Facebook's News Feed algorithm ranks them all, in what it believes to be the precise order of how likely you are to find each post worthwhile. Most users will only ever see the top few hundred. No one outside Facebook knows for sure how it does this, and no one inside the company will tell you.[30]

The News Feed algorithm is one of the most controversial aspects of the site. Some have gone so far as to label it one of the twenty-first century's "weapons of math destruction" (O'Neil 2016). Perusing exposés that have attempted to open the lid on the process gives hints as to what drives the algorithm, but provides few confirmable details.[31] Reports are that the engineers at Facebook responsible for the News Feed algorithm incorporate more than 100,000 highly

---

[29] The News Feed also contains a considerable amount of sponsored content, advertisements that are formatted to look the same as content generated by a person's friends on the site. I do not include the consequences of engaging with this content posted by third parties with which users have not established a direct connection, but this is obviously an area ripe for future study.

[30] Will Oremus, "Who Controls Your Facebook Feed?" *Slate* (January 3, 2016).

[31] In the same post where Zuckerberg celebrated the News Feed's anniversary, he wrote, "Technically, News Feed is one of the most advanced systems we've built. For more than 1 billion people every day, it considers everything your friends are posting and all of the media content you might be interested in, it considers how much you might care about updates from each person or interest, and then it tries to show you what you'll find most important. Nothing like it has ever been built before."

personalized factors[32] when deciding what content to display to a user, all combined to create a "relevancy score." This score focuses on the nature of the relationship between the content creator and the user, the performance of the content among other users, the user's past revealed preference for post type, and the recency of the post. The more "popular" a piece of content in a user's network – in other words, the most people who have liked, commented on, or shared something – the more likely it will make its way into a user's News Feed. Likewise, the users and pages that a person interacts with most frequently are more likely to appear in the feed. The algorithm is responsive to the ways in which a user has engaged in the past and also gives the user a handful of explicit options to shape the kind of content that does or does not appear.

If a user scrolls to the bottom of the News Feed, the algorithm will keep revealing new content, digging deeper into the barrel of possible stories to reveal material with lower and lower relevancy scores. Because of the proprietary nature of the algorithm, no academic studies exist demonstrating the proportion of the universe of content generated by one's contacts to which the average user is exposed on the feed. However, a journalist seeking to answer this question reports that after spending 6 hours on the site in an effort to see everything posted by his friends, he saw less than a third of the content. By his extrapolation, a user spending the average amount of daily time on the site would see much less, perhaps as low as 4 to 5 percent of everything posted.[33]

Part of what makes Facebook so compelling is that every user's News Feed is uniquely tailored to them, based on what the user has chosen to engage with in the past and based on what other users find engaging in the moment. What a particular user sees is then further influenced by the frequency with which she scrolls through her News Feed. But this very feature makes precise measurements of News Feed exposure difficult to collect and study.

First, the algorithm renders the notion of quantifying and characterizing *universal* aspects of News Feed content conceptually and technically difficult. By definition, each user is exposed to a customized feed, unlike traditional forms of mass media or even web pages where everyone can access the same pool of content. Second, users are not in complete control of the content to which they are exposed, which has important implications for our theories of media selectivity. Conversely but simultaneously, the optimization process means that people are served more of what they have consumed in the past, leading to a "rich getting richer" phenomenon that heightens the selection effects into exposure. As long as the algorithm is continually changing and remains proprietary, it will be impossible for scientists unaffiliated with Facebook to systematically and precisely study the outcomes of these competing influences on News Feed exposure.

---

[32] Josh Constine, "How Facebook News Feed Works." TechCrunch (September 6, 2016).
[33] Tim Herrera, "What Facebook Doesn't Show You." *Washington Post* (August 18, 2014).

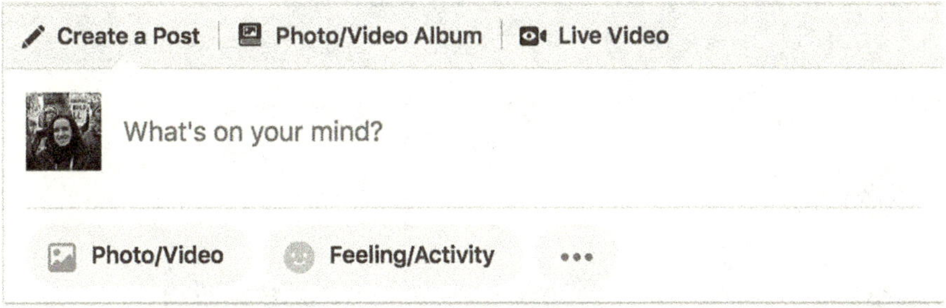

FIGURE 2.2 The status update box
The box in which users can type in a status update or post other content to Facebook appears at the very top of the News Feed.

Articulating the Flow of the News Feed

Now that we have a comprehensive sense of the operation of the News Feed, let's consider the trajectory of a single piece of content introduced by a user. Facebook is constantly developing its interface and features are regularly added or deleted from the user experience. Furthermore, there are many permutations of the way that content can be originally brought into the ecosystem of the News Feed, and each permutation creates slight differences in the information signaled on a particular post. The features outlined here will evolve as Facebook implements changes, but the basic social logic holds regardless of the variation in presentation.[34]

The Generation Phase

The simplest form of communication is a *status update* about a person's opinions, thoughts, or actions. At the top of the home screen of the site when a person is logged in to Facebook is a box in which a user can type a message (Figure 2.2), as well as add photo or video content, which then is circulated to the audience that person selects. Most people choose to have their status updates circulated to all of their friends on the site.

A second option for generating content (text, image, or video) is to visit a third-party website and direct material from that site onto Facebook. Most news sites and many other types of websites include functionalities that allow users to post directly to Facebook, either posting something to their own Timeline,[35] to another user's Timeline, or within a group. All of these ways of introducing content will generate a story that appears in other users' News

---

[34] For an interesting visual retrospective of the evolution of Facebook's design, see www.forbes.com/pictures/edee45edklh/the-evolution-of-facebook-4/#88e936c456dc.

[35] The Timeline is the facet of a user's profile on the site that displays information in reverse chronological order as opposed to other sections that contain personal details, lists of friends, or photos. Facebook defines the Timeline as "where you can see your posts or posts you've been

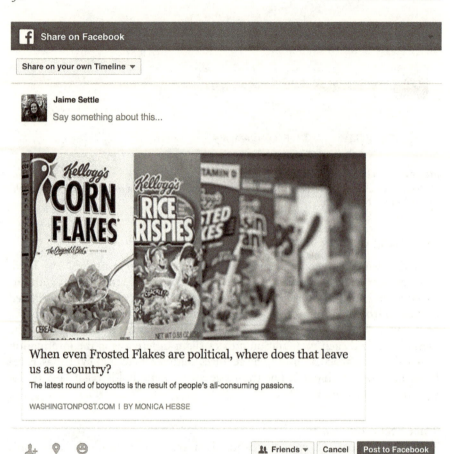

FIGURE 2.3 Content from a third-party source
The appearance of content posted by a third-party organization, such as a media source.

Feeds, indicating the original source of the content as well as the person who brought it into the Facebook environment. Users can post the story without commentary or add their own thoughts and opinions above the image containing the visual link, what I call a *visual lede*, to the original content (see Figure 2.3).

Another option for introducing content into one's network is by following a page or group within the Facebook site. By liking the page of an organization or public figure that creates content – such as a business, a brand, a media

tagged in displayed by date. Your Timeline is also part of your profile. You can post to your Timeline either from the top of your Timeline or from News Feed."

FIGURE 2.4 Mechanisms for social feedback
The buttons featured on the bottom of content posted to the News Feed where users can interact with each other.

organization, or an elected official – content will appear in a user's News Feed directly from that source.[36] A user can then disseminate the content by sharing it with her social connections and adding on commentary if she wants. This spreads the content far beyond those users who follow the original organization that posted it.

The last major way that content gets introduced into circulation is when a user changes something on his or her profile. Not all profile changes will result in a story circulating on a user's friends' News Feeds featuring the change as the "story," but certain alterations do: changing a profile picture or indicating a major life event such as an engagement or marriage.

Content can originate on the News Feed in a variety of different ways. Unlike face-to-face communication, content is not typically directed at a particular individual or individuals and instead is communicated to the social network widely. Everyone is implicitly invited to engage. The consequences of this will be explored in more depth later in the book.

The Social Engagement Phase

This phase, and the consumption phase described below, happen concurrently. Users are presented with the opportunity to engage with content as they are scrolling through their feed. For illustrative purposes, I will begin with the way in which other users can add additional information onto the original content introduced into circulation.

Once a user has introduced content into Facebook, or shared content posted by a group or page already within the site, the content then circulates to his or her friends. Automatically appended to the bottom of almost every type of content that circulates on the feed is an area designed for other users to interact with the content (see Figure 2.4).

Most of the time, friends consume others' posts in a very passive manner: they encounter the posts in the News Feed, but rarely click on the content or engage with it. However, when a friend does want to engage, she has a variety of options. She can "react" to a post, in which case other people reading the post will see that reaction. The original, and most prevalent, "reaction" is to

---

[36] A user can like up to 5,000 pages.

"like" something.[37] Reacting to a post does not permanently attach the post to the friend's profile; only the friend is able to go back on her "Activity Log" to see which posts inspired her to react. A friend also can "share" a post, a behavior that is both visible to the people looking at the original post, but then also becomes a permanent part of the friend's profile. Finally, a friend can "comment" on the original post, which appears as part of the comment thread underneath the post, but is not permanently attached to the friend's profile. A comment can include both a friend's own words, but also any links that they want to include. The user who originally posted the content can join in the interaction among their friends at any stage.

All three behaviors – liking, sharing, and commenting – contribute to the aggregation of social information about the original post that sends potentially important signals to people skimming it in the News Feed. And all three behaviors serve as meaningful responses, even if the response does not necessarily include words.

The Consumption Phase

Depending on the way in which people have configured their privacy settings, the generated content with the addition of social feedback can appear on the News Feeds of the original poster's friends as well as the friends of any of the people who interacted with the original post. In other words, social engagement considerably amplifies the reach of a piece of content. Remember that these two stages happen simultaneously: as friends add social engagement, the content is updated instantaneously to reflect their contribution so that future consumption of the content by other users includes the most updated quantification of social feedback. Furthermore, the more engagement the post gets, the more likely it is to appear in the News Feed of additional users.

Figure 2.5 below shows a stylized schematic of what results from the social engagement process described above. The example includes content that is politically informative – a news story published from a think tank's blog. But any content a user posts directly from third-party sites will look similar. The figure highlights the fact that the core content is only one of several potentially informative components of the post. Others have explored some of these features, such as the importance of media source cues (Iyengar and Hahn 2009) or social cues (Messing and Westwood 2014; Anspach 2017), but have focused primarily on understanding what predicts the content on which a user

---

[37] Most of the time, people still "like" things, even though there are now other emotional reactions available. The expansion from the "like" button to the "react" feature occurred in the middle of data collection for this book. To be consistent, even since the introduction of the expanded react feature, I refer to "liking" content in both the survey and the experiments I've conducted. The Facebook interface displays all reactions together in an aggregated fashion, and the parlance of "liking" something is widely recognized by users. Certainly, a more rigorous analysis differentiating the reactions to political content is warranted.

FIGURE 2.5 Schematic of a Facebook post

clicks. Conversely, the focus in this book is on the consequences of what people *see*. Even without clicking on any content, a user still can be exposed to one or more *signaling mechanisms* simply by scrolling through the News Feed.

When a user scrolls through her News Feed and encounters the most basic form of content, a status update, she has received a straightforward *expression cue* about the opinion, feeling, or behavior of her friend on some topic.

For content other than status updates, the first bit of information a user can consume is the *source cue*, or the media source or origin of the original content. This signal appears whether a friend posted the content directly from the source's web page or whether the friend followed the source on the site.

In addition to the source cue, stories posted directly from news sources, or notifications that a user's friend has liked a story, will carry *aggregated information*: the total number of Facebook users across the whole site who have liked, shared, or commented on that article, without any reference to the user's social network (Figure 2.6).

If a user's friend has posted the story, the content will not contain any aggregated information, but will contain significant social information (Figure 2.6). The first of these I call *endorsements*. The weakest form of endorsement is the implicit endorsement that is created when a person's friend posts an article, which asserts both that the article is worth reading and also

FIGURE 2.6 Comparison of the appearances of aggregated information versus social feedback

If a user follows a third-party source on the Facebook site and shares that with her network, the aggregated information about the total number of users who have engaged with the content is shown. If a user posts a story from a third-party web page, social feedback from the user's network – in the form of social cues and commentary – appears instead.

that the poster implicitly agrees with the content. As we will see in Chapter 6, people do make the connection between the view espoused in a headline and the opinions of the person who posted it, even in the absence of words confirming that endorsement. This endorsement can be made more explicit with the addition of a poster's original words to elaborate on their viewpoints.[38]

Other types of social information can be found on both status updates and posted content. Beyond implicit or explicit endorsement, a post also contains enumerated *social cues*, the number of likes or shares a post has garnered or the length of the comment thread it engenders. Social cues are similar to the aggregated information cue described above, but are distinct because they are quantifiable measures of support from within a person's own social network,

---

[38] Of course, the signals from a user's words and the source cue may conflict, a situation that I test in Chapter 6. However, because of selective exposure to ideologically concordant news, opinion leaders tend to post from sources that align with their beliefs.

either their friends and possibly the friends of their friends, depending on the user's privacy settings. Social cues are quickly consumed metrics of the amount of support or interest a post has generated among the people to whom the user is connected on the site. Finally, a typical post on Facebook contains *social commentary*, or the content of the comments that accompany a post. From the News Feed, only a handful of these comments are visible, but the full commentary can be seen by expanding the post.

Some combination of all six of these signals – expression cues, source cues, aggregated information, endorsements, social cues, and social commentary – are available to users without clicking on content in their News Feed, and the content with the greatest volume of cues is probably more likely to appear based on the algorithm Facebook uses to place stories in the feed. To varying degrees, previous research has investigated how these factors affect information selection, but this book focuses on information *exposure*. In the second half of the book, I show that these signals can be informative about the political views of the user who posted the content to which the signals are attached, even if the content itself is not about politics.

Frequency of Scrolling the News Feed

We've now considered the big picture of the operation of the News Feed and the trajectory of the creation, dissemination, and consumption of a single piece of content in the News Feed. The missing piece in the middle is the volume of content to which a person is exposed. This estimate varies wildly, depending on a number of factors: the platform on which a user accesses the site; a person's scrolling habits and frequency of adding social engagement to the content they see; and the duration that they spend on the site at any one point in time as well as cumulatively over the course of a day or a week. Anecdotally, and based on internal pilot studies,[39] it seems that when a person logs on to Facebook and scrolls through their News Feed, they encounter dozens to hundreds of pieces of content at one time.

It is difficult to quantify the total volume of content that people actually create or consume on Facebook. However, we can measure how frequently they report using the site. Consistent with previous work, in the End Framework Survey fielded in April 2016, more than 80 percent of respondents indicate they use Facebook most or every day. Among those users, over 95 percent say they scroll through their News Feeds, with almost 70 percent indicating that they do so more than once a day (Table 2.1). Any consequences of this scrolling behavior then could potentially affect a broad swath of the American public.

---

[39] My extensive and highly scientific method for making this estimate was to time myself scrolling the News Feed on a desktop computer and calculate how many pieces of content I saw in 60 seconds. Without stopping to engage with anything, I saw twenty-six distinct items.

TABLE 2.1 *Frequency of Facebook Usage*

	Percent of Sample
Log-in Frequency	
A few times a year	2.58%
About once or twice a month	3.97%
About once or twice a week	9.23%
Most days	11.90%
Every day, but only once a day	9.03%
Every day, a few times a day	40.87%
Every day, too many times to count	22.42%
Scrolling Frequency	
I don't scroll through my News Feed	4.83%
Once a day	26.74%
2–4 times a day	39.81%
5 or more times a day	28.62%

The first question assessed users' response to the question, "How frequently do you spend time on Facebook?" The denominator is the 1,008 respondents who answered the question. All users who answered that they logged in to Facebook most days or more frequently (n=849) were asked, "On a typical day when you use Facebook, how many times a day do you scroll through your News Feed, either on a mobile device (like a phone or tablet) or a computer?"

POLITICAL CONTENT ON THE NEWS FEED

The depiction above is intentionally general because most users log on to Facebook for entertainment purposes or to glean information about their social contacts, not to engage in political behavior. This background context is absolutely essential for any analysis of exposure to political material on the site: for most people, the cycle of News Feed consumption and engagement involves *encountering political information while seeking social information.*

How often do users inadvertently encounter content they think is political? On average, users report they see this kind of content about half of the time when they scroll through the News Feed, but aren't looking for it. A slim majority of users, 51.88 percent, report they see political content more than half the time.

Given that most users encounter political content a majority of the time they scroll through their News Feed, what kind of content do they see? Ideally, we could directly assess all the content that a person creates and all the content that circulates through his or her News Feed to get a sense of the political content to which they are exposed, but this is not feasible for a number of reasons.[40]

---

[40] Facebook data scientists do have the access and capability to do this anonymously in the aggregate (Bakshy *et al.* 2015). However, Facebook has restricted its policies over time for

The next best thing is to ask respondents what they generate and what they see most frequently. This self-report measure is almost certainly tainted by recall bias – people are more likely to remember certain kinds of content – but it is likely that what users are able to remember and report is the material that has the most potential impact on them.

Several things apparent in Table 2.2 can be put into context. First, it is clear that while many users generate political content, it is not the most prevalent type of content with which they engage. As a point of comparison, Pew has found that 44 percent of Facebook users like content posted by their friends at least once a day, and 31 percent comment on other people's photos on a daily basis (Smith 2014b), so the incidence rate for these behaviors on political content in a six-month time span is much lower. In fact, approximately 30 percent of subjects report that they haven't posted, shared, or commented on any explicitly political content at all in the preceding six months. Notably, people are much more likely to engage by "liking" political content as opposed to more intense forms of interaction such as posting, sharing, or commenting, but a similar proportion of respondents (27 percent) haven't liked any content.

There is not a one-to-one correspondence between the prevalence of content people post and the prevalence of content that appears in other users' News Feeds because of the role of user engagement in the Facebook algorithm. More than twice as many people report that they post and share news articles than memes or parody videos, but the ratio is attenuated when comparing the rates of seeing news articles versus seeing political images, memes, and videos. This is likely because of the comparatively high rates of user engagement with these other forms of content, which favor their circulation in people's feeds.

But even the political content that is most prevalent is still not encountered as frequently as non-political content. If we assume that users see non-political content 100 percent of the time they scroll through their feeds, then even the most ubiquitous form of political content (news articles, as shown in Table 2.2) is seen only half as frequently. Furthermore, the quantity is considerably less. Although the numbers have increased considerably over time – from 6 percent in 2012 to 25 percent in 2016 who say that much of what they see on Facebook

collaborations with academic researchers, and few social scientists have had access to Facebook's data to test their own research questions. While this data could be obtained directly by accessing Facebook users' accounts with their permission, institutional review boards (IRB) express serious concerns about the fact that a user's friends cannot grant informed consent for their content to be studied. Facebook does have an application program interface (API) that allows programmers to access users' data if they consent to using the application, but the data available to scrape is quite limited. Therefore, it would be nearly impossible to gather content from an individual's News Feed without collecting the very information that many IRBs deem to be off-limits.

TABLE 2.2 *Reported Incidence of Engagement with Political Content*

	Generating Political Content				Consuming Political Content	
	Posted	Commented	Shared	Liked	Seen	Clicked
News article about the election, campaign, or politics in general	20.69%	21.78%	29.50%	47.23%	51.29%	31.49%
Status update	17.13%	17.62%	16.04%	32.87%	38.51%	25.05%
Humorous or parody videos dealing with political issues	10.79%	16.93%	27.23%	43.07%	45.84%	34.95%
Political image	9.41%	15.54%	19.21%	35.15%	46.44%	25.15%
Video of a candidate speech, press conference, or debate	9.01%	13.76%	16.14%	33.76%	38.32%	26.83%
Petition	9.01%	13.56%	20.69%	32.18%	20.59%	19.11%
Political meme	8.32%	14.06%	22.38%	37.72%	45.34%	29.31%
Video news reports about the election, campaign, or politics in general	8.22%	13.76%	19.60%	35.54%	40.39%	28.51%
Informational videos that explain a political issue	7.92%	14.65%	18.32%	33.76%	29.10%	28.51%
Political infographic	7.03%	12.38%	14.26%	30.40%	29.31%	23.07%
Campaign advertisement	6.93%	11.58%	15.05%	34.46%	36.43%	20.40%

The percentages for generating content are all those users who report they have engaged in the behavior in the previous 6 months. The percentages for "seen" and "click" reflect those who reported that they frequently or almost always see this kind of content when they have scrolled through their News Feed in the previous 6 months. The denominator for all columns is all 1,010 respondents in the survey. For full information on the question wording used to generate these statistics, see the online appendices.

is about politics[41] – for most people, political content comprises only a portion of the content that appears in their feed.

POLITICAL INTERACTION ON THE NEWS FEED:
A FUSION BEHAVIOR

Assume for a moment that people don't process political content differently than they would any other content they encounter on the feed. Users have the same motivations for evaluating political content that they would for anything else: looking for interesting or humorous material, providing social feedback on the content their friends post, and learning about the lives of their contacts on the site.

Is this assumption valid? Do people engage with political content just as they engage with any other sort of content on the feed? Should we expect the motivations people have for generating and consuming political content to be the same as for other kinds of content they generate and consume? Should we expect the consequences to be the same?

Political scientists have generally assumed that political behaviors are distinct from other social behaviors because of the features of the domain in which they occur: the inherent contestation of politics, the embedded power dynamic in a given society, and at least in democracies, the overarching importance of questions pertaining to representation. The stakes are simply higher for political behaviors both in terms of the costs accrued and the benefits acquired. In a representative democracy, our attitudes and actions are supposed to have consequences, and the day-to-day ways in which people engage within their political system are theorized to have downstream influences at the ballot box.

If we think political content should be differentiated from other News Feed content, just as we differentiate political behavior from other social behaviors, can we adequately characterize interactions with political content into frameworks we've previously used to study political interactions that precede voting decisions?

Assessing what has been written about political interaction on Facebook reveals a lack of theoretical consensus about how to characterize these behaviors. Most research has selectively focused on a single action of interest without contextualizing that action, and many scholars have left vague their ideas about what precisely people are doing when they generate politically relevant content on these sites. When data extracted from social media is used to make claims

---

[41] The response options on the two Pew surveys differed slightly. In 2012, users could report "all/ almost all," "most," "some," "just a little," or "none at all" (Rainie and Smith 2012). In 2016, they could report "a lot," "some," "a little," or "none" (Duggan and Smith 2016). Perhaps more striking is that in 2012, 63 percent of social networking site users said that none of what they saw was related to politics. That percentage had dropped to 6 percent for Facebook users in 2016.

about aggregate opinions or behaviors of the public, researchers have implicitly assumed that people are engaging in political expression. Others classify interactions on social media as a form of political discussion, noting the conversational-like qualities of comment threads in Facebook groups.

But more commonly, social media behavior has been studied within the framework of mass communications. The origin of much of the political content with which people engage can be traced to political elites and the media, such as campaign materials or news stories. Consequently, media scholars often assume that Facebook is simply a novel platform for traditional producers of political content to distribute it (Gainous and Wagner 2013). A small but growing body of research picks up where these scholars leave off, identifying the factors that make people more likely to follow elites on Facebook, examining the processes through which politically engaged Facebook users receive elite and media messages, or exploring the forces that shape which news stories people are most likely to click. These researchers thus characterize political interaction on Facebook as a form of information seeking, the Web 2.0 version of using the Internet to learn about news and politics. However, there is hardly any previous research focusing on mere exposure to content on the News Feed, when users see it, but don't click on it.

News Feed interactions aren't clear-cut and often fuse together behaviors that are considered distinct in an offline context. Although it is not typically people's primary aim for using the Facebook site, people do report that they engage in a variety of explicitly political ways: liking a candidate's Facebook page, documenting themselves doing silly things to raise money for charity,[42] circulating petitions for particular political causes, or changing their profile picture to show support for a candidate or issue.[43] The list continues to expand as the technology evolves.

The work I have done with my colleagues reveals some of the ambiguities inherent in these kinds of behaviors. For example, on the day of an election, is clicking a button on the top of the News Feed that says "I voted" best thought of as a self-report measure of voting, a measure of political expression, or an attempt to mobilize one's contacts (Bond *et al.* 2017)? Does writing a political status update imply anything about a person's level of political interest (Settle

---

[42] The most classic example of this is the "Ice Bucket Challenge" that went viral during the summer of 2014. According to Facebook's newsroom, between June and August, more than 17 million videos were shared of people pouring ice water on themselves in order to raise money for organizations that do research on the disease ALS (Facebook Press Team 2014). Almost half a billion people worldwide watched these videos for a total of 10 billion views. More information is available at http://newsroom.fb.com/news/2014/08/the-ice-bucket-challenge-on-facebook/.

[43] In response to the Supreme Court's decision in *Obergefell v. Hodges*, more than 26 million people changed their profile picture to one that was overlaid with a rainbow flag to indicate their support for the decision to legalize gay marriage (Dewey 2015). See Robert Barnes, "Supreme Court Rules Gay Couples Nationwide Have a Right to Marry." *Washington Post* (June 26, 2015).

et al. 2016)? Conceptually, does one have to click on a news article in the feed to be engaged in "news-seeking" behavior? What offline behavior is most analogous to "liking" a political meme, to "posting" a news story, to "sharing" a parody video? More fundamentally, given the presence of novel and unconventional content on the site such as political memes, do people even agree on what constitutes "political" content on the News Feed? Previous research suggests that most likely, they don't (Fitzgerald 2013). And what about content that is not explicitly about politics, but is informative of the views of the person who posted it? If people use the site to learn about the lives of their family and friends, might they be inclined to make inferences about the political views of their contacts?

These queries matter because they influence the sorts of effects we should expect to find when people engage on the News Feed. Trying to fit consumption and generation behaviors into the neat boxes established by previous research risks missing the forest through the trees. Until we answer these foundational questions, we will be hard-pressed to articulate theoretically motivated, testable hypotheses about the consequences of engaging with explicitly political or politically informative content. In short, we must better theorize what it is we are measuring so we can look for the kinds of effects that are most likely to result.

In the next chapter, I dive deeply into the characterization of those social media interactions where people *express* their political identities, engage with political *news*, and *discuss* their opinions. I bring together these three conceptually distinct facets of online behavior to propose the *END Framework* of social media interaction from which we can derive novel expectations about the consequences of creating or being exposed to politically informative material on the News Feed.

I argue that generating and consuming politically informative content are distinct political behaviors, albeit ones that fuse together characteristics of more recognizable political behaviors. The way in which people engage with content on Facebook certainly has similarities to the way in which they express their political identities, seek political information, and discuss politics with others. But differences in the content itself, the context in which the behaviors occur, and the constitution of the people who interact with each other are sufficiently divergent as to suggest that we look beyond traditional outcomes – such as agenda-setting, learning, or issue attitude change – and focus instead on how these interactions affect our evaluations of our fellow citizens.

3

The END Framework of Political Interaction on Social Media

Before the development of social media, political behavior scholars could more or less easily classify different forms of political engagement. Political discussion involved two or more people talking about "important issues of the day." News consumption meant that a person sought out access to news, while inadvertent exposure meant that they encountered political information without intending to do so. People expressed themselves politically when they put out a yard sign, affixed a bumper sticker, or wore a campaign button.

Social media upended this neat typology of different forms of political engagement. We express our political identity in a very social and interactive process of consuming information. The affordances on the sites are in many ways designed to blur the lines that differentiate distinct offline political behaviors. As we saw in the previous chapter, people see, post, share, scroll, like, click, and comment in one seamless interface, intermixing their interaction with political content among their interaction with all other sorts of content. Most content that circulates on the News Feed is not about politics. But as alluded to in the previous chapter, the signals attached to Facebook content create the possibility that a considerably larger amount might be informative about the political views of the person who generated it. I will use the phrase "politically informative" to refer to this content to emphasize the idea that people communicate information about their political beliefs – and make inferences about the beliefs of others – even when they are interacting about non-explicitly political topics.

This chapter articulates the *END Framework* of social media interaction. END refers to the characteristics of a subset of content that circulates in a social media ecosystem: a personalized, quantified blend of politically informative *expression*, *news*, and *discussion* seamlessly interwoven into a wider variety of socially informative content. Facebook is a very rich case study in which to explore the effects of END interactions in a social media environment characterized by a particular set of features and norms. It is these affordances of the

TABLE 3.1 *The END Framework: Distinguishing Characteristics of Political Interaction in the News Feed Ecosystem*

Expression	News	Discussion
Highly visible, durable platform	Unintentional exposure to fused social and political information	Multi-person conversations with weak ties
Proliferation of signals	Enhanced information environment	Public forum
Social feedback	Entertainment	Absence of moderating social norms
Catering to an audience	Altered relationship between producers and consumers	Evidentiary support and inflammatory content
	Increased power of opinion leaders	
	Social quantification and curation	

site that facilitate the consequences explored in this book, and the END typology should be generalizable to the extent that other platforms feature affordances similar to those of the News Feed.[1]

The behaviors in the framework are identical to the way in which people engage on the News Feed generally, as noted in Chapter 2. Users *generate* content by posting, sharing, commenting on, or liking content that is politically informative. Users *consume* content when they scroll through their News Feed and encounter content that is politically informative. Importantly, they do not need to click on it; mere exposure is sufficient.

In the previous chapter, we focused on contemporary social media behavior and situated engagement with politically informative content within our understanding of people's experience on Facebook more broadly. In this chapter, I characterize generating and consuming politically informative content in a broader assessment of analogous political behaviors. Engaging with content in the END Framework resembles three offline political behaviors: publicly expressing political views, seeking or encountering political news, and discussing politics.

The approach here is to think about how generating and consuming politically informative content are conceptually similar to and different from the behaviors they most resemble in the offline world, in order to theorize what distinct outcomes might result from the way in which people express their political views and interact with each other about politics in an information-rich environment. There are important differentiations between the traditional behaviors of political expression, information seeking, and political discussion and the comparable facets of those behaviors involving politically informative content on the News Feed. These are depicted in Table 3.1. Despite theoretical

---

[1] The range of ways in which people can engage politically on social media is huge, and a single typology is inadequate to capture the nuances of what people are doing on different platforms. An obvious future extension of this work would be to test these hypotheses on another social media platform.

similarities, these notable differences should inform our study of the consequences of engaging with politically informative content on the News Feed.

POLITICAL EXPRESSION ASPECTS OF NEWS FEED INTERACTIONS

Social media serves to connect people with one another while simultaneously
providing a platform on which people can cultivate their online identities.
Extended to the political realm, the generation of political content allows a
person to define and maintain an online political identity, while consumption of
it facilitates inferences about the political identities of others. The ability to
create a public, political persona – the political expression feature of News Feed
interaction – is perhaps its most novel feature.

What Does Political Expression Look Like Offline?

Political expression occurs when a person makes public some aspect of their
political identity or political views. This broad definition could include many
things. For example, it could encompass such things as attending and holding a
sign at a gathering of people. It could incorporate the behavior of signing a
document containing a political demand or statement of views that is being
publicly circulated. However, we typically would characterize these behaviors
as "protesting" and "signing a petition" respectively, moving them into the
realm of political action, not pure political expression. A more narrow understanding of political expression is therefore restricted to behaviors that are
relatively passive and done independently: displaying a yard sign, ordering a
specialty license plate, affixing a bumper sticker, or wearing an article of
clothing or other identity marker such as a sticker or button. While these
behaviors may be more ubiquitous in other parts of the world, in the American
context, few people engage in them regularly.

What do we know about why, how, and when people choose to publicly
express their political identities, and what kinds of people are most likely to do
so? Pure political expression almost always has been considered as one part of a
broader participatory index of behaviors (Huckfeldt and Sprague 1992; Mutz
2002), and we know relatively little about pure expression in and of itself. In
the United States, the most ubiquitous political identity is one's party affiliation.
Green, Palmquist, and Schickler (2002) demonstrate that people hold the kinds
of identities amenable to expression, but they don't assess the visible or durable
signals of identity. Apart from partisan identity, the next most common signal
to express would be an ideological identity, a candidate preference, or a
position on a particular political issue. Unsurprisingly, based on data from
the American National Election Study, the people with the strongest political
opinions, or strongest partisan identities, are the most likely to engage in

expressive behaviors. The small literature on bumper stickers and yard signs has typically focused on understanding which kinds of people in which kinds of situations (Laband *et al.* 2009; Makse and Sokhey 2014) are most likely to display visible signals, finding that yard sign display is driven not only by political sophistication, but also by a genuine desire to publicly express one's views or a belief that the display can be influential.

What Does Expression Look Like on the News Feed?

Never before have people been able to so visibly and permanently attach specific political content to their identities for their broader social network to see and engage with. Political expression can take many forms on Facebook, and there are several durable and informative markers of a user's political views built into the functionality of the site, such as the ability to like or follow political candidates or groups or to self-identify political views on the profile page. These behaviors only contribute to the News Feed ecosystem, however, to the extent that they are visible when people *interact* with each other. Therefore, the political expression components of END behavior focus on the most visible ways in which people's political identities can be broadcast through their networks.

Written Expression: Status Updates

First, the most direct form of political expression is the written content generated by users: as stand-alone politically relevant status updates or as text accompanying a link that they post. These are generally the most unambiguous signals of political identity. While written commentary has the potential to spark political discussions, before anyone replies, it is simply a statement of a person's political views. Posting a political status update is a less common behavior than posting or sharing content generated by another user or organization, as we saw in Table 2.2 in the preceding chapter. Table 3.2 shows the frequency of status update posting in the END Framework Survey, revealing estimates very much in line with previous work.[2] Despite being less frequent, posting a political status update is a powerful signal to other users about one's political beliefs; nearly two-thirds of respondents who reported that they had learned someone's political views on Facebook indicated that they had done so based on a user's own words, a point further explored in Chapter 5.

---

[2] Pew has found that 34 percent of people report that they have used social media to "post your own thoughts or comments on political or social issues." Relatedly, 31 percent have "encourage[d] other people to take action on a political or social issue that is important to you" and 35 percent have "encourage[d] other people to vote" (Smith 2013). Using data from Facebook collected in 2008–2009, Settle *et al.* (2016) found that over a quarter of users posted a political status update, a proportion that has likely increased in the last decade due to changing norms on the site.

TABLE 3.2 *Incidence of Political Status Update Posting*

Users posted a status update ...	
... containing political views or opinions, written in your own words	39.21%
... containing direct support of a particular political candidate or official, in your own words	29.70%
... containing a direct encouragement to vote, in your own words	34.16%
... requesting others to get politically involved, in ways other than voting, in your own words	29.01%
Combined	
At least one political status update	51.19%

Proportions of the nationally representative sample who report generating various kinds of expressive political content on the News Feed within the last six months. The denominator is all 1,010 respondents in the study.

What are the distinguishing characteristics of these political status updates? It is conceptually difficult to think of appropriate texts with which one could compare the language of status updates. Very few people write newspaper opinion editorials, and even if they did, the style of a long-form editorial would be very different than the short format of the status update. There is no easily accessible written record of the comments people make during informal conversations about politics with family, friends, or acquaintances. Text generated in the comments section of online newspaper articles or blogs are written for a very different audience by a very distinct subset of those people who communicate about politics online.

In the absence of an obvious set of comparison texts, I conducted a study on Amazon's Mechanical Turk[3] service to generate a set of texts to which I could compare political status updates. The premise of the study was to compare the linguistic characteristics of text written to sound like a status update to the characteristics of text motivated by other goals: to be informative, accurate, persuasive, or to elicit engagement from readers. I do not make any assumption about what precisely people are trying to accomplish when they write in the style of a status update. Instead, the linguistic similarity and difference between status updates and other short texts facilitate inferences about the style and tone of political status updates. The details of the study can be found in online Appendix B.

What were the results? Status messages share linguistic similarity with writing that is intended to solicit feedback from readers, and political status updates are even more negatively emotional than are other types of status updates. Self-referential, emotional language is the norm for status updates, but this is not necessarily how people write when they are aiming to be

---

[3] See Appendix A for a description of Mechanical Turk.

accurate, informative, or persuasive. Even though Facebook users report that they are trying to inform or persuade their friends when they generate political content, it appears that the language they use is more similar to language used to encourage other people to respond.

Non-Written Expression: Profile Pictures, Source Cues, and Other Functionalities

People can change their profile pictures to signal political beliefs. Thumbnail profile pictures accompany the information that people post and, most of the time, these pictures are not politically informative, but instead simple headshots or group shots that include the user. However, from time to time, there is viral adoption of a "profile picture" meme, where large numbers of users all transform their pictures in the same way or all post the same profile picture (Leasca 2016). These become very visible and recognizable political signals that accompany a user's posts until she again changes back to a more standard profile picture. Recent examples include the response to the 2012 election of Barack Obama, to the Supreme Court's decision to protect the constitutionality of same-sex marriage, or to attacks on Planned Parenthood. Over 20 percent of users in the END Framework Survey report that they changed their profile picture "to support or oppose a political issue or candidate" in the preceding six months.[4]

People also can signal their political viewpoints by the choice of news outlet from which they post political content. Social media has come of age in one of the most polarized eras of American politics, and the media environment has fragmented in a way that potentially furthers this polarization. Media sources seek to develop a brand as an informative signal of the kind of coverage they post and the niche audience they are trying to reach. As a result, the ideological composition of the people who use particular sources has become more homogeneous, and the public has polarized along ideological lines as to which sources are trustworthy. For example, *Fox News*, the *Drudge Report, Breitbart*, and *The Blaze* have more consistently conservative audiences and are more likely to be trusted by conservatives; the opposite is true for the *New Yorker, Slate, Mother Jones*, and *Think Progress* (Pew Research Center 2014b). Later in the book, we will see that even ideologically moderate people perceive biases in these sources and that a majority of Facebook users impute political slant to a wide variety of media sources.

---

[4] The survey was fielded in April, approximately six months after the viral adoption of a filter that users could place over their profile pictures to show solidarity with France after the terrorist attack in Paris in November 2015 (Feeney 2015). It is unclear if users would consider this a change to "support or oppose a political issue." The frequency of viral profile photo adoption suggests that this particular instance should not bias upwards people's recollection of their behavior. Pew reports that 18 percent of US social media users have changed their profile picture "to draw attention to an issue or event" (Gottfried *et al.* 2016).

Social media users are constantly evolving new norms and adapting the site's features for the purposes of political expression. For example, in the fall of 2016, more than 1 million people "checked in" to the Facebook page maintained by the Standing Rock Indian Reservation, although the number of protestors physically there was considerably less. Due to a rumor circulated that the local police were trying to track activists protesting about the Dakota Access pipeline, users supportive of the protest's cause were indicating their presence at the site to stymie any attempts by law enforcement to do so.[5] As this incident shows, any attempt to systematically catalogue the way in which users signal their political views will be outdated almost immediately, but our conceptualization should be sufficiently flexible to encompass as-yet-undeveloped modes of expression that serve the same purpose as those discussed here.

Unintentional Expression

Finally, as described in Chapter 2, the affordances of Facebook are designed to help users cultivate their public identities. To the extent that non-political aspects of our identity may correlate with our political views, users can post a variety of different types of content – ranging from non-political news stories to cartoons to memes to photos – from which other users could impute political views. In Chapters 5 and 6, we will explore the role of politically sorted and implicitly political content further, but it is possible that users are unaware that they are signaling their political identities when they display this kind of content.

What Distinctions Matter for Our Theorization of the Effects of END Interactions?

Are the aspects of News Feed interaction related to political expression – political commentary, profile pictures, media source selection, and politicized content – simply the social media equivalent of bumper stickers and campaign pins? There are many shared elements. Some of our hypotheses from the offline world should neatly transfer to the social media context. For example, we expect the most partisan people to display these expressions and we would expect an increase in political expression at politically salient times, like election seasons (Settle *et al.* 2016). However, the incredible expansion of the possibilities to express one's political identity, and the distinct features of this public expression, raise the potential of heightened consequences of expressing one's identity or being exposed to the expression of others.

---

[5] Merrit Kennedy, "More than 1 Million 'Check in' on Facebook to Support the Standing Rock Sioux." NPR (November 1, 2016).

What Counts as "Political Expression" and How Often Does It Occur?

The variety of observable signals available to indicate identity on Facebook is much larger than it is in the offline world. During campaign periods, candidates typically make all sorts of tangible goods (such as stickers and signs) for users to display to signal their identities. But at most other points in time, there are many fewer options available, although interest groups and advocacy organizations often solicit donations by offering free goods. Conversely, on Facebook, there is always an abundance of content that a user can link to her public political identity,[6] and there are organizations whose sole purpose is to create politically informative content for users to circulate.

Importantly, it appears that even non-political content can send signals about political beliefs. A few examples may highlight this point. A picture a user posts where she is proudly displaying a hunting rifle could trigger reasoning about what her attitude on gun control might be. An article that a user shares about composting could signal a strong commitment to recycling, and by extension, a concern for climate change. A user's "checking in" weekly at her evangelical church could be interpreted as an expression of religiosity, permitting guesses as to her political views that could be validated via a "like" she posted in response to another's political post.

In studies presented later in the book, Facebook users achieve remarkably high levels of consensus about the political views of anonymous users who post content, even content that is judged to be *apolitical*. Perhaps because of the documented differences in social preferences between liberals and conservatives or because of the social stereotypes people have come to hold about other Americans, it appears that people will draw inferences about the partisanship and ideology of other Facebook users based on a wide range of content.[7]

As a result, we must have a much more expansive understanding of online "political expression" than we have had for its offline counterparts. Even users who don't intend to express their political identities may find that they are signaling their views just by using the site for social purposes. If we only consider the ways in which people explicitly signal their political identities or views, we will miss the wider scope of signals that are *politically informative*.

Who Is the Audience and How Can They React?

In addition to the wider range and increased volume of tangible signals available, political expression on the News Feed has a much more extended reach. Although users do have the option of controlling what content gets

---

[6] Dallas Lawrence, "How Political Activists Are Making the Most of Social Media." *Forbes* (July 15, 2010).

[7] Whether people are aware of the full extent of the signal they send when they post content that is not an explicit statement of their political views is a question that merits future exploration.

shared with which portion of their social network, the default settings on Facebook share content with all of a person's friends on the site. Information that gets shared to the News Feed can then be shared by any of a person's friends. Pew has estimated that the average user can reach 156,569 other individuals through their social network at two degrees of separation: the friends of their friends (Hampton *et al.* 2012).[8]

While the average user probably doesn't realize this, they are very aware of the fact that what they do on Facebook is highly visible and becomes a quasi-permanent part of their online identity. That is, in fact, one of the key reasons for using the site. Thus, political expression on Facebook happens with the full knowledge that it can reach a large audience and that it is durable, not fleeting. Statements of political belief made face-to-face only are recorded for perpetuity by the extent to which the participants or observers remember what was said. Yard signs and bumper stickers are highly visible, but only to the portions of one's network who regularly see a person's home or car. Conversely, the News Feed is expressly designed to circulate people's expression to a wide audience, and the content remains accessible until the user chooses to remove the information.

The audience for political expression on Facebook matters not just because of its scope, but because there is room for public feedback of one's beliefs on the News Feed, unlike in most forms of offline political expression. When a person changes her profile picture or posts content, her contacts have the ability to interact directly with that content, in most cases signaling endorsement via "liking" or "sharing" the content. The incentive to solicit feedback from one's network likely changes how people express themselves as they seek to validate their opinions or assess the level of support for their opinion in their network.

Finally, the audience matters because they can be affected by the political expression they observe to a much larger degree than they have been in the past. Unlike a political discussion, political expression on Facebook is not necessarily seeking to persuade others or provoke a meaningful exchange of ideas. The relatively sparse opportunities for visible or durable signaling of political identity in the offline world has resulted in a dearth of research on the consequence of exposure to the political expressions of others.[9] Given that social psychologists have uncovered profound effects of consuming expressions of identity in other domains, this is a fertile area for investigation.

---

[8] This estimate is skewed by the small number of users who have many friends themselves. The maximum number of friends-of-friends reached was 7,821,772 other people. However, even considering the median reach, the potential impact is large: 31,170 people.

[9] The only study to date focusing on the consequence of public expressions of political identity shows that after being primed with a stimulus evoking partisan disagreement, subjects rate neighborhoods with political yard signs as less attractive places to live (Klar and Krupnikov 2016, ch. 4).

NEWS EXPOSURE ASPECTS OF NEWS FEED INTERACTIONS

A growing proportion of Americans report Facebook is an important part of the way in which they keep up with the news. Users can introduce news into the News Feed ecosystem from third-party websites, help circulate posts from the Facebook pages of third-party sources, or simply encounter news when they scroll through their feeds.

What Does News Exposure Look Like Offline?

The two-step flow of information theory (Lazarsfeld *et al.* 1944) has shaped the way in which scholars of both mass media and interpersonal communication (Katz and Lazarsfeld 1955) understand how the mass public is exposed to political information. Opinion leaders figure prominently in this theory, influencing both what information gets transmitted, as well as interpreting its meaning and significance. We've long known that in addition to elite opinion leaders – politicians and "talking heads" – a small portion of the citizenry is actively engaged in persuading and informing others about political issues (Berelson *et al.* 1954; Katz and Lazarsfeld 1955; Katz 1957; Zaller 1992; Huckfeldt and Sprague 1995; Ahn *et al.* 2010).

Exposure to political information always has occurred intentionally and unintentionally. As a legacy of the golden era of broadcast news – when most Americans had only three television channels from which to select – much of the early theorizing about information seeking assumed that many people were exposed to news not by choice, but because they were a captive audience (Baum and Kernell 1999; Prior 2007). However, in an information-rich environment, our theories changed and the notions of choice – including the decision to pay attention to news in the first place (Mutz 2006a) – became more central in the literature. Some people deliberately and intentionally sought out the news: subscribing to newspapers, watching news programs on television, listening to the radio, or surfing the Internet. Many more encountered the news as a by-product of seeking out entertainment, through "soft news" programming for example, with mixed evidence about whether this inadvertent exposure contributed to increased political knowledge (Baum 2003; Prior 2007).

Simultaneously, the era of choice opened the door for theories of motivation – the differentiation between de facto selectivity and selective exposure (Sears and Friedman 1967) and the process of motivated reasoning (Kunda 1990) – to take hold, explaining the behavior of those people actively consuming political information. The politically interested, when it is available, seek out news that is concordant with their political views (Stroud 2008; Iyengar and Hahn 2009; Stroud 2010; Arceneaux *et al.* 2012; Knobloch-Westerwick 2012; Garrett 2013; Garrett *et al.* 2013; Mummolo 2016) and evaluate political information in biased ways (Meffert *et al.* 2006; Taber and Lodge 2006; Gaines *et al.* 2007; Taber *et al.* 2009; Nyhan and Reifler 2010; Slothuus and De Vreese 2010).

What Does "News Exposure" Look Like on the News Feed?

For the 48 percent of Internet-enabled Americans who report that they go directly to Facebook for political news in a given week (Mitchell *et al.* 2014), information seeking on the News Feed functions largely like the home page of a newspaper's website, where people consume the information readily available (the headline, a short description, and perhaps a photo), clicking on the news that is most interesting to them. The key differences between the feed and the news website – factors that all have important implications for how people process political information – are the intermixture of social and personally relevant information alongside political news, the social signals attached to the political news, and the diversity of news source quality.

For most people, however, information seeking happens when they log in to Facebook for non-political reasons. Most people access Facebook to share information with or glean information from their social contacts. This is the primary motive for the social engagement and consumption phases of the News Feed cycle described in the previous chapter. More often, people scroll quickly through the News Feed, stopping to read the available portions of a post that strike their interest and clicking on a post only if it crosses some threshold of curiosity that justifies the investment of time to read the full post or link.

This "exchange" of information is the core function of the News Feed, although two factors differentiate this exchange in the political realm compared to the way in which people exchange non-political information. First, political communication is heavily imbalanced: many more people consume political information than generate it, and the people engaged in these two distinct behaviors have different characteristics. Second, non-political content is very self-referential and often includes photos or videos of the user and his friends and family. However, almost by definition, political content is more likely to contain content generated by a third party – a news story, a meme, etc. – because the subject matter involves elite actors instead of direct, personal connections.

What Distinctions Matter for Our Theorization of the Effects of END Interactions?

Are the aspects of News Feed interactions related to information dissemination and exposure – elite-generated content, the motivations for opinion leadership, and the psychological processes structuring consumption of political news – simply the social media analogue to the two-step flow of information? There are many shared elements, including the fundamental structure of the information flow from elites to opinion leaders to the uninterested mass public. Many of our hypotheses about the effects of traditional media should neatly transfer to the social media context. However, as Delli Carpini notes in reference to the Internet more broadly, "We cannot gauge the positive or negative consequences of the new information environment on citizens' attitudes and actions without first being able to accurately gauge what information (in the broad sense of the word) people encounter" (2009, p. 55). Not only is the content of "news" qualitatively different on Facebook, but there are several distinct features of news exposure via the News Feed that create the potential for heightened effects on subsequent political attitudes.

Who Controls the Production and Dissemination of Content, and What Are Their Incentives?

Some emphasize the degree to which social media is a tool for elites to control the flow of political information and communicate more directly with the mass public (Gainous and Wagner 2013),[10] while others argue that social media has lowered the cost of news production, empowering a larger and more diverse set of actors to help set the agenda. Scholars have noted the unique "bidirectionality" of the medium for communication between elites and the mass public (Graber and Holyk 2011; Jacobs and Shapiro 2011; Just 2011; Gainous and Wager 2013), and the ways in which the media has increased its reliance on public demand for what is considered news. All of these characterizations are likely accurate.

For news producers, the norms and affordances of social media have altered considerations about what kind of content to produce. When we focus on media and elite-originated content on the News Feed, we must consider the incentives these actors faced when designing it and deciding what to circulate. The primary goal is to elicit as much engagement (i.e. likes, shares, and clicks) as possible among the target audience: most often, a group of like-minded opinion leaders. This has two effects with the potential for fostering psychological polarization: enhancing the role of opinion leaders and creating a role for social curation.

Opinion leaders have never had more tools in their arsenal. As mentioned previously but worthy of repetition, the average Facebook user can reach over 150,000 people through her friends and her friends of friends (Hampton *et al.* 2012). Harnessing the power of one's social network in a highly visible platform greatly increases the possibility for the politically savvy to inform and persuade others. The medium itself is highly conducive for this influence. Beyond the ability to reach large numbers of people, opinion leaders have much more compelling and signal-rich information to transmit. Paired with the increased power of opinion leaders is the concept of social curation: information becomes "newsworthy" when the public endorses it through liking,

---

[10] The conceptualization of social media as a tool of the elites and the media may be facilitated by methodological path dependency: the earliest research in the field focused on analyzing the social media content generated by political elites, favoring a top-down model of political information dissemination on social media. It also may reflect the research design difficulties in measuring politically relevant exchanges by ordinary people on Facebook or Twitter.

sharing, or commenting on it. Media sources use this information to get a sense for public demand and interest, and Facebook's algorithm prioritizes the display of these stories, creating reinforcing cycles for the kind of information that gets widely distributed on the News Feed.

This process stands in stark contrast to the editorial curation of the past. Newspapers and news shows required strict professional gatekeeping, and the decisions of editors and producers about what was considered news – and how to present it – inspired the study of agenda-setting, framing, and priming (Just 2011). This gatekeeping role persisted even into the Internet age, as long as the gateway for people seeking news was the website of a preferred news source. This has shifted, however, in the age of social media. Today, many people go directly to social media and access the news from there. The consequence is that the curation of news has moved from professionals in the newsroom to a form of individually customized crowdsourcing based on the people and news organizations a person is connected to on Facebook.

Has the Democratization of News Production Affected the Quality of the News That Circulates?

There are thousands of media sources and organizations that produce content for the Facebook News Feed. An exact census of these sources would be impossible to conduct. Some of the sources built their reputations in traditional domains, such as cable news shows or newspapers, and others have developed for the ecosystem of the Internet and social media specifically.

Media content always has been a reflection of the incentives and structure of the system in which it is produced (Hamilton 2004), systems sensitive to the effects of the confluence of technology, political institutions, and culture in a given era (Starr 2005). While the need for advertising revenue continues to drive much of the strategic decision-making of what gets covered when, the kind of content that "sells" online is categorically different. Media producers long have known that people prefer human interest stories and scandals to meaty journalistic pieces, and in the era of social media, these preferences are amplified by the demand for visually compelling and interactive news. Organizations that circulate content via Facebook keep a close eye on the metrics monitoring their posts in order to optimize user engagement. Likes, shares, and comments are the currency in the marketplace of political ideas on Facebook. The factors that tend to drive engagement, visual imagery and attention-grabbing headlines, are prevalent. Thus, even the highest-quality media sources grapple with the balance between entertainment and journalism.

Moving down the quality hierarchy is one of the most prevalent types of political content: political humor. Political humor is not a modern invention, although the Internet has led to an explosion of it, perfected by the cartoons, memes, and parody videos circulated on social media. To date, there is little academic research on the novel forms of content that have been created for the

Facebook environment, but we can draw on past research about political humor. Political theorists have explored the virtue of humor in political dialogue, dating to ancient times (Lombardini 2013), and political cartoons have been a staple of the way in which Americans communicate about politics since the printing of the first newspapers. A small literature, rooted in the tradition of the debate over "soft news" (Baum 2003; Prior 2003), has explored the effect of televised humor, primarily in the form of late-night comedy shows, on political learning (Baumgartner and Morris 2006; Young 2006; Esralew and Young 2012; LaMarre *et al.* 2014). Most directly applicable is the finding that humor can make people feel as if they better understand politics because they "get" the jokes (Baumgartner 2008).

Facebook users report that humorous content circulates widely on the site, and that one of users' primary motivations for disseminating political content is because they think that it will make their friends laugh. Presumably, laughing makes people more likely to comment on, like, or share content. In turn, Facebook's algorithm favors content that draws the most user engagement. Since the generators of political content seek to maximize the circulation of their material, they are motivated to learn by trial and error what kind of content receives the most feedback. Over time, this has led to the proliferation of political material designed to be humorous, not necessarily accurate or balanced.

At the bottom of the hierarchy of news quality is "fake news," false information that masquerades as legitimate news. Although this is likely to change moving forward, for many years the Facebook interface has not differentiated content that is produced by reputable news sources from content that is produced by disreputable sources, including single individuals who intentionally circulate factually incorrect information on social media.[11] Concern has become widespread about the implications of the spread of fake news, especially in the aftermath of its prevalence in the 2016 election. A quantitative, albeit journalistic, analysis found that the top-performing fake news stories related to the 2016 presidential campaign received more shares, reactions, and comments than the top-performing news stories from reputable publishers.[12] The formal study of the spread of political misinformation on social media is in its infancy (del Vicario *et al.* 2016), but the empirical findings uncovered by Brendan Nyhan about the difficulties in correcting misinformation (2010) suggest that people may be quite susceptible to biased reasoning after consuming it, especially if the narrative of the false news report comports with their prior political beliefs and opinions.

---

[11] Scott Shane, "From Headline to Photograph, a Fake News Masterpiece." *The New York Times* (January 18, 2017).

[12] Craig Silverman, "This Analysis Shows How Viral Fake Election News Stories Outperformed Real News on Facebook." BuzzFeed (November 16, 2016).

How Prevalent Is Inadvertent Exposure to Political Information, with What Consequence?

It is for politically uninterested individuals that changing technologies have had the largest impact on our assessment about the consequences of information exposure. In an era of media choice, many people "opted out" of watching the news, and we were forced to consider how, or even whether, the politically disengaged were exposed to political news. The advent of social media is not the first technological change to challenge the assumption of intentionality of exposure; the rise of cable television and the Internet did, too. Given that the uninterested simply can opt out of exposing themselves to political information (Arceneaux and Johnson 2013), both the "soft news" (Baum 2003; Prior 2003, 2007) and "by-product learning" literatures (Popkin 1991) sought to identify the extent to which people were exposed to political information incidentally and what the consequence of that was for their political knowledge and attitudes.

The News Feed platform combines the "captive audience" feature of the golden era of broadcast news with the entertainment aspects of soft news with the unintentionality of by-product learning. In other words, political information is presented in a social, entertaining format, but people cannot opt out of exposure to hard news on the site easily, because there are not separate "channels" for hard and soft news on the News Feed. Critically, people now encounter their news when they are seeking entertainment and encounter political information when they are seeking social information. This has not gone unnoticed by the producers of political content, and they have responded accordingly, in many cases, trying to make political information as entertaining as possible in order to compete for people's attention.

If we want to understand the effect of truly inadvertent exposure on the News Feed, we should consider what users encounter when they scroll through their feeds, but don't actively engage with content. It remains a pertinent question whether this incidental exposure affects perceptions of issue salience, political interest, and political knowledge if people do not click on the content and other research has endeavored to find out (Feezell 2018). Importantly, END content contains something that older forms of soft media don't have: social endorsement and feedback from people in a user's social network. These facets of the content are not only more prominently displayed than the pertinent details of the actual news, but are visible even if users don't click, suggesting they are potentially influential for the least engaged users (Anspach 2016).

POLITICAL DISCUSSION ASPECTS OF NEWS FEED INTERACTIONS

The political expression and information exposure aspects of News Feed interactions form the basis on which its third dimension, political discussion, is built. Compared to other political behaviors people report on Facebook, relatively few report engaging in conversations on the site on a regular basis, and as a consequence, most scholars have not studied Facebook interactions through this theoretical lens. But interactions between people are at the core of the site's functionality.

What Does Political Discussion Look Like Offline?

Political discussion has typically been characterized as conversation about politics or public affairs between two or more people who have a social relationship with one another. What do we know about the patterns and consequences of political discussion after decades of study and dozens of publications? Most people don't talk about politics all that frequently. When they do, they tend to talk about politics with people with whom they have close relationships, such as their family and friends (Conover *et al.* 2002). Most people have fairly homogeneous political discussion networks, talking most frequently with those who agree with their presidential candidate choice (Huckfeldt and Sprague 1995; Huckfeldt *et al.* 2004) or share their partisan identity (Huckfeldt and Mendez 2008), but disagreement does persist in discussion networks to varying degrees depending on how it is measured (Huckfeldt and Sprague 1995; Huckfeldt *et al.* 2004; Mutz 2006b). People who engage in political discussion are more likely to be politically engaged in other ways as well. Typically, people who talk about politics more frequently are more informed about politics, and there is some evidence that engaging in political discussion actually can increase political participation (Lake and Huckfeldt 1998). However, the results are mixed as to whether exposure to cross-cutting viewpoints is beneficial or detrimental to downstream political behaviors (McLeod *et al.* 1999; Mutz 2002).

These findings are robust and have been replicated in many different samples in many different settings. However, stemming largely from limitations in our measurement strategies, the scope of inquiry on political discussion has a narrow aperture. While our theories of face-to-face political discussion do not preclude discussions that involve more than two people, in practice, our measurement strategies have typically focused on measuring dyadic discussion between people. The emphasis on two-person conversations between close ties is mostly an artifact of the way in which we can reliably measure political discussion. But this measurement artifact has led to a dearth of theorizing about the kinds of casual political interactions people have face-to-face that may better resemble the discussion aspects of political communication on Facebook.

Measurement constraints on assessing the breadth of a person's "discussion network" often force that network to assume a "starburst" shape, where the respondent is the center of a series of dyadic conversations. We know that this is not necessarily an accurate depiction – that a respondent's discussants may talk with each other, and that a respondent may have a conversation about politics with more than one person at a time – but best practices in survey assessment have dictated that we only capture the kind of political discussion that we can most precisely and uniformly measure.

While scholars recognize that face-to-face political discussion can occur between people who might not identify each other as "discussion partners," the focus of research has been on people who report talking to each other regularly. There is much evidence that the majority of face-to-face conversation does happen between strong ties. Yet the findings that our political discussion partners overlap considerably with our discussion partners for other important topics may partially be a product of first asking about the people, and then asking about the content. This focus on regular discussants means we know more about conversation between close social ties than conversation between more casual acquaintances.

What Does Discussion Look Like on the News Feed?

Research in social psychology and communication shows that a key motivation driving people to post non-political content on Facebook is to solicit feedback from their social network, in the form of likes, shares, or comments. Similarly, one of the biggest incentives to generate expressive or informative *political* content on the News Feed is to spark a reaction from others. While likes and shares on a post create the social cues and social endorsement features of News Feed content, comments on a post are the foundation for the political discussion aspects of News Feed communication.

Although there are very marked differences between face-to-face conversations and the interactions that appear in comment threads on the News Feed, both capture the same fundamental construct: people exchanging ideas and opinions about politics with the hopes of validating their own political views or informing or persuading others about their opinions. One study found that 20 percent of registered voters had sent messages to other users on a social networking site or Twitter "encouraging them to vote for one of the candidates," and that 31 percent have "encouraged others to take action on political/social issues that are important" to them (Smith 2013). These behaviors move from expression to discussion once one or more users reply.

The results from the END Framework Survey validate the idea that Facebook serves as a forum for influence, persuasion, and discussion of political ideas. When asked why they have posted, shared, or commented on political content, 43.72 percent of the sample said they wanted to inform others about political issues, and 34.14 percent report hoping to persuade others to share their opinions. Other frequent responses included the 30.04 percent of the sample who reported that they generate content to see if other people agree with their opinions and the 27.93 percent who want to correct false information that someone else has posted. Although less frequent, about one-sixth of Facebook users reported that they like to provoke agreeable or disagreeable discussions with other users.

Political discussion appears in several places on the Facebook site. Outside the context of the News Feed, a user can comment on the pages of politicians, candidates, and other public figures as well as the pages of major media sources. These comments become relevant when and if they appear on the News Feed of the users' friends who also like that page. When users generate content, their friends have the option of commenting directly on those posts. There can be multiple conversations within a single thread: users can choose to reply directly to the original post or reply to one of the comments that have already been made. Furthermore, users can tag other users in their posts, which is frequently done in multi-person conversations to address comments directly back to a particular speaker earlier in the thread. Beyond commentary, users can share other forms of content – links to news articles, videos, memes, etc. – directly within these conversation threads.

To the extent that our online social network interactions mirror our "real world" connections (Jones *et al.* 2013), it is likely that we are interacting most frequently with strong ties on social media. However, users are connected to hundreds of others on the site and thus are exposed to the discussions that these weak ties have with their own networks. A person who posts a political news article on Facebook with commentary might provoke a conversation thread that is not limited to just the friends of hers who are friends with one another. Social media facilitates political interaction for a user's ties even if those people would not ordinarily talk about politics with each other or might not even know each other. Similarly, conversations that take place in one part of a user's social network, say his friends from high school, are visible to people in a totally separate part of the network, say his work colleagues, if the user contributes to the conversation.

What Distinctions Matter for Our Theorization of the Effects of END Interactions?

Is the political discussion component of the News Feed – the comment threads that form in response to political expression and other forms of political content – sufficiently conceptually similar to face-to-face conversation that we should expect the patterns from the offline world to apply in the social media context? Although political discussion is one of the most fundamental and well-studied behaviors in the political behavior literature, scholars have taken for granted certain implicit assumptions about the concept. Those assumptions have to be revisited in the realm of online communication, and reconciling previous literature suggests that we should expect online political interaction to have several distinct effects on subsequent political attitudes.

Must People Participate in a Discussion to Be Affected by It?
Sharing an opinion about politics with another person always has opened up the possibility for knowledge of those views to be revealed to others, as

conversations can be overheard by third parties not involved in the discussion. We've all sat through Thanksgiving dinner conversations with an insufferable relative or family friend; while the irascible guest may not make our list of regular political discussants, we are certainly affected by the heated conversation that ensues. It's possible to overhear political comments people make in off-handed ways, while waiting in line at a store or in making small talk with strangers. Acknowledging that this happens more frequently to political scientists, most people have had the experience of a seatmate on the bus, train, or plane making a comment about politics that may make us uncomfortable.

However, all of these examples of fleeting instances of interpersonal political communication in the offline world have been understudied. Measurement challenges have kept us from systematically exploring the effects of exposure to the political exchange of ideas that happen between strangers or weak ties. In our conceptualization of traditional political discussion, the possibility of "overhearing" a political conversation – the ability to listen without needing to contribute to the discussion – is incidental. On Facebook, this aspect is foundational to the behavior itself and is much more common. Opinions are expressed and information is exchanged in full awareness – and frequently with full intention – that the interaction is observed by others, and that others may join in without being explicitly invited to do so. Relatedly, most of the political interactions that constitute discussion on the News Feed involve more than two people. The topics, norms, and conventions of political conversation may vary considerably with the size and composition of the group, a topic that is essentially unexplored in face-to-face conversations. We don't have expectations from prior literature on political discussion about how these differences should affect the kind of content that gets exchanged or the characteristics of the people who contribute to the conversation. But even absent participation in it, exposure to this form of interaction could be influential.

What Is the Mechanism through Which Exposure to Disagreement Affects Subsequent Political Attitudes and Behavior?

The definition of "political disagreement" is integrally important to our measurement of how frequently it occurs and what the consequences of exposure to it are. The literature on disagreement in face-to-face discussion networks reveals that the extent of exposure to cross-cutting ties depends in large part on what defines cross-cutting exposure in the first place: disagreement in party affiliation, disagreement in presidential vote choice, or simply self-reported disagreement (Klofstad *et al.* 2013). Most of our theoretical expectations about the effects of this disagreement stem from exposure to points of views with which one does not agree, whether that causes ambivalence and therefore disengagement from the political sphere (Mutz 2002) or encourages them to reconsider their justification for their views (Huckfeldt *et al.* 2004).

If we think the operative mechanism is exposure to points of view that are different than our own, then a person does not necessarily need to participate in the conversation to be affected by encountering those perspectives. To understand the effects of exposure to information with which we disagree on the News Feed, we should focus on the distribution of opinions within a person's network. Because the context of social media opens up the possibility of engagement between weak ties in a way not feasible in face-to-face interactions, and we are more likely to disagree with our weak ties, we should expect that people encounter a higher volume of cross-cutting information than they would in their face-to-face discussions. Additionally, information about the distribution of opinions in a person's Facebook network should be more visible to them than is the distribution of opinions in their offline network. As we saw in the previous chapter, the affordances of Facebook are designed to help make transparent what is popular and "trending" among one's network. Therefore, not only is there more cross-cutting information available to a user on Facebook, but they are better able to characterize the distribution of those opinions.

There is a slightly different literature that addresses the consequence of encountering disagreement, suggesting that some individuals, based on their conflict avoidance (Ulbig and Funk 1999) or their introversion (Mondak 2010; Mondak *et al.* 2010; Hibbing *et al.* 2011; Gerber *et al.* 2012), may have aversive reactions to encountering people who behave in conflictual ways. If exposure to conflict and incivility is a mechanism that we think affects downstream political attitudes and behaviors, then the differential norms and conversational flows of discussion on the News Feed also should matter (Gervais 2015). Data from Pew released in advance of the 2016 presidential election suggest that political interactions on Facebook can be quite contentious and disagreeable. Compared to other forums in which people might discuss politics, 53 percent of users found social media discussions to be less respectful, 51 percent said they are less likely to come to resolution, and 49 percent said they are less civil (Duggan and Smith 2016).

Is Political Discussion on Facebook Deliberative?

If Facebook users were exposed to high levels of contention and disagreement, but those conversations were of a high enough quality to be considered deliberative, our expectations of the consequences of participating or observing END interactions could be optimistic. A deliberative public forum on Facebook would be one in which citizens were able to engage their disagreement in a way that facilitated or prepared them for collective decision-making (Fishkin and Luskin 2005; Thompson 2008). Facebook interactions also would be considered deliberative if citizens take part in a process that creates or reinforces the legitimacy of collective decisions (Thompson 2008). Deliberative forums typically are characterized by public-spiritedness, respectful reasoning, accommodation, and equal participation (Thompson 2008). Successful deliberation is thought to rely upon accurate information, civility, and reflection (Mutz 2008). If successful deliberation were to occur, theorists suggest a plethora of positive outcomes: increased political tolerance, perceptions of the legitimacy of the opposition's viewpoints, and willingness to compromise, to name a few (Mutz 2008).

What we typically define as "political discussion" does not meet the qualifications for democratic deliberation as articulated by political theorists (Delli Carpini *et al.* 2004). Similarly, END interactions are not deliberative for a number of reasons. First, as we will see in Chapter 5, not all citizens are equally likely to contribute to the conversation; the most partisan and ideologically extreme are the most vocal. Second, the expression of political views via the News Feed is more truncated than it would be in face-to-face communication, perhaps due to the increased cognitive task of writing as opposed to speaking. Short expressions of opinion are likely less nuanced than more elaborated explanations, making it difficult to be reflective, let alone identify points of consensus and overlap. Third, the prerequisites for respectful deliberation are rarely met based on the way in which people actually generate political content. Political discussion on social media is ironically less social at its moment of generation; despite the public nature of the interaction, people primarily interact with these sites in geographic and temporal isolation from other users of the site. One of the fundamental problems studied in the field of human-computer interaction is that this depersonalization of communication can adversely affect its quality. There are fewer moderating norms in the social media environment that act to keep interactions civil.

Social media users themselves report outcomes suggesting that their interactions are not deliberative. In addition to the statistics cited above about the quality of Facebook interactions, Pew's report found that 59 percent of social media users find disagreeable political interactions to be stressful and frustrating, and 64 percent find that they have less in common politically than they thought they did (Duggan and Smith 2016). These outcomes are the exact opposite of what should occur if END interactions served as deliberative forums where social media users were able to identify points of consensus and respectful understanding.

CONCEPTUALIZING END INTERACTIONS

Generating and consuming politically informative content on social media are behaviors that share conceptual overlap with the offline behaviors of political expression, news exposure, and discussion and can speak to many of the core debates in the scholarly literature. But the elaboration above reveals that a straightforward application of previous theory is more complex than it may initially appear.

Previous political science research typically has isolated one facet of a behavior on social media and studied it within the framework of the behavior it most resembles offline. Yes, status updates are a form of political expression that should be responsive to the level of competition in the political environment (Settle *et al.* 2016). Yes, the stories that appear on the News Feed do have agenda-setting potential on what issues people consider to be important (Feezell 2018). Yes, clicking on a story in the News Feed can be a measure of selective exposure, and we should care about when that behavior happens and what the effects are on learning and persuasion (Messing and Westwood 2014; Anspach 2018).

Yet focusing only on those facets of behavior that have the clearest analogues to more traditional political behaviors, without respect to the broader context in which the behaviors occur, means we may overlook factors that could be consequential about the use of social media, but that don't fit neatly into our previous typologies. The most novel parts of social media behaviors are those for which there is no clear equivalent offline behavior – such as the quantification of social feedback on our political expression – or those where there is, but the rate of incidence varies markedly between social media and face-to-face interactions – such as the opportunity to be a "fly on the wall" and overhear the political conversations of those people with whom we disagree.

Conceptualizing the END Framework of communication – and its constituent interactions – is an attempt to highlight these potentially consequential and novel facets of social media behavior in order to derive theoretically informed expectations about their consequence on our downstream political attitudes and behavior. END interactions are thus those behaviors in which a person generates or consumes politically informative content in an interactive context, where social and political communication is intermixed, and where the interactions are made visible and quantifiable to become part of the information environment itself. In this book, the focus will be on these interactions in the Facebook News Feed ecosystem, but the argument about the consequences of END interactions should apply to any platform that supports this kind of interpersonal interaction.

The Hallmarks of END Interaction

Synthesizing the distinctions between END interactions and their offline cousins reveals three key factors important for understanding the consequences of these behaviors as they appear on the News Feed. These ideas are previewed here and elaborated on in the next chapter, where I analyze why these changes facilitate the processes underpinning psychological polarization.

The Context of END Interactions Is Social Communication and Inference

Facebook is a social site: people communicate with one another for social reasons and scroll through their News Feeds to learn about the social lives of their acquaintances, friends, and family. Most users thus encounter politically informative content as an unintentional by-product of their broader search for social information about their contacts. They do not intend to become

informed about the news of the day necessarily; rather, they are seeking information about other people's lives. Users are thus primed to make social
inferences and to connect the information they encounter to the person who
posted it.

Increasingly, many users do rely on the site to seek out or disseminate
political news. For those who seek news, their choice of Facebook rather than
another news-aggregating site or the web page of a news source is telling: they
intentionally choose the social curation of news infused with social cues. Other
people desire to use the Facebook site to share political information with their
contacts. This form of engagement with political content also is highly intentional. It is important to remember that they are choosing the platform of social
media over other ways in which they could disseminate political information.
When these users communicate about politics, their motivations extend beyond
the traditional goals of informing and persuading others. Many of them desire
to make visible their political identities and communicate with like-minded
others. If people engage with others to socially validate their own or their
friends' viewpoints, political content is a special category of social information
and we should derive expectations accordingly.

The Content of END Interactions Can Be Subtly Politicized or Unmistakably Polarizing

On the one hand, as we will see in Chapter 5, a wide variety of content has the
potential to be politically informative. This may take the form of *politicized
issues*, content that reveals disagreements between Democrats and Republicans
that have nothing to do with policy. This content also can be *politically sorted*,
such as non-political attitudes or behaviors that are strongly correlated with
political views. A user who posts this implicitly political content may or may
not intend to "be political," and may not even realize the potential of their
content to signal something about their political views. While this kind of
content may be more prevalent on the News Feed than explicit content, the
political signal it sends may be weak or noisy.

Simultaneously, the creators of explicitly political content are driven by
motivations that result in signal-rich and highly polarizing content. The incentives facing content producers on social media are different from those traditionally facing news producers, and the need to chase user engagement has
resulted in content that is optimized to catch users' attention. In the domain of
political content, this results in political "clickbait" news stories or short,
potentially inflammatory statements about political views that are not conducive to the communication of nuance or moderation.

The Constitution of END Interactions Disproportionately Involves Our Weak Ties

Users on social media have hundreds of connections, and the meaning of the
connection varies from site to site. Even on a site such as Facebook where we

primarily interact with people we actually know, we are connected to dozens or hundreds of individuals that we don't know particularly well. Political scientists consistently have found that our weaker ties are more likely to disagree with us politically (Mutz 2002; Huckfeldt *et al.* 2004), and we are therefore connected to a larger number of people on Facebook with whom we potentially disagree than we likely encounter in our face-to-face interactions with people. Facebook users do in fact report that the political content they encounter includes a mix of beliefs, not just viewpoints similar to their own (Duggan and Smith 2016).

Consuming politically informative content facilitates an unprecedented degree of knowledge about the political views of social contacts for whom the topic might never come up in our offline interactions. We also have the chance to observe interactions between people who agree with each other, but whose views are different than our own, something that is quite rare in face-to-face interactions. What's more is that these encounters are quantified, making more visible information about the patterns of political similarity and dissimilarity within people's social networks and those of the people with whom they disagree. Our weak ties – and the friends of our weak ties – occupy a very theoretically important place in our conceptualizations of who our political opponents are and what they believe.

Measuring END Interaction

The studies in this book will take a variety of approaches to elucidate the processes that result from these hallmark characteristics of END interactions. Some of the studies are designed as a "proof of concept" to test as to whether there *are* effects of consuming or generating politically informative content. Given the dearth of research on the psychological processes of engaging with this kind of content, one main goal is to demonstrate what types of evaluations could occur.

However, as elaborated on in the next chapter, the book's central argument is that high rates of engagement with END content should lead to higher rates of psychological polarization. The key then is to accurately and reliably measure variation between individuals on the extent to which they consume and generate politically informative content. The difficulty is that we know people cannot always remember or precisely report on the behaviors that are mundane or habitual parts of their day-to-day lives. How many times did you yawn yesterday? Check your email inbox? Take a sip of water? Could you generalize those behaviors in a survey question that asked you about a "typical" week or month? Accurate and reliable self-reports become even more difficult when we try to measure something subtle. For example, how often have you seen a person wear an article of clothing or jewelry that signaled their religious or political views? For behaviors that are fleeting or pass below our conscious awareness, people may not be able to precisely report their experiences.

While there have been best-practice approaches developed to measure these kinds of behaviors (Juster *et al.* 2003; Csikszentmihalyi and Larson 2014), they are not all suitable for inclusion in the experimental and survey studies used in this book, and I have adjusted accordingly.[13] As I describe below, the measurements are not without flaw and are rather blunt for capturing the dynamic of END interactions. But they are a start. Although the methodological approach varies in each study where the relationship with some facet of psychological polarization is tested, the measurement of END interactions stays largely consistent.

Active Engagement with Political Content

Political scientists have focused much of their attention on active engagement, assessing the extent to which people have clicked on the political content on social media or posted political content themselves. There are more templates for measurement available in this domain.

The emphasis on measurement for active engagement is the frequency with which someone generates political content and the breadth of content with which they engaged. The first construct is measured using a modified version of question that the Pew Internet and American Life Project has used in its previous studies: "Think about all the content you interact with on Facebook when you post material yourself, or share, like, or comment on material posted by others. Of all that content, how much of the content that you interact with do you consider to be political?" Users are given six response options ranging from "none" to "all."

On the END Framework Survey, I included a second measurement approach designed to assess more fully the range of different types of political content with which a user might engage. Building on the various types of content assessed by Pew in its studies, users answered a grid-style question to assess whether they had posted, shared, liked, or commented on each of eleven different types of content in the previous six months.

To assess active consumption of political content, I also used two approaches. The first focuses on the information that users seek out, designed to get a continuous measure of the frequency with which a person uses the Facebook site for news-gathering purposes. The question reads, "Think about all the times you access Facebook on your mobile device or computer and scroll through your News Feed. What percent of those times do you scroll through the News Feed looking specifically for political news and information?" Subjects were provided a sliding scale from 0 to 100. The second mirrors the breadth measure for content generation: users were asked how frequently they had clicked on the same eleven types of content, ranging from "rarely/never" to "almost always."

---

[13] The lack of standardized questions that have been widely used to measure END interactions means that many of these measures are new. But when available, measurement strategies from previous work have been adopted.

As we will see in Chapter 5, these active behaviors are driven largely by the factors that drive other political behaviors: political interest and partisanship strength. While these behaviors will be assessed in relation to measures of psychological polarization, the people most likely to actively engage with content are those most likely to be polarized at the outset. Most of the attention in the book will be on those users who do *not* regularly actively generate political content.

Inadvertent Consumption of Political Content

One of the most prevalent themes in this chapter highlighted the extent to which interaction with politically informative content on the News Feed occurs unintentionally and as a by-product of engagement with other types of content. It is therefore important to assess the extent to which users are exposed, not just their active choice to engage with it.

Pew has previously asked a question that pertains to content exposure, focusing on what proportion of the content posted by a user's friends is about politics. The problem with this question is that it assesses volume, not frequency. A user who sees a handful of political posts every time she scrolls the News Feed will likely report that she doesn't see much political content. But this measure does not assess the regularity of dosage. If this regularity matters as much as the overall volume, then Pew's measure will underestimate the extent to which an individual is exposed.

Instead, in the studies in this book, exposure is measured with a question parallel to that for the active seeking measure: "Think about all the times you access Facebook on your mobile device or computer and scroll through your News Feed. What percent of those times have you seen political news and information, even when you weren't seeking it out?"

On the END Framework Survey, I also assessed the breadth and frequency of what users report that they had encountered on the site. Users were asked how frequently they had seen the same eleven types of content noted above, ranging from "rarely/never" to "almost always." As we will see in Chapter 5, to a certain extent, politics is in the eye of the beholder. Some people are simply more inclined to identify more types of content as political; the broader a person's definition of what counts as "political" content, the more frequently they will report that they encounter it. However, controlling for the factors that may contribute to this breadth of definition – namely, political sophistication – will allow us to isolate the effect of frequency of exposure from the breadth of a person's definition.

Facebook Usage Frequency and News Feed Scrolling

Above all else, the depiction of interaction on Facebook in this and the previous chapter indicates the extent to which END interactions are a regular, integrated component of many people's daily lives. Thus, the most comprehensive measure is to capture the frequency with which someone uses the Facebook site and thus their potential for exposure to the full array of politically informative content that circulates on their feed. A self-report measure of exposure to implicitly political content would likely be very unreliable. The next best thing is to capture their overall level of exposure to the content that circulates on Facebook.

As shown in Table 2.1, subjects were first asked, "How frequently do you spend time on Facebook?" and given a seven-point response set ranging from "a few times a year" to "every day, too many times to count." Users who indicated that they used the site "most days" or more frequently were then asked, "On a typical day when you use Facebook, how many times a day do you scroll through your News Feed, either on a mobile device (like a phone or tablet) or a computer?" with a four-point response set ranging from "I don't scroll through my News Feed" to "five or more times a day." The two measures are highly correlated with one another, but using both helps differentiate high-intensity users. Given that the vast majority of the nationally representative sample reported using the site at least once a day, it is important to capture "dosage intensity" at the high end of the scale.

Establishing a relationship between site usage frequency and psychological polarization is the hardest test, but also the most consequential. This test is the most stringent because frequent Facebook usage is not a behavior into which the politically engaged disproportionately select, nor is its measurement subject to a person's determination of what is considered "political" content – two factors that could affect the conclusions we draw about an observed relationship between psychological polarization and active or inadvertent exposure to political content. Therefore, detecting a relationship between usage frequency and polarization suggests a far-reaching effect of exposure to Facebook, one to which many users are susceptible on a regular basis. A correlation between these measures in the END Framework Survey cannot pinpoint precisely which facet of regular usage could be driving a relationship with psychological polarization, but I rely on the inference and experimental studies to unpack the processes that occur.

CONCLUSION

The growth of social media extends many of the scholarly debates about the political behaviors of expression, news exposure, and discussion. Yet the unique features of the interactions in this domain suggest that we should ask different types of questions about the consequences of this behavior. The END Framework of political interaction on social media shifts our focus beyond traditional dependent variables such as political knowledge, attitude extremity, or voter turnout. Consideration of the hallmark differences of political behavior on the News Feed implies that we should also look at the way in which Americans evaluate each other.

The goal of this book is to analyze the effect of engaging with politicized social information or socially infused political information within the rich case study of the Facebook News Feed. Framing these interactions through their social motivations and gratifications implies turning toward research in social psychology to understand the consequences of inter- and intragroup communication and affiliation. What the literature in that area reveals is that the psychological processes underpinning these interactions are especially conducive to facilitating negative judgment and affective polarization.

4

How Do END Interactions on the News Feed Psychologically Polarize Users?

The evidence is irrefutable about the extent to which political elites have become more extreme in their policy preferences and the extent to which the media environment has fragmented to cater to niche audiences with different ideological preferences. The evidence is more mixed with regard to how polarized the American public has become in its policy views. While most scholars believe that the public has better sorted its ideology and partisanship, there is more disagreement about whether people actually hold more extreme viewpoints or just behave as if they do. The preponderance of evidence suggests some real change, but there remain signs that the public may simply be responding to the choices put forward to them.

Polarization on actual policy preferences is only part of the story. Increasing attention has been channeled toward a change in our affective attitudes and perceptions of our opponents. Iyengar, Sood, and Lelkes (2012) identify this as *affective polarization*, or partisans' increasingly negative feelings and negative trait attribution toward identifiers of the opposing party. Other work characterizes this phenomenon as *social polarization* (Mason 2018), *in-party favoritism* (Iyengar and Westwood 2015), or even *partisan hostility* (Miller and Conover 2015). Conceptually distinct, but related, is the concept of *false polarization* (Levendusky and Malhotra 2016a), alternatively called *perceptual polarization* (Lelkes 2016), where people perceive greater policy or social distinctions between the parties than exist in reality. I group all of these concepts together under the label *psychological polarization*, a term that captures the extent to which Americans think that they are polarized and harbor negative evaluations of the people with whom they disagree.

The early evidence of psychological polarization focused on Americans' increasingly negative views of the symbols in the political system representing the out-group: the political parties, candidates, and politicians themselves. But more disturbing are recent findings about Americans' attitudes toward each other. Partisans discriminate against out-partisans for scholarships (Iyengar and Westwood 2015) and job interviews (Gift and Gift 2015). Americans do not want their children to marry people who identify with a different party (Iyengar *et al.* 2012), nor do they want to live in neighborhoods with partisans (Klar and Krupnikov 2016), especially out-partisans (Pew Research Center 2014a). Partisans evaluate people as being less attractive if they support a dissimilar candidate (Nicholson *et al.* 2016).

How have Americans formed such strong attitudes about individuals who happen to have different political preferences? As the findings above demonstrate, people have *transferred* their antipathy from abstractions of the out-group (e.g. "parties") toward their fellow citizens (e.g. "my crazy neighbor"). Regardless of whether Americans actually hold more extreme policy preferences, they have responded to a polarized political climate by adopting stronger negative attitudes about each other.

The consequence of END interactions could be an important part of the story about why, and in this chapter we'll explore how engaging with the politically informative content found on the News Feed facilitates the processes underpinning psychological polarization. The argument is built on an assessment of the key differentiating features of END communication. In conjunction with one another in the ecosystem of the News Feed, these features provide an optimal environment for the mechanisms we know lead to pejorative judgments of and social distancing from our political out-group: the activation of social identity, interaction in largely homogeneous social networks, and exposure to polarizing and inflammatory political content.

First, using Facebook strengthens people's recognition of political identity. The users generating END content are the most partisan and likely have polarized attitudes at the outset; their motivation to express their identities while informing and persuading other people in their networks only serves to reinforce these already strong identities. The people who consume END content are also influenced, albeit in a different way. Exposure to politically informative content on Facebook provides concrete information about the political viewpoints of a person's weakest social connections and documentation about the symbolic social differences between the left and the right in America. It allows users to make connections between political views and social identities, providing information that crystallizes the differences between people who share their views and those who do not.

Second, encountering END communication biases upwards the amount of perceived difference between the parties and the amount of support for one's own political views. When a user posts content and receives social feedback on it, this further cements in-group identity and pride. But the user who posted the content is not the only person affected by this social feedback. In the aggregate, it provides a window into the distribution of viewpoints among a person's social contacts. This explicit quantification of the amount of support for particular political opinions facilitates the process of the false consensus bias, where people come to believe that their opinion is shared by a majority of others. Furthermore, exposure to END communication facilitates susceptibility to the out-group homogeneity and extremity effects, which biases users to think that out-partisans are more similar to one another and more extreme in their viewpoints.

Finally, END communication fosters instance-based stereotype formation in which people overgeneralize from the characteristics of an individual to a group as a whole. People are exposed to fewer members of the out-group, so those they are exposed to carry disproportionate weight in their evaluations. Simultaneously, Facebook facilitates abstraction-based stereotyping. The process of motivated social consumption of polarizing content encourages people to apply their affective evaluations of the parties and politicians in the abstract to the weak ties in their networks who are members of the out-party. As a way to entrench these negative evaluations, the affordances of the site allow users to socially distance themselves from the people with whom they disagree.

I begin by reviewing the affective origins of American political identities, the social divisions that are known to map onto political identities, the prevalence of psychological polarization, and the structural forces and social psychological explanations that have encouraged its development. I then elaborate on the mechanisms linking END communication and psychological polarization, establishing the expectations and hypotheses that will be tested in the chapters to come.

THE ETIOLOGY OF PSYCHOLOGICAL POLARIZATION

Americans didn't just wake up one morning and decide to loathe their political opponents. The rise of psychological polarization can be attributed to a cascading series of interconnected factors, initiated by structural realignment of political elites in the middle of the twentieth century. This was furthered by strategic decisions of politicians and political operatives at all levels of government and compounded by a media environment that found it profitable to highlight the differences between the parties instead of emphasizing the consensus between them.

"Us" and "Them"

A cultural anthropologist investigating Americans' attitudes about their fellow citizens in the opening years of the twenty-first century would find a nation relying on a series of competing narratives to justify their strong opinions about the political group with which they do not identify. Liberal Democrats would tell her that conservative Republicans are either white, gun-toting, unemployed bigots or elitist, greedy members of the 1 percent, groups who both voted a presidential candidate motivated by xenophobia and misogyny into the highest office of the land. Conservative Republicans would counter that liberal Democrats are out-of-touch, urban snobs, overly sensitive to the least hint of political incorrectness, and willing to run up the national debt to provide government benefits to undeserving people. Each group reports full awareness of the stereotypes the other side holds, although they categorically reject the depiction their opponents have drawn and insist that the vision their side has for America best comports with the values on which the country was founded.

Unsurprisingly, upon systematic investigation of available data to test the veracity of these caricatures, our fictional cultural anthropologist would discover some trends in demographic, social, and geographic factors differentiating the two groups. However, she would likely conclude that while there were members of each group that fit the other side's stereotype, the vast majority did not. How did we reach such a pervasive characterization of who "they" are compared to who "we" are?

Southern Realignment, Sorting, and Deeply Seated Differences

Beginning during the 1970s, elites sorted their ideology and partisanship leading to the consolidation of conservatives in the Republican Party and liberals in the Democratic Party (Bond and Fleisher 2000; Hetherington 2001; Poole and Rosenthal 2001; Stonecash *et al.* 2003; Jacobson 2004; McCarty *et al.* 2006). As a consequence, partisans, and perhaps even broader swaths of the population than the "engaged public," have aligned their partisan identification, ideology, and issue preferences (Jacobson 2006; Abramowitz and Saunders 2008; Bafumi and Shapiro 2009; Abramowitz 2010; Garner and Palmer 2011), in part based on cues provided by elites (Levendusky 2010).

Partisan sorting concentrated liberals in the Democratic Party and conservatives in the Republican Party, based on their shared attitude toward the role of government and policy preferences. But ideological sorting may have resulted in sorting on more deeply seated traits such as philosophical outlook, threat perception, and personality. Political ideology also can be thought of as a reflection of broader psychological dispositions. Thus, sorting created the possibility that the parties now comprise people with different underlying orientations and world views. Ideological differences may reflect different emphases on the moral foundations people use to determine "right" and "wrong" (Graham, Haidt, and Nosek 2009). It can also be thought of as motivated social cognition (Jost *et al.* 2003): political conservatism stresses resistance to change and justifications for inequality that manage uncertainty and threat (Jost *et al.* 2009). The parties may, in fact, have sorted based on attitudes related to authoritarianism (Hetherington and Weiler 2009), which could be related to the fact that liberals are thought to score more highly on openness (McCrae 1996; Jost *et al.* 2003; Mondak and Halperin 2008; Gerber *et al.* 2010; Mondak *et al.* 2010), while conservatives are thought to score more highly on conscientiousness (Jost 2006; Carney *et al.* 2008; Gerber *et al.* 2010).[1]

---

[1] These differences may be self-reinforcing. Ludeke and Deyoung (2014) find that "people with differing views on social and political issues may not be as different in personality as previously thought" (p. 132), but that in self-reports, people tend to over-report the traits they deem to be

Layered on top of partisan sorting is the process of "social sorting," a concept coined by Mason (2018) demonstrating the political consequences of having multiple, reinforcing social identities that align with one's political identity. As the parties have become increasingly socially homogeneous on religious, racial, and ideological divides, there are fewer citizens with cross-cutting identities. Mason labels the result as "mega-parties," where each party has come to represent not only a set of policy preferences, but also a set of people aligned on one side of a variety of social cleavages.

Certain patterns of social and demographic difference between the parties are empirical fact. Younger people, minorities, and unmarried women are more likely to support Democratic candidates. Religious Americans, most particularly evangelical Christians, and people living in rural areas are more likely to vote for the Republicans. The sorting among Americans on a variety of educational, occupational, and regional lines has increased in the past forty years (Mason 2018). But we know very little about whether the sorting extends beyond frequently measured ascriptive or demographic characteristics.

The speculation that partisan sorting has led to observable differences in social behaviors between the parties is circumstantial, supported by piecemeal evidence in a variety of domains. Innate differences between liberals and conservatives supposedly manifest in a variety of ways in day-to-day life, such as dating preferences (Klofstad *et al.* 2012), art preferences (Wilson *et al.* 1973), and even preferences over things such as food (Epstein 2014), product brands (Khan *et al.* 2013), and bedroom décor (Carney *et al.* 2008). Market researchers have discovered differences between members of each political party on their preferred television shows and books (Carter 2012; Facebook Data Science Blog 2014; Katz 2016; Shi *et al.* 2017). There is even evidence that liberals and conservatives use different practices and phonemes when selecting names for their children (Oliver *et al.* 2016).

Red and Blue: Media Depictions of Difference

The pattern between the types of people who identify as Republicans compared to the types of people who identify as Democrats, labeled by political scientists as "sorting," has been dubbed a "culture war" by journalists and pundits (Hunter 1991; Bishop 2008).[2] Political scientists have largely

desirable. To the extent that there are differences in which traits people with underlying differences in socio-political attitudes (such as right-wing authoritarianism and social dominance orientation) deem to be desirable, they may provide self-reports that exaggerate their adherence to those traits.

[2] Similar to the idea of the "culture war," some argue that geographic sorting also is a factor driving Americans apart. But dividing the country into "blue" and "red" states is a gross oversimplification of any geographic polarization that corresponds to political sorting. While dismissing the notion of "red" and "blue," Andrew Gelman's findings reveal nuanced interactions between geography and income at the individual and aggregate level that help explain the perception of the "red vs. blue" divide. Others have also sought to unpack the geographic divides

discredited the notion of a culture war as a driving force for the polarization of political opinions, but some reincarnation of the metaphor appears at every election cycle as commentators attempt to understand the social forces contributing to political beliefs.

The narrative changes over time, and rarely is there agreement in any given election about the exact terms or state of the "war."[3] While pundits and journalists seek to describe the patterns of difference between Americans, campaigns have been exploiting them actively in an effort to identify and target potential voters for persuasion and get-out-the-vote efforts. The popular media has fixated on the predictive power of matching consumer and political data to understand pockets of voter identities. The media's coverage of campaign outreach to voters often gets reduced to discussions of "Soccer Moms" and "NASCAR Dads," the "wired workers" and the "Joe Six Packs."[4] These labels serve to link social, economic, and political characteristics into overly simplified caricatures. The culture war narrative and the popularization of socio-political consumer patterns highlight differences between our political groups. However, these differences are only impactful if coverage of these techniques have crystallized perceptions in people's minds about how Democrats and Republicans differ on non-political behavior. And it turns out that people not only recognize the existence of differences between partisan groups, but that they overestimate those differences.

Perceived Differences

Setting aside the debate about whether or not partisans actually do hold starkly divergent policy preferences, Americans now *perceive* large differences between the political parties. Lelkes (2016) calls this *perceptual polarization* and Levendusky and Malhotra (2016a) label it as *perceived polarization*, borrowing from social psychologists' study of the phenomena more broadly.

---

in more disaggregated ways. The Patchwork Nation project uses Census and survey data to identify types of communities at the county level across the country, arguing that the local culture and economy in sub-state geographic units matter for understanding Americans' political preferences.

[3] In 2008, we were told that evangelicals need to call it off and liberals need to stop pronouncing it over (Berlet and Clarkson 2008), but that we may never be able to escape it (The Economist 2008). In 2012, we were told that the "culture war" returned in 2012 (Younge 2012), but that Republicans have lost it (Bennett 2012). In 2016, we were told simultaneously that "the culture wars are alive and well in America, and in this year's campaigns" (Milligan 2016) and that "the decades-long 'culture war' between religious conservatives and secular liberals is largely over" (Lind 2016).

[4] While journalists often note the oversimplification in which they engage when they characterize campaigning in this way, they do it anyway. From the 2004 election: "From NASCAR Dad to Soccer Mom, Campaigns Drawn to Political Labels" (Armas 2004). From the 2008 election: "One-Armed Vegetarian Live-In Boyfriends: The Quest for This Year's Sexy Swing Demographic" (Beam 2008). From the 2016 election: "Forget Soccer Moms and NASCAR Dads, in 2016 It's about ALICE" (Cherny 2013) and "The Soccer Moms of 2016" (Samuelsohn 2016).

Americans perceive that there are more differences between the parties than they have perceived in the past (Hetherington 2001; Prior 2013; Westfall *et al.* 2015), consistent with cross-national evidence that individuals in more polarized systems recognize political parties as being more polarized (Lupu 2015). In fact, they perceive that there are greater differences – in both policy preferences and group composition – than there actually are. In a nationally representative sample, Levendusky and Malhotra (2016a) find that the mass parties are perceived to be about 20 percent farther apart on the average of a broad set of issues than they are in reality. People perceive both their co-partisans to be more extreme than they actually are, but opposing partisans even more so.

The vast majority of work to date focuses on politically relevant differences, not the multitude of social differences outlined in the preceding section. But, beyond overestimating the policy differences between the parties, Americans also overestimate the share of party-stereotypical groups comprising the parties. For example, most African Americans do identify as Democrats. However, people overestimate the percentage of all Democrats who are African American. When asked to estimate the percentage of Democrats who are black, respondents estimated that closer to 40 percent of Democrats were, when in reality, only 23.9 percent are. On average, respondents overestimated the size of these groups by 342 percent. For six of eight group-party linkages,[5] more than 70 percent of respondents overestimated (Ahler and Sood 2018). This bias affects estimation of group-party linkages for both the in-party and out-party, but out-party overestimation was much larger. In the only work to date examining whether people also perceive purely social differences, there is suggestive evidence that Americans can recognize partisan differences in preferences that have nothing to do with politics – for Internet browsers, restaurants, and art, for example (Hetherington and Weiler 2018).

From Political Identities to Affective Evaluations

The characterization above is built on the notion that partisanship is a meaningful and salient identity. Political scientists have long known that attitudes about politics are in some way connected to how people evaluate others in the political system. Our interpretation of partisan identification moved toward more instrumental explanations in the 1970s and 1980s, perhaps reflecting real shifts in society in response to the dealignment of the political parties in the preceding decades. But our contemporary theories about the origins and function of partisanship now reflect a consensus about the importance of its social identity component.

---

[5] The linkages explored for the Democratic Party were "black," "union member," "gay, lesbian, and bisexual," and "atheist/agnostic." The linkage explored for the Republican Party were "earn over $250,000," "evangelical," "southerner," and "age 65+."

Partisan and Ideological Identities

Both of the seminal works in American political behavior incorporate the idea that people arrive at their primary political identification – partisanship – through social evaluations. Berelson *et al.* (1954) adopt a sociological approach, finding that a person's primary group identities structure how he identifies in the political realm, while Campbell *et al.* (1960) focus on the social psychological foundations of partisan identification. But each notion fundamentally revolves around the idea that people adopt political identities with an eye both toward "people like me" and "people not like me," leading to a relatively stable and long-term psychological attachment to a party (Green *et al.* 2002).

The interpretation of ideological identification is somewhat more complex, although increasingly it, too, is seen as a social identity (Devine 2015; Mason 2018). Most Americans do not have coherent policy-based foundations for their self-reported ideology (Converse 1964). Americans prefer to call themselves "conservative" even when that label does not match the content of their policy preferences. This has been called the "symbolic-operational paradox" (Ellis and Stimson 2012). Self-identified political ideology may be a result of people's evaluation of symbolic reference points in the political environment (Conover and Feldman 1981; Zschirnt 2011) leading to an ideological self-conception that is rooted in identity, not in policy preferences.

Affective Evaluations and Partisanship Stereotyping

Perhaps it is not surprising that Americans have developed stronger affective orientations toward symbolic representations of their political in- and out-groups. Our ideological, partisan, and social identities have come to overlap each other in ways they did not in the middle of the twentieth century. Americans believe that we are more polarized than we actually are. And all this has happened in the context and as a result of a fractious political landscape and a fractured media landscape.

People feel more attached to their political party than they have in the past (Abramowitz 2010). Fewer individuals are indifferent about politics than they were thirty years ago and a larger proportion of the public is "opinionated" about the parties, able to provide at least one positive or negative statement about the political parties when given the opportunity to do so (Thornton 2013). The clearest empirical demonstration of this derives from trends in the American National Election Study (ANES) feeling thermometer data over time. While positive feelings toward one's own party have stayed consistently high, feelings toward the opposition party have become considerably more negative in the last thirty years (Iyengar *et al.* 2012). In 2012, almost half of partisans reported being afraid and almost two-thirds reported being angry at the presidential candidate of the opposition party (Kimball *et al.* 2014). People with both the strongest partisan identities and the most aligned political identities demonstrate the most bias and anger toward the out-group (Mason 2015), but this process has affected a broad swath of the population. Miller and Conover (2015) find that 76.97 percent of the sample in their study agree with the statement that the opposition party is "destroying American democracy."

In addition to increased animosity and negative emotion aimed at the political out-party, Americans are more likely to perceive the other party's candidate as being extreme, but not their own (Hetherington *et al.* 2016). The perception that the parties have polarized may actually further drive the sorting process, especially for the most politically interested, thus providing a feedback-loop element between the perceptions and reality of the differences between partisan groups (Davis and Dunaway 2016). The greater the perceived difference between the parties, the stronger the attachment that people feel to their in-group (Turner 1999; Hogg *et al.* 2004; Lupu 2013, 2015) and the greater the negative affect toward the out-party (Ahler and Sood 2018; Rogowski and Sutherland 2016).

Most of the measures of affective polarization focus on attitudes toward the abstract notion of the political out-group, namely the "Republican Party" or "Democratic Party," or feelings toward the symbolic face of those groups, the presidential candidates. However, it appears that many Americans have transferred these affectively charged opinions to their fellow citizens and have become more negative about each other.

Shanto Iyengar and colleagues have led the way in exploring this notion. In addition to exploring the drop in feeling thermometer ratings for the out-party over the last several decades, they find that approximately 50 percent of Republicans and 30 percent of Democrats report that they would be "upset, displeased, or unhappy if their progeny married someone from another party" (Iyengar *et al.* 2012). Miller and Conover (2015) find that fewer than 15 percent of their sample views the out-party – including both candidates and voters – as possessing core moral traits. People hold negatively valenced stereotypes about members of the other political party in domains related to personality traits, occupations, and even just the general words that "typically describe" people who support the opposing party (Busby *et al.* 2017). As I show later in this book, large majorities of the respondents in my survey agreed with very inflammatory statements about the way in which out-partisans form their political opinions, judging them as being ignorant and dogmatic.

These attitudes spill over into behavior as well. In a series of experiments utilizing behavioral economics games and other tasks, Iyengar and Westwood (2015) show that out-partisans will actually discriminate against each other. Partisans trust their co-partisans more than they do out-partisans (Carlin and Love 2013; Hetherington and Rudolph 2015) and people are prejudiced against those with different ideological beliefs (Chambers *et al.* 2013). Even more worrisome is the evidence that partisan identity affects evaluations that have nothing to do with politics, such as physical attractiveness (Klar and Krupnikov 2016; Nicholson *et al.* 2016), the worthiness of academic scholarships (Iyengar and Westwood 2015), and job interview callbacks (Gift and Gift

2015). There does not appear to be any social desirability encouraging people to underreport their levels of partisan bias either, as explicit measures work just as effectively and sometimes better than implicit measures in capturing out-party prejudice and stereotyping (Lelkes 2016).

THE PUZZLE: WHAT CAUSED PSYCHOLOGICAL POLARIZATION?

How did this happen? How did people translate their negative attitudes about the abstract symbols of the political world (parties and elites) to concrete feelings about their fellow citizens who identify with the out-party? It seems plausible that *something* has changed.[6] The scholars working in this area have rightfully zeroed in on trying to understand the social and psychological processes that could explain this phenomenon. They point to three main factors: the psychological processes embedded within social identity theory; the composition of our social networks; and changes in the broader information environment rendered by elites and the partisan media. I evaluate these explanations in turn, identifying the current gaps in each explanation.

Social Identity Theory

It is possible to imagine a counterfactual world where political and social identities increasingly reinforce one another, but without a concomitant increase in negative affect for the out-group. However, decades of research in social identity theory (SIT) suggest that this counterfactual world is highly improbable.

The root of the explanation for the rise of psychological polarization rests in SIT, drawing on the work of Tajfel and the social psychologists within that paradigm. Briefly, at the core of this theory is the idea that people categorize themselves and others into in-groups and out-groups based on shared characteristics or attributes. These do not need to be enduring traits. Experiments have shown that in-group preferences can be developed for arbitrary identities (Sherif *et al.* 1961; Tajfel 1970) as well as in situations when people know

---

[6] We can't clearly establish a change in affective evaluations of the out-party over time on all of these measures. Iyengar *et al.* (2012) is the only study that looks at over-time change in a survey question that directly addresses the question of whether Americans feel differently about each other than they have in the past, and finds evidence on the limited number of measures for which we do have historical data. We simply do not have the right kind of data to fully test the mechanisms that we think are at play. It is possible that partisans have always harbored these kinds of stereotypic, negative trait evaluations toward each other. However, it seems unlikely that people would simultaneously give the out-party relatively high thermometer ratings – what we observed in the middle of the twentieth century – at the same time they judged them harshly on their moral character.

groups have been randomly assigned (Goette *et al.* 2012).[7] Individuals quickly come to evaluate members of their own group positively, while developing negative affect and evaluations of the out-group, even going so far as discriminating against them.

The theory applied to political identity generally goes like this. In the middle of the twentieth century, a much larger proportion of Americans had cross-cutting identities, where their political views were not aligned with their religious, racial, or geographic identities. This prevented political identity from being particularly salient or indicative of other facets of a person's self. Over time, Americans sorted non-political dimensions of their identities to align with their political views, driven in large part by racial sorting[8] in response to the shift in the parties' policy stances, as well as the alignment of conservative Christianity with the Republican Party during the 1980s and 1990s (Mason 2018).[9]

This multi-faceted sorting process enhances the notion of "comparative fit" (Turner 1999; Hogg *et al.* 2004), where people distance themselves from the out-group and come to see themselves as more closely resembling the prototype of their in-group. They develop expressive identities (Huddy *et al.* 2015) that make them more susceptible to strong emotional reactions in the face of electoral competition. As people's social and political identities came to reinforce one another, people became more vested in the success of their in-group and became more threatened by the idea of the out-group winning (Huddy *et al.* 2015; Mason 2015, 2018).

Social identity theory is a solid foundation for the psychological polarization phenomenon, but is contingent on people being made aware of the boundaries between the in- and out-groups. In the experimental paradigms used in social psychology, especially in the minimal group paradigm, the group identity is often bestowed upon the subjects. But in the real world, how are these differentiations communicated and made salient to Americans? For that, scholars have pointed to the influences of our social networks and our exposure to elite and media communication.

The Role of Social Networks

Consistent with the literature on partisan sorting (Bishop 2008), social sorting (Mason 2018), and the overlay of partisan distributions and economic

---

[7] This line of research is called the "minimal group paradigm" and seeks to understand whether a conflict of interest is a necessary condition to create discrimination between groups.

[8] In brief, the Republican Party's response to the Civil Rights Movement led to the racialization of many political issues and the realignment of the electorate along racial lines (Carmines and Stimson 1982; Sundquist 1983; Stanley *et al.* 1986; Gilens 1999).

[9] A single paragraph cannot do justice to the thorough treatment of this phenomenon in Mason (2018). The reader is encouraged to reference Mason's work for an elaboration of the origins and consequences of social sorting.

inequalities (Gelman 2009), some scholars have turned to study how these broader contextual influences may reinforce the microenvironments in which people find themselves. The context shapes the distribution of opinions within our social networks (Huckfeldt 1983; McClurg 2006), and growing homogeneity could conceivably lead to growing homogeneity in discussion networks, even absent intentional selection by citizens.

Parsons (2015) argues that peer network homogeneity, cohesiveness, sophistication, and density are associated with increased saliency of partisan identity and more polarized intergroup biases. His results about the relationship between partisan social identity and affective polarization are unsurprising: those with more homogeneous networks have stronger partisan identities, and those with stronger partisan identities are more polarized in their affective attitudes toward the parties.

However, the association between the social network composition and level of polarization holds strong, even controlling for the strength of the person's partisan social identity. He argues that the robust association between network homogeneity and attitudinal – and affective – polarization supports the idea that partisan group identity can be reinforced by one's peer group. Even if this simply reflects homophily (that the most affectively polarized individuals gravitate toward one another), this finding establishes a link between a person's perceptions of the attitudes of her discussants and her evaluation of the "political other."

Any argument about negative affect and stereotyping must account for how people reconcile their evaluations of the people they know with their evaluations of the public at large. It is fully possible that our discussion networks are more homogeneous now than they have been in the past, amplifying the process Parsons demonstrates. The problem is that most people do not talk about politics very frequently, and the rates of political talk have not increased over time. When people do talk about politics, they are more likely to do so with like-minded others they consider their close ties; people therefore have exposure to their in-group, but they are less likely to be exposed to many opportunities to observe members of the out-group interacting with another. Our window into "the other side," as Mutz (1998) calls it, must come from influences outside our closest social connections. Historically, our weaker social connections in our workplaces and places of worship have provided these cross-cutting perspectives, although social sorting suggests that opportunities for these sorts of interactions may be decreasing (Mason 2018). The mass media – in large part transmitting the opinions of elites – has traditionally been considered the most effective conduit for helping people make sense of the broader political terrain.

Elite and Media Cues

As political and social sorting proliferated, elites and the media were able to send more coherent signals differentiating Democrats from Republicans on a wider variety of preferences. In a more partisan, polarized political climate, there is evidence that people respond more strongly to elite cues (Druckman *et al.* 2013), perhaps especially out-party cues (Nicholson 2012). Framing effects[10] may be stronger in a polarized climate because motivated reasoning suggests a change to the perception of the relative strength of the in-party's frame compared to the out-party's frame (Druckman *et al.* 2013).

Extant research has linked these sorts of cues with affective polarization. Political campaigning polarizes both favorability and trait ratings of the candidates, leading to a 25-percentage-point growth in the gap over the campaign season. This is driven largely by a drop in affect for the out-party candidate as opposed to an increase in affect for the in-party candidate (Iyengar *et al.* 2012). These effects are larger in battleground states and for people exposed to negative advertising, a finding derived from both observational and experimental data. It appears that these findings are not driven by learning, but more likely by projection (voters imputing greater ideological difference between themselves and the out-party candidate) or strengthened partisan identity.

The media also has played its part. The fractured media environment facilitated the re-emergence of a partisan media, which has strong profit incentives to cue people with the party line. Unsurprisingly, partisan news outlets depict more polarized political views (Padgett 2014). Exposure to partisan media can strengthen partisan attachment (Knobloch-Westerwick and Kleinman 2012) and salience (Horwitz and Nir 2015). Pro-party news exposure is associated with more polarized favorability ratings of candidates and party members, as well as increased social distance measures, including higher levels of objection to inter-party marriage (Garrett *et al.* 2014).

Extending these findings to the consumption of news on the Internet largely confirms the patterns detected in the consumption of news on the television. Access to broadband Internet increases partisans' consumption of partisan media, which in turn drives partisan hostility (Lelkes *et al.* 2017). A study of the effects of news use on perceived polarization found that online news consumption was related to perceived polarization in ten countries (Yang *et al.* 2016). Among regular consumers of online news, those who consume news through social media are more ideologically segregated in their consumption of opinion journalism than are regular users who consume news by directly visiting news web pages (Flaxman *et al.* 2016).

The problem with explanations relating to elite cueing and news consumption is that given the opportunity to do so, most Americans opt out of these exposures. The overall impact of exposure to partisan media is relatively weak. Because the average Republican or Democrat does not report much exposure to

---

[10] Framing is "the process by which people develop a particular conceptualization of an issue or reorient their thinking about an issue" and framing effects occur when "(often small) changes in the presentation of an issue or an event produce (sometimes large) changes of opinion" (Chong and Druckman 2007, p. 104).

partisan media (Kimball *et al.* 2014), cable news has a limited effect since it is "preaching to the choir" (Arceneaux and Johnson 2013). Levendusky (2013, ch. 9) argues that partisan media can affect not only which stories mainstream media eventually cover, but the framing used to cover those stories. While this line of reasoning could extend the impact of partisan media to people beyond regular viewers of cable news, it still does not fully account for the polarization of politically disinterested individuals who do not regularly seek out news of any kind. The "opt-out phenomenon" is likely weaker in the Internet context, but it still exists. Furthermore, elite and media cues are insufficient to explain how the people who receive these cues transfer judgments to out-partisans they personally know. The media excels at vilifying political candidates, but we are missing the connection between how someone goes from loathing Hillary Clinton to loathing his neighbor with the Clinton yard sign.

The existing explanations therefore do not adequately explain why Americans with the least interest and engagement in politics also have become psychologically polarized toward each other. To be sure, it is partisans and political sophisticates who are most likely to have deeply negative evaluations of the out-party and its adherents. But there are signs that even the disengaged public hold strong negative evaluations of the out-party. Remember that three-quarters of Americans agree that the out-party, including its voters, are destroying American democracy (Miller and Conover 2015). In experiments demonstrating the willingness of people to discriminate against out-partisans, even those with the weakest partisan attachments *did* discriminate, even if they were less likely to do so (Iyengar and Westwood 2015). We lack an explanation for the phenomena of psychological polarization among those people who do not care about politics and actively avoid exposure to the media and elite cues.

THE FACEBOOK NEWS FEED ECOSYSTEM: THE PERFECT STORM

The explanations above are not incorrect, but they are incomplete. Insufficient attention has been paid to a phenomenon that brings all of these factors together into one ecosystem in which the average American engages every single day: the Facebook News Feed. As are all scholars studying the "how" of psychological polarization, I am limited in my inferential ability to argue that the mechanisms I explore have caused a *change*, over time, in people's attitudes. I must rely solely on the fact that they have explanatory capacity in our contemporary context and reason how that might have looked different in the past. It is not only the amount of time people spend on Facebook as the extension of the argument and findings in Lelkes, Sood, and Iyengar (2017) imply. The News Feed has distinctive characteristics that are uniquely suited to social inference about politics, fostering mechanisms that reinforce social identity and amplify the polarizing effects of exposure to our social networks, elite cues, and partisan media.

The Prerequisites of Intergroup Interaction Manifest on the News Feed

The starting place for the exploration of the consequences of END interaction on our evaluations of each other is to assess the Facebook ecosystem on its capacity to activate our political identities.[11] What is it about scrolling the News Feed that makes someone more aware of her partisan identity? The majority of Americans do have a social psychological attachment with one of the two major political parties. Even those Americans who do not feel strongly attached to a political party often hold negative views about the party with which they have no attachment. How are these identities made salient in the Facebook context?

Interactions on the News Feed activate many of our social identities. In the process of crafting their online personae, people make deliberate decisions about how to portray themselves to their friends on the site. Likewise, they habitually draw conclusions about other people's various social identities based on the content they post. This general identity-activation process extends to the realm of politics and is further amplified in that the Facebook News Feed weaves together the social influence of interpersonal communication (Katz and Lazarsfeld 1955) with the information about mass collectives typically only derived from impersonal communication (Mutz 1998).

Traditionally, the mass media has served as the key conduit connecting the broader political climate to the average person. Twenty years ago, Diana Mutz made the point, "what media, and national media in particular, do best is to supply us with information about those beyond our personal experiences and contacts, in other words, with impressions of the state of mass collectives" (1998, p. xvi). Ahler and Sood (2018, p. 4) build on her insight to explain how people develop such inaccurate mappings of the social groups comprising the political parties, writing that "political parties cannot be experienced first-hand – we cannot literally meet the party."

The Facebook News Feed has flipped these insights on their head. The line differentiating impersonal from interpersonal influences is blurred. For the first time, interpersonal communication does facilitate inference about mass collectives. We can directly access information about political parties – from the head of the ticket to the man on the street – from both our social connections and the mass media in one fused environment. The News Feed allows us to feel as if we have first-hand knowledge about what broad swaths of the in-party and out-party believe and how they act, helping us recognize where we belong. Facebook users find it hard to *avoid* being reminded about politics (Duggan and Smith 2016).

---

[11] Here, I focus on partisan identities, but the same mechanisms should also apply to our ideological identities. Over time, people have become increasing psychologically attached to their ideological group (Mason 2018), and self-identified ideological attachment likely serves a similar role as partisan attachment.

What is the function of forming this social political identity? Correll and Park (2005) argue that group membership can provide a benefit, even in the absence of a defined out-group, because membership can offer people "a sense of strength, belonging, or merit and so contribute to a sense of personal integrity or worth" (p. 341). In their thoughtful integration of a number of theories explaining the relationship between an individual and her in-group, the authors note that all the theories assume there is a personal advantage to group membership, likely related to self-worth or self-esteem. Furthermore, almost by definition in the political sphere, one's identification with a party implies the existence of an out-group, most especially in a two-party system. Thus, a person's attachment to a political party is best understood as being nested within the system of conflict, which further incentivizes the reinforcement of group identity.

However, not all social interactions between members of different groups can be automatically classified as "inter*group* interactions." Tajfel argues that there is a continuum of social interaction spanning from the interpersonal to the intergroup. At the interpersonal end of the spectrum, the interaction between two or more people is mostly determined by their own characteristics and the nature of their personal relationship (Tajfel 1982, p. 13). At the intergroup extreme, the interactions between individuals are determined mostly by group membership. Intergroup interactions are characterized by (1) the uniformity of the behavior and attitudes displayed by people in the in-group toward the out-group, as well as (2) uniformity in the in-group's perceptions of the characteristics and behavior of the out-group. The processes facilitating depersonalization, dehumanization, a lack of differentiation, and social stereotyping tend to increase when relations between the two groups deteriorate (Tajfel 1982).

Can interactions on the News Feed be thought of as intergroup behavior? Yes. Although not all interactions between individuals on the Facebook site would fall into the domain of "intergroup activations," those in which political identity is made salient do qualify. Generating and consuming END content activates those identities. Remember the description of political expression aspects of News Feed interactions: the language in political status updates was found to use more personal pronouns and emotional words than short bits of text generated for other motivations. The use of words referring to in-group or out-group status has been shown to facilitate intergroup biases (Perdue *et al.* 1990). The fact that political information on Facebook is infused with social information and group-oriented language suggests that political interactions on the News Feed can be identified as a form of intergroup interaction even if much of the non-political interaction may be better identified as interpersonal behavior.

When an individual identifies with a group, they have internalized that identity as part of their self-concept. They are aware of their membership within the group, assign values to group characteristics, and may emotionally identify with the group (Tajfel 1981). Furthermore, although not required for the connection between group identification and intergroup behavior, one mechanism for developing intergroup interactions is in situations of conflict and competition, which aligns very well with our theories of politics. Intergroup conflict can overshadow previous intergroup attachments between individuals (Sherif and Sherif 1953; Sherif *et al.* 1961; Turner 1981).

If END interactions can activate intergroup relations, then our expectations for the effects of those interactions can be guided by previous work on intergroup behavior that focuses on the role of activated identities (Tajfel 1969). First, people categorize, dividing others into discrete groups. Second, they differentiate the groups, and in the process assimilate to learn and internalize the group norms that accompany intergroup attitudes. Finally, they search for coherence, and to explain change in their environment, they attempt to make causal attributions that maintain their own self-concept at the expense of negative evaluations of the out-group.

Here, I preview the argument I will advance in each of the next four chapters in the book, unpacking one part of the process linking Facebook usage with psychological polarization. Each step reflects the integration of what was identified in the previous chapter as the three hallmark distinctions of END communication: the context of by-product exposure and social inference, the signal-rich content, and the disproportionate influence of weak ties in the constitution of the interactions.

The Categorization Phase, Part I: Increased Exposure to Politically Informative Content

The END Framework of communication implies that the more frequently people use Facebook, the more likely they are to encounter content that is informative about the political views of their contacts.

First, unlike other conduits for consuming news, people can't easily opt out of exposure on the News Feed. The politically disinterested simply don't watch cable news (Arceneaux and Johnson 2013), but the vast majority of Facebook users are potentially "dosed" with polarizing and informative content when they log in to the Facebook site for other reasons. Therefore, we should expect exposure to political information on the News Feed to have effects on a much larger segment of the population, including those people who aren't interested or knowledgeable about politics.

Second, this exposure is likely to lead to learning others' views because people are connected on the site to a set of social contacts to whose views they have not typically been privy absent social media. Facebook permits unprecedented access to learning about the weak ties in one's social network. Online discussion facilitates an unparalleled degree of knowing the political views of social contacts for whom the topic might never come up in our offline interactions (e.g. "I had no idea that my child's piano teacher was such a raging liberal!").

Third, exposure to politically informative content disproportionately leads to learning about the views of people with whom we disagree. Although most people share political views with their close family and friends, their broader social networks are not homogeneous. The wider the net drawn around the bounds of the social network, the more likely it is to include people with diverse viewpoints. Although the way in which most people use Facebook reduces the amount of counter-attitudinal information they encounter (Bakshy *et al.* 2015), Messing (2013) finds that people who use Facebook more frequently have more heterogeneous networks.

Finally, heightened exposure to politically informative content widens the scope of what people consider to be about politics. People who use Facebook more frequently should, over time, be exposed to more types of content that have the potential to signal the poster's political views. In essence, using Facebook for learning about others' views becomes a self-reinforcing cycle, furthering a person's awareness of the kind of content that can be informative.

The Categorization Phase, Part II: Increased Recognition of Partisan Identity

The END Framework of communication implies that the more frequently people use Facebook, the more practice they get drawing inferences about partisan identity from content that is potentially informative about the views of the person who posted it.

Explicitly political communication on Facebook constitutes a signal-rich set of content: not only words, but news articles, videos, and imagery. In addition to being partisan, political content is visually compelling. It is likely to be intentionally humorous, controversial, or inflammatory; these characteristics are known to be attention-grabbing. This is especially the case for non-traditional political organizations and groups who create content specifically for an audience on Facebook.

Facebook opinion leaders – who as we will see in the next chapter tend to be more partisan, less conflict avoidant, and less likely to censor themselves – select from this pool of content when they disseminate information to their social networks. This third-party-created content often sends a clear and unambiguous signal about the partisan identity of the poster who circulated it. The expression cues, source cues, and endorsements described in Chapter 2 all contribute to transparent signaling of the political views of the person who posts the content, as well as those who choose to engage with it via likes, comments, or shares. In addition to circulating polarizing information, for those who want one, Facebook is a soapbox in a digital town square. In a context with fewer norms of civility and respect, the power to reach so many listeners at once may encourage these users to be bombastic, expressing their viewpoints in emotional ways without nuance.

Regardless of whether a user is motivated to click on content one of their friends has generated, they are filing away the political signal as a socially pertinent detail about their friend. People tend to be fairly accurate in estimating the opinions of their social connections. While they tend to slightly overestimate the extent to which people agree with them in face-to-face conversations, the more informative signals of Facebook content make it harder to misperceive others' viewpoints.

Inference about implicitly political content works slightly differently. In an era of high levels of political polarization, politics has pervaded even seemingly non-political topics. Consumer and pop culture often become politicized. Posting about something through which politics has been infused (e.g. "checking in" at a restaurant that has been boycotted for its political advocacy), or posting about something that is closely aligned with political views (e.g. environmental conservation or guns) may signal political identity, even if nothing about the post is political.

The more frequently someone uses Facebook, the more likely they are to catalogue bits of social and political information about their contacts and file that information away together. This facilitates the association between the abstract notion of "what the other side believes" and "who those people are." The political component of content is often sandwiched between social signals that create this association. But even when the political signal and social signal aren't conveyed simultaneously, users can make the connection. Once a user has recognized a friend's political identity, through either the explicit or implicit political content with which the person has engaged, the user can then map other social information they post to those political views.

The Accentuation Phase: Increased Biased Processing

The END model of communication implies that the more frequently people use Facebook, and the more frequently they say they encounter political content, the more likely they are to engage in biased reasoning about the viewpoints of Facebook users.

Tajfel (1969) argues that categorization is necessary for perception and that stereotyping results as a part of this process. In other words, inherent to the process of social categorization are three stereotype effects: the potential for intergroup differentiation, in-group favoritism, and differential accuracy in group characterization (DiDonato *et al.* 2011). As DiDonato and colleagues write:

The biases implicit in the three classic stereotype effects are the price paid for social perception being both relatively easy and reasonably accurate. If categories were removed from perception, judgments of individual instances or individuals would be more difficult, less reliable, and less accurate overall. DiDonato *et al.* 2011, p. 66.

When given a task to sort items into categories, people will accentuate the similarities between items if they assign them to the same group and accentuate the differences if they assign them to different categories. In effect, once people have identified different social groups, they are more likely to emphasize within-group similarities and between-group differences. This is exacerbated if there are value differentials associated with assignment to different categories (Tajfel 1982, pp. 20–23).

What does this look like on Facebook? People impute ideological coherence to a person based on their inference about the poster's partisan identity. They've come to recognize which bundle of issue opinions tend to hang together. When a person signals their partisanship, users impute to them overly consistent ideological viewpoints on a broad set of issues, a form of the out-group homogeneity effect. Second, the distribution of content circulating in the News Feed is not an accurate representation of the distribution of beliefs in the network, but people attribute the extreme viewpoints of those who post content to the out-group as a whole. This contributes to the perception of polarization.

Biased reasoning affects not only people's assessments of the out-group, but also the estimation of the amount of support in their networks for the opinions that they hold. Facebook reinforces the tendency to believe that most other people agree with us, called the false consensus effect, because Facebook users encounter that reality in their own networks. Users who post political content can expect that the social feedback they receive on their posts will be disproportionately supportive of the viewpoints expressed, compared to the distribution of beliefs in their network as a whole. Affordances on the Facebook site make this transparent. Aggregated, numeric details have the potential to influence people's beliefs about the popularity of their viewpoints. These cues are the evolution of information such as opinion polls or primary results that convey "information about the attitudes, beliefs or experiences of collectives outside of an individual's personal life space" (Mutz 1998, p. 4).

The Judgment Phase: Increased Out-Group Derision and In-Group Favoritism

The END model of communication implies that the more frequently people use Facebook, and the more frequently they say they encounter political content, the more likely they are to be negatively judgmental about the out-party and to evaluate positively members of their in-group.

Social identity theory suggests that the result of group categorization and differentiation is to negatively characterize the out-group and a desire to "preserve or achieve 'positive group distinctiveness'" which in turn serves to protect, enhance, preserve, or achieve a positive social identity for members of the group" (Tajfel 1982, p. 24). Tajfel concludes, "The behavior of certain individuals often becomes relevant to the stereotype of their group because they are representatives of a category which has a preexisting social significance enmeshed with preexisting value connotations" (p. 7).

Most people don't post much political content on Facebook. Those who do become "representatives" of the political party which they endorse. The evaluations of consistency and extremity people make of their weaker ties, as well as the friends of their friends, are integral to understanding how people have transferred their attitudes from elites to the masses. This group of people represents an important intermediary, people we don't know well or don't know personally, but whose behavior we can readily observe. We have enough information to draw conclusions about "people like them." Weak ties and friends of friends on Facebook put a literal face on the "other side" (Mutz 1998).

What is the pertinent domain in which Facebook users judge members of their out-group? The facet of citizenship that we can easily see on Facebook relates to the quality of the way in which citizens acquire and process information in order to arrive at and express their opinions. Absent a genuine interpersonal relationship with these weak ties and their friends, we don't have any of the kinds of interactions that tend to moderate prejudice and stereotype formation. We can be critical of their levels of political knowledge and the quality of the sources they use to inform themselves, differentiating our in-group by our superiority in using facts to process information and form opinions.

While judgments about the way in which people arrive at their opinions are most directly connected to what we observe of others' behavior on Facebook, social identity theory suggests that we also will become more disparaging about the qualities writ large of the out-group. Consequently, we should expect that Facebook users also see growing social distance between the parties, to the point where they perceive that the parties comprise different kinds of people. The outgrowth of this idea is that we may intentionally structure our social networks to avoid contact with the out-group, preferentially selecting co-partisans as friends and severing communication with out-party members.

CONCLUSION

Some scholars have argued that the perception of partisan disagreement and polarization is greater than its actual existence in our society. Many scholars, most vocally Morris Fiorina, argue that Americans are still largely moderates in their actual policy views. On certain issues, this certainly appears to be the case. However, perceptions matter more than empirical reality for understanding how Americans feel about members of the opposing political party.

A growing body of evidence indisputably demonstrates that many Americans have processed the polarizing messages from political elites and the media in a way that alters their evaluations of their fellow citizens. Regardless of actual levels of divergence in values or policy preferences, Americans believe that there are marked differences between those on the left and those on the

TABLE 4.1 *Central Argument, Demonstrable Mechanism, and Testable Implications of the END Framework of Social Media Interaction.*

	Chapter 5: Exposure	Chapter 6: Recognition	Chapter 7: Inference	Chapter 8: Judgment
Central Argument	People don't report that they post much political content, but users are exposed to a broad range of implicitly and explicitly political content. They are bystanders to the interactions of disagreeable weak ties, providing perspectives and interactions they otherwise would not see.	A potentially large volume of News Feed content is informative about the political views of the person who posts it. Users attribute partisan identity based on both political and non-political content, with high rates of consensus.	END content generators carry disproportionate weight in our instance-based characterizations of the out-group, facilitating the out-group homogeneity effect and perceived polarization. Aggregated social feedback fosters the false consensus effect.	Users make judgments about political competence, based on their observation of how other users engage in END interactions. Facebook use facilitates social categorization and social distancing behaviors.
Demonstrable Mechanism	Users report that they learn the political views of others on the site. Users are most likely to learn the views of their weak and disagreeable social contacts. A wide range of content is considered to be about politics.	A wide variety of content on the feed will be informative to Facebook users about the political views of the person who posted it.	Users make biased inferences based on the content that other users post. Users judge their weak disagreeable ties as being more ideologically extreme than their close disagreeable ties.	Users make negative judgments of their out-party based on the content that other users post. In the construction of their social networks, users prefer ties with agreeable contacts and sever ties with disagreeable contacts.

(continued)

TABLE 4.1 (*continued*)

Chapter 5: Exposure	Chapter 6: Recognition	Chapter 7: Inference	Chapter 8: Judgment
Testable Implications			
People who use Facebook more frequently should . . .			
People who more frequently engage with END content should . . .			
. . . have more heterogeneous networks.	. . . be more likely to attribute partisan identity.	. . . be more likely to attribute ideological extremity.	. . . be more likely to attribute low knowledge judgments to out-group members.
. . . be more likely to report learning the political views of other users, especially their weak and disagreeable ties.	. . . be more confident in their ability to accurately identify a person's partisan identity.	. . . be more confident in their ability to accurately identify a person's ideological views.	. . . be more confident in their ability to accurately identify a person's knowledge level.
. . . have a broader definition of what is considered "political."		. . . characterize a larger portion of the out-group as holding extreme views.	. . . perceive greater social distance between partisan groups.

right. They judge people who are different from them as being less trustworthy, less likable, less employable, less intelligent, and less attractive.

Psychological polarization is a complex phenomenon, and no one factor is to blame for its development or growth. It has occurred as part of a much broader phenomenon of polarization within our political institutions and dramatic changes to the media environment. Social media is certainly not the sole driving force behind the rise in antipathy toward our political opponents; there are millions of Americans who do not use Facebook who detest their opposition and millions of Facebook users who do not.

Yet the fundamental aspects of the way in which people communicate on Facebook – and likely other platforms that incorporate similar features and dynamics – is especially conducive to fostering categorization, differentiation, and negative evaluation of the out-group. The Facebook News Feed environment brings together, in one place, many of the influences that have been shown to drive psychological aspects of polarization. The majority of Americans scroll through their News Feeds on a regular basis, and those who do can't escape being exposed to politically informative content. Therefore, influences from the News Feed have the potential to reach Americans who might opt out of other avenues in which they could be exposed to polarizing forces.

In the chapters that come, we will test these claims about how News Feed interactions facilitate psychological polarization. Table 4.1 outlines the central argument and testable implications. Each chapter will expand the argument about why END communication fosters a part of the sequence forecasted by social identity theory. First, we will test the plausibility of the mechanism to see if the psychological process can result from exposure to prototypical END content. To do this, we will use a set of experimental classification tasks, dubbed the inference studies, introduced in the next chapter and elaborated on in Appendix A and online Appendix B. We will then assess whether the mechanism is more generalizable, using self-report data from the END Framework Survey. At each step, we will test to see whether the measures of END interaction defined at the end of Chapter 3 are associated with an increased propensity to engage in the proposed mechanism. Readers who want a preview of the findings can compare Table 4.1 with Table 8.2 in Chapter 8, where an overview of the results is provided.

We begin our exploration of the consequences of END interactions by elaborating on the concept of politically informative content on the News Feed. This concept is at the core of the generation and consumption behaviors of the END Framework and, before we can proceed to test the effects of interacting with this kind of content, we must have a better idea of what it is.

5

In the Eye of the Beholder: Politically Informative News Feed Content

The Emily Post Institute is a family business that "maintains and evolves the standards of etiquette that Emily Post established with her seminal book *Etiquette* in 1922 ... though times have changed, the principles of good manners remain constant." The company's advice regarding political interaction on social media suggests that it is not "the place to post diatribes that attack one political party or an individual candidate" and that "when you post political opinions or information online, there's a good chance that part of your audience is cringing." The Posts advise that if you find yourself in a political debate, you should change the subject.[1]

It seems that most Americans are inclined to heed the advice of this venerable standard bearer of decorum. In 2016, Pew reported that 78 percent of Facebook users say that none or only a little of what they post to Facebook is related to politics. Only 7 percent of the sample said that they often posted political content (Duggan and Smith 2016). This lack of content generation seems to be driven at least in part by people's deliberate choices not to share their views. In 2012, Pew found that 22 percent of social networking site (SNS) users had decided not to post something to a site because they did not want to offend or upset someone, and that 66 percent of people chose to ignore the disagreeable political content posted by their friends instead of responding or posting information of their own (Rainie and Smith 2012).

Yet, these same surveys report relatively high rates of learning the political views of friends on Facebook. Pew's survey in 2016 found that 50 percent of social media users "say they have been surprised by the political views of someone in their online network because of something that person posted"

---

[1] Anna Post, "Avoid Political Pitfalls When Talking, Working and Posting," available at http://emilypost.com/advice/avoid-political-pitfalls/.

(Duggan and Smith 2016). The survey I fielded during the 2016 presidential primary finds even higher rates of reported learning. Additionally, Pew finds that 81 percent of Facebook users in their sample could provide an answer when asked whether most of their Facebook friends have similar, different, or a mix of political beliefs (Duggan and Smith 2016), indicating that Facebook users are largely able and willing to classify the views of most of their friends on the site.

These statistics create a bit of a puzzle. How is it possible that although most people report they don't post very much about politics, majorities of Facebook users report that they have learned and can characterize the political views of the people they are socially connected to on the site? A parsimonious answer is that people are learning from content that posters do not think is political.

There is little past research about how people perceive the political attitudes of others. But the importance of questions related to perception and interpretation of others' political identities increases as a result of the unique features of online political communication in a context designed for social interaction. In Chapter 2, I highlighted six informative signals of END interaction that could be used to make inferences about the political views of the users who generate content. The studies presented in this chapter and the next test those ideas, focusing on the most basic building blocks of the END Framework: users' own words, the information embedded within visual content, and the source cue provided by the organization that originated the content.

We begin by expanding on Pew's findings to investigate who is most likely to report that they have learned the views of others and whose views Facebook users say they have learned. Consistent with our expectations, the more time people spend on Facebook, the more likely they are to report having learned the political views of others. While users have learned the political views of a wide variety of social connections, they are more likely to report that they have learned the views of people to whom they are weakly connected and users with whom they disagree.

We then turn toward tackling the core of the issue: how is it that people learn so much in the apparent absence of large quantities of explicitly political content on the News Feed? To understand this, we will assess a series of straightforward questions, each building upon the last to make the case that a broad range of content on the News Feed is informative about the political views of the user who posted it:

What kind of content do people consider to be "political"?
What explains the breadth of what a user considers to be political?
How do source cues affect what people consider to be political?
Will people make inferences about the partisanship of Facebook users based solely on the non-political content they post?
Can Facebook content send clear and unambiguous signals about the partisanship of the person who posts it?
How do source cues affect the inferences people make about partisan identities?

The answers to these questions parsimoniously reconcile seemingly contradictory facts about the consequence of interaction on the News Feed. We'll address the first three questions in this chapter and the remaining three in the next chapter.

First, the users who report they post the most political content – however they define it – are the most partisan and most opinionated. The information they post about politics, therefore, likely sends a clear signal about the direction and intensity of their political views.

More importantly, however, is the fact that a much larger proportion of content is potentially *politically informative*. The results of this chapter show that there is a broad and varied definition of what kind of content is considered to be "political." Certain topics are almost universally recognized as pertaining to politics. A much broader set of content can be considered politicized. The strength of someone's partisan identification affects the breadth of what they deem to be about politics, but even politically unsophisticated users identify a wide variety of material to be "political." As we shall see in the next chapter, content does not have to be deemed to be about politics to reveal the partisan identity of the person who posts it.

Facebook has become integrated into users' daily lives. Most users report they log on to the site every day, and many report that they scroll through their News Feeds more than once a day. They are potentially exposed to implicitly political content every time they sign on and they report relatively high rates of exposure to explicitly political content however they might define it. As a consequence, Facebook users are inadvertently but regularly dosed with politically informative content, even those users least vested and interested in politics. There are ample opportunities to learn the political views and identities of those around us.

LEARNING THE POLITICAL VIEWS OF OUR
SOCIAL CONNECTIONS

Try answering this question for yourself: based on the offline interactions you have on a regular basis, is it easier to identify the political leanings of your family and close friends or your more distant connections?

The factors that influence our perception of our discussants' beliefs has not been assessed systematically on surveys over a long period of time. However, there is quite a bit of circumstantial evidence suggesting that we do not need Facebook to learn the political opinions of our closest connections, the "strong ties" in our lives. These conversations happen organically in the course of our daily interactions. When people are asked to name their face-to-face political discussion partners, they are much more likely to name people with whom they have a close relationship, such as members of their family (Marsden 1987; McPherson *et al.* 2006; Brashears 2011). Data from Pew confirms that we tend to know a lot about the viewpoints of our close connections. In a case study examining opinions toward Edward Snowden's accusations regarding the National Security Agency,[2] Pew found that 96 percent of people who live with their spouse or partner report knowing his or her opinion on this particular issue, 87 percent report knowing the opinions of family members, and 88 percent report knowing the opinions of close friends.

Interestingly, social media users are *more* likely to report that they know the opinions of people in their lives (Hampton *et al.* 2014), and 76 percent of Facebook users report that they know the opinions of the people writ large in their Facebook network on the Snowden issue. Since the purpose of Facebook is to share details about our lives with other people, perhaps we should expect a high rate of knowledge of even the weak ties in our network. But on the other hand, this same survey details several interesting facts that make it surprising that people report such high awareness. The authors report that only 14 percent of Americans were somewhat or very unwilling to have a face-to-face conversation about the Snowden-NSA story, but 58 percent of Facebook users reported being somewhat or very unwilling to "join the conversation" online. These effects were even more pronounced among social media users who perceived that their connections on the site did not agree with them, and their reticence to share their opinions online may seep into their interactions offline. Social media users, compared to non-social media users, were actually half as likely to express their views about the issue in face-to-face conversations.

How are Facebook users learning other users' political views if most people aren't communicating about politics? To gain some traction on this phenomenon, we begin by assessing the factors correlated with increased rates of learning, the Facebook activity that is most informative of others' views, and the nature of the relationships where people report learning at the highest rates.

Facebook Usage Correlated with Rates of Learning

The END Framework Survey included a question similar to the one Pew has assessed over time. Respondents were asked if they "have ever learned someone's political beliefs whose beliefs you did not previously know, or learned that someone's political beliefs were different than you thought they were." There were slightly higher rates of political learning in the sample than in Pew's previous work, perhaps because of the timing of the survey during what had been an especially contentious presidential primary season. A very large supermajority of the sample, 68.9 percent, reported that they had in fact learned other people's views.

If increased usage of Facebook implies increased possibility for learning views, then Facebook usage should be associated with learning rates and, in

---

[2] In 2013, Edward Snowden made international headlines when he released evidence of systematic surveillance of Americans' phone and email records by the National Security Agency.

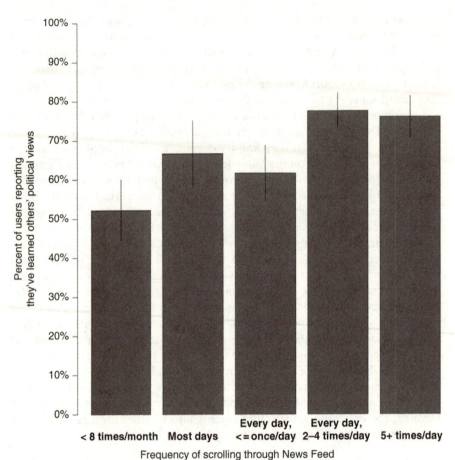

FIGURE 5.1 Rates of political learning, by Facebook activity level
The percentage of people in each category of usage frequency who report that they have ever learned someone's political beliefs whose beliefs they did not previously know or learned that someone's political beliefs were different than they thought they were. Lines depict 95 percent confidence intervals.

fact, it is. Users who scroll through their News Feed more than once on a daily basis are more likely to have learned about others' political views than are people who use the site less frequently (see Figure 5.1). However, even among those users who log on to Facebook the least, only a few times a month, 52.2 percent have learned someone's views or learned someone's views were different than assumed.

Facebook users report that they have learned about others' views in a variety of ways (see Table 5.1). The most obvious manner – a user's direct statement of their political views – is the method reported to be useful for the largest proportion of the sample, but a variety of other signals appear to be informative.

TABLE 5.1 *Manners of Learning the Political Views of Others*

	Learned
Expression of their political viewpoints (in their own words)	63.47%
Expression of disagreement with the political viewpoints of other people (in their own words)	48.59%
Comments they made in response to content someone else posted	40.34%
Political meme, image, or infographic they posted, shared, or liked	39.36%
Media or political source they used when they posted or shared political content	35.42%
Media or political source they followed or liked	28.54%
Candidate or political organization they follow on Facebook	24.72%
Image they used for their profile picture	20.30%

The percentage of Facebook users who have learned the views of others who report that a given kind of content was informative in learning the political views of their social connections. The denominator is the 68.9 percent of the survey sample (n=696) who report that they have learned the views of others.

Many of these methods do not include any words at all. Some Facebook users seem to be sensitive to the signal sent by images, including profile pictures, and some derive meaning from the behaviors that other users engage in, such as following candidates or media organizations on the site.

What else explains whether a respondent reports that they have learned the viewpoints of others? Just as measures of political sophistication are associated with higher levels of knowledge of political issues, so too does increased attachment to the political system seem to make people more receptive to learning the political views of their social contacts. Both partisanship strength and political interest are correlated with a higher likelihood of learning others' views, but neither partisan nor ideological strength is associated with increased reports of any of the particular manners of learning. Individuals who report that they are more interested in politics are more likely to report learning from a user's own words, profile picture, and the source from which a user posts or shares content, as well as the sources they like or follow.

It is unclear what explains this somewhat nuanced relationship between political sophistication and learning. It is possible, even probable, that more politically interested individuals are more likely to have friends utilizing a variety of different content to express their political views, but so too should the strongest partisans and ideologues. An alternative explanation incorporates the idea that we are all political sophisticates (Schreiber 2007) when it comes to inferences from the kind of content that circulates on Facebook. Perhaps the non-written forms of communication are short cuts that do not require much political sophistication to recognize.

Although political sophistication is associated with higher rates of learning overall, even the least politically sophisticated report learning the views of others and learning from a variety of different types of content. Nearly half (48.09 percent) of political Independents and nearly three-quarters (69.13 percent) of partisan leaners report that they have learned others' views, as do over one-third (34.88 percent) of those entirely uninterested in politics and half (50 percent) of those "not very interested" in politics. Of those politically uninterested individuals who do report learning, nearly half (45.45 percent) say that they've learned from a user's own views or when they've expressed disagreement (40.90 percent). The statistically significant relationship between political sophistication and learning shouldn't mask the fact that large proportions of politically unsophisticated individuals – especially those who use Facebook frequently – learn the views of their social connections.

The survey results provide evidence that people are making inferences about the views of others based on what they've observed of their political engagement on the News Feed. We now turn to assessing whether the strength of the relationship between a person and her Facebook social contact is associated with the likelihood of having learned the views of that contact.

The Social Connections Battery

Later in the END Framework Survey, I took another approach to understanding political learning and inference on the News Feed derived from approaches used by scholars who study political discussion in the face-to-face context. The study was designed to assess people's evaluations of their most politically active social contacts on Facebook. This section of the survey began with a short prompt asking respondents to identify their three social connections on Facebook who generate the most political content.[3] This prompt was selected intentionally. Typically, for the purposes of studying face-to-face discussion, the prompt has focused on identifying the people with whom a respondent most frequently communicates. But as argued in Chapter 3, one of the unique aspects of political discussion on Facebook is the ability for a user to listen without contributing to the conversation. The goal was to identify the contacts in respondents' networks who did the most "talking," even if the respondents themselves were not reciprocating.

The respondents were first asked to provide a label for each contact "by the nature of your relationship to them, in a way that you will remember who you listed when we ask you more questions about them." The respondents then answered a series of questions about the political behavior of these contacts, data to which I return later in the book. At present, I focus on the fourth

---

[3] The exact wording was "Think about all the people with whom you are, or have been, connected as friends on Facebook. Now think specifically about the three people who generate (post, share, like, or comment) political content most frequently. These may or may not be people with whom you have a relationship outside of Facebook, but rather are the people who seem the most politically engaged on Facebook."

question in the battery ("Based on what you know about your contacts' political viewpoints, do you tend to agree or disagree about politics?") and the last question in the battery ("Would you have known the person's political viewpoints if you hadn't seen him or her post content on Facebook?").

Asking respondents to identify their social connections "by the nature of your relationship to them" allowed for hand coding the responses to better understand the strength of the relationship with the person they named. Full details of the coding process are included in Appendix B, but strong ties were coded to include close family (spouses/partners, parents, siblings, children, and grandchildren) and friends. Weak ties include more distant relatives, co-workers, acquaintances, and neighbors.

Unlike the study of face-to-face discussion, we do not necessarily expect the people who are "loudest" in a person's News Feed to be their closest connections. In fact, there should be considerable variation in relationship strength. While we do tend to communicate more frequently with the people we are closest to offline (Jones *et al.* 2013), features of Facebook's algorithm may deliver to our News Feeds the content posted by our weaker ties if that content proves popular in the network, if we have engaged with the person's content in the past, or if the person is sharing content from a source that we also follow on the site. Both relationship strength and the amount of agreement between the ties are expected to affect whether the respondent would have known the views of their contact absent the Facebook environment.

Who Learns about Whom?

Table 5.2 shows the results of the first part of the analysis. First, consistent with expectations, many people named strong ties, but nearly as large a proportion of the ties named are considered weak ties. Unsurprisingly, there is less room to learn the views of a person's close family or friends. Facebook users do not need Facebook to learn the views of the people they interact with regularly. They report at very high rates that they would have known the views of their close family members and friends.

Generally speaking, the weaker the tie, the more likely respondents are to report that they would not have known the person's view absent experiences on Facebook. Users report that they definitely would have known the views of nearly 65 percent of the connections identified as strong family ties – their partners, parents, or siblings – but only 46 percent of weaker family ties, such as in-laws, cousins, or grandparents. Similarly, users report that they would have definitely known the views of 40 percent of the people they identify as friends, but fewer than 30 percent of the connections identified as co-workers, classmates, or acquaintances.

From the study of face-to-face political discussion, we expect that our close ties are more likely to share our political opinions. Political views are correlated among family and friends, either as a result of selection (Eliasoph 1998; Ulbig and Funk 1999; Conover *et al.* 2002) or influence (Huckfeldt *et al.* 2004;

TABLE 5.2 *Opportunities for Learning Political Views of Social Connections, by Tie Type*

	Frequency	Yes	Maybe	No
Strong Ties				
Family	7.62% (n=231)	64.94%	27.27%	7.36%
Spouse or partner	1.22%	81.08%	18.92%	0.00%
Parent or siblings	4.89%	62.50%	27.21%	9.56%
Child or grandchild	1.91%	60.34%	32.76%	6.90%
Non-Family	12.87% (n=390)	39.49%	35.13%	24.62%
Close friend	1.82%	69.09%	27.27%	3.64%
Friend	11.06%	34.63%	36.42%	28.06%
Weak Ties				
Family	7.66% (n=232)	45.69%	23.71%	28.45%
In-law	0.83%	52.00%	8.00%	40.00%
Other relative	6.83%	44.93%	25.60%	27.05%
Non-Family	10.56% (n=320)	29.69%	31.25%	39.06%
Co-worker	2.28%	37.68%	39.13%	23.19%
Acquaintance	4.29%	24.62%	26.15%	49.23%
Past friend/acquaintance	2.81%	30.59%	27.05%	42.35%
Neighbor	0.50%	33.33%	60.00%	6.67%

The first column identifies the coded tie type. The second column is the percentage of all dyads that were coded into this category. The denominator is 3,030, the total number of dyads identified. The total N for each tie type is in parentheses, and serves as the denominator for columns 3 to 5. The third through fifth columns are the percentages of dyads in each category where the respondent reports that they would have known the contact's political views without Facebook (Column 3), might have known (Column 4), and would not have known (Column 5).

Mutz 2006b; Lazer *et al.* 2010; Sinclair 2012). There is evidence that people choose their significant others at least in part based on shared political views (Klofstad *et al.* 2012).

Indeed, respondents are more likely to have identified politically vocal Facebook contacts with whom they agree: 49.3 percent of all dyads compared to only 19.4 percent with whom they would disagree. However, respondents report that they are more likely to have *learned* the views of people with whom they disagree some or all of the time.[4] For example, respondents reported that they would not have known the views of only 26.67 percent of their agreeable close family members, but 35.14 percent of their disagreeable close family and 54.39 percent of those family members whose views are a mix of agreeable and

---

[4] Although the network battery was not designed to assess this question, I hypothesize that the dyads in the "neither" category (presumably those with whom the subjects agree sometimes and disagree sometimes) are the least politically sophisticated. Data from the survey show that dyads in this category generate considerably less content than the clearly agreeable and disagreeable dyads named, and that respondents did not consider them to be particularly knowledgeable.

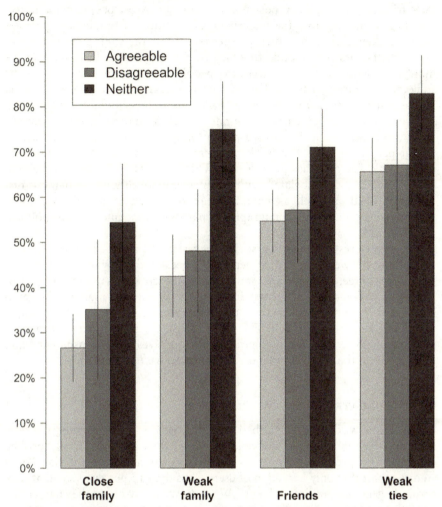

FIGURE 5.2 Opportunities for learning political views of social connections, by tie type and agreement level

Each bar shows the proportion of all dyads in a given category (tie type and agreement status) for which the respondent (ego) said they would not have known the contact's views absent Facebook. Lines depict 95 percent confidence intervals.

disagreeable positions. This pattern holds across all four categories of relationship type, and the importance of Facebook in learning others' views becomes more important the weaker the social connection (see Figure 5.2).

The social network battery asks subjects to name their three Facebook friends who post the most political content. There are likely many factors that influence a subject's selection about which three friends to report, among all their friends who regularly post political content. Most people name agreeable ties, suggesting that the underlying distribution of opinions in people's network likely favors their own perspective. While the study does not disentangle the factors contributing to which friends get named, I assume that the individuals who were named were the people most readily accessible in the subjects' memories. The mechanisms of the END model of social media interaction suggest that more regular Facebook usage should make the political communication of particular kinds of friends more accessible, namely weak ties and those with whom a person disagrees. The testable implication is that people who use Facebook more frequently should be more likely to name weak ties and disagreeable ties. This is, in fact, the case. Facebook usage frequency is associated with an increased likelihood of naming disagreeable dyads as well as naming weak ties, even in logistic regression models controlling for demographics, partisan attachment, and political engagement.[5]

The survey results presented so far suggest that people are most likely to learn about the weak ties in their network, especially those with whom they do not always agree. Pairing these findings with the questions about the kind of Facebook content that has been informative, it appears that a substantial amount of learning happens from the non-textual content posted by people we do not know all that well. This makes sense. Facebook's explicit mission statement is to develop technologies to make our lives more transparent,[6] and at least within the realm of politics, it appears to have succeeded.

WHO GENERATES POLITICAL CONTENT?

The social network study described above focused on characterizing the relationship between average Facebook users and their most politically prolific contacts. This group of contacts is a very small minority on the site: Pew's studies report that only a fraction of users – less than 10 percent – say that they regularly generate political content.[7] What do we know about the characteristics of these opinion leaders, the people who report that they post a large volume of political content?

---

[5] In models predicting whether Facebook usage frequency is associated with naming disagreeable weak ties, the coefficient is in the correct direction, but the relationship is not statistically significant. This may be in part a power issue given that people are more likely to name agreeable friends and close ties.

[6] The entirety of the Form S-1 Registration Statement is available on the Securities and Exchange Commission's website.

[7] In 2016, Pew reports that only 7 percent of social media users report that they often "comment, post, or discuss government and politics with others." In 2012, they report that only 6 percent of users say that "all," "almost all," or "most" of what they post to social networking sites is political.

Opinion leaders are younger, more educated, more likely to be male,[8] and more frequent users of Facebook (measured either as the frequency of using Facebook or the frequency of scrolling through the News Feed). These findings have been confirmed repeatedly in a variety of different ways: in Pew's surveys over the past decade tracking political engagement among nationally representative samples (Rainie 2012; Smith 2013; Pew Research Center 2014b; Smith 2014a),[9] in work derived from unobtrusively studying over 100 million Facebook status updates in the 2008 election (Settle *et al.* 2016), and in the survey used throughout this book.[10]

The Pew Internet and American Life Project has documented that younger people may be more likely to use social media intensely because of their increased familiarity and comfort with the technology itself (Lenhart 2015). However, over time, older people have become increasingly adept at using the site. As of 2016, over 60 percent of people age 65 or older have Facebook accounts (Greenwood *et al.* 2016). Younger people, and to a lesser degree racial and ethnic minorities, also are more likely to identify their use of social media as a "very important" political activity. Black and Hispanic Facebook users are more likely to see social media as an important political tool (Rainie and Smith 2012).

What else do we know about the individuals who generate the most content on Facebook? Personality traits are associated with both face-to-face and online political communication. With regard to face-to-face interactions, extroverts are more likely to talk about politics and to have larger discussion networks (Mondak 2010; Mondak *et al.* 2010; Hibbing *et al.* 2011; Gerber *et al.* 2012). In the END Framework Survey, they are more likely to report a high proportion of their posted content as political and to name more types of political content with which they engage.

We can investigate two other traits measured in the survey that have been suggested by previous findings in the political discussion literature. Conflict-avoidant people do not like to discuss politics (Ulbig and Funk 1999), and neither do those who score highly on a measure of self-censorship.[11] These relationships appear to extend to online communication as well. Individuals

---

[8] While women are more likely to use social media sites and therefore are more likely to report that they have accessed political news on the site, men are more likely to have generated political content.

[9] Although the vast majority of Pew's research has been derived from self-reports, in 2010 they did partner with Facebook to validate whether people's self-reported behavior on Facebook accurately reflected their actual behavior as recorded on the platform. They found that most users are in fact accurate. See Hampton *et al.* 2012, pp. 17–18 and Appendix B for details.

[10] Throughout the analyses in this section, I use three measures of political content generation. A full exploration of the relationship of these variables can be found in Appendix B.

[11] Those with high scores on the Willingness to Self-Censor scale (Hayes *et al.* 2005) are unwilling to confront an opposing majority who holds opinions different than their own and are unwilling to behave in ways that set them apart from a group.

with high scores on these two measures are less likely to report generating political content. Why? Conflict avoidance and a willingness to censor one's views could be associated with low levels of interpersonal political communication because these individuals are more sensitive to the consequences of contentious interactions (Carlson and Settle 2016).

More consequential for the dynamic of the News Feed ecosystem than the demographic or personality differences are the differences in the levels of political engagement between users who generate political content on Facebook and those who do not. Pew's previous research shows that by several measures of political engagement, Facebook users who generate political content are also more likely to be engaged in other ways, both online and offline (Rainie and Smith 2012; Pew Research Center 2014b; Smith 2014a). At times, the differences are substantively very large. These findings are in line with the large literature that has sought to understand the nature of the relationship between online and offline forms of political participation (Conroy *et al.* 2012; Valenzuela *et al.* 2012; Tang and Lee 2013; Gil de Zúñiga *et al.* 2014; Park 2015; Kim *et al.* 2016).

In the END Framework Survey, political engagement – whether measured by self-reported political interest, frequency of reported news seeking, or voter turnout – is a strong and consistent predictor of posting a political status update, of self-reporting a higher proportion of generated political content, and of reporting engagement with more types of political content, controlling for a variety of other variables. However, those who are politically knowledgeable are no more likely to generate political content.

In addition to being more politically engaged, users who generate political content on Facebook also tend to hold political opinions at the extreme ends of the scale. Pew investigated this phenomena in an August 2012 survey, assessing a handful of policy questions in addition to asking respondents about their partisanship and ideology. A greater proportion of users who generate political content identify as strong liberals or conservatives, hold very strong opinions on whether the government should reduce spending or increase services, and have strong opinions about the legality of gay marriage. These same patterns can be detected in the END Framework Survey.[12] The stronger someone's ideological or partisan inclinations, the more likely they are to be engaged in the process of creating and circulating political content on the News Feed.

---

[12] I extend these findings in my own survey. I measure the strength of a respondent's ideology using a four-point scale and measure the respondent's strength of partisanship with two scales, including measuring social psychological attachment to one's party. The measure of ideological strength and the first measure of partisan strength are derived from "folding" the five-point and seven-point scales, respectively, from the standard American National Election Study question battery about these constructs. The second measure of partisan strength is the social psychological battery adapted by Greene (2002). All three measures show a consistently strong and positive relationship to reported political content generation.

The data about political content generation reveal exactly what our intuition suggests. The people who report they are most politically active on Facebook have stronger political opinions and identities. They also are more likely to have personalities that dispose them to be less sensitive to or to derive enjoyment from the experience of engaging with other people about political topics, even when those interactions are contentious.[13] These differences have implications for the dynamics within the News Feed. The opinionated, extraverted minority of users who regularly generate political information have distinct motivations for doing so, which ultimately results in the circulation of more ideological and partisan content (Weeks *et al.* 2017).

THE DAILY DOSAGE OF FACEBOOK

We are now one important step closer to understanding how it is that people report they have learned so much about the political views of others: the people generating political content are opinionated and likely to be circulating information that contains strong political signals. However, they are still a small proportion of users, and we do not have a good sense for how frequently other Facebook users are exposed to the content which they generate.

In an ideal world, we could unobtrusively observe and quantify the political content that appears on a person's News Feed and the extent to which they pay attention to it, while simultaneously ascertaining their perceptions of how much political content they have seen. Unfortunately, there is no feasible way to do that, and we must rely on user self-report about the frequency with which they encounter political content. Table 2.2 in Chapter 2 shows the top-line results from the survey about engagement with various different forms of political content. More than three-quarters of respondents report that they have seen at least one of the various types of political content that circulates on the News Feed "frequently" or "almost always."

Here, I measure exposure to political content in a slightly different way, focusing on the frequency of overall exposure to political content on the News Feed. I ask questions on the survey to assess both inadvertent exposure (encountering political content when not seeking it out) and active exposure (seeking out political content).[14] Below, I break out these results by Facebook usage frequency. Figure 5.3 shows that among all Facebook users, the

---

[13] These survey data are not designed to shed light on the direction of causality between the personality or political characteristics and the frequency of generating political content. It seems plausible that at least for the political engagement characteristics, online and offline behavior reinforce one another.

[14] To assess the degree to which users are exposed to content without seeking it out, I asked two questions. First, I asked, "Think about all the times you access Facebook on your mobile device or computer and scroll through your News Feed. What percent of those times have you seen political news and information, even when you weren't seeking it out?" The measure of active consumption was similar. I asked, "What percent of those times do you scroll through the News Feed looking specifically for political news and information?"

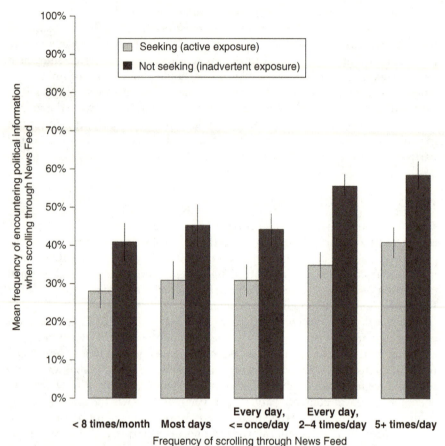

FIGURE 5.3 Exposure to political content, by usage frequency
The percentage of people in each category of usage frequency who encounter political content, actively or inadvertently. Lines depict 95 percent confidence intervals.

frequency with which someone uses the site is very correlated with the frequency with which they see political content, whether they are seeking it out or come across it unintentionally.

The results, so far, group together the users who generate a large amount of political content themselves with the users who say they do not. People who generate political content are considerably more likely to report that they encounter political content as well. There are several likely explanations for this pattern. The first is that political activity on the site creates a higher future incidence of exposure. Since content generators are more likely to follow candidates or media sources on Facebook, they actually see more political content in addition to being more likely to circulate it (Weeks *et al.* 2017). This process may be amplified by the mechanisms of Facebook's algorithm, which could reinforce a person's exposure to political content because they have engaged heavily with similar material in the past. A more psychologically oriented explanation is that people who have posted political content are more aware of and attuned to the political content that circulates because they are motivated to add their own thoughts and share, comment, or like other people's content. The more politically engaged someone is, the more likely they may be to notice and remember seeing political content.

Additionally, the political behavior literature would lead us to believe that because the people who post content regularly are the most politically engaged, they have a wider breadth of understanding of what is considered "political content" and, therefore, report higher levels of exposure to it. As we will see at the end of this chapter, what counts as "political" is in the eye of the beholder, and there is some limited evidence that politically engaged individuals may be more likely to identify Facebook content as "political," consistent with the findings of Fitzgerald (2013).

Therefore, I narrow our focus to those users who do not report posting political content themselves. These are the theoretically most interesting "consumers," as they are not opinion leaders, and as such, we expect that they may be the least likely to be exposed to political content. Here, we restrict the analysis of consumption behavior to the users who do not post any or post very little political content themselves, and characterize the differences between those who report that they see political content and those who do not. A series of regressions assesses the relationship between a variety of explanatory variables and political content exposure, controlling for demographic variables and Facebook usage in each model. The full results are presented in online Appendix D.

Even those people who are most disengaged from politics appear to regularly encounter political material on the News Feed, whether or not they are looking for it. In the overall sample, on average, users report that they encounter political news or information without seeking it out half of the times they scroll through their News Feed, which for most users is more than once a day. Figures 5.4a and 5.4b show that in the sample of users who report that they don't frequently generate political content, that rate of exposure drops. But even Independents see content one out of every three times they scroll, and the least politically interested one out of every five times they scroll.

Not surprisingly, political interest is still correlated with exposure to political content, even among this set of users who aren't opinion leaders on Facebook. Users who are more interested in politics – by self-report and by the number of days a week they report that they seek out news – are more likely to report intentional and inadvertent exposure. However, stronger partisans are only more likely to report *intentional* consumption of political content. The relationship with inadvertent consumption is weak and inconsistent. Political knowledge and voting are not correlated with increased exposure to political content at all.

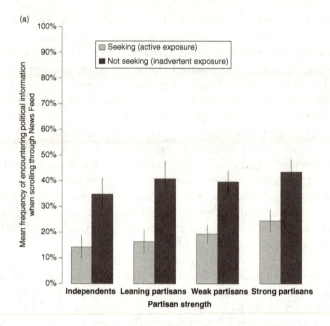

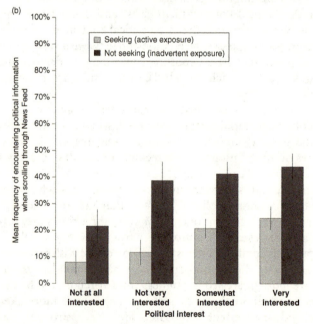

FIGURES 5.4A AND 5.4B. Exposure to political content, by level of partisan strength and political interest

The mean frequency of encountering political information when scrolling through the News Feed, by each category of partisan strength (left panel) and political interest (right panel). Lines depict 95 percent confidence intervals.

Thus, most users experience daily inadvertent exposure to political content. Unlike exposure to cable news or news websites, where people who are uninterested and unattached to the political system opt out of exposure to political information, on Facebook these people regularly encounter content that they think is about politics.

POLITICAL CONTENT OR POLITICALLY INFORMATIVE CONTENT?

Synthesizing what we know so far, we can assert that the more time people spend on Facebook, the more likely they are to learn the political viewpoints of others, most particularly, the viewpoints of the extraverted, conflict-seeking, non-self-censoring politically engaged and opinionated disagreeable weak ties in their networks. As outspoken as these opinion leaders may be, they constitute a small proportion of the overall Facebook-using population. Those users who do not report posting much political content do report being regularly exposed to political content, even those users who are detached from the political system and aren't interested in politics.

What explains this gap between the small proportion of users who say they regularly post political content and the high rates of exposure to political content? One possibility is that everyone is learning the views of only the small subset of people who post a significant amount of political content. This would be difficult to test conclusively, but it seems unlikely to account for the fact that 81 percent of Facebook users in Pew's 2016 study were able to characterize the distribution of political views of the people in their entire network (Duggan and Smith 2016). Another possibility is that the algorithmic features of the News Feed favor political content in some way, inflating the proportion of political content that circulates. While few people post or share political content, a larger proportion of people like it and comment on it, and these actions also convey information about people's political views. However, as we saw in Chapter 2, social feedback is lower on political content than on other types of content. These explanations may be a part of the story, although given most users' stated preferences to avoid explicitly political content on the site, it seems unlikely that the algorithm favors it over the social content that people prefer.

There is a third explanation, but one that questions an unstated assumption about how we learn the political views of other people. Are people only able to learn the political views of other Facebook users from the *explicitly* political content that they post? What about content that might be *implicitly* political? Put another way, what kind of content *do* people consider to be "political" and does content have to be political to be *politically informative*? The possibility that people learn the views of others from content that does not necessarily seem to be about politics on its face means that a much larger proportion of content circulating on the News Feed may be politically informative than is explicitly about politics.

What's Political?

This ambiguity in what is considered "political" always has been embedded in our studies of political interactions, but we have largely ignored the problem of vague definition. With notable exception for case study work (Noelle-Neumann 1974; Walsh 2004) and experimentally induced political conversations (Carlson and Settle 2016; Levitan and Verhulst 2016), most scholars rely on the subjects themselves to define what constitutes a "political" discussion or reading or watching "political" news.

Fitzgerald (2013) conducts one of the first quantitative analyses of how average citizens think about the political and the extent of consensus over the topics that are defined as "politics." She articulates three separate conceptualizations of what "political" means, relating to what government does, what the government should do, and the notion of conflict. In my own work (Carlson and Settle 2016, appendix), open-ended responses indicate that when people think of politics, they think about more than just "issues of the day." "Politics" is construed broadly and includes topics related to the structure of government, the behavior of elites, the substance of policy, and engagement in the political process. Presumably, this broad interpretation extends to the realm of online political communication as well. In fact, it is likely amplified in the signal-rich information environment of the Facebook ecosystem.

A better understanding of what counts as "political content" will aid our interpretation of the self-reported behaviors of generating and consuming political content on the News Feed. If there is variation in what people identify as "political," it is possible that people don't think they post very much political content, but that others interpret what they post as either *implicitly political* or indicative about their views.

Defining and Recognizing Politically Informative Content

What kind of News Feed material might not be about unambiguously political topics, but still be considered to be informative about the political views of the person who posted it? I use the phrase "implicitly political" to describe this kind of content. It exists in a gray zone, highly conditional on the context in which it is generated and subject to the interpretation of the person receiving it more so than the intention of the person who created it.

Implicitly political content could take on several different forms, but here we focus on two. One form is labeled *politicized issues*. In a highly polarized political environment, politics has seeped into seemingly non-political domains. For example, in recent years there have been a number of situations in which companies have received public scrutiny – as well as public defense – for the political views of their owners or corporate board.[15] One of the most prominent examples is Chick-Fil-A. Chick-fil-A always has made its Christian values clear in a number of its business practices, including the closing of all stores on Sundays. But the company's brand was *politicized* after reports of campaign contributions to anti-LGBT politicians in 2010 led many to organize boycotts of the chain to protest those political contributions or the CEO's political viewpoints. In response, there was a strong backlash in support of the chain. The issue went viral on social media in July 2012. Since then, the company has been in the news on occasion for stories related to this narrative.

Is a status update that includes reference to Chick-Fil-A political? Take, for example, a person who writes "How could you not love Chick-Fil-A?!" In June 2012, before the news of the political contributions erupted, neither the person who posted this content nor any of his social contacts on Facebook would necessarily think that this statement was politicized. But for those social contacts who were aware of the politics of the situation in July 2012, and for as long afterwards as any of them remembers, the very same status update may signal the person's support of Chick-Fil-A's politics. By association, posting this status update could be considered an endorsement – or at least toleration – of the political views of the company. The person who posted the status update may or may not consider his status update to be about politics, and likewise the friends who read it may or may not interpret it that way. The ambiguity in what people consider to be political suggests that it is possible that people learn from content that is not necessarily intended to be political by the poster. Politicized issues may be fleeting and public memory may be short, but at any given point in early twenty-first-century America, something in our society is politicized in the way that Chick-Fil-A was in 2012.

A second type of implicitly political content might be called *politically sorted content*. This content could be considered sorted because one political party "owns" the topic. For example, the Republican Party has become the political home for people who advocate for strong gun ownership rights. Might the party's association with gun rights mean that guns themselves have become political? If people know that Republicans are more likely to support gun rights, has the proud display of a gun in a Facebook post – even if the gun was used for hunting purposes – come to be linked with a political statement

---

[15] Other examples include: the Salvation Army's statements regarding homosexuality; the statement made by the chairman of pasta company Barilla regarding the visual depiction of a "traditional family"; Costco's decision to remove a book by conservative pundit Dinesh D'Souza from its shelves; and the politicization of the Oscars with regard to diversity.

about guns themselves?[16] Similarly, the Democratic Party has owned the issue of environmental protection for several decades. When early adopters of hybrid cars or urban dwellers who actively compost boldly share their behavior with their social networks, do some of the people who view that content assume that the person is taking a position on the political issue of environmental protection?

In the next chapter, we more thoroughly consider an extension of the idea of politically sorted content. What if, in addition to the fact that in the aggregate our political views correlate with our non-political preferences, we have learned that these associations exist in our society? In addition to issue ownership, people may have stereotypes in their minds about the kinds of people who belong to the political parties. For example, maybe we think that certain kinds of people shop at certain stores. If these linkages are recognized and considered to be informative, then it is possible that even when people post content to Facebook that is not related to a political issue and is not tied to a politicized episode, they may be communicating a signal about their political views. This content is not likely to be judged as being about politics, but it may be informative about the partisan identity of the person who posted it.

The Expectation of Heterogeneity

A binary distinction between "political" and "not political" is an inappropriate characterization of the content that circulates on the News Feed, and so is the assumption that everyone agrees on what constitutes "political" content. Some people may report posting or seeing more political content because they consider a wider range of topics to connect to politics. Therefore, beyond characterizing the kind of content people deem to be political, we also should explore what drives differences in the breadth of that determination. Fitzgerald (2013) finds wide variation across gender, ideology, and partisan strength in what people consider to be political. Reported political interest, attention to politics, and political discussion behavior also were all correlated with the scope of what people considered to fall within the realm of "politics." Extending this to the realm of the News Feed, we should test for associations between political sophistication, as well as the frequency of Facebook usage, to see what contributes to a user's sense of what counts as political content.

---

[16] An unexplored corollary, one ripe for future study, is whether there are regional differences in perceptions of political sorting. For example, gun ownership may be clearly tied with partisanship in urban areas in the Northeast, but not associated together in rural areas in the South.

THE INFERENCE STUDIES

When we consider the possibility of News Feed interactions to psychologically polarize users, it may be the case that the volume of *politically informative* content is larger than the pool of content that is explicitly about policies or political actors. The first step is to determine the scope of what people identify as "political" and the remaining studies in this chapter probe this idea. The second step is to assess the extent of politically informative content circulating in the News Feed environment, even if that content is not identified as being political. We explore that in the next chapter.

A series of studies, conducted in 2016, was designed to examine the inferences and judgments that Facebook users make about other users, based on the content which they have posted. The studies were all similar in design. I selected from a set of publicly available content on social media, formatted that content to look like typical posts on Facebook, and asked subjects to make a variety of assessments of that material, including whether or not it was "political." In the next chapter, we will return to these same studies, demonstrating that content can be politically informative, even when it is not thought to be about politics, per se.

Based on the reasoning outlined above, the stimuli are drawn from content that has the potential to be politically informative. This designation encompasses both explicitly political and implicitly political content, the latter category including both politicized issues and politically sorted content. Because of the impossibility of randomly sampling from the status updates, memes, and news that circulate on people's News Feeds, I used other approaches to develop the pool of stimuli. For the status update studies, I selected from content that is structurally similar to status updates, but is much more readily available: tweets from Twitter. For the studies using visual content, I scoured the Facebook pages of a variety of different media and other sources to identify news stories or memes that had been disseminated on Facebook in the weeks before a study launched. Table 5.3 provides an overview of the topics. More detail about the specific stimuli used is in online Appendix B.

The basic set-up of an inference study invited subjects[17] to participate in a task to "read and evaluate Facebook posts," making no mention of politics whatsoever. The recruitment text indicated that they needed to be Facebook users to complete the task. The first question in the study asked if the respondent had a Facebook account. Any participants who indicated "no" were excluded from the study. The next screen displayed the stimulus, formatted to look like anonymized Facebook content, underneath the instructions, "Sometimes our first impressions of people are quite accurate. We are

---

[17] Subjects were workers on Mechanical Turk or were part of a student sample. See Appendix A for details.

TABLE 5.3 *Typology of Politically Informative Content*

Politically Informative Content in the END Framework		
Content that can signal the partisan identity and political views of the user who posts it to Facebook		
Explicitly Political Content	**Implicitly Political Content**	
Content about policies or political actors	*Content that is not about policies or political actors, but under certain conditions, can be considered to be about politics or to signal the political views of the person who posted it*	
Political Topics	**Politicized Issues**	**Politically Sorted Content**
News and information about policies, political actors, or electoral politics at the national, state, or local levels	*Cultural situations where politics has seeped into seemingly non-political domains, making support of a product or company indicative of political views or identity*	*Cultural signals tied to a political party's "ownership" of an associated political issue or the stereotypes associated with members of a party*
Example Textual Content		**Example Textual Content**
Muslim immigrant		Gun rack
#blacklivesmatter	**Example Textual Content**	Hybrid cars
Planned parenthood	Chick-Fil-A	Walmart
Income inequality	**Example Visual Content**	Whole Foods
Gun control	For examples, see online	Trader Joe's
Gay marriage	Appendix B. Topics	Car racing
Environment	included the Oscars	**Example Visual Content**
Example Visual Content	diversity controversy,	For examples, see online
For examples, see online	country music stars, and	Appendix B. Topics
Appendix B. Topics	gas prices	included the military,
included taxation,		police, cooking classes
unemployment, voter		for immigrants, and
identification laws, and		students praying on
health-care policy		a bus

This table contains definitions and examples of the content used in stimuli for the inference studies appearing in Chapters 5 to 8 of the book.

interested in your first impressions of the person who posted the following content on Facebook." Below the image appeared a series of six questions.[18] No other information was given about the user who posted the content, and

---

[18] Additionally, I asked the respondent to identify the knowledge level of the poster, the partisanship, the poster's ideological position on five issues, the respondent's confidence in their estimates, and whether the respondent would engage with the content if posted by one of their friends on Facebook.

there were no visual or textual clues about the identity of the individual. Subjects repeated this process – viewing a stimulus and answering questions about the person who supposedly posted it – for several iterations, ranging between six and ten, depending on the study. After the last iteration, they answered a short set of questions about their own Facebook usage and political behavior.

At present, we focus solely on their response to the penultimate question asked after each stimulus, "In your opinion, is this post about politics?" The expectation was that there should be broad consensus that explicitly political content was "political," and more diversity of opinion about whether implicitly political content was. Facebook usage frequency should be positively correlated with a broader definition of political content.

Evaluating Textual Content

To assess the kind of written text that people judge to be political, I gathered ten publicly available tweets on each of fourteen different key words posted in early 2016. Seven of these topics were hypothesized to be explicitly political using keywords associated with key policy debates. Seven were considered implicitly political based on findings from pilot data, media characterizations, or previous research (Moreton 2009). Using Adobe Photoshop, I then formatted these tweets to appear as though they were status updates, blurring out any aspects of the message that in a real status update would reveal the poster's identity. All formatting aspects of the status updates were identical. Figure 5.5 depicts an example. Full information on the stimuli can be found in online Appendix B.

Utilizing a sample from Mechanical Turk, each participant was randomly assigned to ten of the fourteen topics, and then to one of the ten status updates within each of those topics. Approximately ten respondents evaluated each stimulus. Each topic therefore was evaluated 100 times: ten evaluations on ten different stimuli that included the keyword.

Figure 5.6 shows the aggregated results for the respondents' evaluations about whether each topic was "political." Two thresholds are shown for each topic:[19] the proportion of evaluations that said "yes" and the proportion that said "yes" or "maybe" the post was about politics.

A majority of respondents agreed that six of the seven "explicitly political" topics were indeed political. A majority of evaluations indicated "yes," and

[19] The calculation is the overall proportion of evaluations for all ten status update stimuli in a category combined, and it is important to note that some of the tweets in the political category were not clear endorsements of political views. For example, one of the messages in the gun control category was "HELP I accidentally read some comments on a gun control article." This heterogeneity in message clarity was intentional, as there is no way to universally characterize content on a particular topic. This and other research design considerations are discussed in Appendix B and online Appendix B.

2 hrs · 👥

Claiming that Black folks don't care about our own communities or intracommunity violence is racist pandering #BlackLivesMatter

👍 Like   💬 Comment   ↗ Share

FIGURE 5.5 Example status update stimulus
A tweet formatted to appear like a status update.

greater than 80 percent indicated "yes" or "maybe." The seventh topic that was a priori hypothesized to be about a contemporary policy issue, the environment, did not cross the majority threshold for being considered to be definitely about politics, but close to 70 percent of evaluations thought that it was definitely or maybe about politics.

Of the seven implicitly political topics, three appeared to consistently be considered political: Chick-fil-A, hybrid cars, and gun rack. A majority of the evaluations indicated that the status update was or was "maybe" about politics, but there was not a majority who indicated that it definitely was. The remaining four topics were considered to be apolitical by a majority of subjects: Whole Foods, Walmart, Trader Joe's, and car racing. Aggregating the evaluations to the topic level obscures the heterogeneity of opinion at the stimulus level, and there was wide variation within each topic based on the content of the specific tweet.[20]

Facebook users recognize very short and stylized forms of communication as political, even when those messages are not particularly direct, clearly worded, or about contemporary policy issues. Status updates making reference to issues that were frequently in the news at the time the study was fielded were the most likely to be identified as being about politics. However, status updates that made mention of things typically thought to be associated more strongly with one political party over the other, such as gun racks and hybrid cars, could also be political, depending on the wording used. Political controversies from years

[20] Approximately one-quarter of the status updates in the seven non-political topics were considered to be political by 50 percent or more of the people who evaluated them. Take, for example, the status update reading, "Ask Walmart management when hours can stop getting cut, reply is 'we have no idea.' Ask if they know associates are hurting? 'Oh, we know'." This message was considered to be political by 55 percent of respondents, even though it does not include any clear statement of policy preferences. Walmart's labor practices are occasionally in the news. For example, in January 2016, a National Labor Relations Board ruled that the company had unlawfully retaliated against striking employees. That same month, the company was in the news for announcing an impending raise in hourly wages for full-time employees. The particular status update used, however, made no direct reference to either of these situations.

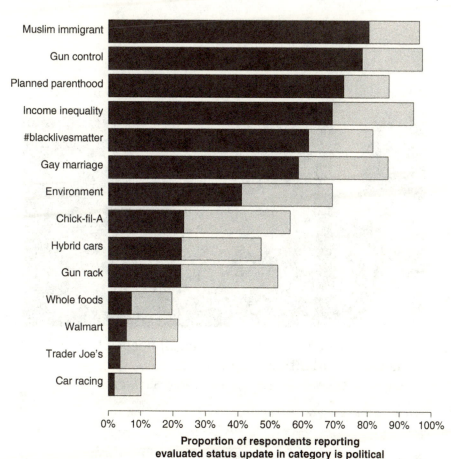

FIGURE 5.6 Mean estimates of the proportion of raters who evaluated status update in category as political

Each bar in the figure is the mean proportion from ten evaluations of ten different status updates in the category (a total of 100 evaluations). The dark portion of each bar is the proportion saying the status update was "definitely" about politics, and the light portion of each bar is the proportion saying the status update was "maybe" about politics.

past, such as the reaction to Chick-Fil-A's financial contributions to political causes, also appear capable of activating people's political judgment years after the initial situation was in the news. "Political" status updates, therefore, appear to encompass a wide variety of topics.

Evaluating Visual Content

Do these inferences extend to non-textual postings, which may be even less direct and clear than a user's own words? Do people recognize political

FIGURE 5.7 Example Facebook lede stimulus

cartoons, memes, and non-explicitly political news headlines as also being political in nature? This sort of content circulates more frequently than do status updates. What I call a "visual lede" is what a typical post on the News Feed looks like if a user has posted it directly from a third-party source. It is visually dominated by a picture, but includes a headline and often a brief one-line statement summarizing or leading the story. An example is provided in Figure 5.7.

The full set of thirty-four stimuli are available in online Appendix B. Stimuli that were so overtly political that I did not expect to see variation among assessments of "politicalness" (e.g. news stories related to presidential or congressional politics) were excluded from the study. Instead, I focused on content about which there might be some ambiguity about how to classify the material. The stimuli can be categorized into one of three types. First, *political memes and cartoons* are visual depictions of political humor. They are about explicitly political topics, but are presented in humorous ways. Example topics include taxes, government regulation, economic policies, environmental policies, and voter identification laws. Second, *policy news* stimuli are visual Facebook ledes for news stories pertaining to politically relevant news – such as immigration, gas prices, and health-care policies. These stimuli have a clear connection to a policy issue, but make no mention of specific political parties, actors, bills, or laws. Finally, *politically sorted* stimuli are visual Facebook ledes for news stories that do not explicitly pertain to politics, but feature topics – such as religion, art, public health, or pop culture – that have the potential to signal information about a person's values or priorities. All the stimuli were edited in Adobe Photoshop to remove any identifying information about the original source or the person who posted it.

The study proceeded in a manner very similar to the approach outlined above. Participants were assigned to see a random subset of these stimuli and then report whether the content was about politics. Approximately thirty subjects evaluated each stimulus. A similar pattern emerges to the results of the status update inference study. People do recognize political content as "political" and, depending on the example, some explicitly non-political content as well. Over 90 percent of the evaluations of political memes and cartoons were deemed to be about politics, as were more than 50 percent of evaluations of policy news and more than one-third of the evaluations of news stories about politically sorted topics.

Thus, despite the possibility that people would be less able to impute political meaning to visual content, it appears that Facebook users readily recognize the political nature of the kind of content that more readily circulates on the News Feed than status updates. While people may not always correctly interpret the meaning of political cartoons (Leroy 1968), they do recognize them as containing political content. In fact, political humor may actually bolster people's confidence that they understand the political world (Baumgartner 2008). News stories extending far beyond those produced by reporters assigned to the "politics" beat are considered to be political by many users. For example, 56 percent of raters judged a story with the headline "Country Music Star Wonders What Happened to America's Work Ethic" (Figure 5.7) to be political in nature, as did 47 percent of raters who evaluated a post declaring "Anti-Beyoncé Protest by Police Supporters Set Outside NFL HQ."[21]

---

[21] The country music star pictured is Charlie Daniels, of the Charlie Daniels Band. The original story connected to this lede was based on an interview with the musician, but there was not widespread attention to it. There was a wider controversy in early 2016 stemming from Beyoncé Knowles's music video to the song "Formation" and her performance at the Super Bowl.

The Role of Source Cue

The two studies described so far use stimuli that emulate content on the News Feed where a user directly posts content that they have written (in the case of the status update study) or from another website (in the case of the visual lede study). However, Facebook users frequently share content with their friends that was originally posted by a third-party source, such as an interest group, political party, or news site. When users circulate content in this way, information about the person or organization who originally introduced the content remains attached to the post in what I call a "source cue."

Does the addition of a source cue to content increase the proportion of users who perceive the content to be political? This is unlikely to be the case for political memes and cartoons, as over 90 percent of those evaluations judged the content to be about politics, even absent a source cue. However, a source cue could change perceptions for the policy news and politically sorted content. I test this idea in a third study, described in the next chapter. Here, I focus on just the portion of it testing whether the addition of a source cue increases the proportion of evaluations that deem implicitly political content to be about politics.

The six stimuli were selected from the visual lede study described above, for which fewer than 60 percent of evaluations had deemed the stimulus to be possibly or definitely about politics. There were four conditions of each stimulus: without a source cue (identical to the study above), with a Fox News source cue, with a Huffington Post source cue, and with a USA Today source cue. The study proceeded in an identical manner as described previously. Approximately sixty evaluations were made of each of the twenty-four stimuli. Here, I collapse together the three media source conditions to form a single "Source Cue" condition.

For five of these six implicitly political stimuli, adding a source cue increased the proportion of evaluations that deemed the post to be definitely or maybe political in nature (see Figure 5.8). I am underpowered to detect statistically significant differences for each paired stimuli separately, as shown in the overlapping confidence intervals in the figure. However, pooling the stimuli, a difference of proportions test comparing all implicitly political stimuli that contained a source cue to those that did not confirms that a larger proportion of sourced stimuli were deemed to be political than were those without (43.99 vs. 36.93 percent, $p < 0.05$).

The implications of this finding are important given that an incredibly large proportion of the content that people circulate on the News Feed is originally created by a news source. Media sources post a mix of stories to their Facebook pages, some about explicitly political topics and others about seemingly non-political topics. When users recirculate implicitly political stories with a source cue – sharing third-party content to their own feeds – their friends are more likely to perceive those stories as being about politics.

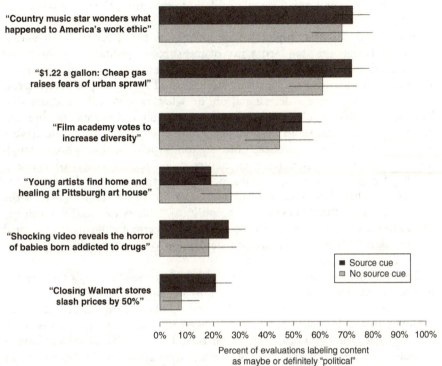

FIGURE 5.8 Effect of source cue on determination that content is political

Each pair of bars presents the proportion of evaluations that deemed the stimulus to be possibly or definitely about politics, with and without a source cue attached. Lines depict 95 percent confidence intervals.

Explaining Heterogeneity

The studies described above permit one further analysis: What explains the breadth of what a user considers to be political? In the status update study, each user evaluated ten stimuli and in the visual lede study, each user evaluated six stimuli. We can therefore assess the extent of a person's conceptualization of the "political," measured by the number of stimuli that a person identified as maybe or definitely being about politics.[22] These counts are normally distributed. Most people identified about half of the stimuli as definitely or maybe being political, while some people said

[22] In the status update study, users were randomly assigned to ten of the fourteen different topics, and thus some users were in fact assigned to a larger number of status updates that were a priori deemed to be about politics. I control for this in the regressions. I collected a very limited set of covariates in this study and did not include demographics.

there were none and some people said that everything they evaluated was about politics.

In her study of what topics people identify as being political, Fitzgerald (2013) finds that the standard array of measures of political sophistication do expand the breadth of what someone identifies as being political. We therefore test whether partisan strength and levels of political interest are related to a user's determination of what is political. Additionally, I hypothesize that regularly using Facebook also should expand the breadth of what people consider to be political. Political sophisticates should have a broader definition of "politics," but so too should people who, through frequent use of the site, have encountered a broader range of content. Finally, I expect that a user's self-report of the frequency with which they encounter political content without seeking it out to be associated with the breadth of what they recognize to be political. This is essentially a validity check, to show that a self-report measure of inadvertent exposure to political content is correlated with increased perception of what counts as political content in the studies.

There is evidence for the validity check in both studies in explaining the number of stimuli that a subject deems to be "maybe" about politics, and support in the visual lede study for the total number of stimuli thought to be definitely or maybe about politics. Users who say they more frequently inadvertently encounter political content on their News Feeds do in fact have a broader conception of the kind of content that could be considered to be political.

Neither political sophistication nor Facebook usage frequency is significantly associated with a broader conceptualization of "political" in the status update study in a regression model. However, there is support for the hypotheses in the meme study. When explaining the total number of stimuli that a user judges to be maybe or definitely about politics, partisan strength is significant. When explaining the number of stimuli that a user judged to be "maybe" about politics, both partisan strength and the frequency of using the site are significant.

Politics Is in the Eye of the Beholder

Although the adage says that "everything is political," the studies in this chapter suggest that we should revise that to "many things are perceived to be political." Certain topics and ideas fall squarely into the realm of politics, such as issues relating to gun control or immigration. People almost universally recognize these topics as political in the written and visual content generated by other social media users. The participants in these studies were also in general consensus that some topics were *not* about politics. But in between these two categories was a wide gray area where participants did not necessarily agree about the political nature of the content. The results in this chapter demonstrate that the definition of what counts as "political" should be considered as a spectrum, not a dichotomy.

This spectrum is not universally defined, and there appears to be considerable heterogeneity in the definition of "political." Facebook users who are politically sophisticated appear to have wider conceptualizations of what counts as explicitly political communication. However, frequent usage of the site can compensate for a lack of political sophistication in expanding someone's horizon about what is political. Even the least partisan users identify some content as political that would not meet a strict definition of communication about policy, candidates, or elected officials. Considerably more work needs to be done to assess the factors that contribute to how people make this determination, but the implications of these basic findings are threefold.

First, the weak but significant correlation between the amount of political content a person reports inadvertently encountering on her News Feed and the identification of evaluated content as "political" in the inference studies, even when controlling for the strength of a person's partisanship, is notable. It suggests that the self-report measures used in surveys to measure political content generation and exposure likely capture both objective exposure and subjective perceptions. Two different people, exposed to identical News Feeds, may report different levels of exposure to political content, depending on their definitions of what counts as "political." Are some people simply predisposed to imputing a political spin on what they encounter, or does encountering content on Facebook one perceives as "political" create a feedback loop that further expands a person's notion of the political domain? This is a fruitful area for future study.

Second, measures of political sophistication alone do not explain the breadth of what is considered political. Partisan strength affects what people identify as "political" to a limited extent. Consistent with Fitzgerald's findings, partisans may be more likely to identify visual content – memes and news ledes – as falling into a political domain. But they are no more likely to impute political overtones to written statements. Furthermore, political interest is not associated with the number of stimuli in the inference study that a respondent deemed to be definitely or possibly about politics. This suggests that even politically unsophisticated individuals identify a wide variety of content populating their feeds as pertaining to the political domain.

Finally, it is unclear if people apply the same conceptualization of "political" to the content they post compared to the content they see. Although I do not test this idea here, it seems plausible that asking Facebook users to report how much political content they generate may grossly underestimate the amount of content they post that *other people consider to be political*. If people are unaware of the extent to which others might recognize what they share as being politically loaded – if, for example, they don't realize that sharing even human interest stories from Fox News makes people more likely to think the story is about politics – then people are more likely to underreport their political content generation than to underreport the extent to which they encounter political content.

CONCLUSION

We are halfway to our answer about how it is that people learn so much about the views of others on Facebook when very few people report that they generate political content on the News Feed.

Political scientists have typically focused on studying explicitly political behaviors. The people who post explicitly political content to the News Feed are the usual suspects: more partisan, ideologically extreme, and predisposed with personality traits that encourage them to share those views with others. When these users generate political content, it likely reflects their more extreme views and sends a clear signal about their partisan identity. The dynamic between those who "talk" and those who "listen" on the News Feed results in a distribution of content that inaccurately reflects the distribution of opinions of Americans at large. Instead, it reflects the more extreme attitudes and increased partisanship of those who are most likely to contribute to the conversation.

Yet explicitly political content posted by partisan and ideological opinion leaders is only part of the content circulating on the News Feed that users deem to be "political." A much larger pool of content appears to be *implicitly* political. The users posting pictures with their guns, their hybrid cars, or their compost heaps probably wouldn't report that they've posted "political" content. But the people who see those pictures might perceive the content to be informative about the political views of the person who posted it, and therefore "about" politics, even if the users who posted the content were not intending to make a political statement. In other words, people may not think that they are posting political content, but their audience interprets what they post to be political in nature.

The consequence of this is that not only might people learn other people's political views from political memes, status updates, and news articles, but also from content that is implicitly political. Certain kinds of content – for example, those that make reference to Chick-Fil-A, gun racks, or hybrid cars – can be considered political, even when there is no explicit reference to any political angle of these topics. The mere reference to a political or politicized topic is sufficient to make a post political.

Therefore, people are exposed to quite a bit more political content on the News Feed than we might imagine if we focus only on the content generated by news organizations about current issues of the day. Even users who are not generating political content online are exposed to it. The more frequently people use Facebook, the more likely they are to report that they have learned the views of other people. Exposure to political content is not driven to the same extent by the factors – like political interest, knowledge, or extremity – that appear to drive traditional political behaviors.

The END model of communication on the News Feed suggests that even communication that is not explicitly about politics can influence viewers' evaluations of the poster if the content sends a signal about the poster's political identity. What matters when assessing the influences of social media communication on psychological polarization is the degree to which content is *politically informative about the views of the person who posted it*. Our focus thus shifts from the intention of the person who posts the content to the perspective of the person consuming that content.

In the next chapter, we turn to study the inferences people make about the political views of others based on a broad set of content that users post on Facebook. Based on the results of this chapter, we will include both explicitly political as well as politicized stimuli. We will also include the third kind of hypothesized politically informative content in the stimuli set, politically sorted content. Regardless of the fact that most of the respondents in the studies did not judge this content to be about politics, it turns out they still make inferences about the political views of the person who posted it.

This inference – a willingness to attribute political identity to another Facebook user based solely on the content of what they post – is the final piece of the puzzle to understanding why such high rates of learning about political views occur on Facebook. When we widen our aperture from communication that is explicitly about politics to communication that is politically informative, we uncover the fact that a substantial proportion of the content circulating on the News Feed may offer clues about the political identities of the people who post it. People are likely underestimating the amount of their own political communication because they only report the content they think is explicitly political, not the larger category of information that is politically informative to others. People may express their political identities without even realizing it, and once political identity is made salient, the processes of social identity theory suggest that negative judgment of the out-group follows suit.

6

Political Inference from Content on the News Feed

The findings in the previous chapter set up a clear, testable expectation: a wide range of News Feed content is informative to people in making inferences about the political views of the Facebook user who posted it. Evidence to support this claim would provide a straightforward, albeit unconventional, explanation for the empirical curiosity with which we began in Chapter 5: that a large proportion of Facebook users report learning the political views of others on the site, when a small proportion of users report that they regularly post political content.

In this chapter we build on the results of the last to show that not only do users consider a broad range of content to be about politics, but that an even broader range of content is informative about the partisan identity of the person who posted it. A key part of the process structuring intergroup inter-actions – the kinds of interactions social identity theory suggests are conducive to psychological polarization – is recognition and categorization of individuals into groups. The argument that News Feed interactions in the END Framework can be considered intergroup interactions is premised on the idea that Facebook users make inferences about the political identities of other users based on the content they post. This chapter provides strong evidence in support of that premise.

We return to the remaining three questions introduced in the beginning of Chapter 5 to more fully elaborate on the idea of inference from politically informative content.

Will people make inferences about the partisanship of Facebook users based solely on the non-political content they post?

Can a variety of Facebook content send clear and unambiguous signals about the partisanship of the person who posts it?

How do source cues affect the inference process?

As a preview of the answers to these questions, people ascribe their political interpretation of content to the partisan identity of the user who posts it. Even when given an option to answer that they "don't know," more than three-quarters of people are willing to ascribe partisanship to a person when the only detail they have about that individual is a single piece of content that user supposedly posted to Facebook. Intriguingly, there is almost always a consensus opinion about what that identity is, implying a consistent signaling mechanism that is generally accurate, but biased in predictable ways. Specifically, subjects recognize the direction of a poster's partisan leaning, but over-attribute identity strength. When source cues reinforce the intuitions people have about the poster's partisan leanings based on the content alone, the cues tend to strengthen the clarity of the signal of the poster's political identity.

The stimuli used in the studies establishing the presence of political inference – and in the analysis of negative judgment later in the book – are designed to resemble the content that circulates in the actual News Feed ecosystem. This content is distinct from solely news articles and status updates, which have received the majority of attention from political scientists to date. Importantly, people make political inference *even from content that is not explicitly political*. Therefore, although political content represents a small portion of all the content that circulates on the News Feed, a potentially much larger pool of content is politically informative.

THEORIZING POLITICALLY INFORMATIVE CONTENT

In the previous chapter, we saw that Facebook users recognize a broad set of content as being "about politics," but that they didn't judge every potentially politically informative stimulus as being political in nature. While the connection between the content someone posts and her attitudes should be more transparent for explicitly political content, there are other ways that people scrolling through their News Feeds might be able to infer the political views of their social contacts.

Explicitly Political Content

The users who post explicitly political content are much more likely to be strongly partisan, ideologically extreme, and opinionated. It is therefore likely that the political content they post sends a clear and unambiguous signal about their political viewpoints and identities. This content might reveal a positive tone about the political news that pleases the poster, or might be largely negative and critical of the candidates, officials, party, or policies with which the poster disagrees. Either way, the poster is likely to make her political views and partisan identity clear. Evidence from the END Framework Survey about the motivations that people have for generating political content support this claim. The most common motivations given by those people who frequently post political content were to inform other people of political issues (50.45 percent), share their political viewpoints with others (43.69 percent), signal to people that they have strong opinions on political issues (40.09 percent), and visibly support a point of view or a political party (40.54 percent).

Implicitly Political Content

Implicitly political content could be about *politicized issues*, information that reveals divisions between people on the left and those on the right that have nothing to do with policy, or contain *politically sorted* information about non-political attitudes or behaviors that are strongly correlated with political views. This content is quite fluid, responsive to stories in the news that highlight the non-political differences between political groups as well as other factors that influence the way in which people map culture and politics onto one another. Facebook users consider some, but not all, of this material to be about "politics." Why might this content be politically informative even if Facebook users do not think it is about politics, per se? Let us return to the examples used in the last chapter.

We will begin with our Chick-Fil-A-loving Facebook poster, who posts his adoration for the company. Depending on what he says about Chick-Fil-A, his friends who view the post may think what he has written is about politics: close to 60 percent of the evaluations of the ten Chick-Fil-A messages tested in the status update inference study reported that the text definitely was or might be political. Even for those statements that do not seem overtly political, what a person communicates about the very act of eating at the restaurant might send a signal about the poster's beliefs. Take the example used previously: "How could you not love Chick-Fil-A?!" To someone who identifies a political reason – support for gay marriage – for not "loving" the restaurant, the perceived dismissal of the company's political actions might signify that the poster does not care enough about marriage equality to alter his consumer behavior.[1]

A similar logic applies for the politically sorted content. A Facebook user posts a picture of herself in her brand-new hybrid car. The findings from the previous chapter suggest that most of her social contacts on the site will not necessarily interpret the act of sharing this picture as posting "political" content. However, the purchase of the car does suggest that the user values fuel efficiency, which implies she might care about the environment. If she cares enough about the environment to purchase a hybrid car, the issue might be especially important to her, and if it is, she is more likely to vote for Democratic candidates over Republican ones.

---

[1] In fact, only 50 percent of evaluations of this message thought that it might be about politics. But of those people willing to attribute a partisan identity to the person who posted it, 80 percent thought the person was a Republican.

Another form of sorted content might rely more on stereotypes than any sort of tenuous connection to a policy preference. This content is unlikely to be considered "political," but may evoke associations to commonly held assumptions about the differences between partisans. Think back to the discussion of social sorting in Chapter 4, where study after study revealed that there are differences between liberals and conservatives (and by extension, Democrats and Republicans) on completely non-political preferences, from baby names (Oliver *et al.* 2016), to art (Wilson *et al.* 1973), food (Epstein 2014), product brands (Khan *et al.* 2013), books (Shi *et al.* 2017), and bedroom décor (Carney *et al.* 2008). Facebook, as a social media site designed to help people express their identities, is especially conducive as a platform for people to send tangible signals about their actions and thoughts related to these preferences. For example, among the stimuli tested, most of the status updates or ledes related to shopping preferences at one of three recognizable chains – Walmart, Trader Joe's, and Whole Foods – were not considered to be about politics. Yet to the extent that these stores align with our notions of what type of people shop at each store – the stereotype that poorer, more rural people shop at Walmart and wealthier, more urban people shop at Trader Joe's and Whole Foods – we might make an association between consumer behavior and political views.

These studies do not actually test the reasoning people use in making these associations and I remain agnostic about where and how they form these connections in the first place. It is easy to imagine that while these sorts of socio-political correlations might have been recognized before social media, social media interactions have amplified the opportunities for mapping what types of people hold which kinds of political preferences. This topic merits considerable future investigation, and this book only scratches the surface. Clearly, there are liberal Walmart shoppers and conservative Whole Foods shoppers. Not all Facebook users recognize those associations that may actually exist in reality. But consensus in the evaluations of the political views of the people who post this politically sorted content would suggest widespread, shared understanding of which types of people "belong" in each political group. Content does not have to be political to be politically informative.

Perceptions of News Source Ideological Bias

The findings in Chapter 5 showed that simply adding a news source cue to content made people more likely to think that content was political. Likewise, these source cues have the potential to figure prominently in the way in which people draw inference from content on the News Feed, but only if those cues are unambiguous signals of political leanings. If we recognize that people's political leanings influence the sources they read, then articles posted from those sites could suggest their political views, even if the article itself has nothing to do with politics.

The theory of selective exposure is predicated on the idea that people can recognize that certain sources are more likely to cover topics they care about or cover those topics in a manner consistent with their a priori attitudes. We know less about whether non-ideologues recognize the ideological inclinations of the plethora of sources preferred by those with ideologically consistent preferences. Stroud (2011) shows that politically knowledgeable individuals are more likely to attribute bias to sources they perceive lean to the other side, but that low-knowledge individuals are much less likely to attribute bias to sources that they perceive support or oppose their ideology. However, the data were collected in 2008, quite soon after the launch of the News Feed on Facebook, and for only six sources. In fact, most of the experiments demonstrating the presence of selective exposure use as stimuli the biggest and most recognizable media sources, such as Fox News or MSNBC. It is unclear whether people recognize the wider range of traditional and non-traditional news sources that circulate in the hyper-fragmented ecosystem on social media.

In the aggregate, the public perceives a liberal bias in the news media,[2] a perception that has increased considerably over time.[3] However, do people recognize the ideological leaning of specific news sources? Is there consensus in the public about which sources are biased toward the conservative perspective, which are biased toward the liberal perspective, and which do not have a bias? These questions are important ones meriting more systematic and in-depth future study. But for the purpose of testing whether source cue affects political inference, I provide a preliminary assessment here.

The focus is on the same media sources used in the 2014 Pew study on polarization and media habits (Pew Research Center 2014b).[4] Participants answered two questions on the END Framework Survey.[5] The first asked them to identify which of the thirty-six sources they recognized. Then, for

---

[2] Historically, more Americans perceive that the media has a liberal bias than a conservative bias or no bias at all. See Justin McCarthy, "Trust in Mass Media Returns to All-Time Low." Gallup (September 17, 2014).

[3] The empirical evidence for the actual existence of liberal media bias is mixed because of the exceptional difficulties in defining uncontroversial measurements of it. Groseclose and Milyo (2005) and Groseclose (2011) argue that there is a strong liberal bias, whereas Budak *et al.* (2016) and Nyhan (2012) do not.

[4] I cannot make any claims about the representativeness of these sources compared to the universe of sources that generate content on Facebook, nor the overall contribution of these sources to the total amount of content that circulates. An exhaustive cataloguing of the sources that disseminate content on Facebook would be nearly impossible, and thus a systematic random sampling of them is not a straightforward exercise. I chose to use sources that had been identified and pilot tested by Pew to maximize variation in platform, audience size, and geography (see Appendix B in Pew Research Center 2014b).

[5] I pilot tested the survey at the end of the visual lede study fielded on Mechanical Turk described in the previous chapter.

any of the sources they said they recognized, they were asked to evaluate the ideological leanings of the source.[6]

Figure 6.1 shows the results from the national sample.[7] The sources are ordered based on the proportion of the sample that identified the source as having a liberal bias. The percentages listed in the right-hand margin are the percentage of all respondents who recognized the source. There are several things to note about the results. First, there is strong face validity to the ordering of bias provided by the respondents. The five sources deemed to have a conservative bias by the greatest proportion of respondents are all considered "more trusted than distrusted" by conservatives in Pew's study and more "distrusted than trusted" by liberals. The opposite is true for the five sources identified as having a liberal bias by the greatest proportion of respondents.[8] Second, network news channels and non-American sources are perceived as being more ideologically unbiased. Interestingly, eighteen of the thirty-six sources are identified by a majority of respondents as having either a liberal or conservative ideological bias.

There is obviously variation in the extent both to which people recognized sources and inferred ideological bias. In the national sample, 43 percent of respondents recognized fewer than ten of the sources, while 12.4 percent recognized thirty or more.[9] Most people perceived that the majority of the sources had an ideological leaning. Only 7.8 percent of respondents who recognized at least one source thought that none of the sources had a slant, and only 23.5 percent thought that fewer than half did. The explanations for what type of people recognize the greatest number of sources and perceive the greatest bias are generally consistent with previous work exploring perceptions of media bias. Those people who are most politically interested and most educated recognize the greatest number of sources. Surprisingly, however, partisanship strength is significantly *negatively* related to the number of sources a respondent could recognize controlling for other variables in a multivariate regression.

---

[6] The exact wording was modeled after Pew's question. I first asked, "Please click on all of the media sources that you have heard of, regardless of whether you use them or not. If you are unsure, please DO NOT click it." I did not include the source logo as Pew did in its study. There were thirty-six sources or shows listed (see Figure 6.1 for the names). For every source that the respondent clicked, I followed up with the question, "Of the sources you listed above that you recognize, do you think these sources tend to report information with an ideological bias? Please drag the source into the box where you think it belongs" and provided boxes marked "Liberal Bias," "No Ideological Bias," and "Conservative Bias."

[7] The rank-ordered results are nearly identical from the pilot study sample using Mechanical Turk.

[8] The results also appear consistent with the crowd-sourced ideological classification conducted by Budak *et al.* (2016), as well as the sources that overlap with those assessed in Gentzkow and Shapiro (2011). The authors conclude that there is more similarity than difference between many sources, but the sources they find as being more slanted are the same sources that appear to be perceived as being most ideological in this study.

[9] In the pooled Mechanical Turk pilot studies, only 11.8 percent of respondents recognized fewer than ten of the sources, while 30.7 percent recognized thirty or more. The discrepancy in media recognition rates between the two samples remains unexplained.

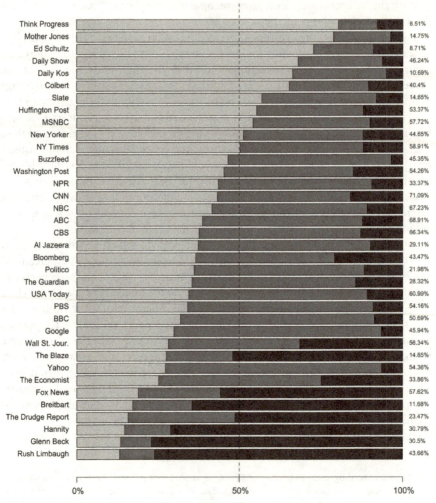

FIGURE 6.1 Perceived ideological bias of thirty-six media sources
The light gray portion of the bar indicates the proportion of the sample that perceived the source to have a liberal bias, the medium gray portion indicates the proportion that said no bias, and the dark gray portion indicates the proportion perceiving the source to have a conservative bias. The percentages listed in the right-hand margin are the percentage of the sample recognizing the source.

Political interest also drives the proportion of sources that a respondent thought had an ideological leaning, but neither partisan strength nor education does. Why doesn't partisan strength appear to matter for the number of sources that a respondent identifies as having an ideological bias? Because the direction of partisanship and ideology do. Consistent with previous research, stronger identification with a conservative ideology, as well as a stronger attachment to the Republican Party, were associated with an increased perception of media bias. Conservatives identify many more sources as being liberally biased than liberals identify as being conservatively biased. In fact, the results for the overall proportion of the sources that a respondent found had a bias is driven almost entirely by the fact that those on the right are more likely to identify more sources as having a liberal bias. The reverse is not true for those on the left.

What is the effect of Facebook usage? Neither usage nor News Feed scrolling frequency is associated with increased recognition or perceived bias of media sources, but reported exposure to political content is. While inadvertent exposure is positively associated with recognizing more sources and perceiving that a greater number of sources are biased, intentional exposure is negatively associated. Further research is necessary to explore this pattern, but the findings suggest that while using Facebook intentionally for news purposes may lead people to seek out sources they already recognize and trust (the echo chamber effect), unintentionally encountering political content on the feed has the effect of heightening people's ability not only to recognize sources, but also to attribute bias to those sources.

This study demonstrates that regardless of the actual level of ideological bias in certain news sources, a notoriously difficult question to answer (Groeling 2013), the public perceives that certain sources lean one direction or the other. It is this perception, as opposed to the objective reality of media slant, that matters for the inferences people make about their social contacts' political views based upon the source of the content they post. Political sophistication matters to a limited extent. Political interest does drive recognition and perception of bias, but political knowledge affects only recognition and partisanship strength matters only for the recognition of bias among Republicans. Furthermore, the estimate that half of the sources are ideologically informative likely underestimates the ideological signaling of the sources producing content that circulates on the News Feed, as many of the non-traditional media sources that prolifically generate content are named in ways that make their leanings more transparent: "Chicks on the Right," "Right Wing News," "Left Wing Nation," etc.

Demonstrating that people identify sources as carrying an ideological bias does not necessarily mean they will infer that a person who shares content from that source adheres to the party aligned with that ideology. As I show below, however, it appears that people do make this assumption.

POLITICAL INFERENCE FROM WRITTEN AND VISUAL CONTENT

Facebook users will evaluate a wide variety of material as political, but will they find News Feed content sufficiently informative to guess the partisan leanings of the person who posted it? When given the option to report that they "don't know," what proportion of people are still willing to draw an inference? The approach used to assess this question may be susceptible to demand characteristics or participant bias, in which subjects guess an experiment's purpose and change their behavior accordingly. But the approach does give a sense of the extent to which people *can* make an inference. It is important to note that in these studies there is no "objective truth" as to the political viewpoints of the original users who posted the tweets and visual content. Yet it appears that people pick up on the same subtleties in the textual and visual stimuli, as there is consensus in inference at a much higher rate than we would expect by chance if people were simply guessing haphazardly.

In the studies described in the previous chapter, in addition to assessing whether subjects thought the content was about politics, they also were asked to provide their assessment of the political views of the person who posted it. Here, we focus on the poster's partisanship, reporting the results of the status update and visual lede study concurrently.

Users were very willing to make evaluations of the partisan identity of the poster, even though they were given the option to report they "didn't know." Overall, approximately three-quarters (76.5 percent) of the responses included an evaluation of partisanship in the status update study, as did 86.2 percent of responses in the visual stimuli study.

Figure 6.2 shows that there was variation across types of stimuli and whether the evaluator thought the stimulus was potentially about politics. But the vast majority of evaluations across all types of stimuli included an estimate of partisanship. For example, even among the implicitly political status updates among people who did not think the status update was about politics, 55.9 percent of evaluators were still willing to wager a guess about the partisanship of the person who wrote it.[10]

Perhaps respondents were willing to ascribe an identity, but only chose the middle or moderate category for each scale. This is not possible to assess for the status update study, as respondents were forced to pick either strong partisan (Democrat or Republican), leans partisan (Democrat or Republican), or "don't know." However, moderation does not appear to dominate the evaluations of ideological viewpoints. Only about 15 percent picked the "moderate" category on each of the five ideological scales also asked.[11] On the visual stimuli study, for which subjects were able to respond that the poster of the content was an Independent,[12] only 19.2 percent of evaluations did so.

---

[10] The lowest percent of a category willing to make a political evaluation – 46.2 percent of evaluations of memes and cartoons by those who did not think the stimulus was political in nature – is somewhat misleading: there were only thirteen evaluations out of nearly 200 that did not consider the stimulus to be political in nature.

[11] In the accuracy study described below, this pattern of results replicates using a student sample instead of a Mechanical Turk sample. Subjects in that study were given the option to evaluate the partisanship of the poster of a status update as Independent, and very few subjects did. This replication also shows that these findings extend to samples beyond Mechanical Turk.

[12] There were trade-offs made in these two different response options. When subjects were not given the option to identify the poster as an Independent (as in the status update study), it is more

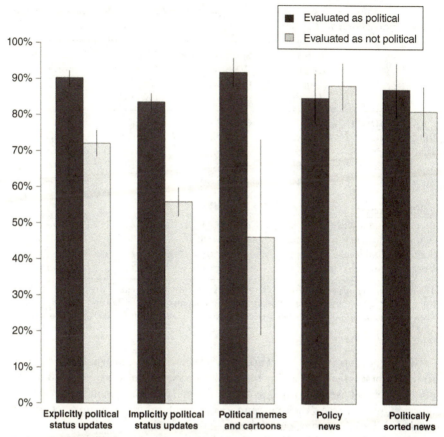

FIGURE 6.2 Willingness to ascribe partisan identity, by stimulus type and judgment that content was political

The proportion of evaluations in each category that supplied an answer other than "don't know" when asked about the partisanship of the person who posted the stimulus. The dark bars show the percentage among those who deemed the stimulus in the category to maybe or definitely be about politics, while the light bars show the percentage among those who did not think the stimulus was political. Lines depict 95 percent confidence intervals.

transparent how to assess aggregate consensus in partisan identity because respondents are forced to make a choice. What we gain in analytic clarity we lose by constraining the poster's partisanship to a restricted, and not entirely realistic, set of choices. In the meme study, subjects are able to identify the poster as an Independent, but this option makes it analytically difficult for the researcher to define what "consensus" means. I chose to split the difference so that we can get estimates of both choices. When given an option, subjects do not overwhelmingly choose to identify the poster as an Independent (only 19.2 percent of evaluations), and when forced to pick from constrained choices, they choose the "don't know" option at a slightly higher rate (about a 10 percent difference).

TABLE 6.1 *Willingness to Infer and Confidence in Inference, by Level of Partisan Strength and Political Interest*

	Status Updates (Out of 10 Possible)	Status Updates Reported Confidence (0–100)	Visual Stimuli (Out of 6 Possible)	Visual Stimuli Reported Confidence (0–100)
Partisan Strength				
Independents	6.52	47.83	4.67	41.11
Leaning partisans	7.04	57.79	5.38	50.63
Weak partisans	7.83	55.88	5.20	58.43
Strong partisans	8.20	66.30	5.41	54.97
Political Interest				
Not at all interested	7.00	41.91	5.40	20.40
Not very interested	8.00	53.18	4.80	42.70
Somewhat interested	7.35	57.08	5.20	53.83
Very interested	8.15	64.77	5.21	58.29

The mean number of stimuli for which respondents provided an estimate of partisanship, and the mean confidence in those partisanship estimates, by strength of partisanship and level of political interest in the status update study (left two columns) and the visual stimuli study (right two columns).

We might expect that strong partisans and those interested in politics are willing to make these inferences about the partisan identities of other users. But what about Facebook users who are less attached to the political system? To answer this question, we can assess the total number of stimuli for which a subject attributed partisanship to the poster, out of the ten status updates they evaluated in the first study or the six visual ledes they evaluated in the second study. While the strength of a subject's partisan identity is correlated with the number of stimuli for which he or she was willing to impute the poster's partisanship, even Independents and those with weak partisan identities were willing to wager guesses the majority of the time (shown in Table 6.1). Political interest was not correlated with people's willingness to make inferences about political views. Even the least politically interested attributed partisanship to the anonymous posters at very high rates.

Political sophistication does matter for the respondents' confidence in the accuracy of their inferences. Respondents were asked to indicate their confidence in their estimates of partisanship, where marking 100 indicated that they were very confident they were correct, and 0 indicated that they were not certain at all. Fewer than 15 percent of evaluations indicated a score of 10 or below. Party strength and political interest did increase respondents' confidence in their estimates, but again, we see that even those with weak partisan identities and lower levels of political interest report at least some confidence in their estimates.

The key implication of the END Framework is that regular usage of Facebook and frequently, but inadvertently, encountering political content in the News

TABLE 6.2 *Willingness to Infer and Confidence in Inference, by Facebook Usage Frequency*

	Status Updates (Out of 10 Possible)	Status Updates Reported Confidence (0–100)	Visual Stimuli (Out of 6 Possible)	Visual Stimuli Reported Confidence (0–100)
Facebook Usage				
Lowest	7.13	50.53	4.59	51.96
Next	7.69	54.59	5.00	49.89
Every day	7.52	61.11	5.32	50.31
Every day, 5+	8.36	62.81	5.62	65.85
News Feed Scrolling				
Lowest	7.60	54.61	5.00	52.08
Middle	7.87	61.66	5.18	50.74
Too many times a day	7.35	58.73	5.56	57.64
Inadvertent Exposure				
Lowest quartile	7.19	52.91	5.12	44.03
Middle 50%	7.65	58.24	4.96	55.40
Highest quartile	8.18	64.53	5.64	55.49

The mean number of stimuli for which respondents provided an estimate of partisanship, and the mean confidence in those partisanship estimates, by site usage, News Feed scrolling frequency, and reported inadvertent exposure to political information in the status update study (left two columns), and the visual stimuli study (right two columns).

Feed also should contribute to users' willingness to infer and confidence in their inferential abilities. The END model of communication suggests that the more people use Facebook, the more practice they get encountering and processing social information based on the content their contacts post to the site. In fact, frequent Facebook usage does appear to matter, especially for confidence (see Table 6.2). In each individual inference study, the relationship between willingness to infer and site usage frequency, News Feed scrolling, and passive consumption of political information is not always robust to the inclusion of other variables into a regression model.[13] However, if the data are pooled together,[14] the relationships are large and robust.

[13] These studies were quite small. There were only 140 subjects in the status update study and 100 in the visual stimuli study. Given the skewed distribution of the usage variables – there were very few infrequent Facebook users in the sample – the lack of statistical significance in the individual studies is not surprising.

[14] As shown in online Appendix E, the responses from the three inference studies are all combined into a single dataset for the pooled analyses. In regression models using this combined dataset, standard errors are clustered at the subject level.

ILLUSION OR REALITY?

Facebook users appear readily willing to draw conclusions about the political identity of another user, based solely on a single piece of content that user posted, absent any other information. This ability to recognize political identity is a critical first step in activating the processes of intergroup interactions that lead to affectively polarized evaluations. But the fact that Facebook users can make an inference does not demonstrate that the inference is anything more than a random guess. To strengthen the argument about the role of politically informative content, it is important to assess whether a variety of Facebook content can send clear and unambiguous signals about the partisanship of the person who posts it. In other words, are these inferences shared and are they accurate?

On the one hand, it really does not matter if people arrive at the same, or accurate, conclusions about the political views of an individual who posts Facebook content. What matters is that people will make the inference and attribute a political identity to someone, not whether they do so correctly or reach the same conclusions as other users. However, if the inferences Facebook users make are neither tethered to reality, nor tethered to a commonly shared mapping between implicitly political topics and political views, the inferences are less meaningful.

At worst, inaccurate or haphazard evaluations could mean that the subjects in the study just were acquiescing to the demands of the experimenter, providing an answer randomly among the provided options. If subjects were doing more than randomly picking responses, but were not in agreement with each other about the signal sent by the content, the argument that people can recognize the politicization of non-political topics would be weakened. This would point to a lack of shared understanding about the very cultural signals that I argue are informative. Likewise, if subjects' inferences were aligned with one another, but totally inaccurate, then the mapping from shared cultural signals to specific instances of those signals would be noisy, questioning whether the inference was in any sense tied to the reality of the poster's views.

These concerns can be put to rest. Subjects achieved both high levels of consensus and high levels of accuracy in their inferences about the political views of anonymous Facebook users.

Consensus in Inference

Respondents clearly were willing to make evaluations about users based on both the political and non-political content they posted. How much consensus exists about the partisan leanings of the poster? If people were guessing, we would imagine that half of the raters would guess the poster was a Democrat and half would guess that the rater is a Republican. Estimates that deviate substantially from a 50/50 split suggest consensus. The lower two panels of Figure 6.3 show that the majority of status updates did achieve consensus (66 percent agreement) as to the partisanship of the respondent (the points,

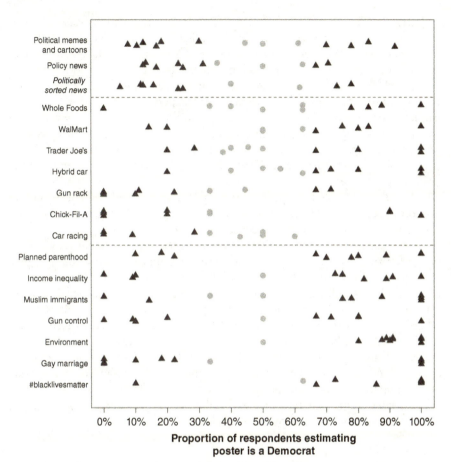

FIGURE 6.3 Consensus in estimates of the partisanship of an anonymous Facebook poster

There were approximately ten individual stimuli within each status update topic or lede category. Each dark grey triangle indicates an individual stimulus (status update or lede) where 66 percent or more of the evaluators agreed about the poster's partisanship (either as a Democrat or a Republican). Each light grey circle indicates an individual stimulus where evaluators failed to reach consensus.

representing individual status updates, that are colored a dark grey and are shaped like triangles). What is more remarkable than inferences based on the political topics (lower panel) is the inferences made based on merely politicized or sorted topics (middle panel). While there was less consensus achieved for the implicitly political topics, consensus was still reached for a majority of the status updates. For example, eight out of ten status updates mentioning Chick-Fil-A achieved consensus, and respondents overwhelmingly thought that people posting about gun racks leaned to the right.

Users' words send informative signals about their political views, even when they write about something that is not explicitly political. Status updates are direct statements of a person's views, and there is rarely ambiguity as to the fact that what the user writes is a reflection of his beliefs. This assumption becomes weaker when a Facebook user is posting content generated by another individual or organization, as it is possible that the person is posting the content ironically or to protest against it. Consequently, people may be less willing to ascribe the message of the content to the viewpoint of the poster. Furthermore, while people report high levels of engagement with humorous political content, it is not obvious whether they can map the humor onto an understanding of the political views it expresses. As the upper panel in Figure 6.3 shows, however, people are in fact able to impute meaning to visual political content, including humorous posts, and to draw conclusions about posters' political views based on the non-textual, non-political content they post.

Overall, the respondents achieved consensus about the political views of the poster for 76.47 percent (26/34) of the implicitly political visual stimuli, 70 percent (49/70) of the implicitly political status updates, and 92.86 percent (65/70) of the explicitly political status updates.[15] These studies cannot shed light on how precisely it is that Facebook users arrive at a shared set of beliefs about what kinds of words and images signal Democratic compared to Republican partisan leanings, but there is strong evidence that they do.[16]

We will return to analyzing the data from these two studies in Chapters 7 and 8, where we move beyond whether subjects were willing to make basic political inferences about the partisanship of the person who posted the content and consider their evaluation of the overall coherency of her policy views and their judgment about the knowledge level of the poster.

Accuracy in Inference

The status update and visual stimuli inference studies presented so far show that individuals are willing to make political inferences about anonymous users.

---

[15] People were least willing to infer a user's partisanship on the implicitly political status updates. Removing those implicitly political stimuli with high proportions of people unwilling to guess (50 percent or more), consensus was achieved for 73.08 percent (38/52) of the implicitly political status updates.

[16] The proportion of stimuli for which consensus was reached obviously depends on the threshold used to determine consensus. Furthermore, it is not a straightforward exercise to conduct a hypothesis test to determine whether these percentages are significantly different from what we would expect if people were randomly guessing. For the status update study, respondents could pick one of five answers (four responses and "don't know") and in the visual lede study, respondents could pick one of six answers (five responses and "don't know"). If respondents were truly randomly guessing, then each response choice should be equally likely to be selected. However, the evidence presented so far indicates that this is not an accurate assumption. Therefore, I do not conduct a statistical test to support this claim.

They achieve a remarkable level of consensus about the partisanship of those posters, based on both written and visual content and about both explicitly and implicitly political topics. But are those inferences accurate? The research designs above do not permit a test of that question because the stimuli were derived from publicly available data from Twitter and Facebook, and the political views of the users who created or shared the content are unknown.

However, that information is available about users who participated in a study in the fall of 2016 that uses explicitly political content. In this study, instead of selecting random or representative content from Twitter or Facebook to serve as stimuli, I tasked Mechanical Turk workers, whom I will call the "posters," to write the content. They were randomly assigned to one of four prompts: two contemporary political issues (the Black Lives Matter movement or gun control) or the 2016 presidential candidates (Hillary Clinton or Donald Trump). Half of the workers assigned to each prompt read a news article and were asked to write a status update in response. The other half were instructed to write a status update without reading an article. After writing their status update, they were asked a set of basic questions about their political partisanship, ideology, and political knowledge.

The short bits of text they generated were formatted in a similar fashion as described above to appear like status updates or ledes, depending on their treatment condition. I selected a set of thirty-four stimuli from the sixty-five that were produced and created nine sets of stimuli, grouped by the partisan and ideological strength of the person who wrote the content.

The remainder of the study was very similar to the inference studies described above, except that a student subject pool (n=340) was used to evaluate the stimuli. These subjects, whom I will call the "judges," were randomly assigned to evaluate one stimulus from each set of nine. This ensured that all the judges evaluated content posted by both co-partisans and out-partisans, and evaluated stimuli created by posters with substantial variation in their partisan and ideological strength. Each of the thirty-four stimuli was evaluated by at least eighty users in order to have enough evaluations to draw meaningful conclusions about the accuracy of the respondents in inferring the political views of the posters. In sum, there were 3,045 complete evaluations to analyze.

The findings from this study show a high rate of aggregate accuracy in the judges' evaluations of the posters' content. The correlation between the posters' self-reported partisanship on a seven-point scale and the judges' evaluation of the posters' partisanship on a seven-point scale is 0.71. When the partisanship scale is condensed to a three-point measure, the correlation ranges between 0.69 and 0.73, depending on whether Independent leaners are coded as Independents or partisans. Consistent with this high correlation, the overall accuracy of the judges on the three-point scale, when Independent leaners are coded as partisans, is quite high: 72.1 percent of all evaluations accurately identified the partisanship of the person who wrote the content.

Aggregating the data at this level misses an important point though. Very few of the judges evaluated the posters as Independents, even when the posters themselves identified that way. Thus, while 82.1 percent of strong partisans were identified accurately on the three-point scale, as were 97 percent of weak partisans, only 65 percent of partisan leaners and only 10.3 percent of Independents were. The more precise conclusion to draw about accuracy, therefore, is that the judges were quite accurate in gauging the self-reported identity of partisan posters, but could not recognize a lack of partisan identity. This is consistent with the fact that the judges overestimated the extremity of the posters' ideology, a point we will explore in the next chapter.

Importantly, the accuracy of the estimations did not vary by the partisan identity of the judge. Democrats and Republicans appear to be able to recognize and identify the viewpoints of the out-party as well as the in-party.[17] There are some effects on accuracy based on the topic of the prompt, whether the posters were writing about the 2016 presidential candidates or about one of two contemporary policy issues. Generally speaking, judges were more accurate when the poster commented about the candidates compared to the political issues (see Figure 6.4).[18]

Some of the judges were more accurate than others. A judge's partisan strength was highly associated with their accuracy. Are more frequent Facebook users more likely to correctly evaluate the partisan identities of the posters? More than 95 percent of the student sample had a Facebook account, so we cannot compare Facebook users to non-Facebook users. Facebook usage intensity was not associated with the judges' accuracy in gauging the partisan identity of posters. This suggests that increased Facebook use does not improve people's accuracy. Subjects who used Facebook infrequently were accurate on average in more than two-thirds of their evaluations. Thus, while Facebook use makes people more confident in their abilities to infer, it does not actually make them more accurate.

In the chapters that follow, we will see that Facebook users are quite biased in their estimations of other people's ideological consistency, extremity, and knowledge levels based on whether they perceive a person to be in their in-party or not. However, they do not appear to be biased in their attribution of identity. At a rate much greater than chance, people appear to be able to correctly perceive the direction of partisan identity based on very short statements of their political views.

---

[17] Because the student subject pool comprised primarily students majoring in Government or Public Policy, a group of knowledgeable and engaged subjects, there were very few political Independents in the sample.

[18] The largest error rate – the 17.98 percent of Democratic judges and 20.08 percent of Republican judges who misperceived the attitudes of Democratic posters – is somewhat anomalous. This appears to be largely driven by a single gun violence stimulus where a poster self-identified as a Democrat, but had very strong (self-reported) conservative views about gun control that were expressed in the content of their status update.

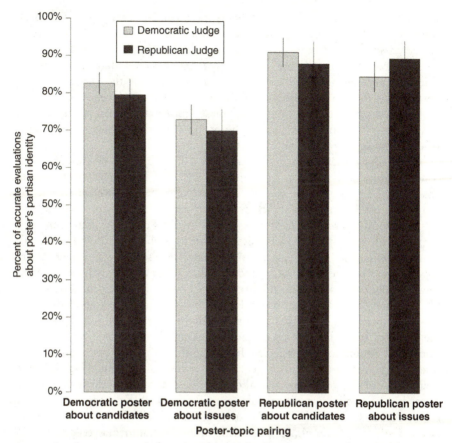

FIGURE 6.4 Accuracy rates of partisanship attribution, by topic and partisanship of judge

Bars show the percentages of evaluations that correctly identified the poster's partisanship. Lines depict 95 percent confidence intervals.

The extent to which the consensus estimate of a poster's political views matches the reality of those views likely varies along a number of dimensions not tested here. The most obvious is the full range of politically informative content. This study only tested the accuracy of inferring partisanship from content that is likely perceived as explicitly political. An open question remains whether Facebook users are accurate in their perceptions of implicitly political content.

SOURCE CUES

People identify a wide range of Facebook content as being "political" in nature. They will make inferences about the partisanship of anonymous users who post both explicitly and implicitly political content.[19] There is broad consensus and relatively high accuracy about those inferences. But the studies presented so far are simplified examples of the content that people encounter on their News Feed and are devoid of a major signal that should further elucidate a poster's political views: the source cue of the original content posted by a third party. People make political inferences even in the absence of source cues, but the addition of these informative signals could either enhance or obfuscate the signal of the poster's political views, depending on whether the signals reinforce or contradict one another.

The results presented in this section are derived from a single large study conducted in April 2016 on Mechanical Turk. The source cues were selected based on the results of the media recognition study presented earlier in this chapter. I used sources that achieved high recognition, with one that was unambiguously perceived to lean left (Huffington Post), one that leans right (Fox News), and one that was perceived to be unbiased (USA Today). The fourth "source cue" condition was the absence of a source cue. I next selected stimuli from the visual stimuli study discussed previously, varying the perceived "politicalness" of the content and the consensus about the partisanship of the poster.[20] I sorted the stimuli based on "political ambiguity," the extent to which there was consensus about the partisanship of the user who posted the content. In each of three categories (Clearly Democrat, Clearly Republican, and Ambiguous), I selected four stimuli, ranging from examples that raters said were not political (i.e. were potentially implicitly political or politically sorted, but were not about political topics) to those raters considered to be explicitly political. The overall design of the study is outlined in online Appendix B, and all of the stimuli are available there. In addition to evaluating a set of stimuli, subjects also completed the media recognition task described above.

Adding a source cue could either clarify or muddy the signal sent by the content alone. I therefore analyze the effects of the source cue for three different conditions: where the source cue contradicts the perceived partisan leaning of the content; where the source cue reinforces the perceived partisan learning of the content; and where the source cue might reduce the ambiguity of content that does not by itself send a clear signal of the partisan leanings of the poster.[21]

---

[19] Perhaps it is not surprising that people will make inferences when asked to do so on a survey. Remember that subjects had the option to indicate that they "didn't know" or to provide moderate evaluations.

[20] This study also included a fourth manipulation – the addition of an explicit endorsement of the third-party content. However, because there were null results, I collapse the study across that condition. More information is available in the online Appendices B and E.

[21] For example, in the absence of any information about source or endorsement, most people thought the story about the "Art House" was posted by a Democrat and that the Voter Identification meme was posted by a Republican, but there was no consensus about the story describing babies born addicted to drugs (see online Appendix E). Signal-reinforcing stimuli

In the first situation, we should expect lower rates of consensus about the partisanship of the person who posted the content, whereas in the second and third conditions, we should expect the source cue signal to enhance consensus.

In the first two conditions – where the signal sent by the content and the source cue potentially interact with one another – our expectation is that there should be higher rates of consensus about the partisanship of the poster in the signal-reinforcing conditions (Huffington Post and Democratic-leaning content, Fox News and Republican-leaning content) compared to the signal-contradicting (vice versa) conditions. I calculate the proportion of evaluations for a given stimulus in signal-reinforcing and signal-contradicting conditions that estimate that the poster identifies with the party signaled by the content, based on the results of the pilot study.

I repeat the calculation using only those evaluations made by a subset of the respondents in the study, whom I call the "media sophisticates," the respondents who identified the ideological bias of all three news sources in a way consistent with the biases perceived by the majority in the media recognition study: the Huffington Post leans left, Fox News leans right, and USA Today does not have a bias. This reduces the number of evaluations considerably, but is a useful comparison.

In Figure 6.5, look first at the signal-reinforcing conditions (the darker bar in each pair), where the aggregate perception of the partisanship of the content aligns with the aggregate perceived ideological bias of the source cue. When assessing the "Democratic" content with the Huffington Post label, approximately three-quarters of the evaluations are in consensus that the person who posted the content is a Democrat. The rates are slightly higher among the sophisticates. When the Fox News signal aligns with Republican-leaning content, sophisticates still arrive at high levels of consensus about the partisanship of the poster, but the overall sample does so at a lower rate.[22]

Turning to the signal-contradicting conditions (the lighter bar in each pair), we see that rates of consensus decline markedly for the content deemed to be posted by a Democrat, when the exact same content is paired with the signal-contracting source cue of Fox News compared to the Huffington Post. Whereas 72.62 percent of evaluations deemed the political content to be posted by a Democrat when it had the Huffington Post banner, only 46.02 percent do when it has the Fox News banner. Only sophisticates appear to respond dramatically

would be the addition of a Fox News label to the Voter ID meme or the addition of a Huffington Post label to the "Art House" story. Signal-contradicting stimuli would be the opposite. And the addition of either of the source cues to the ambiguous article about drug-addicted babies might increase the strength of the signal sent.

[22] Because respondents were given the option to mark "Independent," if respondents were truly guessing, we would expect a three-way split between Democrat, Independent, and Republican. Thus, these figures do indicate some consensus that the poster leans to the right, just not as much consensus.

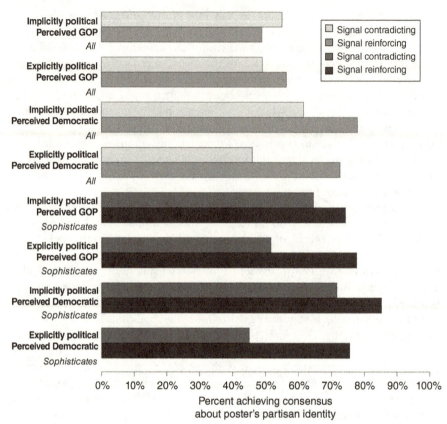

FIGURE 6.5 Comparing signal-reinforcing and signal-contradicting stimuli on consensus in perceptions of partisanship

Bars are labeled by the perceived partisanship of the content.

to the signal-contradicting condition for Republican content, arriving at reduced levels of consensus when content perceived as leaning to the right appears alongside a Huffington Post banner. Unsophisticated users appear to be less responsive to both the signal sent by content perceived in the aggregate to lean to the right as well as the reinforcing signal sent by a Fox News source cue, at least for these particular stimuli on this particular Mechanical Turk sample.

Those people who perceived bias in the sources for the cues in the study (the sophisticates) behave exactly as anticipated. Even those people who did not recognize all three of the sources or impute bias to all three of them behave as expected in three of the four cases, suggesting a more complex psychological phenomenon than simple perception of an ideological bias and attribution of that bias to those people who share content from that source. It seems likely that

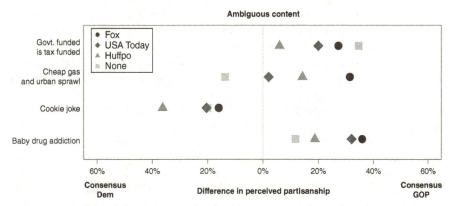

FIGURE 6.6 Effect of source cue on clarifying partisan signal sent by otherwise ambiguous stimuli

The dark grey dots tend to appear to the right of the medium grey triangles and medium grey diamonds, suggesting that the Fox News label made subjects more likely to perceive that the content was posted by a Republican.

there is more signal-reinforcing content than signal-contradicting content circulating on the News Feed, although this claim should be tested in future research.

Finally, we turn to the third condition of content-source cue interaction, where source cue could matter because there is no clear partisan signal being sent by the content. Here, I calculate the difference between the proportion of people who estimated the content was posted by a Republican as compared to the proportion of people who thought the content was posted by a Democrat. A difference of "0" means that there were no differences in the estimate, where a positive difference can be interpreted as a larger proportion of people estimating the poster was Republican, and a negative difference indicating that the poster was thought to be a Democrat.[23] Figure 6.6 visualizes this, showing the differences for each of the four source cue conditions for the four stimuli evaluated in the pilot test to be ambiguous.

Examining Figure 6.6, a general pattern emerges. Identical content with a Fox News banner is more likely to be judged to be posted by a Republican than is content with a USA Today banner or content with the Huffington Post banner. This generally had the effect of yielding higher consensus among respondents, except in cases where high consensus already was achieved (the

[23] Note that this is different than the consensus measures used in the original meme study. A stimulus could show a difference of "0" if everyone thought it was posted by an Independent or if the respondents were equally divided about whether the poster was a Democrat or Republican (50/50). Similarly, a relatively high value on the difference measure does not necessarily imply broad consensus if subjects were equally divided between one of the partisan categories and the Independent category (45 Republican – 45 Independent – 10 Democrat, for example).

"Government Funded Is Tax Funded" meme, for example). Difference of proportion tests aggregating evaluations of all four stimuli reveal statistically significant differences between conditions: 49.76 percent of all evaluations for the Fox News stimuli thought the poster was Republican compared to 37.73 percent for Huffington Post stimuli ($p < 0.05$) and 40.09 percent for the stimuli without a source cue ($p < 0.10$).

We know that people select news sources that align with their ideological beliefs (Iyengar and Hahn 2009). This study shows that Facebook users – most especially politically sophisticated Facebook users – recognize that people do this. In other words, the average Facebook user understands the concept of selective exposure and makes inferences based on that knowledge. A user who posts a story from Fox News sends a signal to those in her social network that she is likely to be a Republican, even when she is posting content that has nothing to do with politics.

CONCLUSION

People report considerable amounts of learning about the political views of their contacts on Facebook – particularly their weak ties, and the people with whom they disagree – at the same time that most people say they don't post much about politics. Why? This puzzle can be explained in a relatively straightforward manner. The pool of content that circulates on the News Feed contains a small volume of polarizing, explicitly political content. But it contains a much larger volume of implicitly political content. Therefore, even the least politically interested and politically engaged Facebook users receive consistent and regular inadvertent exposure to politically informative content on their News Feeds, presenting ample opportunity for learning.

At very high rates, and even on content that they do not think is about politics, Facebook users are willing to attribute a partisan identity to an anonymous stranger based on a single piece of Facebook content they have posted. These inferences are not haphazard guesses. The amount of consensus of these evaluations suggests that Facebook users perceive clearly and widely recognizable signals about the kinds of preferences that map to partisan views. The rate of accuracy for inferring views from explicitly political content is also high, suggesting that people are not biased in their identification of the political in-group and out-group. Furthermore, adding a source cue to content, even content that has nothing to do with politics, affects the conclusions that people draw about the user who posted it. Political sophistication makes people more confident in their inferences, but so does the frequency with which they use Facebook. Consequently, this inference process is not limited to the most politically interested and engaged. Facebook users engage in this behavior even if they do not normally pay much attention to politics.

The evidence in this chapter and the one before provides the foundation underpinning the END Framework and the argument about why consuming News Feed content has the effect of polarizing our attitudes toward each other. For people to make judgments about the users who post content, and to generalize and stereotype based on that content, they must be exposed to information that has the possibility of sending a signal about the political views of the poster. It is clear that a wide variety of content – from status updates to political memes to news stories about non-political topics – has this potential, and that people are regularly exposed to it. And in instances where the ideological bias of the source that created the content aligns with the perceived partisanship of the person who posted it, these signals are even stronger.

The most important implication of this finding is that if we focus only on the communication of explicitly political content, we will miss a large part of the story about how people evaluate the political views of others. When people report that they have posted, shared, or commented infrequently on political content on the News Feed, the findings of this chapter suggest that we interpret their self-report in a very specific way: they do not intend to engage with much political content. Yet, what matters is not their intention, but rather how their content is perceived. What counts as "political" is sensitive to the eyes of the beholder and depends to a great degree on the context of the polarized culture in which we live. Most users do not regularly post content that they consider to be explicitly about politics. However, these very same users may use a broader definition when identifying what content posted by others is considered political. And they very likely make inferences about political views even on content that they do not think is about politics.

The studies reported in this chapter ask people to make inferences about the political views of anonymous strangers. While the results unambiguously demonstrate that people *can* make these inferences and that there is broad consensus about the political views associated with even non-political content, the question remains whether people *do* make these inferences about those in their social network outside the experimental context. In the studies presented, respondents had no other contextual or biographical information about the poster with which to situate their inference based on the content the anonymous user created. In the Facebook ecosystem, even for the weakest of ties in a person's social network, most people have a variety of information about their contacts that may bolster or contradict the political interpretation of the content those contacts post.

I do not test directly whether these effects hold when people evaluate the content posted by their actual social connections on Facebook. For inference to matter in the real world, two things must be true. Exposure must actually occur in people's News Feed, and inference must be weighed against the information that people already have about their social connections. Creating a study sufficiently realistic to mislead participants in which I manipulate the content that a person's friends had posted would involve a considerable amount of deception.

In the absence of this direct evidence, the self-reported results from the survey data in the previous chapter suggest that people are being regularly "dosed" with exposure to the News Feed and that they report substantial exposure to political content. Supermajorities have in fact learned the views of their family and friends, or learned that those views were different than they anticipated, implying that inference has occurred. Assessed in conjunction with one another, the findings give us a more complete picture of how, and how frequently, people make inferences about the political views of their social connections. This inference is most common among the weaker ties in their network, about whom users are the least likely to know political opinions in the absence of Facebook.

In the next chapter, we turn to exploring the basis for the cognitive heuristics that facilitate the connection between inference and judgment. The finding that people over-attribute partisan identities to people who identify as political Independents foreshadows the results to come. Although people achieve consensus and are largely accurate on the direction of a person's political views, they are biased in their estimates of the consistency and the extremity of those views. As the predictions of social identity theory suggest, once we have identified our political out-group, it appears that we assume they are all similar to one another: extremely and consistently ideological.

7

Biased Inference from END Interactions

Facebook users may unintentionally signal their political views by posting content that others perceive to be politicized or indicative of their political inclinations, resulting in a potentially large volume of content circulating on the News Feed that is informative about the partisan identity of the person who posted it.

If the fidelity in this inference process were high, we could imagine that, over time, Facebook users would become increasingly aware of the ideological heterogeneity[1] within each political party. While they would be quick to identify someone's partisan identity, they could accurately differentiate partisans who hold extreme views from those who do not. Understanding the nuance and complexity of others' political opinions would lead them to realize that there is considerable overlap in Americans' views on many contentious issues, opening up the possibility for building consensus across party lines. With realistic interpretations of other users' political viewpoints derived from the bits of information they post, the News Feed might facilitate Facebook's vision to make the world more open and connected in the political realm, ushering in a new era of moderation and a push for cooperation, where American voters hold their elected officials accountable for representing those in the middle of the political spectrum.

Sound farfetched? Social psychologists would agree. While Facebook users' interpretation of others' political views is not completely untethered from reality, we have already seen evidence that the inference process is neither perfectly accurate nor particularly well-honed in making fine-grain differentiations between people. In the previous chapter, we saw that while

---

[1] Self-reported (symbolic) ideology and partisanship have clearly sorted into one another (Abramowitz and Saunders 1998; Levendusky 2009; Mason 2015), but there remains a considerable diversity of policy preferences within each party.

Facebook users could, for the most part, correctly identify the direction of a person's partisan identity; they attributed partisan identities to those who had none. In other words, they overestimated the intensity of people's affiliations with the political parties. The results in this chapter confirm and extend this finding.

These patterns are entirely predictable based on prior research in the social identity theory framework. Identity recognition facilitates biased thinking that shapes the evaluations we make of others. Tajfel (1959, 1969) argued that the process of categorizing people accentuates the differences between the groups as opposed to highlighting the variation within them on the dimensions associated with what differentiates the groups in the first place (the "accentuation principle").

As soon as a user has identified another Facebook user as a member of the out-group – whether they have made that inference based on explicitly or implicitly political content – they are more likely to attribute excessive ideological consistency and extremity to that individual. Users perceive the friends of their friends with whom they disagree as being more extreme than the friends of their friends with whom they agree. The more frequently someone uses Facebook, the larger their estimate of the proportion of the out-party that supports exaggerated portrayals of the party's political stances.

These biases also affect evaluations of the in-group. Rooted in the fact that our social networks are homophilous – that we associate more with people who are similar to us – most people have more Facebook friends who share their political views than who disagree with them. Thus, most people reside in a Facebook "neighborhood" that disproportionately features members of their own party. But layered on top of that empirical reality, the features of the News Feed highlighted in the END model of communication reinforce the perception of a widely shared political worldview. The social cues provided on content that users post – the high levels of social feedback on their political expression – skew their estimation of the extent to which their viewpoints are supported by others. This social feedback also reinforces their partisan identities and increases their partisan pride.

In this chapter, I begin to test the implications of the END Framework of interaction on attitudes toward the political out-group and in-group, guided by the expectations derived from social identity theory. Decades of research have demonstrated that once group identity is made salient, we should expect people to think and behave in ways that elevate their own group and denigrate the out-group, heightening the distinction between "us" and "them."

REALITY VERSUS PERCEPTION: IDEOLOGICAL LEANINGS IN A
POLARIZED ERA

In our contemporary polarized era, do Americans hold more extreme political opinions than they have in the past or do they just think they do? At the nexus of the research of opinion polarization and psychological polarization is a body of research, perceptual polarization, demonstrating that although most members of the public are still ideologically inconsistent or moderate, they have come to believe that they are more polarized than they are.

Americans are Ideologically Scrambled, But Think Others are Ideologically Pure

Political scientists have long known that most Americans do not have consistent ideological preferences (Campbell *et al.* 1960; Converse 1964). Although the processes structuring elite polarization have contributed to ideological and partisan sorting in the mass public, leading to higher levels of ideological consistency, rates of ideological coherence among the mass public are still low. Pew's Political Polarization in the American Public study (2014a) estimates that only 12 percent of Americans are consistently liberal and 9 percent are consistently conservative, based on their answers to a set of questions about their political values.[2] Moreover, Americans' symbolic ideology, the extent to which they identify with an ideological group, often does not match their operational ideology, the actual content of their policy preferences. As a result, even those who identify with an ideological group don't always hold policy preferences that align with it.

Nor are Americans markedly more ideologically extreme than they have been in the past. In fact, the distribution of partisanship and ideology has remained remarkably consistent over time. The American National Election Study (ANES) data from 2012 show that 3 percent of Americans consider themselves to be "extremely liberal" and 13 percent consider themselves to be "liberal" or "extremely liberal," while 4 percent consider themselves to be "extremely conservative" and 22 percent consider themselves to be "extremely conservative" or "conservative." Symbolic self-identified ideological extremity is conceptually different from operational ideological extremity. But Americans are even less extreme when their stated preferences over policies are examined. People may have become better at mapping their ideological preferences to their party identification over time, but one of the most persistent arguments in the debate over levels of issue polarization in the mass public was that most Americans hold moderate viewpoints on many issues (Fiorina *et al.* 2008).

---

[2] Using data from the 2012 National Election Study, rates of ideological consistency are even lower. The survey includes questions that relate to the five policy issues assessed in the analysis in this chapter: gun control, health care, immigration, abortion, and tax policy. Just over 3 percent of respondents provided answers that would be considered consistently liberal or consistently conservative. Even when removing the tax policy question – to which more than 70 percent of Americans gave the liberal answer – the rate of consistency is only slightly above 10 percent. The rate of ideological extremity is obviously even lower.

Yet many Americans appear to believe the opposite of these empirical realities about the high rates of moderation and inconsistency in self-reported ideological identities and issue-based measures. Using data from the ANES in the 1970 to 2008 range, Westfall and colleagues (Westfall *et al.* 2015) find that Americans overestimate the magnitude of differences in policy preferences between the Democratic Party and Republican Party on most issues by a factor of two. The actual difference in the preferences expressed by partisans has increased over time, but the perception of polarization has increased more.

The fact that non-Facebook users also inaccurately attribute extremity to the out-party attests to how widespread these biases are. Facebook clearly is not the only contributing factor skewing our perceptions of the distribution of opinions of our fellow citizens. But many of the explanations underlying the belief in false polarization are more likely to affect those who are strongly partisan or are interested in politics. And far more Americans than just the politically sophisticated inaccurately believe that the parties are polarized. For people who do not pay too much attention to politics and are not particularly interested in it, Facebook provides the necessary information to distort perspectives of what other Americans believe.

Cognitive Processes in Social Identity Theory

That Americans misperceive the beliefs of their fellow citizens is exactly what the "accentuation principle" of social identity theory would predict. The very act of categorizing people into groups has the effect of making the groups seem more distinct than they really are (Tajfel 1959; Tajfel and Wilkes 1963; Corneille and Judd 1999; Rutchick *et al.* 2009).

In addition to the effect of pushing characterizations of the group further apart, there also is evidence that the categorization process decreases estimates of the variability of members of the out-group, a phenomenon called the out-group homogeneity effect. In short, the existence, recognition, and salience of partisan identification increases the likelihood of perceiving that one's political opponents are "all the same." As described in Chapter 4, a media narrative has developed about the persistence of a culture war. Seyle and Newman (2006) argue that the use of "red" and "blue" labeling in media characterizations of American politics makes it difficult for Americans to accurately perceive and differentiate variation within their political out-group.

Why do group differentiation and out-group homogenization occur? Tajfel argued that while cognitive processes are "both necessary and sufficient for the understanding of the formation and functioning of social stereotypes," they must be contextualized with the value-laden social differentiations that people form (Tajfel 1982, p. 31). Researchers have argued that people are motivated to differentiate their in-group from the out-group on characteristics that favor their in-group (Tajfel and Turner 1979; Turner *et al.* 1987). Thus, social identity theory predicts affective polarization, in conjunction with the perceptual evaluations people make to justify those value judgments. In the realm of politics, disparaging the out-group may relate to the way in which people form their political opinions. Robinson *et al.* (1995) argue that people gauge opposing partisans as being driven by ideology and therefore inclined to process information from the "top down" as opposed to forming evaluations from the "bottom up." People attribute to their own group more reasoned and methodical processes for forming their opinions (Ross and Ward 1995). As a consequence of this, people perceive the political out-group as being more ideologically extreme.

Learning Stereotypes

How might people arrive at stereotyped judgments of out-partisans? Park and Hastie (1987) argue that our stereotypes about a particular group fall on a continuum between abstraction-based stereotypes, where we glean stereotypes from our environment and then apply them to individuals, to instance-based stereotypes, where we form characterizations of individuals that we then apply to generalize their group. It is not immediately obvious where our learned perceptions of partisan groups should fall on this spectrum. Do people have perceptions of the variability and extremity of political opinions among members of political parties and use that information to evaluate individual Facebook users who are members of the party? Or is their impression of the variability and extremity of the out-party based more on the particular experiences they have had with individual out-partisans in their networks?

Abstraction-Based Learning

Consuming the news leads to plentiful opportunities for learning characterizations of the out-party. If our learning about an out-group is rooted in abstraction-based stereotypes, we first learn information about the group and then use that pre-formed stereotype in our perception of individuals within that group. Park and Hastie write that learning on this end of the spectrum often occurs when we have little contact with individual members of an out-group, and that learning is a result of information provided by "socializing agents such as parents, teachers, and the media" (1987, p. 622).

The contemporary media environment is full of cues to signal partisan stereotypes. We are bombarded with information from the media about what the out-party is like as a group. We can observe characterizations of each party's members of Congress,[3] or even its interns,[4] and draw conclusions about what type of people might support each party. As outlined in Chapter 4, there are plenty of group-based characterizations of the supporters of particular

---

[3] David Wasserman, "House Democrats Are Getting More Diverse. Republicans Aren't." FiveThirtyEight.com (November 6, 2016).

[4] Quoctrung Bui, "The Demographics Behind #InternsSoWhite." TheUpshot.com (July 22, 2016).

candidates in every presidential election. Any time we read or watch news reports typifying groups of people based on political identity, we digest a message about what types of people belong on each side of the political spectrum.

Facebook reinforces many of these group-based signals. The ecosystem of the News Feed may foster the transmission of what Jones and McGillis (1976) call "culturally transmitted category-based expectancies." In other words, in-group members communicate about out-group members in ways that reinforce the stereotypes of the out-group, reinforcing a person's perception that all members of the out-group are similar. There is little research systematically examining the characteristics of content that is most likely to circulate on the News Feed, but it is plausible that stories denigrating a partisan group hold a particular appeal, especially during a political campaign.

Instance-Based Stereotyping

Facebook may facilitate abstraction-based stereotype learning, but it is not the only game in town doing so. Newspapers, websites, cable news, and face-to-face discussion also have vital roles to play in perpetuating common understandings of who "they" are compared to who "we" are. Where the News Feed ecosystem has the greatest comparative influence is on the other end of Park and Hastie's typology – instance-based stereotype learning. If we learn stereotypes in an instance-based way, we develop stereotypes about an out-group based on what we've learned from isolated interactions with people in that out-group. Our perception of the out-group is built upon aggregating our impressions of individuals.

In the absence of Facebook, can instance-based stereotype formation of members of the out-party occur? Certainly, although with considerable less material upon which to draw. As the literature about political discussion shows, most people have at least one person in their discussion network who identifies with a different political party or votes for a different presidential candidate. Our country is residentially segregated based on class and race, and we may actively geographically sort ourselves based on political views (Bishop 2008; Hui 2013; Gimpel and Hui 2015), but partisans are not entirely separated from one another and, at least occasionally, interact with someone whose views are very different from their own.

However, this exposure is amplified on Facebook for all of the reasons described in Chapters 3 and 4. The site is designed to allow people to observe the opinions and behaviors of others without needing to reciprocate. Weak ties are considerably more influential and represent an important source of instance-based impressions, devoid of the personal details that could moderate instance-based stereotyping of closer ties. Users also readily can observe the behavior of the friends of their friends, who represent an important linkage between the members of the out-group they personally know and their impressions of the out-group collectively.

These instance-based impressions could affect both our perceptions of the variability of the out-group as well as its extremity. Quattrone and Jones (1980) speculate that because people interact more frequently with members of their in-group, they have been exposed to more diversity within their group. Most friends who post explicitly political content to the News Feed are partisan and ideological, but the relative importance of any one of these individuals in shaping stereotypes of their group may differ based on whether a person agrees or disagrees with their friend. On Facebook, as we shall see below, most users have more agreeable ties in their networks than disagreeable ties, leading to more opportunities for instance-based learning of the heterogeneity of their own in-group. With fewer chances to observe out-party members, when users encounter extreme members of the out-group, there is less opportunity to counterbalance those extreme views with observations of more moderate people. If users do not realize the extent to which these extreme individuals are not prototypical of the group overall, they might make a biased inference about the out-group based on the behavior of these few.

Beyond differences in rates of exposure to in-group versus out-group members, we may rely on different kinds of information to categorize people. Park and Rothbart (1982) argue that perceptions of out-group homogeneity may arise because we use a wider variety of information to encode our evaluations of in-group versus out-group members. We are more likely to use subordinated or differentiated characteristics – such as occupation, personality, or education level – when we evaluate in-group members, as compared to the superordinate, general, or undifferentiated characteristics – such as race or gender – used to evaluate out-group members.

What does this look like on Facebook? Users know many characteristics of their strong ties on Facebook, but fewer about their weak ties, and even fewer about the friends of their weak ties. As we saw in Chapter 5, the weaker the tie, the higher the likelihood of perceived political disagreement. The very people whom users know least about are the most likely to represent the out-party on their Facebook feed, and in the absence of knowledge of these individuals' other traits, users may be more likely to use partisan identity as a superordinate characteristic.

Facebook use should be associated with increased exposure for opportunities to form stereotypes based on instances, but these instance-based impressions are not entirely independent from the abstract-based influences of the broader media environment. This generalized sense of the extent to which members of a party are similar to each other is important for understanding the consequences of encountering instance-based information from the Facebook News Feed. Park and Hastie (1987) show that differences in perceived variability of group members affect the way in which subjects make generalizations and classifications about group members, even if subjects all hold the same stereotype about the group. The more likely an evaluator is to think that members of the group are similar to one another, the more susceptible they are to generalize away from observation of a single actor's choice (Nisbett and Borgida 1975; Quattrone and Jones 1980). This suggests that the Facebook users who already hold strong preconceptions about members of the other party – namely, strong partisans – are likely to be those most willing to attribute their stereotypes of the group to their evaluations of an individual user's behavior and attitudes.

In the sections below, we will explore the presence of these biases within the context of generating and consuming information from the Facebook News Feed. First, we shall see evidence for the out-group homogeneity effect, whereby we perceive members of the out-group to be of the same "type." In the realm of ideological views, this means that we over-attribute ideological consistency to members of the out-group. Next, we will examine the complementary bias of perceived polarization in which we think that the other side is considerably more extreme in their viewpoints than is our side. Finally, we will explore the process of social feedback in reinforcing our identification with and pride of our political in-group, demonstrating that people are susceptible to the "false consensus" phenomena, in which they believe that their opinions are in the majority.

THEY ARE ALL THE SAME: THE OUT-GROUP HOMOGENEITY EFFECT

In one of a series of studies conducted in the early 1980s designed to understand how people perceived their in-groups compared to their out-groups, Bernadette Park and Myron Rothbart (1982) visited three sorority houses at the University of Oregon. After assuring the women that their responses would not be revealed, the researchers asked them to rate how similar the women were in their own sorority, as well as the other two sororities. What did they find? The women in each sorority rated themselves as being more dissimilar than did the women in the other two sororities. The sorority members themselves were able to recognize the diversity of attitudes and behaviors within their own houses, but thought that the women living in the other houses "were all the same."

This study captures a very extensively researched and consistent finding: people recognize more diversity within their in-group than they do within their out-group. Dubbed the out-group homogeneity effect, there is a mountain of evidence that people less accurately characterize the out-group because they underestimate the variation of traits within it. Research characterizing this phenomenon in non-political domains has measured out-group homogeneity in a number of different ways. Some studies have asked subjects to estimate the proportion of target groups who would agree with attitude statements thought to be stereotypic of the groups (Park and Rothbart 1982). Others have asked subjects to estimate distributions of a group on particular attribute dimensions, sometimes followed up by calculating the standard deviation or variance of those placements (Linville *et al.* 1989). A similar approach is to ask subjects to indicate the range of values on a specific trait scale on which members of the out-group might fall. Other studies more simply ask subjects to rate how similar members of a group are to each other (Park and Rothbart 1982).

We do not have extensive research in political science using analogous measures to capture perceptions of the extent of variation between members of the political parties,[5] but we do have much circumstantial evidence suggesting that the pattern extends to the political realm. The prior findings most similar to the concept of "out-group homogeneity" come from Ahler and Sood (2018). Americans appear to attribute more social sorting than occurs in reality and overestimate the extent to which the parties are composed of party-stereotypic groups. For example, Americans report that 32 percent of Democrats identify as LGBT, when only 6.3 percent actually do. Similarly, people report that 38 percent of Republicans earn more than $250,000 a year, a figure nearly twenty times larger than the actual 2.2 percent who do. While this overestimation occurs for one's own group, it is even more pronounced for characterizations of the out-group. Americans thus think of the parties as being overly homogeneous based on social characteristics, although we do not know if this extends to their evaluations of the homogeneity of their policy beliefs.

In the realm of partisan identity, what does it mean for members of our political out-group to "all be the same"? It likely means that we overestimate the likelihood that a given member of the out-party ascribes to the stereotypic ideology and views of that party. Recognizing heterogeneity among members of the out-party would mean that a partisan label should not be particularly indicative of any given individual's preferences. And, in fact, previous findings suggest that Americans attribute extremity and overly consistent ideological opinions to others, most especially opposing partisans. Facebook clearly is not a necessary condition for this sort of biased reasoning to occur. However, the prevalence of opportunities for instance-based impressions suggests that people might be more confident in their judgments about out-partisans. Facebook, in essence, gives users a great deal of practice in evaluating individual members of the out-group.

To what extent do people think the out-party is more homogeneous than their own? Will they make attributions of consistency at the individual level?

---

[5] There are many papers that ask subjects to place themselves, the political parties, or presidential candidates on issue or ideological scales (Ahler 2014; Westfall *et al.* 2015). These studies are useful for assessing perceived distance between the parties, but not for assessing homogeneity. The 1997 ANES pilot study did ask questions about perceived group variability, modeling a question off that used in Park and Judd (1990). However, subjects evaluated the political homogeneity of social groups – such as women, Blacks, and Christian fundamentalists – not the homogeneity of the beliefs held by partisans.

Are people who use Facebook most frequently more likely to perceive members of the out-group as overly consistent? We return to the inference studies described in the preceding chapters to test these questions.

Ideological Consistency in the Inference Studies

As the statistics in the beginning of this chapter show, most Americans are not ideologically consistent. Knowing their stance on one issue does not necessarily increase the odds of predicting their opinion on another issue. Yet Americans perceive that their fellow citizens are ideologically consistent and coherent. In the broader political information environment in which we have ample abstraction-based information about the political groups, Facebook offers opportunities for instance-based learning to characterize the attitudes and behaviors of individuals in the out-party. There is considerable work to be done to fully map this process, but here I show that Facebook usage is associated with increased confidence in instance-based stereotyping of ideological consistency.

We begin by assessing the extent to which people will attribute ideological consistency to anonymous others based on the content which they post to Facebook, using the data from the status update and visual lede studies described in the preceding chapters and detailed in online Appendices B and E. Respondents were asked to estimate the ideology of the poster on five issue domains: abortion, taxes, Obamacare, gun control, and immigration. Ideology was reported on a five-point scale, with the option for marking "don't know." The respondent attributes *ideological consistency* to the poster when (a) she provides an estimate about ideology for all five issue positions and (b) all five estimations fall to one side of the midpoint (e.g. the respondent marks all "1's" and "2's" or all "4's" and "5's").

First, respondents were very willing to make inferences about a poster's ideology based on a single piece of Facebook content. Nearly 200 different stimuli were tested between the three inference studies, representing a wide variety of textual and visual content. There is some variation in the extent to which people were willing to make ideological inferences based on the type of content, but respondents were willing to impute ideology even from the content that they did not think was about politics. Very few subjects left the ideological estimates blank. Across the three studies, approximately 75 percent of evaluations included an assessment for each of the five issues.

Combining the data from the status update and visual lede study, subjects evaluated all five ideological issues for 85.07 percent of all stimuli for which they attributed a partisan identity to the poster, compared to only 36.49 percent of the stimuli for which they said that they did not know the partisan identity of the poster. Subjects also provided evaluations at a higher rate for the content deemed a priori to be "political." Moreover, as shown in Figure 7.1, if a subject herself deemed the content to "be about politics," she also was more likely to ascribe

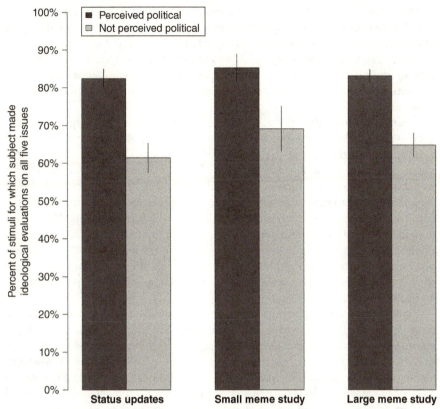

FIGURE 7.1 Willingness to make ideological inferences, by stimulus type and perception of political content

The percentage of all evaluations in a category for which the subject provided an inference about the ideological views of the poster on all five issues. Dark bars depict evaluations for which the subject thought the content was "definitely" or "maybe" about politics. Lines depict 95 percent confidence intervals.

ideological views for all five positions. However, a majority of evaluations were complete even for content that was not thought to be about politics.[6]

In the remainder of the analysis, we will focus on the set of complete evaluations. Based solely on a single piece of even non-political content, if a subject was willing to hazard a guess about the poster's ideology on one issue, the subject tended to ascribe a consistent ideology across all five issues. Across all three studies, there is remarkable consistency in subjects' evaluations of

[6] Unexpectedly, subjects were more likely to attribute ideological stances to posters they deemed to be Democrats than Republicans. In other words, both Republicans and Democrats were less likely to complete the ideological issue evaluations for perceived Republican posters. The reasons for this are unknown and merit future exploration.

ideology across all five issues. Each pairwise correlation between the five issues is higher than 0.70.[7] This is not driven by a tendency to report the middle value of the scale for all five evaluations: approximately 10 percent of evaluations are all "3's," but nearly two-thirds (64 percent in the status update study, 57 percent in the visual lede study, and 61 percent in the source cue study) are evaluations that are consistently on one side of the ideological scale or the other.

Figure 7.2 shows that subjects generally attribute more ideological consistency to posters they deem to be members of the other political party.[8] Although there was no difference in the status update study, in the two studies using visual stimuli, Democrats are more likely than Republicans to think that Republican posters are ideologically consistent. Republicans are more likely than Democrats to think that Democratic posters are more likely to be consistent in the two meme studies, although they actually were more likely to think that members of their in-group were consistent in the status update study. Pooling across the studies, a difference of proportions test shows that a greater proportion of the out-party evaluations were ideologically consistent than were evaluations for posters perceived to be part of the in-party (70.72, 59.62, p < 0.001).

Exploring these relationships in a regression framework controlling for some basic characteristics of the evaluator shows that this pattern persists. The more interested in politics a subject was and whether the subject deemed the stimulus to be "political" in nature, the more likely they were to report that a poster was ideologically consistent. Partisanship strength mattered in some but not all models. In some models, the frequency with which a person encounters political content or posts it herself also is associated with evaluations of consistency.

Finally, another way to think about the out-group homogeneity effect is to assess the variance in the evaluations that subjects made about the stimuli they perceived to be posted by members of their in-group compared to the stimuli they perceived to be posted by members of their out-group. While each subject did not assess enough stimuli to assess the variance of each subject's evaluations, we can assess variation in the aggregate. A statistical test for the ratio of the variances reveals that both Republicans and Democrats reported higher levels of heterogeneity (larger variance in response) for members of their in-group compared to members of their out-group. In other words, we think that

---

[7] These correlations are very inflated compared to the empirical reality found in the ANES. There, the strongest overlap was between attitudes on abortion and immigration. Nearly 60 percent of subjects had ideologically consistent viewpoints on those two issues.

[8] Interestingly, both Democrats and Republicans think that posters perceived as Republican are more likely to be ideologically consistent than are posters perceived as Democrats. However, the pattern holds that out-party evaluations attribute more ideological consistency than do in-party evaluations.

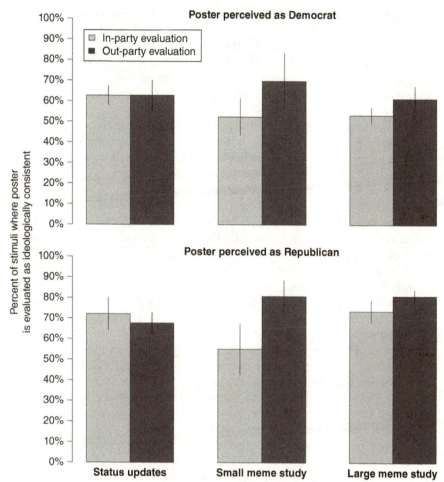

FIGURE 7.2 Ideologically consistent evaluations, by stimulus type, perceived partisanship, and in-group status

The percentage of all evaluations in a category for which the subject reported that the poster had ideologically consistent opinions on all five policy issues. Dark bars depict evaluations when the subject perceived that the poster was a member of their out-party. Lines depict 95 percent confidence intervals.

there is more heterogeneity of opinion within our own political party than there is among members of the opposition party.

THEY ARE ALL EXTREME: PERCEIVED POLARIZATION

False polarization, or perceived polarization, is a distinct concept from out-group homogeneity and focuses more on the extremity of the measure of central tendency for an out-group's opinion as compared to the perception of variability of the out-group itself. When affiliation with the in-group is an important part of a person's social identity (Ellemers *et al.* 2002; Jetten *et al.* 2004), or when levels of uncertainty are high (Sherman *et al.* 2009), we would expect categorization effects on perceived polarization to be amplified. This is likely the case in terms of our political identities in a polarized political era, and there is ample evidence to support this.

Americans think the parties are farther apart on issues than they actually are and attribute extremity both to their own party, but even more so to opposing partisans. There are many examples of studies demonstrating that subjects overestimate the difference between partisan groups on issues such as support for war, abortion, affirmative action, environmentalism, and the role of government (Dawes *et al.* 1972; Robinson *et al.* 1995; Sherman *et al.* 2003; Chambers and Melnyk 2006; Chambers *et al.* 2006; Ahler 2014). The perception of difference might be greatest on the issues that are closest to the values that group members find central to their own beliefs (Chambers and Melnyk 2006). In a more comprehensive study on a nationally representative sample, Levendusky and Malhotra (2016a) find that the two political parties are perceived to be about 20 percent farther apart on the average of a broad set of issues than they are in reality.

In the abstract, the pattern is clear for Americans' evaluations of the parties and members of those parties. But do these evaluations of extremity transfer when making assessments about people who have posted Facebook content? Do we ascribe more extremism to the people in our networks with whom we disagree? Evidence from both the inference studies and the social network battery on the END Framework Survey suggests that we do. And frequent usage of Facebook is associated with estimating that a greater proportion of the out-group adheres to stereotypic characterizations of policy viewpoints.

Ideological Extremity in the Inference Studies

We return to the inference studies, where the analysis proceeds in a very similar fashion to the evaluation of ideological consistency just described. Whereas consistency was measured by placing a poster on one side of a five-point ideological scale for all five issue evaluations, the respondent has attributed *ideological extremity* to the poster when (a) she provides an estimate about ideology for all five issue positions and (b) all five estimations fall to the extreme ends of the scale (e.g. the respondent marks all "1's" or all "5's").

People attribute more ideological extremity to posters they deem to be members of the other political party (see Figure 7.3). Across all three studies, Democrats think that Republican posters are more likely to be ideologically extreme than are Democratic posters. Republicans think that Democratic and Republican posters are about equally likely to be extreme, except in the source

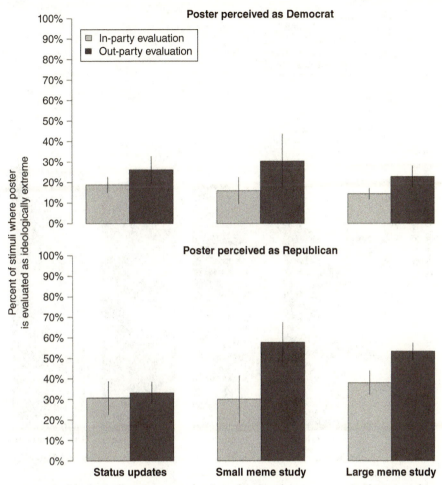

FIGURE 7.3 Ideologically extreme evaluations, by stimulus type, perceived partisanship, and in-group status

The percentage of all evaluations in a category for which the subject reported the poster had ideologically extreme opinions on all five policy issues. Dark bars depict evaluations when the subject perceived that the poster was a member of their out-party. Lines depict 95 percent confidence intervals.

cue study, where a greater proportion of evaluations of Republicans report extremity. Similar to the results testing the effects of political interest and partisanship strength on evaluations of consistency, these traits of the evaluator also were associated with an increased likelihood of attributing extremity to the out-group.

Were subjects who use Facebook frequently more inclined to make ideological attributions? While Facebook usage and News Feed scrolling were not

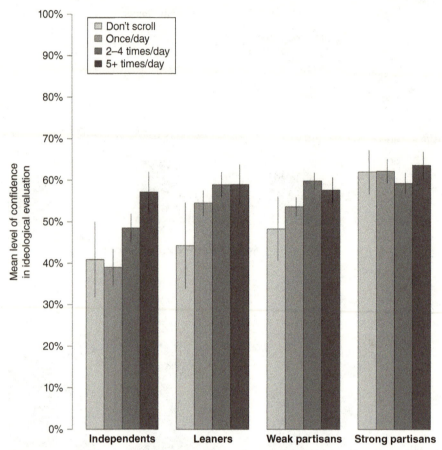

FIGURE 7.4 Confidence in ideological estimates, by partisanship strength and News Feed scrolling frequency
The mean confidence level in the accuracy of ideological estimations, on a scale of 0 to 100 percent. Lines depict 95 percent confidence intervals.

associated with an increased likelihood of attributing ideology for all five positions, inadvertent and intentional exposure to political content were, as was the amount of political content subjects report that they post. Moreover, all five usage variables were consistently and positively related to subjects' confidence in the accuracy of their ideological evaluations. Figure 7.4 depicts this relationship, separating out the effect by partisanship strength. Strong partisans were very confident in their ideological evaluations even if they say that they do not regularly scroll through their News Feeds. But among those with less attachment to the parties, the more frequently they scroll through the News Feed, the more confident they are that they have accurately characterized the poster's ideology.

Ideological Extremity in Social Network Study

Facebook users attribute too much ideological extremity to anonymous posters they perceive to be members of the out-party, but is that attribution moderated by the presence of a social connection? In other words, do people think that their own social ties with whom they disagree also are extreme?

To test this, we can use the social network battery assessed on the END Framework Survey. In addition to reporting whether they agreed or disagreed with the contacts they named, respondents also reported their perception of the extremity of their contacts' friends, answering the question, "Thinking about the friends of these contacts on Facebook, do you think that the contacts' friends' viewpoints are more ideologically extreme than those of your friends, about the same, or more moderate?"

Why ask about the friends of their friends? One of the most unique features of the Facebook News Feed is the ability to be a "fly on the wall" and invisibly watch others interact. While the majority of the content on the feed is produced or shared by people users personally know, they are regularly exposed to interactions between the people they know and the people *their friends* know. These "friends of friends," whom social network scholars have called our second-degree alters, represent an important intermediary in the conceptual framework used to characterize the out-group. The evaluations users make of these second-degree alters are nestled between the impressions they have of the cross-cutting ties in their personal networks and their perceptions of the abstract notion of the out-party and its voters. Instead of focusing solely on people's evaluations of individuals they personally know, the study is designed to assess people's perceptions of the groups of people with whom their friends identify.

Overall, subjects reported that their second-degree alters were more extreme than their own friends about one-third of the time (29.30 percent) and that these friends-of-friends had about the same level of ideological extremity most of the time (59.55 percent of all named dyads). However, whether or not the subject agreed with the political views of their contact is very strongly correlated with their evaluations of the extremity of the contact's friends. Subjects report that those people with whom they disagree are more likely to have friends that are more extreme than their own. A majority (52.81 percent) of all disagreeable dyads were thought to have more extreme friends, a figure that increases to 61.70 percent of those contacts listed with whom the subject "strongly disagreed." Conversely, agreeable friends were thought to have friends similar to the subjects' own friends. Only 27.22 percent of the friends of agreeable friends were perceived to have friends who were more extreme and nearly two-thirds (64.11 percent) were thought to have friends who were about the same.

These statistics reflect the implication of social identity theory. We perceive members of our in-group to be like us, while we perceive members of the out-group to be extreme. We can get more leverage on this question by incorporating the information about the nature of the relationship between the subject and the contact they named. The friends of our family and close friends are likely to be "weak ties" themselves, people whom we are likely to have met face-to-face even if we do not know them well. The friends of our extended family and weak ties are more socially distant, and we are less likely to have interacted with them ourselves. Facebook facilitates users in putting names and faces to these otherwise unfamiliar individuals. But the lack of direct interaction with them provides fewer opportunities to learn details about them that could moderate evaluations of their political opinions.

People are more likely to perceive the friends of their weak ties to be more extreme than the friends of their close ties. While only 25.93 percent of the friends of close family and friends were perceived to be more extreme than a subject's own friends, 38.04 percent of the friends of distant family and weak ties were perceived as being more extreme ($p < 0.001$). These differences are amplified when we focus just on disagreeable social ties. In addition to the fact that users are more likely to disagree with weak ties than close ties, they also are more likely to perceive that the friends of their disagreeable weak ties are more extreme than the friends of their disagreeable close ties (see Figure 7.5).

Remember from Chapter 5 that frequent Facebook users were more likely to identify disagreeable and weak ties in the network battery than were people who used Facebook less frequently. Frequent Facebook usage also is associated with an increased likelihood of thinking that a contact's friends are more extreme than one's own friends. While this is only marginally significant for evaluations of disagreeable ties overall, it is statistically significant for evaluations of weak ties.

The people who most readily name disagreeable Facebook friends, and perceive that the friends of their weak ties are extreme, are those who use Facebook most frequently, not those who are the strongest partisans.[9] Using Facebook more frequently gives people more confidence in their inferential abilities and makes certain kinds of contacts more salient. There is considerably more work to be done to understand the nuances of why disagreeable and weak ties are more accessible to more frequent Facebook users. But these initial results suggest not only will people assess anonymous Facebook users as ideologically extreme if they perceive they disagree with them, but they actually make those judgments of the people within their Facebook networks.

Opinion Extremity of Facebook Users

The two research designs above show that people identify anonymous others and their social contacts as being ideologically extreme. Do they also think that

[9] Strong partisans are more likely to have politically homogeneous networks, so they are more likely to agree with the friends of their friends and thus perceive them as being similar.

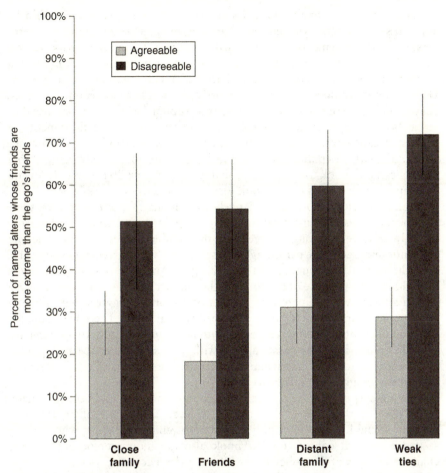

FIGURE 7.5 Percentage of named contacts whose friends are more extreme than subjects' friends, by dyad type and agreement level

Dark bars depict the percentage of disagreeable dyads; light bars depict the percentage of agreeable dyads. Lines depict 95 percent confidence intervals.

out-partisan Facebook users, as a group, are more likely to hold extreme views? Demonstrating that subjects are moving from instance-based judgments to stereotyping a group is an important part of our understanding of the psychological polarization on Facebook. We saw in Chapter 5 that the users who post the most political content are more likely to be strong partisans and hold more ideological views. So, users' perceptions of individuals with whom they have interacted may be based on the extremity those individuals have actually demonstrated on the site. But if people impute extremity to out-partisan Facebook users overall, it is clear that they are generalizing based on the extreme cases to make conclusions about the viewpoint of the group as a whole.

Pilot testing of strongly worded statements about the viewpoints held by adherents of each party yielded such high rates of agreement that more extreme versions of the statements were included in the final END Framework Survey. These statements are rooted in the actual policy view held by each party, but characterize those views in stereotyped and judgmental ways. For example, the Democratic Party does advocate for more open access to abortion. However, characterizing Democratic Facebook users as supporting abortion because they see it "as a solution to careless behavior without considering the sanctity of life" is an exaggerated and stylized depiction of why Democrats support the policy. Similarly, Republicans do typically advocate for "family values," but Republican Facebook users would probably not say they do because they want to "impose their morals on everyone else's reproductive choices."

Table 7.1 below shows the relatively high levels of agreement with these statements.[10] Respondents answered on a five-point Likert scale, ranging from strongly disagree to strongly agree, with the middle category reading "neither agree nor disagree." The percentage of respondents who agree or strongly agree with the statement about the out-partisan group is in the parentheses in the table. I created a variable of the count of the number of statements with which a person agreed. Approximately 25 percent of respondents agreed with none of the statements and about 13 percent agreed with all eight. There were roughly equal numbers of respondents agreeing with between two and seven statements. Overall, on average, Democrats agreed with 3.79 statements about Republicans compared to 3.91 statements for Republicans evaluating Democrats, a statistically insignificant difference.

It is not surprising that people who generate more political content themselves agree with more of the statements, even when controlling for their partisan strength or levels of political interest. Similarly, people who actively seek out political content on Facebook also are more stereotyped in their characterizations of the policy beliefs of out-party Facebook users.

However, a user does not have to be actively engaged with political content on Facebook to be influenced by her exposure to the News Feed. Facebook users who unintentionally see higher levels of political content on the News Feed agree with more of the statements, even when controlling for their partisanship strength, political interest, and demographics.

Most importantly, simply using the site more frequently is associated with higher levels of agreement with the statements. The relationship depicted in Figure 7.6 shows the mean number of statements with which subjects agreed, by frequency of using the site. This pattern is incredibly robust in regression models and holds however usage is measured and whatever control variables are included, including demographic variables, partisan attachment, and

---

[10] The exact wording was, "Think about [Democrats/Republicans] you've seen post political material on Facebook. Please indicate the extent to which you agree with each of the following statements about these users." The label for the out-group was piped into the question.

TABLE 7.1 *Percent Agreement with Exaggerated Statements about Out-Party Political Views*

Stereotypes of Republicans *(asked of Democrats)*	Stereotypes of Democrats *(asked of Republicans)*
They use "family values" as a justification to try to impose their morals on everyone else's reproductive choices (48.5%)	They see abortion as a solution to careless behavior without considering the sanctity of life (49.7%)
They are right-wing religious nut jobs who are anti-science and believe in creationism (36.2%)	They are anti-religious atheists devoid of the good Christian values America was founded on (37.8%)
They are warmongers (32.3%)	They are spineless and cowardly in their views about foreign policy (38.0%)
They are against equal rights for women and minorities (42.6%)	They care so much about minorities that they disadvantage white Americans (55.2%)
They are elitists who favor advantages for the top 1 percent and are uncaring with regard to everyone else (42.7%)	They want to give government benefits to people who don't deserve them at the expense of hardworking Americans (60.5%)
They don't care about the environment or climate change (41.3%)	They care so much about the environment that they try to force us all to "go green" (44.3%)
They say that they oppose immigration to protect American jobs, but really they just dislike immigrants (44.9%)	They want to take jobs away from Americans and give them to illegal immigrants (45.6%)
They want an unregulated free market, even when it is shown to fail (50.0%)	They want socialism, even if it means more government control in our lives (57.33%)

Subjects were presented with a grid of caricaturized statements of the policy opinions of members of the out-party and asked to assess their level of agreement with the statement on a five-point scale. The percentages indicate the percentage of each partisan group who agrees with each individual statement about the out-party group.

political engagement. This pattern holds even when controlling for the manner in which subjects get most of their political news and how frequently they get news. Interestingly, while relying primarily on the Internet for news is associated with higher rates of stereotype agreement, relying primarily on the television for news is negatively associated with the agreement count.

Taken together with the findings from the inference studies, these results bolster the case for inference-based stereotyping based on engaging with the content that comes across the Facebook News Feed. Above and beyond the contribution of partisan strength and reliance on the Internet for political information, using Facebook is associated with higher rates of agreement with

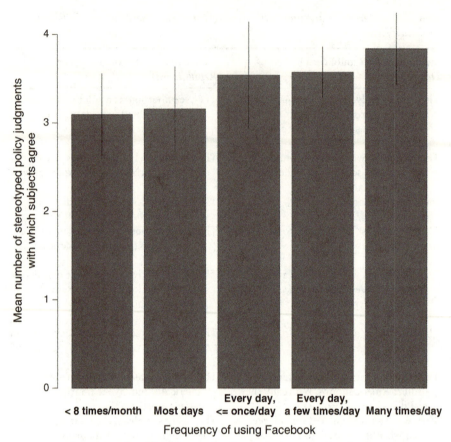

FIGURE 7.6 Mean number of stereotyped policy judgments, by Facebook usage rate
The mean number of stereotyped statements with which a subject agreed about members of the
out-party, by the frequency with which a user logs in to the Facebook site. Lines depict 95 percent
confidence intervals.

statements about the extremity of the out-party's beliefs. In the next chapter, we
will assess whether Facebook users' evaluations of each other as extremists
carries over into their assessments of the members of the political parties. It
appears that Facebook users not only abstract away from the Facebook users
they have interacted with to out-party Facebook users generally, but also to
their judgments of the out-party as a whole.

We turn next to the way in which engaging on the Facebook News Feed
bolsters evaluations of the political in-group. Just as Facebook users are biased
in thinking that members of the out-group are more extreme and more similar
to one another than they are in reality, they are biased in thinking that their
own opinions are shared more broadly than they actually are.

EVERYBODY AGREES WITH ME: FALSE CONSENSUS EFFECT

It is a proud American political tradition to claim that one's views are in the majority. Several presidents in the past century have spoken of the support of a "silenced majority" for their cause, from Warren Harding, to Richard Nixon, to Donald Trump. Similarly, Jerry Falwell dubbed his movement the "Moral Majority," claiming that most Americans supported the group's vision of traditional values and culture. After the 2016 election, Democrats consoled themselves with the fact that Hillary Clinton won 3 million more votes than Donald Trump, even if that was only a plurality of the votes cast. We desperately want to believe that most of our fellow citizens share our political views.

These claims are likely encouraged by the zero-sum game created by the American institutional structure, fostering a winner-take-all political system. But it also is related to a phenomenon that social psychologists have dubbed the false consensus effect. In its simplest conceptualization, the false consensus effect is the tendency for people's estimates of the prevalence of an attitude or behavior to be positively correlated with their own (Gilovich 1990). Research on this phenomenon began as early as the 1930s, was studied intensely in the 1970s and 1980s (Ross *et al.* 1977; Mullen *et al.* 1985; Marks and Miller 1987), and continues to be influential today.

Although the reasons are unclear, it appears that the false consensus effect is especially pernicious in the realm of politics (Mullen *et al.* 1985) and cannot be erased by education or the provision of statistical information about others' views (Krueger and Clement 1994). Diana Mutz explored this idea comprehensively in her work studying the way in which people perceive mass collectives (1998), unpacking the contribution of our personal experiences, our interpersonal interactions, and the mass media to our perceptions of collective opinion. There is substantial evidence for the existence of the effect in the domains of candidate preference (Lazarsfeld *et al.* 1944; Brown 1982; Granberg and Brent 1983; Granberg 1987), presidential performance evaluations (Fields and Schuman 1976; Goethals *et al.* 1979), specific policy decisions (Manstead 1982; Koestner *et al.* 1995), and support for political movements (Judd and Johnson 1981).

Why are people so likely to "see their own behavioral choices and judgments as relatively common and appropriate to existing circumstances while viewing alternative responses as uncommon, deviant, or inappropriate" (Ross *et al.* 1977, p. 280)? There are complementary veins of thought explaining the prevalence of the false consensus effect: the way in which people are either exposed to, or access, information and the motivations they face for believing that their views are in a majority (Marks and Miller 1987).

Homophily and Information Accessibility

The selective exposure and cognitive availability explanations for the false consensus effect draw on the fact that because people are similar to their social connections, a classic example of homophily (McPherson *et al.* 2001), people are exposed to a biased sample of the population that is more likely to agree with their political preferences. This can lead people to make biased inferences about the prevalence of particular attitudes or behaviors in the population writ large. If a person is surrounded by a majority of people who hold a particular attitude, she may be led to believe that the attitude is in the majority in the population overall, even if the attitude is actually rare. Lerman, Yan, and Wu (2016) call this the "majority illusion" paradox and demonstrate in simulations that it is prevalent in the kinds of networks that structure our social world, such as the structure of the political blog network.

Political scientists have long known that most people have homophilous social networks and political discussion networks. It has been a subject of debate whether this is the result of active selection into our networks or whether the homophily results from the correlation between political views and traits for which we do select our social ties. Just as our networks in real life, our social networks on Facebook are somewhat homophilous.

That being said, networks on Facebook appear to be more politically diverse than in-person discussion networks, presumably because of the larger volume of weak ties. Users who logged in to Facebook more frequently also had more politically diverse networks (Messing 2013). Using data derived from Facebook's servers on a sample of politically engaged individuals,[11] Messing finds that on average, about 60 percent of the friends of liberals and conservatives share their ideology. The rates of cross-cutting friendships – approximately one-quarter – is higher than the rate within face-to-face discussion networks, although there is considerably more homophily in Facebook networks based on ideological affiliation than there is on age, gender, religion, education level, or relationship status. Furthermore, users' tendency to cultivate networks of people to whom they are similar has been demonstrated to be a larger contributing factor than Facebook's algorithm to the "echo chamber effect" (Bakshy *et al.* 2015).

The rates of homophily in this unobtrusively collected data from Facebook is significantly higher than the rates of homophily in self-report data collected by Pew, a function not only of the way in which the data were collected, but also the sample itself. In a report released in advance of the 2016 presidential election, Pew reported that 23 percent of Facebook users say that most of the people in their networks have political viewpoints similar to their own, while 53 percent say there is a mix of beliefs (Duggan and Smith 2016). The 2014 American Trends Panel showed that among those who pay attention to

---

[11] Messing assesses 10.1 million Facebook users who self-reported their political ideology on the site and clicked on a political news article. Thus, since this sample comprises disproportionately people who are politically interested or engaged, it should overestimate levels of homophily, based on work showing that the most politically partisan and engaged are more likely to communicate with like-minded others.

political content on Facebook, 23 percent said that most or all of what they saw was in line with their own views, but this rate jumps to 47 percent of consistent conservatives and 32 percent of consistent liberals. The people surveyed using the social network battery in the END Framework Survey also reported more homophily among the most vociferous contacts in their social network. About half of the dyads named were agreeable ties compared to less than 20 percent of disagreeable ties and about 30 percent of dyads where the respondent reported that the tie was neither agreeable nor disagreeable.

To the extent that Facebook helps users learn the views of people around them, this political similarity may become more visible. Of course, counteracting this is that users also have more weak ties on Facebook, and, as we saw in Chapter 5, users are more likely to learn the political views of these weak ties, especially those who disagree with them. Exposure to disagreement could plausibly lower the false consensus effect (Wojcieszak and Price 2009). On the surface, these ideas may seem contradictory, but they are not. Facebook users can simultaneously learn the views of their disagreeable weak ties while understanding that those views represent a minority in their network.[12] Thus, one very concrete reason they may overestimate the proportion of people who agree with their political views is that a majority of their contacts on the Facebook site actually do agree with them.

Motivated Perception

In addition to the fact that users are exposed to significantly more agreement than disagreement in their Facebook feeds, they may be motivated to believe that most other people agree with them because this perceived similarity can "bolster perceived social support, validate the correctness or appropriateness of a position, maintain self-esteem, maintain or restore cognitive balance, or reduce tension associated with anticipated social interaction" (Marks and Miller 1987, p. 73).

Motivated perception is built on many of the same psychological principles as is the study of motivated reasoning in the selection and processing of political news, but it also is infused with social motivations that are a less prevalent part of the news-processing instances of motivated reasoning. For example, people who have a high need to belong are more susceptible to the false consensus effect, and priming people that they have a commonly shared belief may actually reduce their need to belong (Morrison and Matthes 2011). Although

---

[12] Of course, the exact balance between these two factors varies from individual to individual. An individual who has radically changed her social milieu – by moving across the country, obtaining high levels of education or income, or altering her religiosity – is much more likely to have a News Feed with a wider mix of viewpoints. Understanding the effects of this heterogeneity – controlling for all the factors that likely induce it in the first place – is an important next step in understanding the consequences of exposure to the News Feed.

attitude certainty and issue importance are associated with the false consensus effect, the desire to perceive similarity could exist regardless of our confidence in our own opinion. If we are not certain about our beliefs, we may desire the validation of others. If we are certain in our beliefs, we may want to believe that most other people agree with us to reinforce that our opinion is the correct one.

Like Breeds Like

Both of these theoretical perspectives could help explain the tendency of Facebook usage to intensify the false consensus effect. In addition to the structural features of users' social networks – that their News Feeds disproportionately feature content they are inclined to agree with – the END model of communication suggests that the feature of the News Feed most likely to drive the false consensus phenomenon is the effect of aggregated social cues. The ability to "react" to what other users have posted, most commonly through "liking" it, is especially important because of the prominent display on a piece of content of the total number of users who have reacted to it.

The very concept of a "like" button is expressly designed to provide the validation humans seek from others by believing that others agree with our opinion. As social psychologists have found, it "feels good" to have people like the content one has posted on Facebook. But it is not just the validation users receive from individual members of their networks. The effects of homophily and motivation may be further amplified in the News Feed environment because this social feedback becomes quantified in the form of aggregated information about the number of people who have reacted to or shared the comment a user posts. This feedback could have an effect both on the person who posted content and also on the people who view it. In addition to biasing people's perception of the popularity of particular viewpoints, this information also may lead to the anchoring effects described by Tversky and Kahneman (1974).

"Liking" content is an extremely frequent action on the Facebook site. Referring back to Table 2.2 in Chapter 2, remember that "liking" content is the most common way in which people engage with political content on the News Feed. Between one-third and one-half of the sample reported they had liked each of eleven different types of political content in the previous six months and over 70 percent had liked at least one type of political content.

This rate is consistent with what was reported in the social network battery about the rates at which people engage with the content posted by their most politically prolific contacts on the site. Approximately two-thirds of the contacts named by respondents (67.24 percent) posted something which the respondent had in turn clicked, liked, or shared to express agreement or disagreement. People were twice as likely to report they commented, liked, or shared content from one of their contacts to show agreement (49.93 percent of all contacts named) than disagreement (24.48 percent of all contacts named).

And respondents also were much more likely to have responded to the content posted by the contacts with whom they agreed (82.66 percent) compared to the contacts with whom they disagreed (43.37 percent).

What kind of content are people most inclined to "like"? In the three inference studies described where respondents were asked questions about Facebook content supposedly posted by other Facebook users, I included a question about whether the subject would "like" the content.[13] Overall, rates of liking were quite low – only 25.6 percent of all evaluations indicated that the subject would "like" the content – but several patterns are evident when we look at which kinds of content was most popular.

Most obvious in Figure 7.7 is that people were much more inclined to "like" content they perceived to be posted by a co-partisan. Perhaps surprisingly, people actually were more inclined to "like" the *political* content posted by their perceived co-partisans than the content they did not think was about politics. Also apparent in the figure is that people reported they would like visual content – memes, cartoons, and news stories – at a higher rate than they would like status updates. This is entirely consistent with our expectations about the kind of content that is generally most compelling on the News Feed, as well as the self-reported rates of liking content in the survey.

Although extensive covariates about the subjects in the inference studies were not collected, we can assess the effects of subjects' Facebook usage behavior on the pattern of what kind of content they were most inclined to like. Focusing first on just the set of content perceived to be political, the most important explanations for whether a subject liked the content is the intensity with which someone uses Facebook, namely how frequently they scroll through the News Feed and what percentage of those times they are seeking out political content. However, partisanship strength, political interest, and posting political content are not statistically significant.

What about the content users perceived to be posted by an in-party member? Again, we see that Facebook users who scroll through their News Feeds more, as well as those who post more political content themselves or seek out more political content on the Feed, were more inclined to "like" in-party content. The strength of a person's partisanship is also associated with her tendency to like in-party content, although her level of political interest was not.

Finally, what explains the behavior of liking content perceived by people to be posted by members of the out-group? Again, the frequency of scrolling through the News Feed and the proportion of times a user seeks out political information is positive and significantly related. However, for out-party content, partisan strength is very significantly negatively correlated, as is political interest. Most people indicate that they would not "like" content they perceive

---

[13] The exact question wording was "Would you take any of the following actions if one of your Facebook friends posted this status update and you saw it on your News Feed?" A grid-style response allowed subjects to report if they would like, share, or comment on the content.

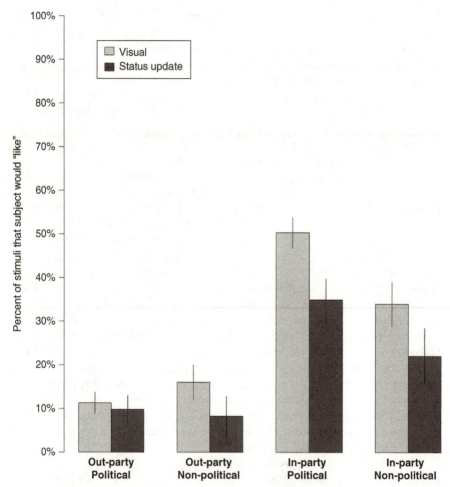

FIGURE 7.7 Rate of "liking" on stimuli in inference studies, by in-group status, content type, and stimulus type

For example, approximately half of all evaluations of in-party visual stimuli that were perceived to be about politics indicated that the subject would "like" the content. Lines depict 95 percent confidence intervals.

to be posted by members of their out-group. Those people who would are those who use Facebook frequently, but are the least politically interested and partisan.

In the END Framework Survey, I followed up on these findings by asking respondents why they "liked" political content on the News Feed. In short, even though people say that they don't generate much political content, they readily "like" political content if they think that it has been posted by someone with whom they agree. If we take users at their words about why they say they

TABLE 7.2 *Reported Reasons for "Liking" Political Content*

	Proportion Who Have Liked for that Reason
I want to show support for the person who posted the content	39.62%
I want to signal agreement with the content	38.13%
I thought the content was funny or would make people laugh	37.04%
I want to signal that I agree with the political views of the person who posted the content	35.84%
I want to visibly support a point of view or a political party	31.21%

Subjects were asked the question, "Which of the following are reasons that you click the 'like' button on political content?" The response options were randomized. The top five most prevalent reasons are reported in the table. The denominator is the 737 people who indicated that they had liked at least one of the eleven categories of political content.

like content, much of this behavior appears to be driven by social utility, an effort to support their friends and to help circulate humorous content (see Table 7.2).

The act of liking a piece of content on the News Feed is an individual one, intended to send a signal to the friend who posted the content. In and of itself, this behavior is important and suggests one mechanism for further development of strong in-group identification and attachment to one's party. But it also takes on importance because of the way in which "likes" aggregate in the News Feed environment. People who post political content not only note who likes their content, but the total number of "likes." While a user scrolling through the News Feed looking at content posted by others can click on the post to figure out who liked it, the more immediately available and visually prominent piece of information is the total number of reactions that a piece of content garnered. These individual behaviors accumulate into quantifiable information infused with affect.[14] It is this feature of the News Feed ecosystem that I argued in Chapter 3 should be especially powerful in signaling information about the distribution of the viewpoints within a person's network.

What is the consequence of receiving quantifiable, public feedback on the political content one posts to Facebook? Does seeing higher rates of feedback on other people's posts affect users' estimates of the rate of agreement with the content? I expect that Facebook users who receive higher levels of social

[14] Historically, quantified social feedback was infused with positive affect because of the connotations of the word "like." With the introduction of reaction buttons, a broader range of affect can be conveyed. However, the visual depiction of quantified feedback does not make clear which emotion is most prevalent unless a user actually clicks on it. Thus, the total number of reactions still likely conveys positive reinforcement for a user's post.

feedback on their Facebook posts will feel more attached to and proud of their political party affiliation. I also expect that Facebook users who see content with a higher level of social feedback will estimate that a larger proportion of people agree with the opinions they expressed in their post.

Social Reinforcement

It is incredibly difficult to design experiments that maintain the authenticity of the Facebook environment, but allow the researcher to manipulate salient features of the experience of engaging on the site. Scholars have tried a variety of creative research designs, such as snowball sampling (Anspach 2018) and recruiting subjects to join dedicated Facebook groups where experimental treatments can be introduced (Feezell 2018).

I took a slightly different approach, hoping to mimic the experience of sharing content with one's network by leveraging the student subject pool at the university where I work. In the first part of the study, subjects were randomly assigned to one of four treatments: reading an article, reading an article and writing a status update, writing a status update, or a control condition where they were not exposed to a stimulus. Subjects in all four treatment groups then proceeded to complete an inference task, namely the Accuracy Study described in the previous chapter. The users who had written status updates were told that they were evaluating content written by other study participants,[15] while those who had not written anything were simply instructed that they would evaluate status updates written by Facebook users.

In the time between the pre-survey and the portion of the study taking place in the lab, the users who generated political content were randomly assigned to one of two conditions: a low social feedback condition (two likes) or a high social feedback condition (fifty-two likes).[16] Users who read a news article but did not write a status update also were assigned to a low or high feedback condition. However, they received a version of the article they had read in the pre-survey, formatted to look like Facebook content.

---

[15] The instructions were, "Every semester, about 500 students are invited to participate as subjects in the Omnibus Project. In the next section of the study, you will evaluate some responses that previous study participants wrote. We've formatted what they wrote to look like status updates and kept their identities anonymous."

[16] This study focused on the number of likes for a post, but future work could consider the impact of comments, as well. The combination of homophily among the people in their network, paired with the Facebook algorithm, appears to go hand-in-hand to contributing to the fact that most people report that the conversation threads they see also are largely agreeable. When asked to consider the comment threads of the posts they see, people reported on average that over 80 percent of the comment threads they see contained comments that entirely supported the views in the original post or was a mix of comments that support and oppose the views expressed in the original post.

When subjects came to the lab for the second portion of the study, they were handed an envelope with a printed copy of their customized stimulus. They then were asked a series of questions to measure the dependent variables related to strength of their partisan attachment, pride in their political identity, and perceptions of support for their viewpoints. Finally, subjects in all three treatment groups also were asked for their evaluation of the number of subjects who read the post in order to be able to estimate their perception for the rate of support for the article in the subject pool. There were no significant differences between the groups in terms of their estimates of how many subjects had read the content, suggesting that the operationalization of high and low social support was meaningfully distinct.

Partisan Pride

Receiving higher levels of social feedback on a political post should increase feelings of pride and attachment to one's political party and that is, in fact, what we observe. Subjects in the high feedback condition reported increased social psychological attachment to their political party, but the result is driven by the respondents in the treatment groups who wrote their own political content. Thus, in and of itself, seeing high rates of social feedback on content does not appear to increase partisan attachment, but seeing high rates of feedback on one's own words does.

Users who received higher levels of social feedback not only felt more attached to their party, but also indicated an increased likelihood that they would post their content to their actual Facebook accounts. Among participants in the treatment groups who had written their own content, those who received higher levels of feedback were more willing to let the researcher use their content as an example.[17] Figure 7.8 plots the raw data, showing the percentage of subjects in each condition who indicated a willingness to actually post their content or share it with the researcher. The treatment effects actually are strengthened in regression models, since including covariates – such as demographic variables, partisanship, and personality – makes the standard errors of the estimates for the treatment effect more precise.

Everyone Agrees with Me

Did higher levels of social feedback increase subjects' estimates of the proportion of their network who agree with their viewpoints? In this study, the relevant "network" is defined as the student body at the university where the study was conducted. Perceptions of the partisan distribution are important background information to contextualize the results. There was a broad consensus among subjects that their fellow students were more likely

---

[17] "The researcher conducting this study is looking for example Facebook posts to include in research presentations and papers about the project. Would you be interested in letting her use your post as an example?"

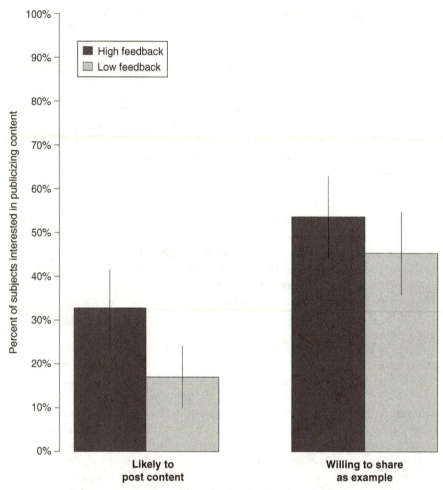

FIGURE 7.8 Subjects' interest in publicizing their political content, by treatment group
Subjects in the high social feedback condition were more likely to say they actually would post the content they generated in the experiment and were more willing to let the researcher use their content as an example. Lines depict 95 percent confidence intervals.

to be Democrats. In the pre-survey, on average Democrats thought that 61.28 percent of their fellow students were Democrats and, on average, Republicans thought that only 26.53 percent of their fellow students were Republicans. Thus, going into the study, Democrats could reasonably perceive that their opinions were likely to be in the majority, while Republicans could not.

After subjects wrote political content in the pre-survey, they were asked to report the percentage of their fellow students who would agree with what they wrote. Despite the perceived partisan imbalance on campus, both Democrats and Republicans thought that a majority of their peers would agree with their

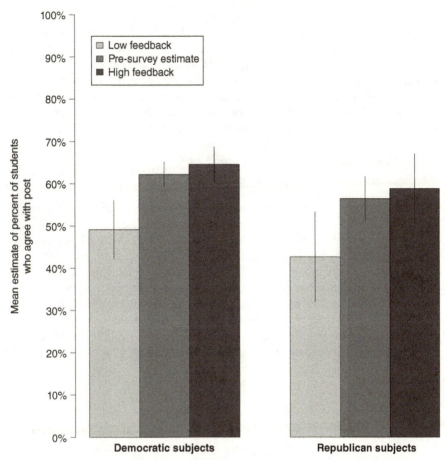

FIGURE 7.9 Subjects' estimations of the rate of support for their expressed political views, by partisanship and treatment group

Both Democrats and Republicans perceived that a majority of their peers would agree with their views in the pre-survey. Low levels of social feedback lowered estimates of support. Lines depict 95 percent confidence intervals.

statement about the political candidates. Although Democrats estimated a slightly elevated level of support compared to Republicans – 62.17 to 56.51 percent – the difference was not statistically significant.

Receiving social feedback on their posts in the lab portion of the study altered these expectations. As shown in Figure 7.9, low social feedback depressed the subjects' estimate of the amount of support among their peers for their views, while high levels of feedback slightly increased it. Subjects – even those who know that they are in a political minority in their community – are inclined to think that most people will agree with their stated political opinions. High levels of social feedback appear to reinforce that belief.

Does this effect extend to their estimates of the distribution of partisanship among their peers? In other words, does high social feedback increase their estimate of how many co-partisans there are? This question also was asked in the pre-survey, so we can construct a variable of the difference of the subjects' estimates of their in-group before and after receiving social feedback on their post. Overall, the high feedback treatment did not appear to alter subjects' estimates of the size of the in-party on campus, but the results are significant if we focus just on those students who pass a manipulation check. Among these respondents, the results of a linear regression show that social feedback did increase their estimates of the proportion of students in their in-party by an average of seven percentage points, and the effects appear to be stronger among Republicans compared to Democrats.

These results are suggestive and based on a relatively small sample. Nothing conclusive can be drawn without replication and extension. It is possible that the perceived partisan imbalance of the student body created a heterogeneous treatment effect for the high social feedback condition. Republican students recognized they were in a minority. Only 2.3 percent of the entire sample (seven students) thought there was more support for Donald Trump than Hillary Clinton among students. It is possible that high levels of social feedback signaled to Republicans that there was more support for their opinions than they had originally perceived and that it is this facet of the treatment that caused them to revise upwards their estimate of the proportion of students who were Republican.

CONCLUSION

People do not post comprehensive statements of their overall political views, but rather post short statements about specific political issues. Consequently, Facebook users rarely get a comprehensive picture of all the views their contacts hold. Instead, they make judgments based upon single snapshots of what their friends write. The studies in this chapter were designed to emulate that reality about the Facebook ecosystem, and the findings reiterate an important point about communication on the News Feed: moderation and nuance are hard to convey in a short bit of text, a meme, or a news lede.

Political content generators – whom we know are already the most partisan and opinionated – receive significant positive reinforcement for their partisan identities from the outpouring of social support on their posts. Generating political content and receiving social feedback on it appear to increase generators' estimates of the proportion of people who agree with them and increases their confidence and willingness to share their views. This creates a reinforcing cycle for those people who do post political content. Consistent with the expectations of social identity theory, generating political content appears to bolster one's identification with the in-group.

But it is not only those users who generate political content that are susceptible to the biased processing inherent in social identity theory. Encountering political content, even unintentionally, also is sufficient to activate these effects. What have we learned about the way in which Facebook users process the politically informative content that comes across the News Feed? In the aggregate, they are quite accurate and achieve high levels of consensus about the partisan views of the person who posted the content, although users are too likely to ascribe partisan identities to people who say they are political independents. Facebook users impute too much ideological extremity and consistency to people based on the content of what they post. The weaker the connection they have to another Facebook user with whom they disagree, the more likely they are to think that their viewpoints are extreme. These perceptions extend to evaluations of Facebook-using members of the out-party as a whole.

One critique of the inference studies presented so far is that they do not isolate the effects of the information from the medium. In other words, these studies may simply demonstrate a specific instance of a generalized phenomenon: people think members of their out-group are more homogeneous and extreme than they are in reality. The experimental stimuli do not isolate the Facebook environment as a necessary condition, and it could be the case that simply asking people to make any sort of inference about an out-group member based on isolated information about her would result in the same finding, absent any pretense of the out-group member using Facebook to advertise the content. In short, I have not identified nor tested these results against an appropriate counterfactual.

This is a valid critique. But in this case, the counterargument is related to the core of the END Framework: communication about politics on Facebook is similar to, but distinct from, other forms of interpersonal political interaction. The appropriate counterfactual in day-to-day life is difficult to conceptualize because of the hallmark characteristics of News Feed communication outlined in Chapter 3. Does biased inference occur as a result of the more traditional ways in which people learn the political views of the people in their lives? Do we make similar judgments based on comments overheard in line at the grocery store or based on our neighbor's yard sign or bumper sticker? Probably. But the incidence of opportunities to learn on Facebook is simply much higher than these one-off observations from other parts of our day-to-day lives. Unlike many experiments with potentially artificial stimuli, subjects actually encounter structurally identical "stimuli" in their daily usage of the Facebook site as they encountered in the inference studies. Thus, even if the "Facebook ruse" is not necessary to obtain these results, when considering when and how people actually encounter this kind of information outside the experimental context, we know that a large majority of Americans do on a daily basis on Facebook.

Careful readers also will have picked up on an important trend in the data. Increased usage of Facebook and higher reported inadvertent exposure to political content on Facebook is not consistently associated with increased willingness to make inferences about the political views of others, increased accuracy in doing so, or increased imputation of ideological extremity or consistency to posters. However, increased site usage and inadvertent exposure to political content *is* associated with higher confidence in making inferences about the partisan identities and ideological views of posters.

Thus, what I have demonstrated is not that Facebook teaches users how to make these inferences, but rather that Facebook gives them practice in doing so. The more content, explicitly political or otherwise, a user reports that they see, the more confident they are in their abilities to make accurate inferences about the views of Facebook users, even if they are not actually any more accurate in doing so. These studies do not rule out the possibility that there are differences between practiced and novice Facebook users in the way they process politically informative content. There are many more related questions to be explored. Are Facebook users faster at the process of assigning identity or inferring beliefs? Are they better able to reconcile multiple bits of information about users? These important follow-up questions merit future study.

The results of the inference studies suggest that everyone is capable of making these evaluations and falling into these patterns of biased thinking. The goal of this chapter is to demonstrate that the phenomena social psychologists have studied for years related to biased processing of out-group members are alive and well in the social media age. These processes are not isolated to social media. Quite the opposite is true. END communication has, in fact, provided an ideal platform for phenomena that have long been demonstrated in the laboratory environment.

Social identity theorists focus on affective processes, arguing that cognitive processes are a result of motivation to enhance our self-esteem, not the driver of the negative attitudes toward the out-group. However, political scientists have long been interested in the way in which cognitive biases affect other aspects of political behavior. Whether people first respond affectively and then reason in a biased way or vice versa, it appears that the information to which people are exposed on Facebook is sufficient to trigger estimations that the out-party is more ideologically consistent and extreme than they are in reality. What is the consequence of the fact that Facebook users think members of the out-party are all the same and are inclined to believe they are extreme in their views? In the next chapter, I turn to those affective evaluations, focusing on the negative judgments that Facebook users make about the people with whom they disagree. It turns out that while Facebook use does not increase people's willingness to infer, it does increase their willingness to be pejorative.

8

Judging the Other Side

Decades of research on intergroup interactions suggests that an almost inevitable result of categorizing people into groups is affective polarization, the development of positive evaluations of one's in-group and negative evaluations of the out-group. Given that Facebook users classify each other as Democrats and Republicans based on even the non-political content they post to Facebook and that the News Feed ecosystem can activate group identities, we should expect that users also form stereotyped, value-laden judgments about the political out-group.

The literature in affective polarization outside the realm of politics finds that in an effort to positively differentiate their in-group, people will form negative judgments about the out-group that run the gamut from intelligence to skill level to moral values. However, the context in which the in-group interacts with the out-group is thought to be of great importance for the characteristics of the out-group that get stereotyped (Leyens *et al.* 1994). Our search for the issue domain in which Facebook users are most likely to judge out-partisans should thus be sensitive to the value-laden judgments that are most salient in the context of END interactions on Facebook.

Just as we evaluate candidates and elected officials on the traits pertinent to their role in the political system, I argue that we should judge other members of the public on the performance of their role as citizens. We assess our candidates on their experience, leadership, and personal qualities. What traits are most important when we evaluate our fellow Americans on the dimension of citizenship?

The END model of communication suggests that the Facebook platform facilitates behavior at the nexus of political information acquisition, discussion, and expression. The facet of citizenship that users readily can observe on Facebook, therefore, relates to the quality of the way in which citizens acquire and process information in order to arrive at and express their opinions. This can be thought of as political competence. That this dimension is closely tied to two of the most important contemporary popular debates about the consequences of using social media – the presence of "echo chambers" and the rise of "fake news" – supports the argument about the salience of this facet of judgment.

Narrowing to the dimension of political competence does not imply that this is the only important category of judgment, nor that it is the most important one. But it is the most relevant domain for what people can observe of their fellow Facebook-using citizens and it is a natural outgrowth of the findings presented in the previous chapter about the biases shaping user characterizations of the out-party.

The findings in this chapter demonstrate that people readily report that hypothetical Facebook users are ill-informed if they perceive those users are members of the out-party. This negative judgment about knowledge levels extends to members of the partisan out-group in their own Facebook networks, where it also appears to be the case that we believe out-partisans use less credible information sources. Contrary to the idea that increased social contact is supposed to reduce antipathy toward an out-group, it does not appear to do so in users' judgments about the information-processing skills of their out-partisan friends and family. In fact, Facebook users believe information-processing stereotypes better characterize members of the out-party than do non-Facebook users, and increased usage of the site exacerbates this belief.

While judgments about the way in which people arrive at their opinions most directly are connected to what people can actually observe of others' behavior on Facebook, social identity theory suggests that also we will become more disparaging about other qualities of the out-group. The high rate of agreement with some of the opinion-extremity stereotypes presented in the previous chapter – statements hinting at moral failures and character flaws – implies that this may, in fact, be the case. Consequently, we should expect that Facebook users also see growing social distance between the parties, to the point where they perceive that the parties comprise different types of people. The outgrowth of this idea is that people may intentionally structure their social networks to avoid contact with the out-group, preferentially selecting co-partisans as friends and severing communication with out-party members. The results presented below confirm many of these troubling predictions.

JUDGING THE RESPONSIBILITIES OF CITIZENSHIP

Tajfel's seminal studies led him to conclude that as a result of the differentiations people make between groups, they are motivated to pass judgment in order to elevate the position of their in-group vis-à-vis the out-group. This involves both positive evaluations of the characteristics and traits of one's own group, as well as denigration of those of the out-group. These evaluations occur on multiple dimensions, beyond those related to the characteristics that distinguished the groups in the first place. While we would, therefore, expect out-party judgment on a wide variety of factors, we begin with a factor directly tied to what Facebook users observe of their fellow citizens' behavior: how people navigate the political information environment.

Negative Judgment in Social Identity Theory

Out-group judgments occur even within the minimal group paradigm – where groups are assigned completely arbitrarily – so it is clear that a meaningful differentiation defining the groups is not integral to the out-group judgment process. However, in scholarship that moves beyond the minimal group paradigm and explores more salient category differentiations, it is common practice to assess the extent to which group members judge each other on the dimension pertinent to how the groups were initially distinguished.

In the realm of politics, what salient characteristics that distinguish "us" versus "them" are readily available for observation? Robinson *et al.* (1995) argue that the way in which people process information to form their opinions is an integral part of how partisans differentiate themselves from the out-group. As they write:

... individuals may feel that whereas they themselves have proceeded from available evidence to reasonable interpretations and beliefs, those who hold opposing beliefs ... have done just the opposite ... People should tend to believe that they alone struggle with the ambiguities, complexities, and even inconsistencies of objective reality, that others tend to perceive the world in simple, ideologically consistent, black or white terms ... Robinson *et al.* (1995), p. 405

The authors find that people overestimate the homogeneity and extremity of the opinions of the people with whom they disagreed. People also discounted the reasoning process their opponents had used to arrive at their opinions, claiming that their opponents relied too heavily on ideology as opposed to measured consideration of the evidence.

Most Americans place great value on the idea that we are all entitled to our own opinions. We may not like the views other people have and we may not always agree that they have a right to act on those opinions, but a core notion of American identity is that we have a constitutionally protected right to believe what we want and to express those opinions. In and of itself, holding strong opinions may actually be thought of as an asset of good citizenship. When we judge people based upon their opinions, we are not judging the fact that they have that opinion, but rather *why* or *how* they arrived at the content of that opinion. In other words, we are focused on their opinion formation process. Our judgments about a person's views are rooted in the motives we attribute to them and their ability to make reasoned evaluations about political topics. Making reasoned evaluations implicitly assumes making informed decisions, and the manner in which citizens gather information about politics is, therefore, implicitly a key component of "good citizenship."

Forming Opinions in the Age of Digital Media: Echo Chambers, the Filter Bubble, and "Fake News"

The study of what Americans actually know about politics reveals a simple and clear answer: not much. Trivially small proportions of the population are able to answer factual questions about either civics or contemporary political issues (Delli Carpini and Keeter 1997). If one must be informed to be a good citizen, then most Americans fail the qualification exam. Many of the most important debates in the field of political behavior in the last thirty years have revolved around the notion of how Americans compensate for this lack of knowledge: examining the role of heuristics in opinion formation, studying the consequences of inadvertent exposure to "soft news," and assessing the reliance on knowledgeable opinion leaders in discussion networks. If Americans can compensate for their lack of information and still arrive at the opinion they would have if they were well-informed, perhaps they can fulfill the duties of citizenship demanded of them, albeit in a suboptimal way.

The nexus of the debate over good citizenship thus turns toward how people are able to make order and meaning out of their information environments. On the one hand, as a result of elite polarization, citizens may only need a single heuristic in order to "vote correctly": partisanship. However, vote choice is the one behavior in American politics that remains entirely private. We cannot observe the markings on the ballots of our family, friends, neighbors, and colleagues, but we can observe many facets of their process arriving at that decision.

If we care about the evaluations Americans make of each other, we should focus on the behaviors that are observable. Thus, even if political scientists are satisfied that Americans can make sufficiently informed decisions using heuristics, everyone else is focused on the less-than-optimal way that most people navigate their search for political information. While polarization has made partisanship an exceptionally valuable heuristic, over-reliance on that heuristic is deemed normatively undesirable. Klar and Krupnikov (2016) make a strong case that many Americans eschew the expression of partisanship by portraying themselves as Independents to make a better impression on others because it is socially desirable to do so.

Simultaneously, the rise of the Internet and media fragmentation have created an increasingly complex information environment through which citizens must navigate. The imperative to process information in a rational way remains the same, whether a citizen is faced with a context of information abundance or information constraint. But as the production of news has proliferated, the most challenging aspect of this component of citizenship has changed. The challenge is no longer how to use heuristics to form opinions in the absence of information, but rather how to sift through the vast amount of information available. The difficulty has moved from acquiring enough information to acquiring the right kind of information and knowing how to parse through it.

Information complexity is compounded on Facebook by concerns that the information people encounter is shaped by structural forces outside their direct control. Much attention has been paid to the problem of biased information search, either as a result of the active choices individuals make about accessing news[1] or the intervention of technology into what people see.[2] The 2016 election further complicated the information quality debate by revealing the extent of stories written to sound like authentic news stories that were, in fact, completely false.[3] On Facebook, citizens are inadvertently exposed to bountiful information, but information that may not be accurate or complete. A good citizen in the age of social media should be able to parse through what is true and what is not in order to consume a balanced news diet to form opinions based on reasoned judgment after exposure to the complete set of facts.

These assessments are more than an academic exercise. Facebook users watch each other navigate these choices on a daily basis. They observe what news sources their social connections follow on the site, and from which sources they post stories. They get snapshots of others' opinions through the commentary they add to those stories. They have a window into the deliberative – or not-so-deliberative – processes through which other people form their opinions by reading the comment threads created in response to explicitly political posts. They glean insight into a friend's level of political sophistication based on their selection of a meme. Even those who refrain from engaging about politics are not immune to judgment. Facebook users know which of their social connections appear to be completely disinterested in politics, when the rest of the world is up in arms about the news of the day.

Now we can judge not only whether someone *is* informed, but how they *became* informed. The way in which users traverse the complex information environment easily can be observed by the people in their network, and, thus, the domain of citizenship related to how people form their opinions potentially takes on a critical role. If people implicitly value the process through which others make their decisions, we should expect that judgments about how our in-group versus our out-group navigates the information environment could be a relevant dimension. Within the realm of politics, being well informed is a socially desirable trait that indicates that one's opinions are rooted in fact and truth. In an effort to bolster in-group concept and value, we

---

[1] This is the "echo chamber" concept, where as a result of the people to whom they are connected or the news sources that they follow, individuals only see information that reaffirms their views.

[2] This is the "filter bubble" concept, defined as algorithmic distortion of the information individuals encounter due to a platform's attempt to deliver the content that a person wants to see.

[3] This is the "fake news" concept. This label should not be confused with the epithet of "fake news" used by those who seek to delegitimize news organizations such as CNN by claiming that the stories they report are "fake news." This label reveals a pernicious problem in its own right, but one that is driven by perceptions of media bias.

expect that Facebook users will attribute higher levels of both political knowledge and source reliability to co-partisans.

KNOWLEDGE JUDGMENTS OF ANONYMOUS OTHERS

The initial test of these hypotheses can be conducted on the inference studies described in the previous three chapters on the evaluations people make in response to the content posted by anonymous others. As a brief review of the set-up of each study, subjects were asked to evaluate between six and ten different stimuli, answering a set of questions about the anonymous Facebook user who posted each stimulus. The results reported here are based on the question gauging the knowledge level of the person who posted the status update or visual content. After asking subjects to rate the poster's knowledge level, they were asked to report on their confidence level in their judgment, in order to ascertain if they were simply guessing. In order to increase the power of the study to detect differences based on content type and respondent characteristics, I pool together the data from all three studies, although the pattern of results is consistent when each study is analyzed separately.

Social identity theory predicts that as soon as group identity is made salient, people are triggered to derogate the out-group in order to enhance estimations of the in-group. It would not be surprising, therefore, to tell people the partisanship of the person who posted a piece of content and find that they are more critical of the person's knowledge level when the person is identified as a member of the out-party. By priming the subject with the hypothetical Facebook user's partisanship, we would induce the negative judgment.

Four facets of the studies' research design set up a harder test to establish that Facebook users make judgments about the knowledge levels of people who post content to the News Feed. First, instead of making the poster's identity salient to the subject, subjects impute it themselves. In other words, I did not assign group identity to the anonymous poster. Subjective reality is what matters. If the subject thinks the poster is a member of the out-party, that should be enough to trigger judgment.

Second, the ordering of the questions intentionally put the knowledge judgment question first and the partisanship inference question later. The judgment question therefore assesses the subjects' instincts before being primed to think about partisan identity.[4]

Third, the inclusion of implicitly political content in addition to explicitly political content tests the scope condition about what kind of content is sufficient to induce judgment. The studies test people's willingness to make

---

[4] I argue that people become aware of their intuition of a poster's partisanship based on the content of the stimulus. Thus, the knowledge judgment reflects their recognition of the poster as a member of the in-group or out-group, but the subject has not yet been asked to think intentionally about this recognition.

judgments about political knowledge even when the content the hypothetical Facebook user posts is deemed not to be political in the eyes of the subject. Again, SIT predicts that people should make this judgment, but the implication is that the non-political content circulating on Facebook – if implicitly informative about the poster's partisan identification – may contribute to the negative judgment underpinning partisan stereotyping.

Finally, we can test whether the discrepancy in in-group versus out-group knowledge evaluation holds for those subjects who are weakly identified as partisans. Demonstrating that even people who identify as political Independents, and only lean toward a political party when pushed, also discriminate between in-group and out-group members' knowledge levels suggests most Facebook users engage in this process, not just those who feel strong bonds toward their party.

Are Users More Judgmental about Their Out-Group than Their In-Group?

Participants were asked to rate the poster's knowledge on a three-point scale and were given an option to report that they did not know. Overall, a small proportion, only 16.08 percent, of the responses failed to include a knowledge evaluation. While subjects were slightly less willing to make an evaluation about posters they perceived to be members of their out-group, the magnitude of the overall difference was small.

There is variation in this willingness to make an evaluation based both on the characteristics of the content as well as the characteristics of the respondent, depicted in Figure 8.1. Subjects were very willing to make knowledge evaluations about people who posted political content, regardless of whether that person was perceived to be a member of the in-party or out-party. Both weak partisans and partisan leaners were willing to make knowledge judgments. There was a difference between in-party evaluation rate and out-party evaluation rate for content that was deemed to "maybe" be about politics, but subjects' partisan strength was not related to their willingness to make a judgment for this middle category of content.

It is only among the non-political content that we see an effect of both in-party status and partisan strength. Strong partisans made knowledge evaluations approximately 80 percent of the time for non-political content they perceived to be posted by a co-partisan. Partisan leaners made evaluations only 60 percent of the time for non-political content they perceived to be posted by a member of the other party. Although the difference is very significant, in all instances, a majority of subjects made evaluations based on the content.

Beyond the type of stimulus and whether the respondent perceived the content to be posted by a co-partisan, what other individual characteristics predicted willingness to make an evaluation of knowledge? In addition to a subject's partisanship strength, her level of political interest also significantly

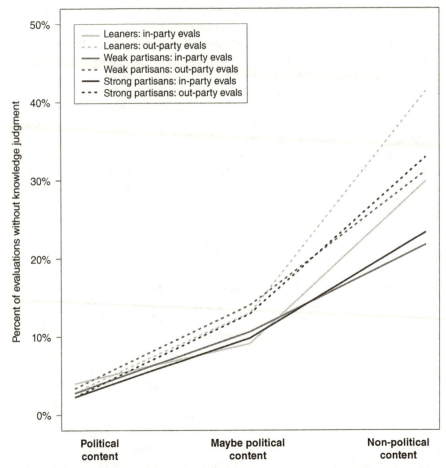

FIGURE 8.1 Missing knowledge evaluations, by content type, evaluators' partisanship strength, and in-party perception

Over 90 percent of all subjects made evaluations for political content regardless of their partisanship strength and their perception of whether the poster was a co-partisan. The rate is considerably lower for other types of content.

predicted her willingness to make these evaluations. While Facebook usage, News Feed scrolling, and inadvertent exposure were not associated with an increased willingness to wager a knowledge evaluation, both intentional seeking and generation of political content were.

For the remaining assessment, we focus only on those evaluations where subjects marked the knowledge level of the poster on a three-point scale: "very knowledgeable" (2), "somewhat knowledgeable" (1), or "not very knowledgeable" (0). Figure 8.2 shows the mean level of political knowledge attributed to posters, by content type, in-party status, and subject's partisan strength. The

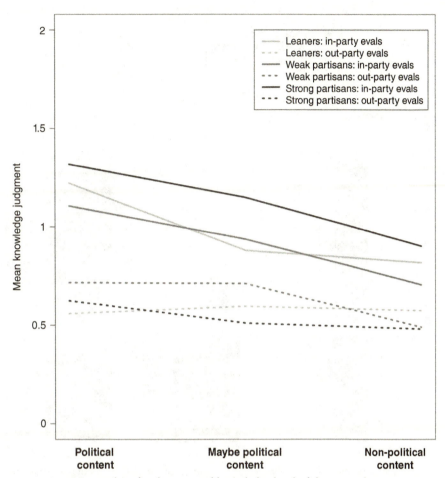

FIGURE 8.2 Mean values for the reported knowledge level of the poster by content type, respondents' partisanship strength, and in-party perception
All stimuli are pooled together across all three inference studies.

figure shows the pooled results of all three studies, but the results hold across all three studies individually: the status update study, the visual lede study, and the source cue study.

Across content type and all levels of partisan strength, subjects attributed higher levels of knowledge to their co-partisans. Content type mattered less for evaluations of out-partisans than it did for co-partisans, and while strong partisans were more polarized in their evaluations, even partisan leaners attributed higher levels of knowledge to their co-partisans based on their perception of the non-political content they posted. The magnitude of these differences is depicted in Figure 8.3. Partisan leaners perceive nearly as much difference in

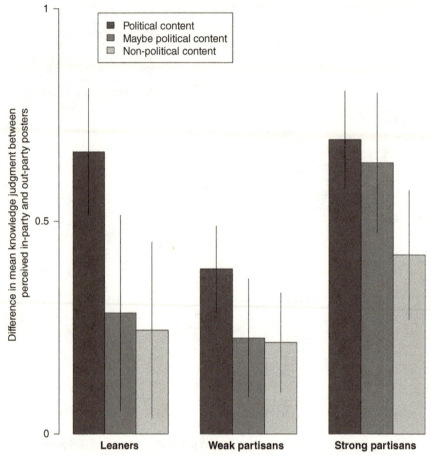

FIGURE 8.3 Difference in mean knowledge judgment of the poster by content type and partisanship strength

All stimuli are pooled together across all three inference studies. Lines depict 95 percent confidence intervals.

knowledge level between in-party and out-party posters as do strong partisans, but both leaners and weak partisans are much less polarized in their judgments of content that is not or is only possibly about politics. While the mean perceived differences are smaller, they are still substantial and are very statistically significant.

Just as predicted by social identity theory, Facebook users show a strong in-group bias in attributing a characteristic that is important to the differentiation between groups – the perception of being politically knowledgeable – even when they are not given any information pertinent to the poster's actual level of political knowledge.

Can Users Recognize Knowledgeable Members of Their Out-Group?

Gathering information from the well-informed opinion leaders in our networks is supposed to be one of the most important factors compensating for the lack of widespread political knowledge. How might politically knowledgeable people make themselves known to others? This question has not been pursued in the face-to-face discussion literature, so we cannot search for analogous offline signals, but presumably opinion leaders communicate knowledge by the frequency and quality of information they communicate.

What might this look like in the Facebook environment? In Chapter 5, we saw that people who post large proportions of political content were no more likely to be politically knowledgeable than are people who do not post much political content. The act of regularly posting political content is not a reliable heuristic in and of itself to identify the most politically knowledge-able people in the network. What about the characteristics of the content that opinion leaders post to Facebook? Political knowledge is generally correlated with education level, so it is possible that when users consume Facebook content, they use heuristics associated with educational attainment – such as proper spelling, grammar, and sentence complexity – as a proxy for the political knowledge level of the person who posted it. The kinds of details that a person includes in her post, such as the use of proper names or official titles, also may signal that a person pays close attention to the nuances of politics.

The first step in assessing if people are able to recognize the politically knowledgeable out-partisan opinion leaders in their networks is to see if people are able to differentiate the posts of politically knowledgeable Facebook users from those who are not. To test this question, we use the Accuracy Study data to examine whether the poster's actual knowledge level is correlated with the judges' estimations of her knowledge level. In this study, first introduced in Chapter 6, a group of Mechanical Turk workers, the "posters," generated political content related to their attitudes about the 2016 presidential election candidates or about one of two contemporary political issues. A second group of subjects in a student subject pool, the "judges," evaluated the content. Because we collected information about the posters, including their political knowledge level, we can assess whether they were able to signal their status as a potential opinion leader through their Facebook post.

In the previous section with the inference data, we saw that perception of in-group identity appears to drive the judges' evaluations of the knowledge level of the poster. But will judges be able to differentiate between posters in their own parties who know a lot about politics compared to those who do not? Similarly, although we expect the judges to attribute lower levels of knowledge to people they perceive to be part of their out-group, are they able to recognize variation in knowledge levels of the out-group?

A difference of means test, splitting the knowledge level of the posters at the median, shows that judges do attribute higher levels of political knowledge to the posters who objectively have higher levels of political knowledge (0.75, 0.61, p < 0.001).[5] Clearly, some sort of signal is being communicated by what the posters write. However, the poster's objective knowledge level does not appear to shape evaluations nearly as much as a shared partisan identity. In Figure 8.4, there is a much greater difference between pairs of bars than within them, suggesting that perceived in-group status matters considerably more than objective knowledge level in the judges' evaluations. In fact, the judges attribute twice the political knowledge level to low-knowledge co-partisans than they do to high-knowledge out-partisans.

Further exploration of these phenomena is necessary, but what these initial results suggest is that users are not willing to give credit where credit is due to members of their out-group, and they attribute political knowledge to co-partisans without cause. Recent experimental work on communication in political networks suggests that people weight expertise more than shared preference when selecting informants. But while subjects in those experiments may have selected expertise when incentivized to vote correctly, they were less likely to trust the information coming from the well-informed but disagreeable experts (Ahn *et al.* 2010, 2014).

The present results suggest that in the organic Facebook ecosystem, people are much less willing to recognize when their political opponents know what they are talking about. In the context of the Facebook News Feed, it appears that people are not willing to acknowledge the value of these cross-cutting opinion leaders. As soon as they have deemed them to be in their out-group, they discount what they know about politics. Conversely, users pad their estimations of the political knowledge level of their co-partisans, even when they objectively know less about politics. The implications for the flow of information in the environment are profound and suggest that not only do people end up situated in echo chambers, but they might refuse to acknowledge the merits of the voices coming from outside.

---

[5] The mean knowledge attribution level was significantly lower in this study compared to the pooled results of the inference studies. There are three possible explanations for this. First, they were run on different samples. The pooled inference studies were conducted on Mechanical Turk, while the Accuracy Study was conducted on a sample of undergraduates taking political science courses at an elite university. The student sample had objectively higher levels of political knowledge and also were likely stronger written communicators. So, when evaluating status updates that had been posted by Mechanical Turkers, they may have been more judgmental. Second, the Accuracy Study assessed direct statements of people's views about the political candidates or contemporary policy issues as opposed to implicitly political content. Finally, the Accuracy Study was conducted six months after the inference studies, in the middle of a heated general election campaign.

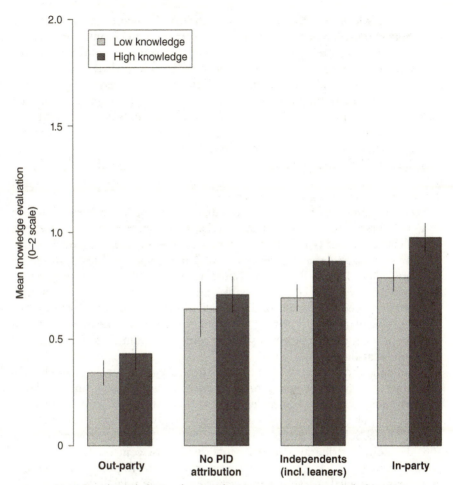

FIGURE 8.4 Mean knowledge evaluation, by in-party perception and objective knowledge level

Subjects who perceived that the poster was a co-partisan attributed higher levels of knowledge to the poster, regardless of her actual level of political knowledge. "No PID attribution" refers to all those evaluations in which subjects said they did not know the partisanship of the poster. Lines depict 95 percent confidence intervals.

The Role of Frequent Facebook Use

While Facebook usage frequency is not associated with more positive knowledge judgments for in-group members and more negative judgments for out-group members, engaging with political content is. Inadvertent exposure, intentional exposure, and political content generation are all associated with increased positive knowledge evaluations for co-partisans and increased negative knowledge evaluations for out-partisans. We will return to this question shortly to explore it further using data from the END Framework Survey.

These data also are conducive to evaluating a subject's confidence in her ability to correctly gauge a poster's level of political knowledge based on the content she posts. While some subjects indicated that they were just guessing, it appears that most respondents have moderate levels of confidence about their estimates of posters' knowledge levels. This confidence only is responsive to the type of content posted, not the perceived partisanship of the person who posted it. Subjects have higher confidence in their knowledge estimations for content they deem to definitely be about politics than about non-political content, but there are few differences in confidence levels between evaluations of those deemed to be in the in-group versus the out-group.

Facebook usage is very related to subjects' confidence in their ability to accurately assess posters' knowledge levels. As Figure 8.5 shows, the effects almost entirely are driven by the fact that Facebook usage makes Independents, partisan leaners, and weak partisans as confident in their estimates as are strong partisans. This effect is incredibly robust, no matter how Facebook usage is measured and whatever control variables are entered into a regression model. The more engaged someone is on Facebook – in every way from using the site on a more regular basis to posting more political content – the more confident they are in their ability to correctly gauge someone's political knowledge level based on what they post.

Combining these results with the results from the previous chapters, the role of engagement on Facebook can be more narrowly identified. Using Facebook regularly does not appear to make users more likely to recognize content as being about politics. There is mixed, although mostly supportive, evidence that frequent Facebook usage makes users more likely to attribute partisan identities and ideological attributions to the people who post content. Engaging with political content on Facebook, not usage alone, appears to polarize evaluations of posters' knowledge levels. However, there is unambiguous evidence that simply using Facebook regularly makes people more confident in their inference capabilities. It is not that people who use Facebook more frequently are necessarily more likely to attribute partisan identity, biased ideological beliefs, or low levels of political knowledge to individual members of the out-party. But they are more confident they are good at doing this, perhaps because of the practice they receive multiple times a day in doing so.

DOES CONTACT MATTER? JUDGING OUT-PARTISANS IN SOCIAL NETWORKS

In the study above, subjects had no other information about the person they were evaluating except for the content the anonymous individual posted on Facebook. This is not entirely unrealistic, as one of the features of the Facebook ecosystem is

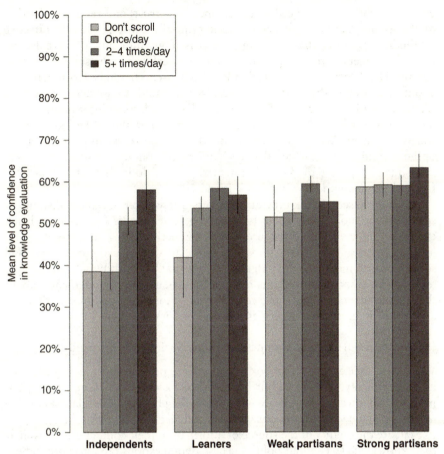

FIGURE 8.5 Mean level of confidence in accuracy of knowledge evaluation, by subjects' partisanship strength and News Feed scrolling frequency
Independents who scroll through the News Feed more regularly are as confident in their knowledge assessments as are strong partisans. Lines depict 95 percent confidence intervals.

the opportunity to observe the communication of people with whom a user does not have a personal relationship. However, it is more telling if these judgments of the out-group persist, even in the face of additional information about the individual that could mitigate harsh judgments of their political views.

Contact theory (Allport 1954; Pettigrew 1998) suggests that under the right set of conditions,[6] increased contact with members of our out-group can lead to

---

[6] Allport (1954) asserts that the four conditions for optimizing intergroup contact are equal group status within the situation, common goals, intergroup cooperation, and authority support.

greater acceptance, enhanced empathy, increased trust, and reduced prejudice of the group. Contact appears to work primarily through altering affective attitudes, suggesting that over time, increased warmth and positive feeling toward members of the out-group are more powerful than the stereotypes that remain. The theory thus predicts that Facebook users should be less judgmental about the people they know personally compared to unidentified others (Pettigrew and Tropp 2006). Because users have additional information about individuals to whom they are socially connected, they should be less likely to stereotype them. While interactions on the Facebook site do not meet the optimal conditions to foster the mechanisms of contact theory, presumably individuals may have the kinds of interactions that do in their offline, face-to-face encounters with their Facebook friends.

As we have seen in the previous chapters, the weaker and more distant the social tie, the more likely subjects were to perceive the tie's contacts as being extreme. However, Facebook users were perfectly willing to attribute ideological extremity to people with whom they had some social connection. Will social distance moderate the judgment people pass about the political competence on their social connections? Are people as negatively judgmental about their family members and close friends with whom they disagree as they are about the disagreeable weaker ties in their networks?

Judgments about Political Competence in the Social Network Study

We should expect that Facebook users will be pejorative about people they know personally, not just about hypothetical Facebook users in a study, but perhaps at a lower rate for those with whom they have a close relationship. To test this, I included two questions on the Social Network Battery asking subjects to evaluate the quality of the source of information their contact uses as well as their knowledge level about politics. These two questions tap into both dimensions of the relevant judgments about the information-processing capabilities of our fellow citizens. The question about knowledge level mirrors the judgment that subjects in the inference studies made about the anonymous posters. However, in this study, there was no option to mark "don't know" about how knowledgeable the social contact was. The question about source reliability assesses the dimension related to a person's use of credible sources to form her opinions. On this question, subjects were given an option to indicate that they did not know if the sources their contact used were reliable, an option availed in evaluations of approximately 20 percent of the dyadic relationships.

Nearly 60 percent of the contacts were deemed to be very or somewhat knowledgeable about politics. Remember, though, that most people named

Subsequent research has questioned whether these conditions are essential or simply facilitate interaction and has better specified the mechanism through which contact actually changes attitudes (Pettigrew 1998; Pettigrew *et al.* 2011).

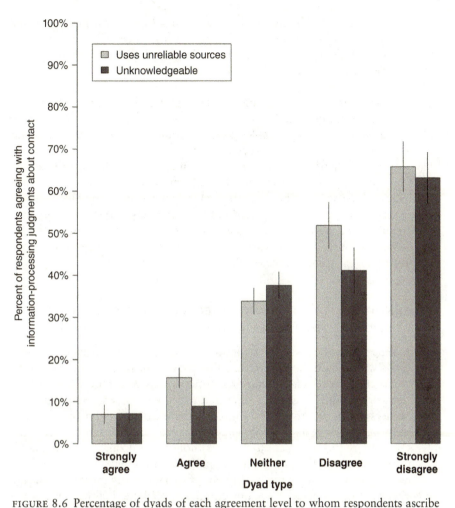

FIGURE 8.6 Percentage of dyads of each agreement level to whom respondents ascribe negative judgments about knowledge level and source reliability

Dark bars indicate the percentage of named contacts whom the subjects said were somewhat or very unknowledgeable. Lines depict 95 percent confidence intervals.

contacts with whom they agreed. When we separate out assessments by the level of agreement the respondent had with his or her contact, we see a strong correlation between agreement levels and evaluations of the contact's knowledge level and use of reliable sources (see Figure 8.6). Subjects report that those people they disagree with are more likely to use unreliable sources and are less politically knowledgeable.

Critically, it does not appear that people report that their close ties – their immediate family and friends – are any more knowledgeable than their more distant relatives or their weak ties. There are no significant differences in judgment of knowledge levels of disagreeable ties by relationship status and only a 10 percent, but statistically insignificant, difference when judging one's close family compared to other types of ties. People were equally critical of their disagreeable close ties and weak ties when it came to assessing whether they utilized reliable sources.

Social proximity, therefore, only partially mutes the effects of out-party judgment. While fewer than 10 percent of agreeable dyads are thought to be unknowledgeable or use unreliable sources, about half of disagreeable dyads are even when they are family and close friends. Facebook users may love and hold dear their close ties who disagree with them, but they still judge the way in which their contacts navigate the political information environment.

Subjects who used Facebook more regularly were not more likely to be judgmental of the political competence of their contacts. However, users who more regularly engaged with political content – via inadvertent exposure, intentional exposure, and generation of political content – were more likely to report that their disagreeable contacts used unreliable sources.

FROM INDIVIDUALS TO GROUPS: INFORMATION-PROCESSING STEREOTYPES OF THE PARTISAN OUT-GROUP

The evidence presented so far suggests that people are judgmental about individuals with whom they disagree, either hypothetical Facebook users who posted particular pieces of content, or the individuals who they know in their social networks. While it is concerning that Facebook users are so judgmental about others – whether they are evaluating them isolated from other bits of social information or in its presence – judgment is a fundamental part of social interaction. Were this judgment to occur without generalizing those judgments into stereotypes about the out-group, we might be less concerned.

However, consistent with the predictions of social identity theory, people *are* stereotyped about members of the out-group. On the large Political Discussion Survey fielded to over 3,000 subjects,[7] I asked respondents a set of questions about their stereotypes of the way that out-partisans process political information. In this study, I choose to focus on the evaluative and homogeneity dimensions[8] of stereotypes to ascertain the extent to which people thought

---

[7] Of the 3,310 respondents in the original survey, 2,349 reported that they had Facebook accounts. Any difference between Facebook users and non-Facebook users could be attributed to the selection factors that predispose people to create a Facebook account. As explored in Chapter 1, certain demographic factors are associated with increased usage of Facebook and those same factors – including race, age, and income – are associated with having a Facebook account. Party strength is also positively associated with having a Facebook account, but not with the intensity of usage of the site.

[8] Questions assessing stereotypes about the out-group could be formatted a number of ways, but Leyens *et al.* (1994) argue that no single measurement technique can capture the five aspects of

judgmental characterizations about how others form their opinions were wide-spread among members of the out-party.[9] Subjects were asked to estimate what proportion of the out-partisan group conformed to a list of six different statements about information processing, which were used to create a mean estimate of the proportion of the out-party that conforms to negative stereo-types. Subjects on this first survey had not been asked anything about Facebook at this point in the study except whether they had an account. It is, therefore, unlikely that they were in any way primed to be thinking about partisans on Facebook in particular.

A regression with this mean estimate as the dependent variable reveals that Facebook users are more stereotyped about the information processing of out-party voters than are non-Facebook users, even controlling for their partisan-ship, strength of partisanship, voter turn-out, political interest, age, race, income, and education. Holding all other variables at their means or modes, Facebook users report that 2.64% more of the out-party adhere to the stereo-types. The magnitude of the difference is not huge, but it is very statistically significant.

Focusing only on the 1,010 respondents who completed the END Frame-work Survey about Facebook usage, it also appears that increased Facebook *usage* is associated with higher levels of judgment about information process-ing. No matter what measure of engagement is used, this pattern holds. Using several different measures of content generation, the more politically engaged a person is on the site, the higher the proportion of out-party voters they think adhere to the stereotypes.

Even more interesting, users who are exposed to more political content on Facebook also are more stereotyped. Both measures of passive consumption – the percentage of times political content is seen when it is not sought and the count of types of material seen – are positively and significantly related to the information-processing stereotypes. Both measures of active consumption – the percentage of times political content is sought and the count of types of

---

stereotypes they consider to be essential: stereotypes must be descriptive; they must be evaluative; they must identify the homogeneity of members of the target group; they must identify the distinctiveness of the target group from other groups; and there must be consensus about the content of the stereotype. A researcher's decision of what measurement technique to use reflects her priorities about what aspects of the definition matter most.

[9] The format of the question was, "Think about [Democratic/Republican] voters. What percent of all [Democratic/Republican] voters in the United States are ... ?" Subjects then filled in a grid-style table to provide a sliding scale ranging from 0 to 100 for each of six statements: ideologic-ally driven; narrow-minded; well informed about politics; ignorant; don't think for themselves and just blindly accept what [conservative/liberal] media and politicians tell them; would change their opinions if they understood more about important policies. Descriptive analysis of the data revealed that the reverse-coded question ("well informed about politics") was not inversely correlated with the other questions, so that item was dropped. The remaining five items were averaged to yield a mean for the percentage of out-partisans who conform to the information-processing stereotypes.

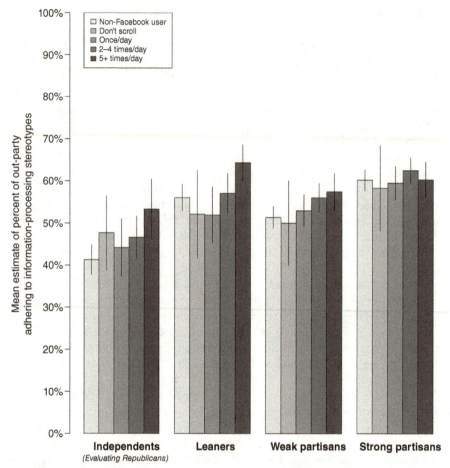

FIGURE 8.7 Mean estimate of percentage of out-party adhering to information-processing stereotype, by partisanship strength and Facebook usage
Lines depict 95 percent confidence intervals.

material clicked – also are positively and significantly related. The count variable of material clicked drops below significance only when political interest is added to the model.

Most critically, this relationship holds just with the measure of how frequently someone scrolls through her News Feed. As shown in Figure 8.7, strong partisans are judgmental, even if they are not Facebook users. But for those less attached to the parties, increased frequency of scrolling through the News Feed is associated with increased levels of stereotype attribution.

Using Facebook, and using Facebook more frequently, is associated with believing that a larger proportion of out-partisans arrive at their opinions while being uninformed and insufficiently critical of the information they encounter.

What people observe on their News Feeds leads them to the conclusion that a majority of the out-party fails in one of the most important tasks of citizenship.

DISTINGUISHING "US" AND DISTANCING "THEM"

The problem runs deeper than merely reflexive judgments of how other people navigate their information environments. SIT suggests that in addition to passing judgment on the domains most relevant to the factors that differentiate our in-group from our out-group, people actively construct narratives on a much wider set of dimensions. True affective polarization suggests that not only are we judgmental about our out-group, but we come to see a true distinction between "us" and "them" as people.

Social Categorization

Here, I focus on a very narrow domain of the possible range of differences, evaluating whether Facebook users are more likely to perceive a difference on the demographic and social composition of the two political parties.

On the same large survey where the information-processing stereotypes were assessed, subjects also were asked a battery of questions about their perception of partisan differences. The question was phrased, "Think about American voters. What percent of all voters in each party in the United States ..." Below the text appeared a grid-style table, where the row order was randomized. The purpose of this question was to assess the extent to which subjects saw the parties comprising distinct types of people, similar to the approach used in Ahler and Sood (2018), although the focus here was primarily on social characteristics, not demographic characteristics.[10]

The statements can be divided into two categories. The first set contains two statements related to demographics: the proportion of each party that comprises white men and the proportion that are immigrants or racial minorities. The second set refers to perceived social differences in sports and consumer preferences. This list is certainly incomplete and does not reflect the full extent of the kinds of non-political differences that might correlate with partisan orientation.

For the purpose of measuring social distinction, the differences reported between the compositions of the two parties are more meaningful than the raw estimates themselves. The absolute value between the respondent's perceptions of Democrats and Republicans captures the extent of the difference she perceives between what types of people identify with the parties. A value of zero

---

[10] There was overlap on one of the group characterizations. Ahler and Sood (2016) asked what proportion of Democrats are Black and found that, on average, respondents reported that 41.9 percent were. The survey fielded here asked what proportion of Democrats are immigrants or racial minorities and revealed a mean estimate of 45.89 percent. Given how little work there is in this area, comparable results suggest that the effects are not sample-specific.

TABLE 8.1 *Mean Absolute Difference in Social and Demographic Composition of Parties*

	Mean Absolute Difference
Are white men	20.04%
Are immigrants or racial minorities	25.83%
Watch NASCAR races	18.74%
Watch the FIFA World Cup	11.27%
Shop at Walmart	16.43%
Shop at Whole Foods	15.95%

Subjects were asked to assess what percentage of each party group was or behaved in the described way.

means that, in her mind, the two parties comprise equally people from a particular group or engage in a particular behavior at the same rate. The larger the absolute value of the difference, the greater the distinction between the types of people who associate with each party in the subject's mind. I construct two separate measures of the mean absolute difference: one for the demographic variables and one for the social variables (see Table 8.1).

Because the battery was used in the study that included non-Facebook users, we can assess both the effect of having a Facebook account as well as using the site more intensely (see Figure 8.8). Even controlling for the factors that could explain increased perception of differences between the parties – partisan strength, political interest, past voting behavior, and a variety of demographic variables – a simple linear regression demonstrates that Facebook users report higher average levels of difference for the social difference variable, although not the demographic difference variable.

While not a definitive test of causality, focusing just on Facebook users reveals that increased rates of political content generation on the site are associated with higher levels of the recognition of social differences between the parties. Among Facebook users, using the site more frequently does not appear to increase people's perceptions of social differences. Instead, it is the frequency which users *post* political content that does so. Thus, in addition to facilitating the perception that the out-group is more ideologically extreme and more consistent, it appears that, at least for users who report posting political content, Facebook also may contribute to users' perceptions that the two parties are composed of different types of people.

Can We Be Friends?

Facebook users recognize more social differences between partisans. But does using the site alter people's preferences for friendship formation? Social network scholars have long debated whether the political homophily in our social

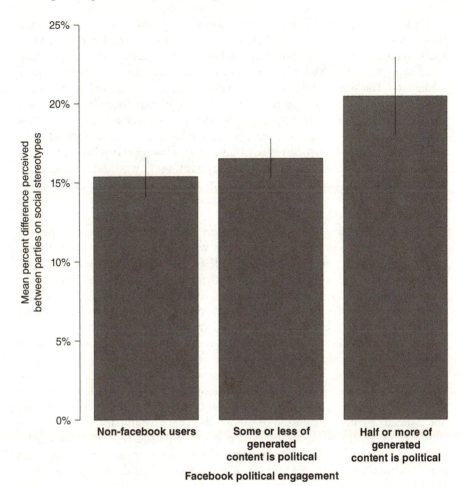

FIGURE 8.8 Mean absolute percentage difference in party composition based on social stereotypes, by level of Facebook political engagement
Lines depict 95 percent confidence intervals.

networks is a reflection of active choice based on political views or simply an unintended consequence of other active choices or structural forces that shape the types of people we tend to befriend. If Facebook users have become so judgmental of the out-partisans they know, are they more inclined toward friendships with people whose views are similar?

A collaborator and I fielded a study in the late fall of 2014 to assess how people communicated face-to-face about politics in the context of their holiday (Thanksgiving or Christmas) celebration. We were interested in studying whether exposure to disagreeable family at the holiday time altered the social evaluations people made of the out-party. We thus included an array of measures about people's inclination to form friendships across party lines.

We happened to include a single question about people's social media usage. Survey respondents were asked, "Did you post on Facebook, Twitter, or other social media about your [holiday] celebration this year?" The respondents could reply that they had, that they had not, or that they do not use a social media site. The way in which social media usage was measured in this study was admittedly blunt, as the purpose of the study was to collect data for a research project on a different topic. Whether a subject posted about their holiday celebration is a proxy measure for a user's general frequency of using the site, although there are obviously frequent Facebook users who did not post about their celebration and infrequent Facebook users who did. However, to the extent that this creates a noisy measurement of Facebook usage, it should be harder to detect effects between those who use Facebook regularly and those who do not.

Facebook users were more likely to report affinity with members of their in-party (see Figure 8.9). When asked, "To what degree do you enjoy having an average [in-party member] as a friend?" those who used Facebook more frequently indicated a higher level of enjoyment. Likewise, when asked, "To what degree are you and an average [in-party member] similar?" Facebook users indicated higher scores. These results persist in a regression model controlling for a user's partisan strength and demographics and seem to be unique to political party friendships compared to friendships based on other forms of affiliation such as a shared sports team.[11]

These findings suggest that Facebook users indicate stronger preferences for being friends with their co-partisans. Although this study cannot rule out the possibility of reverse causality, as shown in Chapter 1, political covariates are not associated with the decision to use Facebook frequently and the results are robust to the inclusion of measures of political sophistication. Facebook users perceive more social difference between the partisan groups, and it appears that Facebook usage may encourage users to build friendships with these like-minded others.

Severing Ties

Perceptions of the partisan groups likely matter for evaluations of the merits of the policies that each party pursues and the determination of what type of

---

[11] The survey asked the same friendship question about the extent to which the respondent would enjoy being friends with a fan of their same sports team, with a fan of their rival sports team, and with a member of the political out-party. Facebook use predicted an increased propensity for enjoying these other kinds of friendships as well, suggesting that perhaps Facebook users simply enjoy forming friendships. However, when the paired type of friendship is included in the regression model (sports team friend for same party friend, and rival sports team friend for opposition party friend, and vice versa) in order to control for this propensity toward friendship enjoyment, only the result for the relationship between Facebook use and same-party friendship remains significant.

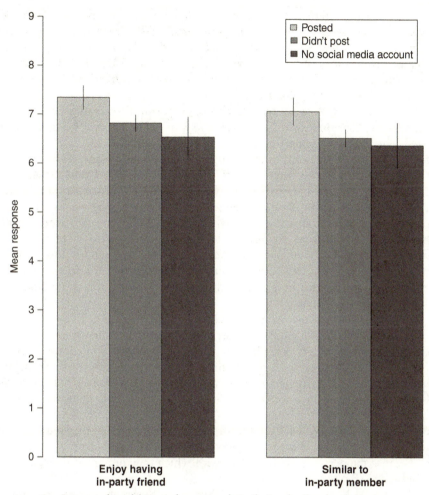

FIGURE 8.9 In-party friendship preference and similarity, by Facebook usage
Subjects answered questions about their perceived similarity to and enjoyment of a friendship with the average co-partisan on a scale of 1 to 9. Lines depict 95 percent confidence intervals.

people will benefit if a particular party is in power. People's preference for befriending like-minded others may incline them to privilege nurturing certain friendships over others. However, given the high rate of homophily in the social environment, these tendencies may have little actual effect on the construction of their social networks. People never have been particularly likely to encounter others who differ drastically and, therefore, they were not befriending these individuals at high rates before Facebook.

But neither have people's networks been totally homogeneous either, and schooling and workplaces have typically provided opportunities to get to know people who are different. This exposure to difference is amplified on Facebook. What if the consequence of the feelings of perceived similarity with the political in-group and perceived social difference with the out-group leads people to change their pattern of behavior within their networks? Do affective attitudes ever lead people to limit contact with or even sever ties of friendship with the people with whom they disagree?

There are multiple ways that Facebook users can distance themselves from their connections on the site. The most mild is to "hide" content from the News Feed. This removes the particular piece of content and gives the user the option to alter Facebook's algorithm so that they see less content from the person who has been hidden. It also is possible to completely "unfollow" the presence of content from a particular person, preventing it from appearing on the News Feed at all. Both of these actions reduce the amount of exposure to a friend's posted content without signaling anything to the friend. In other words, both hiding and unfollowing are private actions. Facebook also gives users the option to "unfriend" the users to whom they are connected. At the moment of "unfriending," no notification is sent to the friend, but the friend immediately loses access to the user's account. It is therefore possible to determine if someone has "unfriended" you.

The Pew Internet and American Life Project has tracked these behaviors over time, and the percentage of users who report that they have distanced themselves from others for political reasons has more than doubled since 2012.[12] In an October 2016 report, they find that 31 percent of social media users have altered settings to see fewer posts from someone in their feeds because of something related to politics, and 27 percent have blocked or unfriended someone for that reason. Combined, 39 percent of users report doing one of these behaviors. Of those users, 60 percent said they were driven to do so by offensive content the person posted, and 39 percent said they did so because the person posted content with which they disagreed (Duggan and Smith 2016).

The Social Network Study also allows us to assess these network-culling behaviors. Overall, the reported incidence of these behaviors is quite low. Only 13.64 percent of named contacts have been hidden, 3.92 percent unfollowed, and 3.36 percent unfriended, for a combined total of roughly one in five contacts (19.1 percent) that have been distanced in some way. Not surprisingly, Facebook users are much more likely to distance themselves from the contacts with whom they disagree. But even when comparing rates of social distancing for contacts deemed to use unreliable sources or who are not considered knowledgeable, people are more likely to distance themselves from those with whom they disagree. In fact, more people report distancing themselves from

---

[12] In 2012, 18 percent of users had blocked, unfriended, or hidden someone (Rainie and Smith 2012). By 2014, the estimate was up to 26 percent (Pew Research Center 2014b).

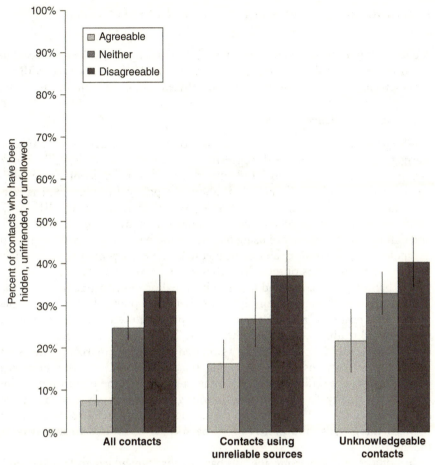

FIGURE 8.10 Social distancing behaviors, by dyad agreement level and political competence judgments
Lines depict 95 percent confidence intervals.

reliable or knowledgeable disagreeable contacts (27.18 percent) than report distancing from unreliable or unknowledgeable agreeable contacts (17.01 percent, difference significant at p < 0.01, results shown in online Appendix G).

This pattern holds in a regression framework, and contrary to previous findings, the traits of the Facebook user, such as her level of partisan strength or political interest, are not robustly associated with the likelihood of having hidden, unfollowed, or unfriended one of the top three most prolific political posters in one's network. Neither is the frequency of using Facebook, nor the strength of the social connection. Even the least active Facebook users appear willing to cull their networks of their family and friends in this way.

BUILDING THE CASE FOR THE POLARIZING EFFECTS OF USING FACEBOOK

We have now reached a point where we can holistically assess the evidence that has been presented linking engagement on the Facebook News Feed with the development of polarized attitudes toward citizens affiliated with the out-party.

Assessing the Evidence

Synthesizing together the results from the previous chapters, what have we learned? The END Framework suggests a causal mechanism. Using Facebook facilitates the processes of social identity theory that make people more judgmental and psychologically polarized about the political out-group. The testable implications of this theoretical framework are that, on average, Facebook users should be more psychologically polarized than are non-Facebook users, and that increased intensity of using the site should be associated with increased psychological polarization, all else held equal. Table 8.2 provides an overview of the results from tests of these hypotheses in Chapters 5 to 8.

In Chapter 5, we discovered that a substantial proportion of content on the News Feed is sufficiently informative to signal the political identities of the people who posted it, and the results in Chapter 6 showed that these political identities are readily inferred by other users. The salience of this identity then triggers the cascade of processes associated with the polarizing effects of intergroup interactions demonstrated in this chapter and the one previous: overestimating the differences between the in-group and the out-group; attributing homogeneity to members of the out-group; negatively evaluating the characteristics of the out-group; perceiving greater social differentiation between the groups; and preferring to be socially connected to members of the in-group.

In addition to unpacking the mechanism through which these judgments could be formed, we also have learned a considerable amount about how prevalent these evaluations are among Facebook users. Unlike cable news, which has potent effects (Levendusky 2013), but effects that appear to be strongest among the people least likely to be watching cable news (Arceneaux and Johnson 2013), the polarizing effects of Facebook usage are widespread. Users make political inferences and judge people even based on the non-political content they have posted. Weak partisans and independent leaners who use Facebook are less likely to negatively judge members of the out-party than are partisan users of Facebook, but they still do. Users judge their socially close, but politically disagreeable, social contacts at nearly identical rates as they do their weaker disagreeable ties.

What is the role of using Facebook on a regular basis on the process of recognition, inference, evaluation, and judgment? Facebook usage frequency does not consistently predict the extent to which someone can or will make

TABLE 8.2 *Overview of Relationship between Facebook Usage and Facets of Psychological Polarization*

	Strength of partisanship	Political interest	Facebook account	Frequency of site use	Scrolling through the News Feed	Inadvertent exposure	Intentional exposure	Content generation
Exposure (Chapter 5)								
Broadened definition of "political" content	(+)	(−)		(+)		(+)		(+)
Increased number of weak ties		+		+			−	−
Increased number of disagreeable ties		+		+			−	
Recognition (Chapter 6)								
Increased recognition and perceived bias in media	−	+				+		+
Willingness to make a partisan identity attribution	+			+	(+)	+	−	−
Confidence in partisan identity attribution	+	+		+	+	+	+	+
Inference (Chapter 7)								
Willingness to make ideological attribution	+	+		(+)	(+)	+	+	+
Confidence in ideological attribution	+	+		+	+	+	+	+
Identifying second-degree alters as extreme	+	+		+	+		+	
Agreement with policy extremity statements	+	+		+		+	+	+
Perceived ideological differences between parties *	+	+	+	+			−	+
"Liking" political content	+		+		+		+	
"Liking" content posted by co-partisans	+		+		+		+	+
Judgment (Chapter 8)								
Willingness to make knowledge attribution	+	+		+	+	+	+	+
Polarized knowledge evaluations	+	+				+	+	+
Confidence in knowledge attribution	+	+				+	+	+
Negative judgment of disagreeable social contacts	+	+		+	+	+	+	+
Information-processing stereotypes	+	+	+					
Partisan social differences	+	+	+					
In-party friendship and perceived similarity	+	+	+	(+)				(+)
Social distancing behavior				+				
*Decreased out-party feeling thermometer	+	+	+					+
*Increased in-party feeling thermometer	+	+	+					

Plus signs in the columns between Facebook usage behaviors and dependent variables indicate the presence of a statistically significant relationship, even controlling for partisanship strength, levels of political interest, and demographic variables (if available). Plus signs in parentheses indicate relationships that are significant in bivariate regressions, but are not robust to the inclusion of covariates. Blank cells indicate no significant relationship. Reports from the inference studies (attribution and confidence) are from the pooled studies.

* indicates results from ANES data presented in Chapter 8.

inferences about the political views of others, nor does it make them more accurate in doing so. It appears that people are capable of making these inferences and evaluations even if they do not regularly use the site, and the most partisan Americans are judgmental about their political out-group even in the absence of Facebook.

Yet Facebook users are more judgmental about the out-group than are non-Facebook users. So what precisely is it about frequent Facebook usage that impacts the way in which they learn about and judge people on their News Feeds? In limited cases, frequent Facebook use is associated with an increased propensity to identify or evaluate a member of the out-group, but the magnitude of the effects is not always large, nor are the effects always robust to the inclusion of control variables in the model. The most likely mechanism appears to be that regular Facebook use is associated with increasing people's exposure to the political out-group and bolstering their confidence in the inferences they make about people based on the content that they post to the site. Frequent Facebook users are much more confident in the accuracy of their estimates of partisanship, ideology, and knowledge level in the inference studies, but they were no more likely to *be* accurate.

Is it possible to move beyond demonstrating a possible mechanism to show that using Facebook actually causes people to become more psychologically polarized than they would have been absent engagement on the site?

Looking Backwards: Causality and the Missing Data Problem

Social scientists typically care about causality, not just association. Our first assessment should be to rule out reverse causality. Could the people most likely to be psychologically polarized select into using Facebook most intensely? Engagement in the political system – as measured by political knowledge, political interest, or voting – is not correlated with having a Facebook account. Likewise, these measures are not associated with more frequent use of the site. While partisanship strength is weakly associated with having a Facebook account in the END Framework Survey, no association exists in the ANES data. In neither sample is partisan strength associated with the frequency with which someone uses the site. It is, therefore, unlikely that a latent propensity toward polarized attitudes is causing people to join the Facebook site at significantly higher rates or use it more regularly.

The designs of the studies in the book do not cleanly demonstrate that using Facebook *causes* people to become more polarized. The inference studies demonstrate that people are capable and willing to ascribe identities, evaluate others' political views, and assess their levels of political knowledge. The social network battery suggests that people do make these kinds of evaluations of the most prolific political content generators in their networks. The survey data establish a correlation between Facebook usage and holding negative evaluations of the out-party. But none of these research designs actually demonstrates *change within an individual over time* as a result of using Facebook, nor the contribution of social media usage vis-à-vis other factors.

What would be the critical test to demonstrate this? A strong test would be a panel study tracking the same people over time to measure their social media behavior and their levels of psychological polarization. Absent that, cross-sectional surveys conducted at regular intervals could be analyzed to assess whether or not Facebook usage has become increasingly associated with psychological polarization. Unfortunately, the datasets from the years 2005 to 2015 on the major cross-sectional studies – such as the American National Election Study, the General Social Survey, the Cooperative Congressional Election Study, or Pew – did not ask the kinds of questions we would need to make these inferences. The questions measuring aspects of psychological polarization are inconsistent across time and survey sponsor and do not capture Americans' attitudes about each other, only about the abstract notions of the parties. Furthermore, while not all of these surveys include questions about social media, the surveys that do include social media questions only ask about explicitly political social media behaviors – such as following a candidate's page or encouraging other people to vote – not the general usage patterns that the evidence in this book suggests should be relevant for the majority of Facebook users.[13]

In the absence of data suitable to demonstrate that Facebook users have become more psychologically polarized over time than have non-Facebook users, we are left with evidence from a single snapshot of time on a nationally representative sample where we can assess Facebook usage compared to other factors that might contribute to polarization. The 2016 ANES study was the first to include a measure of whether respondents had a Facebook account, which can be coded as a very blunt measure of Facebook usage frequency.[14] Two other questions can be roughly mapped onto END Framework behaviors: a measure of political content generation[15] and a measure of political context exposure.[16] The survey also contains feeling thermometer scales for the political parties – a measure of affective polarization – as well as ideological placement questions for the parties – a measure of perceived polarization. These variables are theoretically correlated with the measures of psychological polarization used in this book.

---

[13] For a more thorough assessment of the historical data unavailability, see Appendix B.

[14] "Do you have a Facebook account that you have used in the past month, a Facebook account that you have not used in the past month, or do you not have a Facebook account?"

[15] "During the past 12 months, have you ever posted a message on Facebook or Twitter about a political issue or have you never done this in the past 12 months?"

[16] "During a typical week, how many days do you use social media such as Twitter or Facebook?" This question was asked in the section of the survey assessing news-seeking behavior. The distribution of the variable shows that only about half of users report they use Facebook every day, an estimate considerably lower than the figure estimated by Pew or found in the END Framework Survey. It therefore seems likely that given its placement in the survey, subjects interpreted the question to be assessing their use of the site for news, not their general usage.

In a regression controlling for a wide variety of demographic and political covariates – including a respondent's report of whether she watches television news programs[17] or uses the Internet to get news information – Facebook usage was strongly associated with both perceived and affective polarization. Furthermore, those users who had generated political content also reported much lower thermometer scores and greater ideological distance between the parties. There was no effect among Facebook users based on the number of days they used the site for news about the presidential campaign. Turning to examine in-party evaluations, the usage measure in the ANES data is not associated with a higher feeling thermometer rating for one's own party. Neither is the content exposure variable or the content generation variable. All results are shown in online Appendix G.

This pattern is generally consistent with the predictions of the END Framework. That Facebook users – and Facebook users who are most active – are more polarized about the out-group is a strong confirmation of the psychologically polarizing effects of using the site. Consistent with other work using the feeling thermometer measure, it appears that affective polarization may be driven more by increased negativity toward the out-party than increased positivity toward one's own party.

What explains the lack of effect of Facebook engagement for in-party thermometer ratings? Two explanations seem plausible. The first is simply poor operationalization of the key concepts. The independent and dependent variables in the ANES are measured in ways that do not fully capture END Framework behaviors and outcomes. For example, the Facebook-content-generation variable cannot differentiate people who simply reminded their friends and family to vote from those who post political diatribes on a regular basis. More importantly, the party feeling thermometer scores are proxy measures for attitudes toward our fellow citizens. One could speculate that evaluations of in-party voters and the in-party itself might diverge more than usual due to the idiosyncrasies of the 2016 election: historically unpopular presidential candidates, as well as infighting and scandal plaguing both parties.

The second explanation more deeply engages the predictions generated by the findings in this book. While the studies show more positive evaluations of in-party posters and in-party social contacts, the only study that tested and found direct effects on in-group identity was the Generation Experiment, where receiving social feedback on one's posted content bolstered partisan attachment and pride. It is possible that a simple measurement of content generation or content consumption may not capture the salient aspect of News Feed behavior that affects in-party evaluations: the extent to which a user's network reinforces her identity by positively engaging with political content. It is also possible that while posting content and receiving feedback on it may increase partisan pride

---

[17] Measured as "television talk shows, public affairs, or news analysis programs."

in an experimental setting, the effect in the real world is tempered by other factors. A likely candidate for moderating effects would be Facebook network composition, for example. Those users who have networks with higher rates of attitudinal congruity are the most likely to see identity-reinforcing content and are more likely to receive positive feedback when they post or see content.

The evidence for a relationship between increased Facebook usage and negative evaluations of the out-party are clear and robust. The effect of Facebook usage on in-group identity and positive evaluations of one's own group seem more contingent and is an area ripe for future research.

Looking Forward: Rigorously Studying Psychological Polarization in the Era of Social Media

This book shines a light on the process in which regular Facebook use is associated with increased judgment about the people whose political views differ from our own. The studies presented unpack some of the mechanisms and offer a variety of different types of evidence. However, to truly understand the process – both its antecedents and its consequences – will require sustained work extending the preliminary assessment presented here. There is much more to study about how regular and prolonged usage of the Facebook site leads to judgment of our fellow citizens. This book postulates some processes through which this could happen, showing that Facebook takes the social evaluative skills with which humans have been endowed and gives us much practice in using them. Pushing further on this idea is a task to which people with a variety of interests in intergroup interactions, social cognition, and political behavior could attend. In the sections below, I identify some fruitful areas for further exploration.

Conceptualizing and Measuring Social Media Behavior

We cannot correct the absence of past data about social media usage to explore the development of these phenomena over time, but we can be mindful of measuring the right kind of behavior moving forward. The studies in this book indicate that exposure to both explicitly and implicitly political content can lead to the cascading processes that result in psychological polarization. The Pew Internet and American Life Project regularly has asked about exposure to explicitly political content, and that question should be standardized and more widely adopted. Additionally, the findings of this book point to two other recommendations for changes to how we measure politically consequential social media usage.

Measuring Exposure to Implicitly Political Content
Before we can better measure exposure to implicitly political content, we must better conceptualize what it is. This will be difficult, given the complexity in

predicting what will become politically informative in the future. But a stronger typology built on more systematic study of what has been politically informative in the past is a good place to start.

Of course, capturing the nature of relatively fleeting exposure to this content also will be a challenge. The concept evokes Justice Potter Stewart's concurring opinion in *Jacobellis v. Ohio* regarding pornography, "I know it when I see it." Quantifying exposure to content that is so subject to individual interpretation will be difficult and, before we can assess levels of exposure in the organic environment of the News Feed, we likely need considerable work to better understand the mechanism of exposure so that we can measure its most pertinent facets. The nature of this kind of exposure lends itself to experimental studies in controlled designs. The remaining questions are plentiful. Is there a decay effect in which people are more judgmental immediately after using the site and encountering this kind of content? At what rate do the effects recede? Are there variations in the way in which people consume information? Focusing more on the nuances of the way in which people communicate may yield more leverage to understand why increased exposure to politically informative content on the News Feed leads to psychological polarization.

To get a sense of the generalizability of these findings, ideally we would develop measures of exposure to implicitly political material that could be included on observational studies and survey instruments. The studies in the book use a measure that focuses on frequency of exposure and leaves the characteristics of the content that users see up to their own definitions.[18] As with any measure, there are both strengths and weaknesses in this approach. Communications scholars have debated for decades the most valid ways to assess news exposure on television and in print. A similarly rigorous debate is needed for exposure to content on social media.

In practice, we may need to rely on the best proxy measure possible to capture inadvertent exposure to politically informative content. The findings in this book suggest that Facebook usage frequency is a better proxy than Facebook political content generation to capture the extent to which someone is exposed to implicitly political content. Yet political scientists have rarely included this construct in their studies.

Social Media Usage as a Proxy

For good and understandable reasons, political scientists always have focused on the political facets of behaviors. Generally speaking, we are not interested in how much TV one watches, but how many programs one watches with possible

---

[18] The exact question reads, "Think about all the times you access Facebook on your mobile device or computer and scroll through your News Feed: (a) What percent of those times do you scroll through the News Feed looking specifically for political news and information? (b) What percent of those times have you seen political news and information, even when you weren't seeking it out?"

exposure to political news. We care about discussion networks, but focus on measuring the discussions that are about politics. Consequently, we have largely focused on explicitly political behaviors on social media.

One key takeaway message of this book is that there are implications for political attitudes on even the non-political usage of Facebook. Therefore, if we cannot measure both general and political usage of the site, depending on the research question in which we are interested, we should prioritize measuring the intensity of social media usage itself, not just political activity on social media. This is a major conceptual shift. The vast majority of the political science work on social media has focused on the way in which people have used social networking sites for explicitly political behaviors. For most people, though, the effects of Facebook center on the content to which they are exposed, not the content which they themselves generate.

There are several justifications for this shift. First and foremost, in Chapter 5 we saw that there is wide variation in the content people consider to be about politics. Therefore, we should have serious concerns about simply asking them about their own generation of political content, a conclusion in line with Fitzgerald's (2013) cautions. Second, in Chapters 6 to 8, we saw that implicitly political content has the potential to initiate the cascade of evaluations that result in psychological polarization. If we only measure engagement with explicitly political content, we will systematically bias our measurement. In short, if the most prevalent and consequential effect of social media on our political attitudes is what we see, not what we post, then we should structure our measurement to focus on accurately capturing content exposure, not creation.

A person's overall frequency of usage on the site is a better proxy to capture her exposure to implicitly political material than is the amount of political content she says she posts. Generating content appears to be explained largely by the predictors that always have been of interest to political behavior scholars, such as strength of partisanship and interest in politics. But inadvertent exposure to political content appears to be a function of other factors. Without directly measuring the content that a person sees on Facebook – a task difficult even for the data scientists at Facebook themselves – the amount of time that a person spends on the site may be a useful proxy for the amount of political content they inadvertently encounter.

Finally, refining our measures of Facebook usage will become increasingly important if the penetration of the Facebook site continues to grow. As of August 2016, 79 percent of Americans with Internet access had a Facebook account. While a decade ago, it may have been analytically useful to try to understand the factors predicting who has a Facebook account, now there are likely systematic differences associated with the few Facebook "hold-outs." If the vast majority of Americans use Facebook, and the vast majority of those use Facebook on a daily basis, we should continue to refine our measures of usage intensity. If we think of the END model of communication as a dosage treatment, then we could imagine that the most intensive users of Facebook might be most susceptible to its effects.

Conceptualizing and Measuring Psychological Polarization

There has been a surge of interest in the study of psychological polarization since the phenomenon was articulated several years ago. The bundle of phenomena that I group together as psychological polarization – affective polarization, false polarization, and social sorting – are clearly interconnected, and we should continue to explore the origins and consequences of each construct, as well as the relationships between them. To do that, however, we need to reach some consensus about the way in which we describe and measure these various concepts.

The only survey question that has been asked over time is the feeling thermometer assessment of the candidates and parties. This question is straightforward and robust, and it has been shown to be associated with a range of outcomes. Continuing to ask this question will help us assess the changes in our affective attitudes over time. But only asking this question short-changes the field of study and is insufficient for the exploration of such a multi-faceted concept. Feeling thermometer assessments may serve as the fastest and broadest proxy measure, but we should push beyond that. Many scholars are working on the puzzle of how to capture these attitudes, and measurement pluralism has its benefits. But to ensure that different veins of research are able to be assessed against one another, it would be helpful for a wider variety of measures to be consistently used.

The Target of Our Wrath

Polarization has tainted our attitudes of our fellow citizens in addition to our attitudes about elites. Therefore, in addition to asking about elites or the abstract notion of the party, we also should measure attitudes toward each other. There is a good reason to think that Facebook use might not predict changes in feeling thermometer scales of political elites. The American public is quite negative about our political leaders, based on congressional approval ratings and measures of trust in government. It is quite possible that those attitudes already have reached a floor for large segments of the population, apart from any new information they might glean from using Facebook.

Rather, the hallmark of Facebook is interacting with our fellow citizens, and we should expect the greatest effects on judgments of the targets for which we learn the most on Facebook. Facebook sheds light on other members of the public, so we should shine our light there. A feeling thermometer measure may be appropriate if the correct target is identified, although the numeric rating itself does not tell us much about the content of the negative judgments we hold, which makes it difficult to theorize ways in which to remedy the problem.

Differential Stereotypes

I have focused on one facet of psychological polarization – judgments about how others navigate the information environment to arrive at their political opinions. Social identity theory suggests that many more attitudes may be affected. One obvious area for exploration relates to our judgments about the moral values of out-partisans. Graham *et al.* (2012) find that liberals and conservatives correctly recognize the direction of moral differences. Liberals are more concerned about compassion and fairness, while conservatives are more concerned with in-group loyalty, respect for authority and tradition, and purity. However, subjects exaggerate the ideological extremity of moral concerns for both the in-group and the out-group.

There also is growing evidence for stereotyped trait judgments. Eriksson and Funcke (2015) show that Democrats rate the average Democrat as being warmer than they rate themselves, and that Republicans rate the average Republican as being more competent than they rate themselves. We can model the study of partisan stereotyping on the voluminous body of work exploring the development of and remedy to stereotyping of other groups, such as women or ethnic minorities.

Partisan stereotyping might not be perfectly balanced. In other words, Democrats' unfounded stereotypes about Republicans may stem from different factors than those guiding Republicans' unfounded stereotypes about Democrats. Similarly, not all of the informative signaling indicating stereotypes will be understood the same way in different parts of the country. In urban areas, Democrats may typecast gun-lovers as Republicans, but in more rural areas this signal may not be informative. The content of these stereotypes matters because it may inform our measurement of the implicitly political content discussed above.

Behavioral Consequences

The studies in this book barely scratch the surface of the behavioral measures of social distancing that are the natural consequence of sustained affective dislike for our out-group. The social psychological research on the processes of stereotyping is broad and deep, but there is little work specifically examining the stereotyping of partisan groups. Iyengar and Westwood (2015) use an Implicit Association Test to demonstrate support for increased positive affect for one's in-group. They also show that people are very sensitive to partisan cues and will readily discriminate against out-partisans. While not focused on the content associated with the negative evaluations, in two papers using behavioral economics techniques to measure the concept, in-group favoritism has been shown to be present among partisan groups (Iyengar and Westwood 2015) and even between factions within the same party during a party primary (Dunham *et al.* 2016).

Ultimately, we care about how people's attitudes affect their behavior. If affective polarization is severe enough that we discriminate against our out-group, it is important to tackle the root of the problem in a way that will address its behavioral manifestations.

CONCLUSION

More important than the empirical findings presented in the second half of the book are the implications for how we should study the effects of social media on political polarization moving forward.

This chapter reveals the final stage of the cascading process initiated the moment someone identifies another user as a partisan based on the content she posts to Facebook. Identity recognition leads to political inferences, which leads to negative judgment about the way in which that user has formed her political opinions. Beyond judgments about the extent to which the out-party fails to perform the functions of citizenship, it appears that increased Facebook use also disposes people toward recognizing differences in the composition of each party and makes people more likely to say they prefer like-minded friends. As a consequence of identifying "us" as opposed to "them," they further the process that led to a social gulf in the first place, pruning their social networks to limit continued exposure to the out-group. Contrary to the findings of Barbera (2015) about the way in which Twitter users increase the heterogeneity of their networks, on a platform designed for social interaction with people we know personally, it appears that users draw the wagons closer together.

In the next chapter, we will take a step back from the study of Facebook to consider the effects of social media communication more broadly. What do the findings of this book portend for the larger dynamics at play in twenty-first-century American politics? What can we learn by studying past eras of polarized politics? Are the patterns of interaction uncovered here inevitable, or are there ways to alter the technology – or the way we use it – to reverse the trajectory of psychological polarization in which we find ourselves?

9

Erasing the Coast of Bohemia in the Era of Social Media

... the adjustment of man to his environment takes place through ... a representation of the environment which is in lesser or greater degree made by man himself ... the real environment is altogether too big, too complex, and too fleeting for direct acquaintance. We are not equipped to deal with so much subtlety, so much variety, so many permutations and combinations. And although we have to act in that environment, we have to reconstruct it on a simpler model before we can manage with it. To traverse the world men must have maps of the world. Their persistent difficulty is to secure maps on which their own need, or someone else's need, has not sketched in the coast of Bohemia.

Lippmann (1922)

Written nearly a century ago, Lippmann's seminal contribution to the field of political behavior continues to be relevant today. Lippmann was well aware that the pictures people form in their minds characterizing the world around them are distorted representations of reality. His book endeavored to understand the formation of *Public Opinion*,[1] which Lippmann defined as the aggregation of *public opinions*, or "the pictures inside the heads of these human beings, the pictures of themselves, of others, of their needs, purposes, and relationship," into the depictions that are acted upon in the realm of public affairs.

Lippmann noted that "the picture inside so often misleads men in their dealings with the world outside," a phenomenon he attributed to two factors. First, he pointed to constraints that limit people's access to facts:

... artificial censorships, the limitations of social contact, the comparatively meager time available in each day for paying attention to public affairs, the distortion arising because events have to be compressed into very short messages, the difficulty of making a small

---

[1] With capital letters.

vocabulary express a complicated world, and finally the fear of facing those facts which would seem to threaten the established routine of men's lives.

Second, he assessed

... how this trickle of messages from the outside is affected by the stored up images, the preconceptions, and prejudices which interpret, fill them out, and in their turn powerfully direct the play of our attention, and our vision itself ... how in the individual person the limited messages from outside, formed into a pattern of stereotypes, are identified with his own interests as he feels and conceives them.

Lippmann's proposed remedy to the systematic distortion of reality was a separate system of intelligence to balance that of the press, one based on a "system of analysis and record" so that a re-education based on objective expert reporting and information organization could help people reconcile their pseudo-environment with the actual environment. Would Lippmann argue that social media is better thought of as part of the problem or part of the solution? Does the way in which politically informative content gets created and circulated on social media bring our pseudo-environment better in line with objective reality or distort it further?

On the one hand, social media is certainly a separate "system of intelligence" and a system of "analysis and record," one with long historical roots in providing an additional, and at times alternate, commentary on the official public record (Standage 2013). Social media in the twenty-first century disrupts every facet of what Lippmann identifies as the limitations structuring how we glean insight into the world outside: censorship, privacy, contact, opportunity, time, attention, speed, words, and clarity. In many instances, these changes should make it easier to form accurate depictions by increasing the amount of information available and lowering the time and financial cost to access that information. Most notably, scholars studying the Arab Spring attribute the use of social media in oppressive regimes with making public opinion more transparent and accelerating the desire and potential for revolution. In these cases, social media provides complementary evidence to simplify and organize the complex world of which we are a part with greater fidelity than relying on mass media alone.

But, on the other hand, the END Framework of social media communication, in the context of twenty-first-century American politics, suggests distortion in the insights we gain into the political realities that we do not personally experience. People draw political inferences based on even the non-political content that their social contacts post, and the recognition of that identity begins a cascade of processes that result in strengthened attachment to one's own political party and heightened negative judgment of one's opponents. Facebook facilitates people in making biased evaluations of the beliefs of other people, and using the site gives people practice in mapping social and political identities in stereotyped ways.

The findings of this book suggest that social media is part of the problem. It further distorts the pictures in people's heads, metaphorically increasing the odds of them incorrectly assigning coast lines to land-locked countries. But could social media instead realize its potential as a "separate system of intelligence" to facilitate more accurate mappings? I am not optimistic. But neither am I convinced that the trajectory we are on is irreversible. Social media technology did not create the processes that lead to psychological polarization. Rather, it is the way in which people use technology that has amplified the cognitive and affective biases to which we already are predisposed. Altering the affordances of social media to counteract the way in which people misinterpret the information circulating within it, and thinking seriously about how to incentivize the kinds of political communication we normatively prefer, could change the course on which we find ourselves.

MAPPING AFFORDANCES TO OUTCOMES

The theorization in this book suggests that the confluence of affordances on Facebook facilitates a series of processes that result in psychological polarization. In Chapter 2, I assessed the evolving role of social media in our lives, hinting at the wide variety of social media platforms in use. I justified the decision to focus on Facebook because of the confluence of features on the site that foster interactions most conducive to polarization. To what extent are the patterns detected in this book generalizable to other social media platforms, those containing similar affordances, but in different configurations and with different emergent norms?

Table 9.1 presents a structure to think about future tests of the END Framework on other social media platforms or in other political contexts. It displays a subset of the suggested relationships between selected features of the Facebook platform and the processes of psychological polarization. Not every relationship has been tested explicitly, but the accumulation of the theory and evidence suggests the pattern depicted. This table is an oversimplification of the argument. The features do not operate in isolation, and no feature is directly responsible for an outcome without reinforcement from other features of the platform.

Testing the generalizability of the END Framework of communication requires thinking deeply about platform specificity. Why do people choose to use a particular social media platform? Who connects to whom and what does connection mean? What kinds of topics are considered appropriate for interaction, and as a result, what kind of content tends to circulate? What is the distribution of content production and how vital are third-party producers to the content that circulates? How do users provide social feedback to one another? In what ways are norms and engagement quantified and made visible?

Scholars interested in further testing the END Framework could capitalize on variation between the features on social media platforms to test some of the proposed mechanisms above. For example, Twitter shares with Facebook the same fusion of social and political content, has similarly stylized political content, provides for social feedback, and visually depicts quantification. But other comparisons reveal stark differences. Connection on Twitter is

TABLE 9.1 *Suggested Relationships between Social Media Affordances and Processes of Psychological Polarization*

	Platform design facilitates identity maintenance and inference	Fusion of social and political content	Stylized political content (inflammatory, humor, etc.)	Structural importance of opinion leaders	Structural importance of weak ties	Social feedback	Quantification
Users come to believe that their own political views are more popular than they are						X	X
Posting, or receiving social feedback, on political content reinforces a person's political identity	X		X			X	X
People recognize the political identities of others based on the political content they post	X	X	X	X		X	
People recognize the political identities of others based on the non-political content they post	X	X			X	X	
Users learn the political views of those they otherwise would not	X		X		X	X	
People attribute ideological extremity to out-group members based on the content they post			X	X	X		

Each column represents a feature on a social media platform, and each row represents one step of the process outlined in this book.

unidirectional, and users follow many others whom they do not know personally. While Twitter users certainly cultivate identities on the site, users' profiles are de-emphasized compared to the content they circulate. This particular configuration of features suggests that while people will come to recognize the political identities of other users, the relationships they have with those users may be less conducive to stereotyping processes. The structural role of personal weak ties on Facebook – and the resultant characterization of the outgroup based on friends of friends – and the emphasis on self-presentation – and the resultant possibility for identity reinforcement – suggest that psychological polarization may be more likely on Facebook than on Twitter. Conversely, unlike Facebook posts, tweets are public and anyone can comment in response. These features may incentivize especially vitriolic and ideological reactions, untethered by any moderating forces of social connection and in turn increasing the psychologically polarizing aspects of Twitter engagement.

Another way forward would be to manipulate the salience of particular features within a given platform to understand the relative contribution of an affordance, holding other aspects constant. For example, the results presented here suggest that the actual political composition of a person's network on Facebook should be related to the frequency with which users recognize out-party members and gain experience evaluating them. Users vary widely on the dimension of network heterogeneity, potentially leading to opportunities to refine our understanding of the consequence of exposure to disagreeable connections. Others might want to exploit variation in usage patterns across groups of users on the same platform to understand the influence of norms on behavior within a given structure of affordances. Younger people use social media in qualitatively different ways. Drawing connections between usage patterns and polarization outcomes could suggest which particular kind of interactions on the site are most influential.

Much more research is needed before we can fully understand the extent to which the processes described in this book are generalizable to other social media platforms in a broad range of political contexts. The best-case scenario is that the effects are contingent on a particular configuration of affordances or dependent on particular aspects of contemporary American political culture. If this is the case, then few other social media sites have the potential to be as psychologically polarizing as Facebook. The worst-case scenario is that individual affordances, even in isolation, tend to incentivize particular forms of behavior, suggesting that future social media platforms integrating those features in a wide range of political contexts could be susceptible to the processes described here.

ASSESSING THE TRADE-OFFS

However widespread or circumscribed the processes may ultimately turn out to be, the fact remains that psychological polarization is a pervasive problem in America. Using Facebook appears to exacerbate it. What are the potential adverse consequences of psychological polarization? How do those negative effects compare to the widely noted benefits of social media on political participation?

The Consequences of Psychological Polarization

Other forms of polarization, namely ideological divergence and consistency, have been blamed for many of the ills in our contemporary political climate. Polarized members of Congress are thought to prioritize party goals over policy goals, causing gridlock and reduced policy production. A gridlocked legislature cedes power to the executive branch, unable to fulfill its constitutionally pro-scribed role as a check and balance. Strongly partisan state legislatures are incentivized to gerrymander districts in ways that facilitate policy extremists winning election to Congress, furthering polarization. Citizens are less likely to communicate with their cross-partisan elected officials, reducing pressure on members of Congress to represent more than just their base.

Deeper consideration of the effect of psychological forms of polarization suggests equally dire consequences and a similarly pervasive reinforcing cycle. When we detach partisanship from issue preferences and rely more on its expressive and identity aspects, qualitatively different kinds of political behavior emerge. Expressive partisan identities are more likely to drive campaign involve-ment and to be associated with strong emotional reactions to political events, particularly the reaction of anger to the perception of threat (Huddy *et al.* 2015). While expressive partisanship is not necessarily undesirable to those looking to mobilize the public, as Huddy *et al.* (2015) write, "the advance of normative democratic ideals is less clear and far less certain if partisanship is more expres-sive than instrumental in nature" (p. 2). Partisans are hostile toward each other and harbor considerable anger and rivalry toward the out-party. The competi-tion of elections only serves to generate increased hostility and to raise the stakes of winning. Those partisans who most negatively judge the other party on moral traits support the use of any political tactics to win elections and they are the most likely to participate in campaigns and vote (Miller and Conover 2015).

Thinking about politics as a "team sport" also changes people's preferences for the behavior of their elected officials. Gallup's polling over time suggests that while people endorse the need for political leaders to compromise in the abstract, when asked about specific instances of compromise, they are much less supportive. For example, in March 2017, only 15 percent of Democrats wanted their congressional leaders to compromise with President Trump, even though 56 percent of Democrats had endorsed the principle of compromise six months earlier.[2] Pew notes that for partisans, "compromise" implies that their

---

[2] Frank Newport, "Democrats Say Their Leaders Should Not Compromise with Trump." Gallup (March 31, 2017).

party should get more of what they want when negotiating with the other party, not that both sides should sacrifice equally. This is most true among those partisans who rate the out-party group very coldly (Pew Research Center 2016a).

Not only does polarization reduce people's desire for compromise and thus their willingness to demand it of their elected officials, but it may make them less accepting of political outcomes. Experiments have shown that elite endorsements from the opposing party cause people to be less supportive of policy (Nicholson 2012). This appears to be the case for Supreme Court decisions as well (Nicholson and Hansford 2014). The framing that likely occurs for much of the content circulating on Facebook therefore could have the effect of further reducing acceptance of policy and court decisions with which a person disagrees. This extends beyond evaluations of any single policy to evaluations of the system as a whole. Hetherington and Rudolph (2015) argue that the concept of political trust itself has become polarized. Americans who identify with the party that controls the White House trust government, and those who identify with the party out of power do not. The concern is that those who distrust government are not willing to make policy sacrifices, suggesting the near impossibility of compromise on important issues.

Strong dislike of political opponents, paired with the attitude that only the in-party can be trusted to do what is right, lends itself to a reduction in the perceived legitimacy of our institutions. Pew found that 56 percent of registered voters who supported Donald Trump had little or no confidence that the presidential election would be open or fair. Perceptions of illegitimacy may beget further erosion of the system. Only 48 percent of Trump supporters thought that it was very important for the losers of elections to recognize the legitimacy of the winners in order to maintain a strong democracy. Along with this reduction in the perceived legitimacy of our institutions is a loss of respect for our political opponents. In the 2016 election, 58 percent of Clinton supporters said they would "have a hard time respecting someone who supports Donald Trump for president," as did 40 percent of Trump supporters with regard to Clinton's voters (Pew Research Center 2016b).

What is the forecast for a country whose citizenry perceives wide social differentiations between people affiliating with different political parties and is so entrenched in their beliefs that they have delegitimized their political opponents? Mason (2018) notes that a lack of cross-cutting social identities is associated with an increased risk of civil war. Heightened recognition of sorting due to political communication on social media may accelerate the problems she identifies. The consequence of perceiving the system as illegitimate, and losing respect for the political opposition, cuts to the core of the foundation on which liberal democracy is built. The situation in the United States is far from a violent clash between political groups. I am not suggesting that civil war is on the horizon or inevitable. But taken to its extreme, the trajectory we are on is deeply troublesome.

The Baby in the Bathwater

Given the dire picture painted above – anger, hostility, obstructionism, distrust, and de-legitimization – it would be easy to conclude that the deleterious effects of social media on our political system are so pervasive as to merit the technology's extinction. Certainly, that was the tone of many pundits in the aftermath of the 2016 presidential campaign, when writers across the political spectrum, from *The Federalist*[3] to the *New York Post*[4] to the *Washington Post*,[5] suggested that political interaction on Facebook should cease. However, those views are short-sighted. Situating the findings of this book in the bigger picture of what we know about the effects of social media on political attitudes and behavior suggests a much more complex story. Social media has brought about many benefits to the American political system that would be lost with the eradication of political communication.

There may be informational benefits of accessing political content on social media. Barbera convincingly shows that Twitter users have ideologically heterogeneous networks of friends and family and are presumably exposed to cross-cutting political messages. In a very careful study, he shows that ideological heterogeneity in a user's personal network subsequently leads to an increase in the ideological heterogeneity of the verified political elite and media accounts that a user follows.[6] Similarly, Facebook exposes people to information they might not otherwise encounter. The ability for friends to share and recommend news content may expose users to news they would not select on their own. Based on their study showing the power of personal recommendations over source cue to influence selective exposure, Messing and Westwood argue that:

The widespread sharing of news content (a) limits the extent to which individuals can simply ignore hard news altogether as when watching television (Prior 2003), (b) makes it less likely for individuals to fall victim to falsehoods intentionally reinforced by a single news source (Kull *et al.* 2003), and (c) suggests that attitudinal polarization should decrease as source diversity increases (Stroud 2010). Social media may not be a panacea for democracy's ills, but their technological affordances are a spot of hope in an otherwise dark media landscape ... Messing and Westwood (2014), pp. 17–18

Scholars who have looked for effects on political learning and knowledge argue that social media is uniquely suited to exert agenda-setting influence on users,

---

[3] Bethany Mandel, "Facebook Dead at 12, a Victim of 2016." *The Federalist* (February 1, 2017).

[4] Karol Markowicz, "You're Ruining Facebook (and Friendships) with Political Rants." *New York Post* (October 9, 2016).

[5] Caitlin Dewey, "The Most Compelling Reason to Never Talk Politics on Facebook." *Washington Post* (August 4, 2016).

[6] Barbera argues that this is evidence of political moderation, but this is predicated on the assumption that following a new account with a different ideological persuasion means a user has changed his or her underlying political views, a claim for which Barbera presents no direct evidence.

especially those users who are less politically interested (Feezell 2018). These effects may do more than raise the salience and importance of issues to users. Munger *et al.* (2015) find that exposure to more information from media does increase political knowledge on a set of key issues, although exposure to more information from politicians does not. Dishearteningly, though, there is some evidence that exposure to too much information may actually confuse people and lead to lower levels of knowledge.

Social media has affected much more than just our knowledge and attitudes. It also has profoundly shaped the behavior of actors in the political system. Facebook has altered how campaigns and candidates engage potential voters, reaching people who otherwise would not be contacted and groups that have historically been detached from the political system, such as young people. Although it is difficult to establish that social media engagement actually causes people to become more politically participatory, at minimum there is certainly much evidence of a positive feedback loop (Conroy *et al.* 2012; Valenzuela *et al.* 2012; Tang and Lee 2013; Gil de Zúñiga *et al.* 2014; Park 2015; Kim *et al.* 2016). Social media platforms also are conducive for interventions that nudge people to change their behavior. Studies show that Facebook is an effective tool for voter registration[7] and voter mobilization (Bond *et al.* 2012; Jones *et al.* 2017), and that Twitter can be, under certain conditions (Coppock *et al.* 2016).

A PATH FORWARD

What is the net effect of the integration of social media into our political environment? That is a hard question to answer and worthy of a book-length treatment itself. The positive aspects we attribute to social media – exposing people to more political information and expanding the opportunities people have for political engagement – are the very things that the END Framework suggests contribute directly to the polarizing effects of social media communication, given the configuration of affordances on the site. Are the benefits described above enough to counteract the adverse effects on psychological polarization I have chronicled in this book?

The optimal scenario would be to eliminate the need for considering such trade-offs by remedying the root of the polarization problem. Is it possible that we could reap the participatory and learning benefits of the technology without a concomitant increase in our polarized evaluations of our political out-group? Or is it inevitable that social media causes us to form negative attitudes about those who disagree with us?

---

[7] David Becker, "New State Data to Celebrate National Voter Registration Day." ElectionInnovation.org (September 28, 2016).

The consequences of END Framework communication are almost certainly context dependent. If America depolarized – if our political identities became less aligned with our social identities, if new cleavages formed that traversed party lines to create cross-cutting coalitions in Congress, and if electoral incentives changed to favor moderation over extremity – it is likely that the culture of our political communication would follow suit. Psychological polarization stems from and reinforces the recognition of two or more highly distinguishable socio-political identities. Take away that reality and the decline in identity salience should moderate the polarizing forces of the News Feed.

Others have thought long and hard about what kinds of institutional changes could effect this depolarization – from changes in our electoral rules, our methods of redistricting, to our approach to financing campaigns. Scholars of mass polarization have considered what cultural and societal factors might serve to reduce partisan antipathy, such as priming national identity (Levendusky 2018) or practices of self-affirmation (Mason 2018).

I leave the monumental task of addressing polarization writ large to others. Although polarization may not be here forever, it is here for the foreseeable future. I therefore address changes to political communication on social media, assuming the existence of polarization in the broader society. The framework presented in Table 9.1 is useful here as well, for identifying the features of the site that are most integral to the effects of END behaviors on psychological polarization, highlighting which affordances could be altered to have the largest effect on changing the trajectory of the political communication patterns on the site. Certain factors are unlikely to change and other factors are those, as a society, we should not want to change. But there is a path forward, examining changes to the affordances that could incentivize different communication patterns, which optimistically might disrupt the accompanying flow of recognition, inference, and judgment of our political out-group.

Intractable Factors

Is the solution to abandon Facebook? No. Even if Facebook ceases to control the largest share of the social media market, another platform will take its place. Humans' fundamental desire to connect with one another, facilitated by the power of the Internet, is unlikely to disappear. Technologies evolve and supplant older forms, but changes in our expectations about what kind of communication is possible rarely regress. Interaction on online social media is likely here for the long haul until it is complemented or displaced by the next technological shift. As Standage (2013) points out, it is actually the era of broadcast media in the twentieth century that is the anomaly in a long historical progression of media forms that fuse together objective information with social commentary. Denouncing social media as an ill to society clearly is not the answer.

Similarly, certain aspects of the Facebook platform are unlikely to change. For example, referring back to Table 9.1, even though the structural importance of weak ties facilitates various processes of polarization, this feature is such an integral part of Facebook that it would be difficult to alter it without eliminating the motivation that draws people to the site in the first place. Connecting users to the friends of their friends is in large part the point of Facebook. The company is likely to be resistant to any platform changes that would reduce the ability of or inducements for its users to connect and communicate with their weak ties.

Not only is technology durable, but so is human psychology. While awareness of the processes of polarization might encourage people to be more reflective in their communication, it will not stop the cognitive and affective biases to which humans are predisposed. Signal sending is so fundamental to the very purpose for which communication evolved that it seems absurd to suggest that we should attempt to stop recognizing identity on the basis of what and how others communicate. Social media has optimized a platform for social identity management, but in its absence we would still seek to learn about the people in our networks. Similarly, as long as there are cues in the broader environment that help people map social and political identities, people will continue to make inferences. Neither can we eliminate the forces of evolution that help us pass judgment in order to identify friends and distance enemies. The strategies designed to combat stereotyping more generally tend to build upon this framework instead of fighting its existence. It is unrealistic to expect people to change these ingrained dispositions without active alteration to the system that structures their behavior.

Any proposed remedy must take these realities into account. Humans are human, and social media – in some way, shape, or form – is here to stay.

Illiberal Solutions

Is the solution to stop communicating about politics on Facebook? It seems infeasible that Facebook could somehow prohibit political content from entering the News Feed ecosystem and highly unlikely that the company would consider it profitable to do so. But it could be possible for the norms on the site to shift sufficiently to discourage people from posting political content. As Pew has demonstrated, there is wide variation in the extent to which different social media sites are used for political communication, and Facebook has not always been the hub for political content that it is currently.

Even if this were possible, it is not a solution we should pursue. First, it would not solve the whole problem. Even non-political communication in a polarized environment is informative, potentially triggering the cascade of processes that lead to judgment of the out-group. More importantly, we should not want to abolish online political dialogue. To do so would be fiercely illiberal and anti-democratic. We should aim to foster political dialogue, not stifle it. One of the tenets of a democratic society is that people can and do express their political opinions on the issues of the day. The tools to reach a large audience, whether a literal soap box in a town square or a digital soapbox on Facebook, should be fiercely protected for people seeking to exercise their freedom of expression. As pernicious as the consequences are, suppressing political communication on Facebook would do more harm than good.

Incentivized Behavior: Altering Affordances to Foster Democratically Desirable Behavior

We cannot eradicate the human desire to harness available technology for social connection and we cannot alter human psychology to eliminate social inference. We choose not to suppress political interaction on social media, even if the technology facilitates processes leading to polarization. What is left? The set of possible solutions that remain involves changes to the technology that encourage desirable forms of interaction and discourage our natural inclinations toward biased inference and stereotyping.

I don't have a panacea to remedy the adverse consequences of the way in which we interact about politics on Facebook. But after thinking about this problem deeply for several years, it seems to me that we need to change *how* people use the site to alter the norms of acceptable and appropriate political communication. Norm changes rarely happen spontaneously, however. They require psychological nudges and changes to the incentive structure that motivate people to behave in different ways, gradually shifting what is considered to be socially desirable behavior.

How do we make false and inflammatory content unprofitable for news producers? How do we encourage opinion leaders to be more civil, nuanced, and moderate in their expressions of political opinion? How do we alter the norms about providing social feedback, so that only the highest quality information circulates on the site?

Because Facebook is not used primarily for political communication, any modifications aimed at reducing the polarizing dynamics on the site would need to apply to all interactions of a particular form. For example, it is possible to imagine that Facebook could make a change to the visual presentation of all content posted from third-party web pages, but it is difficult to imagine that they could easily make distinctions between political and non-political third-party content. In a similar way, they could change which reaction buttons are available for a whole class of content – say status updates – but it would be nearly impossible to target that change solely toward status updates expressing political opinions.[8]

---

[8] The necessity stems not from the technical limitations, but from the public relations ones. Machine learning techniques could be trained to recognize political content, probably in real time. But revelation of the fact that Facebook was making decisions about what counted as "political content" would likely provoke a significant backlash. Furthermore, as long as non-political information is politically informative, altering only explicitly political content might be insufficient.

Below, I offer five concrete recommendations about how changes in the affordances of the Facebook site could incentivize interactions that are more conducive to constructive political dialogue, reducing the potential for psychological polarization.

Increasing Information Quality

The evidence in Chapter 8 suggests that one of the ways in which Facebook users negatively evaluate each other is in the domain of the quality of the information they access. It is unlikely that we will return to an era when a handful of media sources are considered highly credible and trusted by most of the American public. But changes to the Facebook platform could weed out the worst offenders of information quality, even if people disagree about which sources are most credible.

Much of the information that gets injected into the News Feed ecosystem comes from third-party sources whose motivations for information production are not to foster knowledge and civilized debate. The issue of informational quality became most visible as part of the national conversation about "fake news" during the 2016 presidential election. Moving beyond concerns about echo-chambers on social media, many became alarmed by the apparently intentional spread of false information. Not only was this disinformation[9] circulating, but in several instances, went "viral" and inspired more user engagement than legitimate news stories. The fact that the Facebook News Feed algorithm likely helped fake news go viral made the situation especially worrisome.[10]

In the aftermath of the election, a number of technological solutions on a variety of different social media platforms were proposed to address the fake news problem.[11] To its credit, Facebook took several steps to address the problems of information quality on its site. It announced the formation of the Facebook Journalism Project, committing itself to "collaborating with news organizations to develop products, learning from journalists about ways we can be a better partner, and working with publishers and educators on how we can equip people with the knowledge they need to be informed readers in the digital age."[12]

---

[9] Misinformation – information that is unintentionally incorrect – is also a problem. However, it seems less pernicious.

[10] Timothy Lee, "Facebook Is Harming Our Democracy, and Mark Zuckerberg Needs to Do Something About It." Vox.com (November 10, 2016).

[11] For example, in December 2016, the *Washington Post* announced that they had created a tool – an Internet browser extension for Google Chrome and Firefox – that automatically provides more context when then President-elect Trump tweeted something that was factually inaccurate or misleading. The extension inserts a box below the tweet with additional information and links to the *Post*'s news articles that provide details and factual corrections.

[12] Fidji Simo, "Introducing: The Facebook Journalism Project." Facebook.

The company also announced that it would introduce features to directly combat fake news. In December 2016, it began a series of internal experiments to identify ways to stem the tide of the spread of fake news[13] and in March 2017 introduced a "disputed" tag on third-party content.[14] This feature will certainly evolve over time. It is not entirely clear how disputed sources are identified or recognized, but it appears that the company is working in conjunction with well-known and well-respected fact-checking organizations.[15] At least in part, the identification of fake news is relying on user report, a form of crowdsourcing.

This is an important step. The problem is that any adoption of a system to rate information quality will quickly become politicized.[16] The history of Facebook's management of the trending topics tool suggests that employing human fact-checkers will be controversial. If the tool is structured so that the site itself alerts a user that she is posting a disputed news story, Facebook opens itself to criticism of censorship and political bias. One alternate option that may be less politicized is to deploy social pressure to motivate people to use higher quality news sources. Presumably, Facebook data engineers compile user reports about fake news in their determination of credible sourcing. Further modification to the tool could harness the power of social sanction to change the norm of sharing fake news.

Users share fake news for two reasons: because they do not realize the news is fake or because they do not care if it is. Direct intervention from the site administration will address users in the first category, but may actually backfire for users in the second category, who are likely driven by partisan motivations to circulate certain kinds of information. To address these individuals, Facebook's disputed news tool could be modified so that the user who shared the fake content receives a notification that what they posted had been flagged as unreliable by (anonymous) people *in their social network*. Thus, for every Facebook friend who communicated positive reinforcement by liking the content or writing a supportive comment, the user could be reminded that there were others who were passing negative judgment. This essentially counters one social motivation – partisan-motivated reasoning – with another equally powerful social motivation – the desire to avoid derision by our peers.

---

[13] Mike Isaac, "Facebook Mounts Effort to Limit Tide of Fake News." *The New York Times* (December 15, 2016).

[14] "How Is Facebook Addressing False News through Third-Party Fact-Checkers?" available at www.facebook.com/help/733019746855448.

[15] "International Fact-Checking Network Fact-Checkers' Code of Principles," available at www .poynter.org/fact-checkers-code-of-principles.

[16] Hudson Hongo, "Facebook Finally Rolls Out 'Disputed News' Tag Everyone Will Dispute." Gizmodo (March 3, 2017).

Increasing Political Transparency

The results presented in Chapters 6 to 8 show that weak ties play a very important role in the polarizing effects of using Facebook. By connecting identities and personas to the "other side," we facilitate the link between judgments about out-group members we do not know well and negative evaluations of the out-group as a whole. Facebook did not teach us how to do this. It is not the News Feed that bequeathed us with the capacity to evaluate one another based on very little information. As the studies in the chapters show, people who use Facebook less frequently are just as willing to form impressions of one another as are people who use the site multiple times a day every day. What Facebook appears to do is give users much practice linking our inferences to judgments.

The question then is how to channel our skills at inference – which serve us well and are essential to many domains of our social lives – in a way that does not make us more judgmental about people based on their political views. At present, we generalize away from incomplete information to draw conclusions that only have a tenuous connection to reality. Scrolling through the News Feed makes "System 1" (Kahneman 2011) processing too easy because it provides the exact kind of information to us that undeservedly bolsters our confidence in our assessments.

Counterintuitively, one solution to the problem of biased inference on the News Feed may be to incentivize *more* disclosure and transparency of political attitudes. What if instead of hiding their political views, people regularly and clearly made the ambivalence of their political opinions (Zaller 1992; Lavine *et al.* 2012) known? What if – instead of just a single question on people's profiles to indicate their political ideology, reducing the complexity of their views to a single self-identified report on a scale – people fully identified the variability of their political views? Quizzes abound on the News Feed, including those that allow users to see where they fall on the political spectrum. What if it was possible – and socially encouraged – to share one's specific answers on that type of quiz with one's social network instead of just the political label the quiz computes based on our answers?

Ideally, this transparency would take much of the guesswork out of the process of inference. Yes, your uncle's friends seem to share his extreme views on immigration, but it turns out that they have a mix of views on other issues. They are not all alike and are not all extreme. They just happen to all share views on one particular policy domain.

Doing this would require an abrupt shift in the norms of political dialogue in the United States. The adage goes that we are supposed to keep our thoughts on religion and politics to ourselves in polite company. But this adage is misguided in an era in which everything we do is subject to politicization. If people cannot eat lunch at Chick-fil-A without sending a signal about their attitudes toward gay rights, or eat organic kale without implying they support Obamacare, we should not attempt to keep politics out of the conversation. Given the likely prevalence of implicitly political material in a polarized political context, most people are probably unaware of the extent of the political signals they send.

This also could turn the structural importance of weak ties into a strength in combating our misperceptions. Because the people we know not as well are more different from us, they could offer unprecedented opportunities to form more realistic perceptions. Being more transparent about what we actually believe might reduce the ambiguity of our explicit political expression and reduce the relative importance of implicitly political content. We know that Americans' political opinions are not as extreme as those of the politicians they elect. We know there are plenty of people who eat kale who think the corporate tax rate should be lowered, and who eat at Chick-fil-A and oppose "bathroom bills." Those Americans need to speak up. Making a concerted effort to create more links between our social identities and our political identities could reveal the heterogeneity of the linkages that are diverse and the homogeneity of linkages that are not. This should weaken poor-quality signals and strengthen those that are meaningful.

Incentivizing Moderation

One of the major dynamics contributing to polarization is the lack of temperate voices and the inability of moderates to communicate their non-extreme viewpoints. As the studies in Chapter 7 show, Facebook users have a tendency to impute too much extremity and consistency to the political views of other people. The voices of Americans in the middle of the political spectrum – whether as a result of ambivalence, dispassion, or even conflict avoidance – are not contributing to the conversation on the site. When they do, it is unclear that their fellow users recognize their more nuanced views.

What would it take to change the composition of people posting political content? Introducing moderators into comment threads has been shown to be effective (Stroud *et al.* 2015), but that model is not feasible given the structure of the News Feed. Moderates would need to be incentivized to speak up. To find the right enticement, we need to know why it is that they do not express their opinions more frequently. Research I have conducted with my colleague Taylor Carlson on political interaction in the face-to-face context suggests that the factors most likely to make people uncomfortable in political discussion are concern about their ability to defend their opinions, concern that others will judge them for their opinions, and concern that expressing disagreement will make other people uncomfortable. These factors all are rooted in social considerations: the desire to be perceived positively and to maintain relationships. It is no wonder that many people do not want to express their political views on social media.

How could we make the Facebook environment a context where people are not concerned about being attacked for their opinion, where people with more middle-of-the-road viewpoints feel comfortable speaking up? This issue actually speaks to a much larger problem in our polarized environment (Prior and

Stroud 2015). Moderate voices are not only quiet on Facebook; they appear to be silenced everywhere. It seems unlikely to change the dynamic on the Facebook site without changing this societal phenomenon simultaneously. Until such time, how could moderation be encouraged? A straightforward idea would be to alter the News Feed algorithm to lower relevancy scores for emotional political speech, ensuring that dispassionate communication is more likely to circulate on the site.

One promising finding in Chapter 7 is that the people most inclined to "like" content posted by out-party members are frequent Facebook users who are the least partisan and politically interested. Another solution might be to harness the judgment of these moderates by altering the News Feed algorithm to assign a higher relevancy score to political content that these users like. This might be especially beneficial because moderate users, who do not frequently post political content themselves, are more likely to be situated in cross-cutting networks. The social feedback they provide could thus serve as a bridge to help partisans communicate across the aisle.

Reasonable people might disagree about whether Facebook should alter its algorithm to favor particular kinds of communication, not just to maximize user engagement. Making these changes in secret would cause an outcry that a corporation was attempting to police the public sphere. How might Facebook avoid this inevitable backlash? If the company were to conspicuously and with great fanfare introduce the feature change on the premise that it wanted to make political communication more civil, its motives might help mitigate the inevitable criticism that it sparked.

It bodes well for this remedy that many people seem to desire a qualitatively different kind of interpersonal political communication on social media. Pew reports that people have largely negative attitudes about political discussions on Facebook. In a report released in advance of the 2016 election, they find that 37 percent of social media users are "worn out by how many political posts and discussions they see," and that 59 percent of social media users find disagreeable interactions on the site to be "stressful and frustrating." Most users – 84 percent – report that social media encourages people to say things about politics they would never say in person (Duggan and Smith 2016). In the months preceding the 2016 election, and in the wake of its surprising outcome, there was a spate of journalistic attention paid to how to "play nicely in the sand box" of social media. And perhaps most tellingly, there are a number of browser plug-ins for Facebook that are designed to silence the political outbursts on a person's Facebook feed.[17] Thus, if Facebook was to offer functionalities within the site itself to moderate the tone of conversation, they might encounter widespread support for the idea.

---

[17] Michael Ansaldo, "4 Ways to Block Political Posts on Facebook." *PCWorld* (February 20, 2017).

Reacting Deliberatively

Filtering out low quality information and incentivizing more and more moderate expressions of political opinion could begin to alter the dynamic on the News Feed. However, the problem runs deeper than the information that is provided by third-party organizations or the explicit statement of political views by opinion leaders. While the characteristics of the content set the tone for END Framework interaction, the driver of the process is the exchange of information with the addition of social feedback. It also is likely that this social feedback is more responsible for reinforcing users' political identities than the act of posting political content itself. Therefore, any comprehensive remedy must also address the social engagement process, not just the content that gets introduced into the Facebook ecosystem.

In Chapter 7, we saw that a disproportionate amount of the "liking" that occurs is in response to content posted by our in-party contacts, the people with whom we agree. This merely serves to reinforce social aspects of people's partisan identities. Relatedly, although not studied here, is the potential for the addition of the "angry" reaction button to add fuel to the fire of expressive partisanship. Anger seems especially poorly suited to constructive political dialogue, and allowing users to signal that response undermines the possibility for cool-headed interactions.

Facebook overhauled its "reaction" buttons in mid-2016, moving from the inclusion of a simple "like" button to a panel with options for more appropriate reactions to people's expressions. Building on this, Facebook could introduce a "deliberative reactions" feature that people could opt in to when they post something political.

Scholars of deliberation have spent years optimizing procedures to facilitate constructive political conversations. Their insights could be applied to the way in which people communicate about politics on Facebook. Subtle changes to the options Facebook users have to respond to one another might change the tenor of the conversation. One possibility might be to include options for more constructive feedback, such as a "this is interesting" button. Other changes might elicit more sustained engagement, such as a "clarify" button or a "tell me more" option. To encourage more cross-cutting dialogue, another option could be a "respectfully disagree" button or a "provide a validating source" button. The goal of these new reaction options would be to move political interaction away from the mentality of cheering on co-partisans and more into the realm of a sustained dialogue.

Eliminating Highly Visible Quantification

Enhancing the quality of political content and changing the norms about how we interact with it would create a qualitatively different information environment on Facebook. However, even these changes would probably not be enough to reverse the outcomes outlined in this book. The END Framework suggests that social inference is integral to the process of information exposure.

Increasing the civility of interactions, and reducing the presence of inflammatory content, would not change one of the fundamental dynamics that drive our perceptions of political reality: the quantification of opinion. The results in Chapter 7 suggest that these signals bolster in-group pride and identity and may lead to overestimation of the amount of support for particular views in the network.

There are two distinct facets of quantification: the extent to which a social media platform bases its algorithms on the popularity of information and the way in which users interpret quantified signals. Quantification is too vital for the operation of the News Feed algorithm to dismiss it entirely. There are hundreds, perhaps thousands, of pieces of content generated by the average user's network each day, and the site needs some systematic way to figure out what content is most likely to be relevant in order to keep the site engaging and profitable. The necessity of user-generated quantification for the back-end operation of Facebook will most likely be a permanent feature.

What if that quantification were made less visible to users, however? Removing quantification from such a prominent position on the News Feed, making it only visible by clicking on the post itself, could significantly limit its influence. Users could still react, comment, and share content, but they would not know if other people had done the same simply by scrolling through their feed. They would have to take the extra step of clicking on the content to see whether others had engaged. Similarly, news articles could include additional contextual information. The interpretation that 10,000 Facebook users have liked an article is quite different if users are reminded how many millions of people saw it on their News Feed and did not like it.

The upshot of reducing the visibility of quantification would be twofold. It could de-incentivize "expressive" reacting, where the point of engaging is not to directly communicate with the person who posted the content, but rather to publicly and symbolically show support for a political team. Second, it would break the cognitive link between the expression of an opinion and the perception of widespread support for it. The value of quantified signals pales in comparison to their pernicious effects in the way in which we process information. De-emphasizing these signals might reduce the appeal of posting information solely for the purposes of social feedback. Making this functionality less prominent also would mean that when we encounter cross-cutting information posted by one of our disagreeable social connections, we are not immediately reminded of the size of the out-group, which is likely threatening.

The downside would be that this change could lead to a decline in engagement. Users post content seeking validation from others. Allowing them to see that validation is important, but I suspect that it also is important for people to know that their friends see them receiving social validation. In other words, a Facebook user posts content not only to feel good about the fact that people liked the post, but also to feel good about the fact that other people saw that people liked the post. In the realm of politics, this is part of the problem.

But for the broader patterns of communication on the site, reducing quantification may have unintended consequences.

CONCLUSION

Academic study alone will not solve the problems chronicled in this book. Ivory tower solutions to pressing social issues entail remedies that must be carried out by others. The glimmer of optimism for solving the problem of psychological polarization on social media is that the people responsible for implementing alterations to the platforms – the social media companies themselves – may face incentives that motivate them toward meaningful change.

These companies seek to maximize revenue streams without alienating their users. They wield enormous power, but power entirely derived from the size and engagement of their user base. As a consequence, users can demand change through their engagement choices. Of course, this presents a classic collective action problem. As long as everyone coordinates on using a social media platform, an individual user has little incentive to defect and take a symbolic stand, no matter how frustrated she is with her experience on the site. But widespread abandonment of the site is not the only way for users to collectively signal their preferences. Facebook has been responsive in the past to feedback from its users and pressure from the media to improve the site's functionality.

Social media companies can no longer deny their responsibility in shaping the way in which news and political information are generated, disseminated, and consumed. Facebook has insisted repeatedly that it is a tech company, not a media company.[18] In the classic sense of the term, the company is correct. But as the lines between news production and news consumption blur, the distinction matters less and less, and their unconventional position in the media environment does not abdicate Facebook of its responsibility to facilitate civic dialogue.

Twenty-first-century corporate responsibility for social media companies demands a sense of obligation to improving the quality of the public sphere. Just as the institutions of American government are designed to channel human nature to act as a check upon itself, so too must those designing the social institutions of public political deliberation aim to bring out the better angels of our nature. A good start is intentional platform design that acknowledges the way in which humans, being human, will use the technology in undesirable ways in the political sphere. There is a role for business leaders and entrepreneurs to be mindful of the ways in which they can use their innovation in a capacity for good. Corporate leaders in the Gilded Age demonstrated their civic virtue with a legacy of constructing public spaces befitting the promise of a

---

[18] Giulia Segreti, "Facebook CEO Says Group Will Not Become a Media Company." Reuters (August 29, 2016).

nation on the rise. Tech leaders in the digital age should follow suit by developing online public spaces that inspire us to fulfill our duties as citizens.

It is not just the companies who have a responsibility to the public sphere. Improving the quality of our political communication also demands individual commitments to behavioral change. A complete solution will not be found simply by altering the technology. Ultimately, it is up to us to mold the public sphere the way we want it to be shaped by modeling the behavior we desire to see. It necessitates moderates to be willing to express their views and serve as bridges between groups of their friends who disagree with one another. It calls on opinion leaders to make responsible choices about what political content they choose to post. And it demands that all of us work to override the psychological processes that come so naturally in a polarized era.

Social media facilitates mechanisms that have long been at work in human interaction. Humans are wired for social inference and will do it in the presence or absence of technology. But we can recognize that we engage in these automatic processes and actively endeavor to counter them. Research on stereotype formation suggests that one of the most promising ways to dispel biases are encounters where people seek to understand the perspective of those who they are inclined to judge (Broockman and Kalla 2016). The affordances of social media, while susceptible to facilitating polarization, also seem ripe for encounters encouraging active perspective taking. If the effect of this technique is found to be durable and replicable, it may be a tractable way forward in thinking about how to overcome the polarizing processes to which we are all predisposed. Social media companies must address how people use technology to undermine our better instincts, but ultimately it is up to those of us who have integrated social media into our daily lives. We all have a responsibility to our fellow citizens to be mindful about the consequences of our political communication, to ensure that we are not leading others to secure maps on which we have sketched in the coast of Bohemia.

References

Abramowitz, Alan I. 2010. *The Disappearing Center: Engaged Citizens, Polarization, and American Democracy*. New Haven, CT: Yale University Press.
  2008. "Don't Blame Primary Voters for Polarization." *The Forum* 5(4) (online).
Abramowitz, Alan I. and Kyle L. Saunders. 2008. "Is Polarization a Myth?" *The Journal of Politics* 70(2): 542–555.
  2005. "Why Can't We All Just Get Along? The Reality of a Polarized America." *The Forum* 3(2) (online).
  1998. "Ideological Realignment in the US Electorate." *The Journal of Politics* 60(3): 634–652.
Abramowitz, Alan I. and Walter J. Stone. 2006. "The Bush Effect: Polarization, Turnout, and Activism in the 2004 Presidential Election." *Presidential Studies Quarterly* 36(2): 141–154.
Abrams, Samuel J. and Morris P. Fiorina. 2012. "'The Big Sort' That Wasn't: A Skeptical Reexamination." *PS: Political Science & Politics* 45(2): 203–210.
Ahler, Douglas J. 2014. "Self-Fulfilling Misperceptions of Public Polarization." *The Journal of Politics* 76(3): 607–620.
Ahler, Douglas J. and Gaurav Sood. 2018. "The Parties in Our Heads: Misperceptions about Party Composition and Their Consequences." *The Journal of Politics* (forthcoming).
Ahn, Toh-Kyeong, Robert Huckfeldt, and John Barry Ryan. 2014. *Experts, Activists, and Democratic Politics: Are Electorates Self-Educating?* Cambridge University Press.
  2010. "Communication, Influence, and Informational Asymmetries among Voters." *Political Psychology* 31(5): 763–787.
Allport, Gordon W. 1954. *The Nature of Prejudice*. Reading, MA: Addison-Wesley.
Ansaldo, Michael. 2017. "4 Ways to Block Political Posts on Facebook." *PCWorld* (February 20).
Anspach, Nicolas. 2017. "The New Personal Influence: How Our Facebook Friends Influence the News We Read." *Political Communication* 34(4): 590–606.
  2016. "The Facebook Effect: Political News in the Age of Social Media." PhD Dissertation. Temple University.

Arceneaux, Kevin and Martin Johnson. 2013. *Changing Minds or Changing Channels?: Partisan News in an Age of Choice*. University of Chicago Press.

Arceneaux, Kevin, Martin Johnson, and Chad Murphy. 2012. "Polarized Political Communication, Oppositional Media Hostility, and Selective Exposure." *The Journal of Politics* 74(1): 174–186.

Armas, Genaro C. 2004. "From NASCAR Dad to Soccer Mom, Campaigns Drawn to Political Labels." nwi.com (June 20), www.nwitimes.com/news/opinion/from-nascar-dad-to-soccer-mom-campaigns-drawn-to-political/article_d7c70776-5b70-5bb4-8e2d-286162f31545.html.

Bafumi, Joseph and Robert Y. Shapiro. 2009. "A New Partisan Voter." *The Journal of Politics* 71(1): 1–24.

Bakshy, Eytan, Solomon Messing, and Lada A. Adamic. 2015. "Exposure to Ideologically Diverse News and Opinion on Facebook." *Science* 348(6239): 1130–1132.

Barbera, Pablo. 2015. "Birds of the Same Feather Tweet Together. Bayesian Ideal Point Estimation Using Twitter Data." *Political Analysis* 23(1): 76–91.

Bareket-Bojmel, Liad, Simone Moran, and Golan Shahar. 2016. "Strategic Self-Presentation on Facebook: Personal Motives and Audience Response to Online Behavior." *Computers in Human Behavior* 55: 788–795.

Barnes, Robert. 2015. "Supreme Court Rules Gay Couples Nationwide Have a Right to Marry." *Washington Post* (June 26).

Baron, Naomi. 2008. *Always On: Language in an Online and Mobile World*. New York: Oxford University Press.

Baum, Matthew A. 2003. "Soft News and Political Knowledge: Evidence of Absence or Absence of Evidence?" *Political Communication* 20(2): 173–190.

Baum, Matthew A. and Samuel Kernell. 1999. "Has Cable Ended the Golden Age of Presidential Television?" *American Political Science Review* 93(1): 99–114.

Baumgartner, Jody. 2008. "American Youth and the Effects of Online Political Humor," in Jody C. Baumgartner and Jonathan S. Morris (eds.), *Laughing Matters: Humor and American Politics in the Media Age*. New York: Routledge.

Baumgartner, Jody and Jonathan S. Morris. 2006. "The Daily Show Effect: Candidate Evaluations, Efficacy, and American Youth." *American Politics Research* 34(3): 341–367.

Beam, Christopher. 2008. "One-Armed Vegetarian Live-In Boyfriends: The Quest for This Year's Sexy Swing Demographic." *Slate*, www.slate.com/articles/news_and_politics/politics/2008/07/onearmed_vegetarian_livein_boyfriends.html.

Becker, David. 2016. "New State Data to Celebrate National Voter Registration Day." ElectionInnovation.org (September 28).

Bennett, William J. 2012. "Republicans Lost the Culture War." CNN (November 14), www.cnn.com/2012/11/14/opinion/bennett-gop-election/.

Benton, Joshua. 2011. "'Like,' 'Share,' and 'Recommend': How the Warring Verbs of Social Media Will Influence the News' Future." NiemanLab (February 28).

Berelson, Bernard Reuben, Paul Felix Lazarsfeld, and William N. MacPhee. 1954. *Voting: A Study of Opinion Formation in a Presidential Campaign*. University of Chicago Press.

Berinsky, Adam J., Gregory A. Huber, and Gabriel S. Lenz. 2012. "Evaluating Online Labor Markets for Experimental Research: Amazon.com's Mechanical Turk." *Political Analysis* 20(3): 351–368.

Berlet, Chip and Frederick Clarkson. 2008. "Culture Wars, Evangelicals, and Political Power: Lessons from the 2008 Presidential Election." *The Public Eye Magazine*, www.publiceye.org/magazine/v23n4/culture_war_2008.html.

Bimber, Bruce. 2001. "Information and Political Engagement in America: The Search for Effects of Information Technology at the Individual Level." *Political Research Quarterly* 54(1): 53–67.

Bishop, Bill. 2008. *The Big Sort: Why the Clustering of Like-Minded America Is Tearing Us Apart*. New York: Houghton Mifflin Harcourt.

Bond, Jon R. and Richard Fleisher (eds.). 2000. *Polarized Politics: Congress and the President in the Partisan Era*. Washington, DC: CQ Press College.

Bond, Robert M., Christopher J. Fariss, Jason J. Jones, *et al.* 2012. "A 61-Million-Person Experiment in Social Influence and Political Mobilization." *Nature* 489(7415): 295–298.

Bond, Robert M., Jaime E. Settle, Christopher J. Fariss, *et al.* 2017. "Social Endorsement Cues and Political Participation." *Political Communication* 34(2): 261–281.

Bond, Robert M. and Solomon Messing. 2015. "Quantifying Social Media's Political Space: Estimating Ideology from Publicly Revealed Preferences on Facebook." *American Political Science Review* 109(1): 62–78.

Bourdieu, Pierre, Robert Castel, Dominique Schnapper, *et al.* 1965. *Un art moyen: essai sur les usages sociaux de la photographie*. Paris: Les éditions de Minuit.

Boyd, Danah. 2014. *It's Complicated: The Social Lives of Networked Teens*. New Haven, CT: Yale University Press.

Boyd, Danah and Nicole B. Ellison. 2007. "Social Network Sites: Definition, History, and Scholarship." *Journal of Computer-Mediated Communication* 13(1): 210–230.

Brashears, Matthew E. 2011. "Small Networks and High Isolation? A Reexamination of American Discussion Networks." *Social Networks* 33(4): 331–341.

Broockman, David and Joshua Kalla. 2016. "Durably Reducing Transphobia: A Field Experiment on Door-to-Door Canvassing." *Science* 352(6282): 220–224.

Broockman, David E. and Timothy J. Ryan. 2016. "Preaching to the Choir: Americans Prefer Communicating to Copartisan Elected Officials." *American Journal of Political Science* 60(4): 1093–1107.

Brown, Clifford E. 1982. "A False Consensus Bias in 1980 Presidential Preferences." *The Journal of Social Psychology* 118(1): 137–138.

Budak, Ceren, Sharad Goel, and Justin M. Rao. 2016. "Fair and Balanced? Quantifying Media Bias through Crowdsourced Content Analysis." *Public Opinion Quarterly* 80(S1): 250–271.

Bui, Quoctrung. 2016. "The Demographics Behind #InternsSoWhite." TheUpshot.com (July 22).

Bullock, John G., Alan S. Gerber, Seth J. Hill, and Gregory A. Huber. 2015. "Partisan Bias in Factual Beliefs about Politics." *Quarterly Journal of Political Science* 10(4): 519–578.

Busby, Ethan, Adam Howat, Jacob Rothschild, and Richard Shafranek. 2017. "Putting People into Boxes: The Correlates and Effects of Partisan and Racial Stereotypes." Prepared for the annual meeting of the Southern Political Science Association New Orleans, LA, January 12–14.

Butler, Daniel M. and Eleanor Neff Powell. 2014. "Understanding the Party Brand: Experimental Evidence on the Role of Valence." *Journal of Politics* 76(2): 492–505.

Campbell, Angus, Philip E. Converse, Warren E. Miller, and E. Donald Stokes. 1960. *The American Voter*. New York: Wiley.

Carlin, Ryan E. and Gregory J. Love. 2013. "The Politics of Interpersonal Trust and Reciprocity: An Experimental Approach." *Political Behavior* 35(1): 43–63.

Carlson, Taylor N. and Jaime E. Settle. 2016. "Political Chameleons: An Exploration of Conformity in Political Discussions." *Political Behavior* 38(4): 817–859.

Carmines, Edward G. and James A. Stimson. 1982. "Racial Issues and the Structure of Mass Belief Systems." *Journal of Politics* 44(1): 2–20.

Carney, Dana R., John T. Jost, Samuel D. Gosling, and Jeff Potter. 2008. "The Secret Lives of Liberals and Conservatives: Personality Profiles, Interaction Styles, and the Things They Leave Behind." *Political Psychology* 29(6): 807–840.

Carpenter, Christopher J. 2012. "Narcissism on Facebook: Self-Promotional and Anti-Social behavior." *Personality and Individual Differences* 52(4): 482–486.

Carter, Bill. 2012. "Republicans Like Golf, Democrats Prefer Cartoons, TV Research Suggests." *The New York Times* (October 11).

Chambers, John R., B. R. Schlenker, and B. Collisson. 2013. "Ideology and Prejudice: The Role of Value Conflicts." *Psychological Science* 24(2): 140–149.

Chambers, John R. and Darya Melnyk. 2006. "Why Do I Hate Thee? Conflict Misperceptions and Intergroup Mistrust." *Personality and Social Psychology Bulletin* 32(10): 1295–1311.

Chambers, John R., Robert S. Baron, and Mary L. Inman. 2006. "Misperceptions in Intergroup Conflict: Disagreeing about What We Disagree about." *Psychological Science* 17(1): 38–45.

Cherny, Andrei. 2013. "Forget Soccer Moms and NASCAR Dads, in 2016 It's about ALICE." HuffPost (October 29), www.huffingtonpost.com/andrei-cherny/forget-soccer-moms-and-na_b_4174225.html.

Chong, Dennis and James N. Druckman. 2007. "Framing Theory." *Annual Review of Political Science* 10(1): 103–126.

Clinton, Joshua, Simon Jackman, and Douglas Rivers. 2004. "The Statistical Analysis of Roll Call Data." *American Political Science Review* 98(2): 355–370.

Conover, Pamela Johnston, Donald D. Searing, and Ivor M. Crewe. 2002. "The Deliberative Potential of Political Discussion." *British Journal of Political Science* 32(1): 21–62.

Conover, Pamela Johnston and Stanley Feldman. 1981. "The Origins and Meaning of Liberal/Conservative Self-Identifications." *American Journal of Political Science* 25(4): 617–645.

Conroy, Meredith, Jessica T. Feezell, and Mario Guerrero. 2012. "Facebook and Political Engagement: A Study of Online Political Group Membership and Offline Political Engagement." *Computers in Human Behavior* 28(5): 1535–1546.

Constine, Josh. 2016. "How Facebook News Feed Works." TechCrunch (September 6).

Converse, Philip E. 1964. "The Nature of Belief Systems in Mass Publics," in D. E. Apter (ed.), *Ideology and Discontent*. London: Free Press of Glencoe.

Coppock, Alexander, Andrew Guess, and John Ternovski. 2016. "When Treatments Are Tweets: A Network Mobilization Experiment over Twitter." *Political Behavior* 38(1): 105–128.

Corneille, Olivier and Charles M. Judd. 1999. "Accentuation and Sensitization Effects in the Categorization of Multifaceted Stimuli." *Journal of Personality and Social Psychology* 77(5): 927–941.

Correll, J. and B. Park. 2005. "A Model of the Ingroup as a Social Resource." *Personality and Social Psychology Review* 9(4): 341–359.

Csikszentmihalyi, Mihaly. 1975. "Play and Intrinsic Rewards." *Journal of Humanistic Psychology* 15(3): 41–63.

Csikszentmihalyi, Mihaly and Reed Larson. 2014. "Validity and Reliability of the Experience-Sampling Method," in Mihaly Csikszentmihalyi, *Flow and the Foundations of Positive Psychology: The Collected Works of Mihaly Csikszentmihalyi*. Dordecht: Springer, pp. 35–54.

Darnton, Robert. 2011. *Poetry and the Police*. Harvard University Press.

Davis, Nicholas T. and Johanna L. Dunaway. 2016. "Party Polarization, Media Choice, and Mass Partisan-Ideological Sorting." *Public Opinion Quarterly* 80(S1): 272–297.

Davis, Richard, Christina Holtz Bacha, and Marion R. Just (eds.). 2016. *Twitter and Elections around the World: Campaigning in 140 Characters or Less*. New York: Routledge.

Dawes, Robyn M., David Singer, and Frank Lemons. 1972. "An Experimental Analysis of the Contrast Effect and Its Implications for Intergroup Communication and the Indirect Assessment of Attitude1." *Journal of Personality and Social Psychology* 21(3): 281–295.

De Castella, Tom. 2012. "Five Ways the Digital Camera Changed Us." BBC News (February 28).

Delli Carpini, Michael X. 2009. "Something's Going on Here, But We Don't Know What It Is: Measuring Citizens' Exposure to Politically Relevant Information in the New Media Environment," in Gary King, Kay L. Schlozman, and Norman Nie (eds.), *The Future of Political Science: 100 Perspectives*. New York: Routledge.

Delli Carpini, Michael X., Fay Lomax Cook, and Lawrence R. Jacobs. 2004. "Public Deliberation, Discursive Participation, and Citizen Engagement: A Review of the Empirical Literature." *Annual Review of Political Science* 7(1): 315–344.

Delli Carpini, Michael X. and Scott Keeter. 1997. *What Americans Know about Politics and Why It Matters*. New Haven, CT: Yale University Press.

Del Vicario, Michela, Alessandro Bessi, Fabiana Zollo, *et al*. 2016. "The Spreading of Misinformation Online." *Proceedings of the National Academy of Sciences* 113(3): 554–559.

Devine, Christopher J. 2015. "Ideological Social Identity: Psychological Attachment to Ideological In-Groups as a Political Phenomenon and a Behavioral Influence." *Political Behavior* 37(3): 509–535.

Dewey, Caitlin. 2016. "Facebook Has Repeatedly Trended Fake News Since Firing Its Human Editors." *Washington Post* (October 12).

2016. "The Most Compelling Reason to Never Talk Politics on Facebook." *Washington Post* (August 4).

2015. "More than 26 Million People Have Changed Their Facebook Picture to a Rainbow Flag. Here's Why That Matters." *Washington Post* (June 29), www.washingtonpost.com/news/the-intersect/wp/2015/06/29/more-than-26-million-people-have-changed-their-facebook-picture-to-a-rainbow-flag-heres-why-that-matters/.

Dickey, Megan Rose. 2013. "It's Hard to Believe How Drastic the Changes to Facebook Have Been over the Years." Business Insider, www.businessinsider.com/facebook-evolution-2013-3.

DiDonato, Theresa E., Johannes Ullrich, and Joachim I. Krueger. 2011. "Social Perception as Induction and Inference: An Integrative Model of Intergroup Differentiation, Ingroup Favoritism, and Differential Accuracy." *Journal of Personality and Social Psychology* 100(1): 66–83.

Doherty, David. 2013. "To Whom Do People Think Representatives Should Respond: Their District or the Country?" *Public Opinion Quarterly* 77(1): 237–255.

Dowling, Conor M. and Amber Wichowsky. 2015. "Attacks without Consequence? Candidates, Parties, Groups, and the Changing Face of Negative Advertising." *American Journal of Political Science* 59(1): 19–36.

Druckman, James N., Erik Peterson, and Rune Slothuus. 2013. "How Elite Partisan Polarization Affects Public Opinion Formation." *American Political Science Review* 107(1): 57–79.

Duggan, Maeve and Aaron Smith. 2016. "The Political Environment on Social Media." Pew Research Center Report, released October 25.

Dunbar, Robin. 2016. "Do Online Social Media Cut through the Constraints that Limit the Size of Offline Social Networks?" *Royal Society Open Science* 3(1): 150292.

1998. *Grooming, Gossip, and the Evolution of Language.* Harvard University Press.

Dunham, Yarrow, Antonio A. Arechar, and David G. Rand. 2016. "From Foe to Friend and Back Again: The Temporal Dynamics of Intra-Party Bias in the 2016 U.S. Presidential Election," https://papers.ssrn.com/sol3/papers.cfm?abstract_id=2846915.

The Economist. 2008. "Endless Culture War: Pastimes and Preachers May Matter as Much as Guns and Butter," www.economist.com/node/12321661.

Eliasoph, Nina. 1998. *Avoiding Politics: How Americans Produce Apathy in Everyday Life.* Cambridge University Press.

Ellemers, Naomi, Russell Spears, and Bertjan Doosje. 2002. "Self and Social Identity." *Annual Review of Psychology* 53(1): 161–186.

Ellis, Christopher and James A. Stimson. 2012. *Ideology in America.* Cambridge University Press.

Epstein, Reid J. 2014. "Liberals Eat Here. Conservatives Eat There." The Wall Street Journal Online, http://blogs.wsj.com/washwire/2014/05/02/liberals-eat-here-conservatives-eat-there/.

Eriksson, Kimmo and Alexander Funcke. 2015. "A Below-Average Effect with Respect to American Political Stereotypes on Warmth and Competence." *Political Psychology* 36(3): 341–350.

Esralew, S. and D. Young. 2012. "The Influence of Parodies on Mental Models: Exploring the Tina Fey–Sarah Palin Phenomenon." *Communication Quarterly* 60(3): 338–352.

Evans, Heather K. and Jennifer Hayes Clark. 2016. "'You Tweet Like a Girl!' How Female Candidates Campaign on Twitter." *American Politics Research* 44(2): 326–352.

Facebook Data Science Blog. 2014. "Politics and Culture on Facebook in the 2014 Midterm Elections." October 28, www.facebook.com/data/.

Facebook Press Team. 2014. "The Ice Bucket Challenge on Facebook." Facebook Newsroom, http://newsroom.fb.com/news/2014/08/the-ice-bucket-challenge-on-facebook/.

Feeney, Nolan. 2015. "Facebook's New Photo Filter Lets You Show Solidarity with Paris." *TIME,* http://time.com/4113171/paris-attacks-facebook-filter-french-flag-profile-picture/.

Feezell, Jessica T. 2018. "Agenda Setting through Social Media: The Importance of Incidental News Exposure and Social Filtering in the Digital Era." *Political Research Quarterly*, forthcoming.

Fields, James M. and Howard Schuman. 1976. "Public Beliefs about the Beliefs of the Public." *Public Opinion Quarterly* 40(4): 427–448.

Fiorina, Morris P. 2013. "America's Polarized Politics: Causes and Solutions." *Perspectives on Politics* 11(3): 852–859.

Fiorina, Morris P. and Samuel J. Abrams. 2008. "Political Polarization in the American Public." *Annual Review of Political Science* 11: 563–588.

Fiorina, Morris P., Samuel A. Abrams, and Jeremy C. Pope. 2008. "Polarization in the American Public: Misconceptions and Misreadings." *The Journal of Politics* 70(2): 556–560.

Fishkin, James S. and Robert C. Luskin. 2005. "Experimenting with a Democratic Ideal: Deliberative Polling and Public Opinion." *Acta Politica* 40(3): 284–298.

Fitzgerald, Jennifer. 2013. "What Does "Political" Mean to You?" *Political Behavior* 35(3): 453–479.

Flaxman, Seth, Sharad Goel, and Justin Rao. 2016. "Filter Bubbles, Echo Chambers, and Online News Consumption." *Public Opinion Quarterly* 80(S1): 298–320.

Gaines, Brian J., James H. Kuklinski, Paul J. Quirk, Buddy Peyton, and Jay Verkuilen. 2007. "Same Facts, Different Interpretations: Partisan Motivation and Opinion on Iraq." *Journal of Politics* 69(4): 957–974.

Gainous, Jason and Kevin Wagner. 2013. *Tweeting to Power: The Social Media Revolution in American Politics*. Oxford University Press.

Gardiner, Bryan. 2015. "You'll Be Outraged at How Easy It Was to Get You to Click on This Headline." *Wired* (December 18).

Garner, Andrew and Harvey Palmer. 2011. "Polarization and Issue Consistency over Time." *Political Behavior* 33(2): 225–246.

Garrett, R. Kelly. 2013. "Selective Exposure: New Methods and New Directions." *Communication Methods and Measures* 7(3–4): 247–256.

Garrett, R. Kelly, Dustin Carnahan, and Emily K. Lynch. 2013. "A Turn Toward Avoidance? Selective Exposure to Online Political Information, 2004–2008." *Political Behavior* 35(1): 113–134.

Garrett, R. Kelly, Shira Dvir Gvirsman, Benjamin K. Johnson, *et al.* 2014. "Implications of Pro- and Counterattitudinal Information Exposure for Affective Polarization." *Human Communication Research* 40(3): 309–332.

Gee, Laura K., Jason Jones, and Moira Burke. 2017. "Social Networks and Labor Markets: How Strong Ties Relate to Job Finding on Facebook's Social Network." *Journal of Labor Economics* 35(2): 485–518.

Gelman, Andrew. 2009. *Red State, Blue State, Rich State, Poor State: Why Americans Vote the Way They Do*. Princeton University Press.

Gentzkow, Matthew and Jesse M. Shapiro. 2011. "Ideological Segregation Online and Offline." *Quarterly Journal of Economics* 126(4): 1799–1839.

Gerber, Alan S., Gregory A. Huber, David Doherty, and Conor M. Dowling. 2012. "Disagreement and the Avoidance of Political Discussion: Aggregate Relationships and Differences across Personality Traits." *American Journal of Political Science* 56(4): 849–874.

Gerber, Alan S., Gregory A. Huber, David Doherty, *et al.* "Personality and Political Attitudes: Relationships across Issue Domains and Political Contexts." *American Political Science Review* 104(1): 111–133.

Gervais, Bryan T. 2015. "Incivility Online: Affective and Behavioral Reactions to Uncivil Political Posts in a Web-Based Experiment." *Journal of Information Technology & Politics* 12(2): 167–185.

Gibson, James J. 1977. "The Theory of Affordances," in R. Shaw and J. Bransford (eds.), *Perceiving, Acting, and Knowing: Toward an Ecological Psychology*. Hillsdale, NJ: Erlbaum, pp. 67–82.

Gift, Karen and Thomas Gift. 2015. "Does Politics Influence Hiring? Evidence from a Randomized Experiment." *Political Behavior* 37(3): 653–675.

Gil de Zúñiga, Homero, Logan Molyneux, and Pei Zheng. 2014. "Social Media, Political Expression, and Political Participation: Panel Analysis of Lagged and Concurrent Relationships." *Journal of Communication* 64(4): 612–634.

Gilens, Martin. 1999. *Why Americans Hate Welfare: Race, Media, and the Politics of Antipoverty Policy*. University of Chicago Press.

Gilovich, Thomas. 1990. "Differential Construal and the False Consensus Effect." *Journal of Personality and Social Psychology* 59(4): 623–634.

Gimpel, James G. and Iris S. Hui. 2015. "Seeking Politically Compatible Neighbors? The Role of Neighborhood Partisan Composition in Residential Sorting." *Political Geography* 48: 130–142.

Gladwell, Malcolm. 2010. "Small Change: Why the Revolution Will Not Be Tweeted." *The New Yorker* (October 4).

Glassman, Matthew E., Jacob R. Straus, and Colleen J. Shogan. 2013. "Social Networking and Constituent Communications: Members' Use of Twitter and Facebook During a Two-Month Period in the 112th Congress." Congressional Research Service report R43018.

Goethals, George R., Shelley Jean Allison, and Marnie Frost. 1979. "Perceptions of the Magnitude and Diversity of Social Support." *Journal of Experimental Social Psychology* 15(6): 570–581.

Goette, Lorenz, David Huffman, and Stephan Meier. 2012. "The Impact of Social Ties on Group Interactions: Evidence from Minimal Groups and Randomly Assigned Real Groups." *American Economic Journal: Microeconomics* 4(1): 101–115.

Goffman, Erving. 1959. *The Presentation of Self in Everyday Life*. Garden City, NY: Anchor.

Golbeck, Jennifer, Justin M. Grimes, and Anthony Rogers. 2010. "Twitter Use by the U.S. Congress." *Journal of the American Society for Information and Technology* 61(8): 1612–1621.

Gottfried, Jeffrey and Elisa Shearer. 2016. "News Use across Social Media Platforms 2016." Pew Research Report, released May 26.

Gottfried, Jeffrey, Michael Barthel, and Elisa Shearer. 2016. "Changing a Social Media Profile Picture is One Way to Express Support or Solidarity." Pew Research Center's Fact Tank Blog (March 28).

Graber, Doris A. and Gregory G. Holyk. 2011. "The News Industry," in Robert Shapiro and Lawrence Jacobs (eds.), *Oxford Handbook of American Public Opinion and the Media*. Oxford University Press.

Graham, Jesse, Brian A. Nosek, and Jonathan Haidt. 2012. "The Moral Stereotypes of Liberals and Conservatives: Exaggeration of Differences across the Political Spectrum." *PLoS ONE* 7(12): e50092.

Graham, Jesse, Jonathan Haidt, and Brian A. Nosek. 2009. "Liberals and Conservatives Rely on Different Sets of Moral Foundations." *Journal of Personality and Social Psychology* 96(5): 1029–1046.

Granberg, Donald. 1987. "Candidate Preference, Membership Group, and Estimates of Voting Behavior." *Social Cognition* 5(4): 323–335.

Granberg, Donald and Edward Brent. 1983. "When Prophecy Bends: The Preference–Expectation Link in US Presidential Elections, 1952–1980." *Journal of Personality and Social Psychology* 45(3): 477–491.

Green, Donald P., Bradley Palmquist, and Eric Schickler. 2002. *Partisan Hearts and Minds: Political Parties and the Social Identities of Voters*. New Haven, CT: Yale University Press.

Greene, Steven. 2002. "The Social-Psychological Measurement of Partisanship." *Political Behavior* 24(3): 171–197.

Greenwood, Shannon, Andrew Perrin, and Maeve Duggan. 2016. "Social Media Update 2016." Pew Research Center Report, released November 11.

Groeling, Tim. 2013. "Media Bias by the Numbers: Challenges and Opportunities in the Empirical Study of Partisan News." *Annual Review of Political Science* 16: 129–151.

Groseclose, Tim. 2011. *Left Turn: How Liberal Media Bias Distorts the American Mind*. New York: Macmillan.

Groseclose, Tim and Jeffrey Milyo. 2005. "A Measure of Media Bias." *The Quarterly Journal of Economics* 120(4): 1191–1237.

Gulati, Girish J. and Christine B. Williams. 2013. "Social Media and Campaign 2012: Developments and Trends for Facebook Adoption." *Social Science Computer Review* 31(5): 577–588.

Gye, Lisa. 2007. "Picture This: The Impact of Mobile Camera Phones on Personal Photographic Practices." *Continuum: Journal of Media & Cultural Studies* 21(2): 279–288.

Halpern, Daniel, Sebastián Valenzuela, and James E. Katz. 2016. "'Selfie-ists' or 'Narci-Selfiers'?: A Cross-Lagged Panel Analysis of Selfie Taking and Narcissism." *Personality and Individual Differences* 97: 98–101.

Hamilton, James T. 2004. *All the News that's Fit to Sell: How the Market Transforms Information into News*. Princeton University Press.

Hampton, Keith N. 2011. "Comparing Bonding and Bridging Ties for Democratic Engagement: Everyday Use of Communication Technologies within Social Networks for Civic and Civil Behaviors." *Information, Communication & Society* 14(4): 510–528.

Hampton, Keith N., Lauren Sessions Goulet, Cameron Marlow, and Lee Rainie. 2012. "Why Most Facebook Users Get More than They Give." Pew Research Center Report, released February 3.

Hampton, Keith N., Rainie, L., Lu, W., *et al.* 2014. "Social Media and the 'Spiral of Silence.'" Pew Research Center Report, released August 26.

Hayes, Andrew F., Carroll J. Glynn, and James Shanahan. 2005. "Willingness to Self-Censor: A Construct and Measurement Tool for Public Opinion Research." *International Journal of Public Opinion Research* 17(3): 298–323.

Heimlich, Russell. 2012. "Number of Americans Who Read Print Newspapers Continues Decline." Pew Research Center's Fact Tank Blog (October 11).

Herrera, Tim. 2014. "What Facebook Doesn't Show You." *Washington Post* (August 18).

Hersh, Eitan D. and Brian F. Schaffner. 2013. "Targeted Campaign Appeals and the Value of Ambiguity." *Journal of Politics* 75(2): 520–534.

Hetherington, Marc J. 2001. "Resurgent Mass Partisanship: The Role of Elite Polarization." *American Political Science Review* 95(3): 619–631.

Hetherington, Marc J. and Jonathan D. Weiler. 2009. "Threat and Authoritarianism: Polarization or Convergence," in *Authoritarianism and Polarization in American Politics*. Cambridge University Press, pp. 109–133.

2018. *Prius or Pickup?: How the Answers to Four Simple Questions Explain America's Great Divide*. Boston: Houghton Mifflin Harcourt.

Hetherington, Marc J., Meri T. Long, and Thomas J. Rudolph. 2016. "Revisiting the Myth." *Public Opinion Quarterly* 80(S1): 321–350.

Hetherington, Marc J. and Thomas J. Rudolph. 2015. *Why Washington Won't Work: Polarization, Political Trust, and the Governing Crisis*. University of Chicago Press.

Hibbing, Matthew V., Melinda Ritchie, and Mary R. Anderson. 2011. "Personality and Political Discussion." *Political Behavior* 33(4): 601–624.

Hogg, Michael A., Dominic Abrams, Sabine Otten, and Steve Hinkle. 2004. "The Social Identity Perspective Intergroup Relations, Self-Conception, and Small Groups." *Small Group Research* 35(3): 246–276.

Hongo, Hudson. 2017. "Facebook Finally Rolls Out 'Disputed News' Tag Everyone Will Dispute." Gizmodo (March 3).

Horwitz, S. Nechama and Lilach Nir. 2015. "How Politics-News Parallelism Invigorates Partisanship Strength." *International Political Science Review* 36(2): 153–167.

Huber, Gregory and Celia Paris. 2013. "Assessing the Programmatic Equivalence Assumption in Question Wording Experiments: Understanding Why Americans Like Assistance to the Poor More than Welfare." *Public Opinion Quarterly* 77(1): 385–397.

Huckfeldt, R. Robert. 1983. "Social Contexts, Social Networks, and Urban Neighborhoods: Environmental Constraints on Friendship Choice." *American Journal of Sociology* 89(3): 651–669.

Huckfeldt, Robert and Jeanette Morehouse Mendez. 2008. "Moths, Flames, and Political Engagement: Managing Disagreement within Communication Networks." *The Journal of Politics* 70(1): 83–96.

Huckfeldt, Robert and John Sprague. 1995. *Citizens, Politics, and Social Communication: Information and Influence in an Election Campaign*. New York: Cambridge University Press.

1992. "Political Parties and Electoral Mobilization: Political Structure, Social Structure, and the Party Canvass." *American Political Science Review* 86(1): 70–86.

Huckfeldt, Robert, P. Johnson, and John Sprague. 2004. *Political Disagreement: The Survival of Diverse Opinions within Communication Networks*. New York: Cambridge University Press.

Huddy, Leonie, Lilliana Mason, and Lene Aarøe. 2015. "Expressive Partisanship: Campaign Involvement, Political Emotion, and Partisan Identity." *American Political Science Review* 109(1): 1–17.

Hui, Iris. 2013. "Who Is Your Preferred Neighbor? Partisan Residential Preferences and Neighborhood Satisfaction." *American Politics Research* 41(6): 997–1021.

Hunter, James Davison. 1991. *Culture Wars: The Struggle to Define America*. New York: Basic Books.

Hutchinson, Andrew. 2016. "New comScore Traffic Report Underlines the Strength of Facebook, Rise of Snapchat." Social Media Today (March 31).

Ingram, Mathew. 2015. "TV Engagement Secrets from Twitter, Everyone's Favorite Second Screen." *Fortune* (September 21).

Isaac, Mike. 2016. "Facebook Mounts Effort to Limit Tide of Fake News." *The New York Times* (December 15).

Iyengar, Shanto, Gaurav Sood, and Yphtach Lelkes. 2012. "Affect, Not Ideology: A Social Identity Perspective on Polarization." *Public Opinion Quarterly* 76(3): 405–431.

Iyengar, Shanto and Kyu S. Hahn. 2009. "Red Media, Blue Media: Evidence of Ideological Selectivity in Media Use." *Journal of Communication* 59(1): 19–39.

Iyengar, Shanto and Sean J. Westwood. 2015. "Fear and Loathing across Party Lines: New Evidence on Group Polarization." *American Journal of Political Science* 59(3): 690–707.

Jacobs, Lawrence and Robert Y. Shapiro. 2011. "Informational Interdependence: Public Opinion and the Media in the New Communications Era," in Robert Shapiro and Lawrence Jacobs (eds.), *Oxford Handbook of American Public Opinion and the Media*. New York: Oxford University Press, pp. 3–21.

Jacobson, Gary C. 2006. "The Polls: Polarized Opinion in the States: Partisan Differences in Approval Ratings of Governors, Senators, and George W. Bush." *Presidential Studies Quarterly* 36(4): 732–757.

2004. "Explaining the Ideological Polarization of the Congressional Parties in the Postwar Era." *Legislative Studies Quarterly* 29(3): 474–475.

Jenkins, Henry. 2006. *Convergence Culture: Where Old and New Media Collide*. New York University Press.

Jennings, M. Kent and Vicki Zeitner. 2003. "Internet Use and Civic Engagement: A Longitudinal Analysis." *Public Opinion Quarterly* 67(3): 311–334.

Jetten, Jolanda, Russell Spears, and Tom Postmes. 2004. "Intergroup Distinctiveness and Differentiation: A Meta-Analytic Integration." *Journal of Personality and Social Psychology* 86(6): 862–879.

Jones, Edward E. and Daniel McGillis. 1976. "Correspondent Inferences and the Attribution Cube: A Comparative Reappraisal," in J. H. Harvey, W. Ickes, and R. F. Kidd (eds.), *New Directions in Attribution Research*. Hillsdale, NJ: Erlbaum, vol. 1, pp. 389–420.

Jones, Jason J., Jaime E. Settle, Robert M. Bond, *et al.* 2013. "Inferring Tie Strength from Online Directed Behavior." *PLoS ONE* 8(1): e52168.

Jones, Jason J., Robert M. Bond, Eytan Bakshy, *et al.* 2017. "Social Influence and Political Mobilization: Further Evidence from a Randomized Experiment in the 2012 U.S. Presidential Election." *PLoS ONE* 12(4): e0173851.

Jost, John T. 2006. "The End of the End of Ideology." *American Psychologist* 61(7): 651–670.

Jost, John T., Christopher M. Federico, and Jaime L. Napier. 2009. "Political Ideology: Its Structure, Functions, and Elective Affinities." *Annual Review of Psychology* 60(1): 307–337.

Jost, John T., Jack Glaser, Arie W. Kruglanski, and Frank J. Sulloway. 2003. "Exceptions that Prove the Rule – Using a Theory of Motivated Social Cognition to Account for Ideological Incongruities and Political Anomalies: Reply to Greenberg and Jonas (2003)." *Psychological Bulletin* 129(3): 383–393.

Judd, Charles M. and Joel T. Johnson. 1981. "Attitudes, Polarization, and Diagnosticity: Exploring the Effect of Affect." *Journal of Personality and Social Psychology* 41(1): 26–36.

Jungherr, Andreas. 2016. "Twitter Use in Election Campaigns: A Systematic Literature Review." *Journal of Information Technology & Politics* 13(1): 72–91.

Just, Marion R. 2011. "What's News: A View from the Twenty-First Century," in Robert Shapiro and Lawrence Jacobs (eds.), *Oxford Handbook of American Public Opinion and the Media*. New York: Oxford University Press, pp. 105–121.

Juster, F. Thomas, Hiromi Ono, and Frank P. Stafford. 2003. "An Assessment of Alternative Measures of Time Use." *Sociological Methodology* 33(1): 19–54.

Kahneman, Daniel. 2011. *Thinking, Fast and Slow*. New York: Macmillan.

Katz, Elihu. 1957. "The Two-Step Flow of Communication: An Up-to-Date Report on an Hypothesis." *Public Opinion Quarterly* 21(1): 61–78.

Katz, Elihu and F. Paul Lazarsfeld. 1955. *Personal Influence: The Part Played by People in the Flow of Mass Communication*. Glencoe, IL: The Free Press.

Katz, Josh. 2016. "'Duck Dynasty' vs. 'Modern Family': 50 Maps of the U.S. Cultural Divide." The Upshot in *The New York Times*, www.nytimes.com/interactive/2016/12/26/upshot/duck-dynasty-vs-modern-family-television-maps.html.

Kaye, Barbara K. and Thomas J. Johnson. 2004. "A Web for All Reasons: Uses and Gratifications of Internet Components for Political Information." *Telematics and Informatics* 21(3): 197–223.

Kennedy, Merrit. 2016. "More than 1 Million 'Check in' on Facebook to Support the Standing Rock Sioux." NPR (November 1).

Kenski, Kate and Natalie Jomini Stroud. 2006. "Connections between Internet Use and Political Efficacy, Knowledge, and Participation." *Journal of Broadcasting & Electronic Media* 50(2): 173–192.

Khan, R., K. Misra, and V. Singh. 2013. "Ideology and Brand Consumption." *Psychological Science* 24(3): 326–333.

Kim, Tonghoon, David J. Atkin, and Carolyn A. Lin. 2016. "The Influence of Social Networking Sites on Political Behavior: Modeling Political Involvement via Online and Offline Activity." *Journal of Broadcasting & Electronic Media* 60(1): 23–39.

Kimball, David C., Bryce Summary, and Eric C. Vorst. 2014. "Political Identity and Party Polarization in the American Electorate," in John C. Green, Daniel J. Coffey, and David B. Cohen (eds.), *The State of the Parties*, 7th edn. Boulder, CA: Rowman & Littlefield, pp. 37–54.

Klar, Samara and Yanna Krupnikov. 2016. *Independent Politics: How American Disdain for Parties Leads to Political Inaction*. New York: Cambridge University Press.

Klofstad, Casey A., Anand Edward Sokhey, and Scott D. McClurg. 2013. "Disagreeing about Disagreement: How Conflict in Social Networks Affects Political Behavior." *American Journal of Political Science* 57(1): 120–134.

Klofstad, Casey A., Rose Mcdermott, and Peter K. Hatemi. 2012. "Do Bedroom Eyes Wear Political Glasses? The Role of Politics in Human Mate Attraction." *Evolution and Human Behavior* 33(2): 100–108.

Klofstad, Casey A., S. D. McClurg, and M. Rolfe. 2009. "Measurement of Political Discussion Networks: A Comparison of Two 'Name Generator' Procedures." *Public Opinion Quarterly* 73(3): 462–483.

Knobloch-Westerwick, Silvia. 2012. "Selective Exposure and Reinforcement of Attitudes and Partisanship before a Presidential Election." *Journal of Communication* 62(4): 628–642.

Knobloch-Westerwick, Silvia and Steven B. Kleinman. 2012. "Preelection Selective Exposure: Confirmation Bias Versus Informational Utility." *Communication Research* 39(2): 170–193.

Koc, Mustafa and S. Gulyagci. 2013. "Facebook Addiction among Turkish College Students: The Role of Psychological Health, Demographic, and Usage Characteristics." *Cyberpsychology, Behavior, and Social Networking* 16(4): 279–284.

Koestner, Richard, Gaëtan F. Losier, Nicolay M. Worren, *et al.* 1995. "False Consensus Effects for the 1992 Canadian Referendum." *Canadian Journal of Behavioural Science / Revue Canadienne des Sciences du Comportement* 27(2): 214–225.

Kosinski, Michal, David Stillwell, and Thore Graepel. 2013. "Private Traits and Attributes Are Predictable from Digital Records of Human Behavior." *Proceedings of the National Academy of Sciences* 110(15): 5802–5805.

Kramer, Adam D. I., Jamie E. Guillory, and Jeffrey T. Hancock. 2014. "Experimental Evidence of Massive-Scale Emotional Contagion through Social Networks." *Proceedings of the National Academy of Sciences* 111(24): 8788–8790.

Kreiss, Daniel. 2016. "Seizing the Moment: The Presidential Campaigns' Use of Twitter During the 2012 Electoral Cycle." *New Media & Society* 18(8): 1473–1490.

Kriner, Douglas and Francis X. Shen. 2012. "How Citizens Respond to Combat Casualties: The Differential Impact of Local Casualties on Support for the War in Afghanistan." *Public Opinion Quarterly* 76(4): 761–770.

Krueger, J. and R. W. Clement. 1994. "The Truly False Consensus Effect: An Ineradicable and Egocentric Bias in Social Perception." *Journal of Personality and Social Psychology* 67(4): 596–610.

Kull, Steven, Clay Ramsay, and Evan Lewis. 2003. "Misperceptions, the Media, and the Iraq War." *Political Science Quarterly* 118(4): 569–598.

Kunda, Ziva. 1990. "The Case for Motivated Reasoning." *Psychological Bulletin* 108(3): 480–498.

Laband, David N., Ram Pandit, John P. Sophocleus, and Anne M. Laband. 2009. "Patriotism, Pigskins, and Politics: An Empirical Examination of Expressive Behavior and Voting." *Public Choice* 138(1): 97–108.

Lake, Ronald La Due and Robert Huckfeldt. 1998. "Social Capital, Social Networks, and Political Participation." *Political Psychology* 19(3): 567–584.

LaMarre, Heather L., Kristen D. Landreville, Dannagal Young, and Nathan Gilkerson. 2014. "Humor Works in Funny Ways: Examining Satirical Tone as a Key Determinant in Political Humor Message Processing." *Mass Communication and Society* 17(3): 400–423.

Lane, Robert E. 1955. "Voting: A Study of Opinion Formation in a Presidential Campaign. By Berelson Bernard R., Lazarsfeld Paul F., and McPhee William N. (Chicago: The University of Chicago Press. 1954. Pp. Ix, 395)." *American Political Science Review* 49(2): 529–531.

Lassen, David S. and Adam R. Brown. 2010. "Twitter: The Electoral Connection?" Paper prepared for presentation at the annual meeting of the Midwest Political Science Association, held in Chicago, Illinois, April 21–25.

Lawrence, Dallas. 2010. "How Political Activists Are Making the Most of Social Media." *Forbes*, www.forbes.com/2010/07/15/social-media-social-activism-face book-twitter-leadership-citizenship-burson.html.

Lavine, Howard G., Christopher D. Johnston, and Marco R. Steenbergen. 2012. *The Ambivalent Partisan: How Critical Loyalty Promotes Democracy*. Oxford University Press.

Lazarsfeld, Paul F., Bernard Berelson, and Hazel Gaudet. 1944. *The People's Choice: How the Voter Makes Up His Mind in a Presidential Election*. New York: Duell, Sloan and Pearce.

Lazer, David, Brian Rubineau, Carol Chetkovich, *et al*. 2010. "The Coevolution of Networks and Political Attitudes." *Political Communication* 27(3): 248–274.

Leasca, Stacey. 2016. "Here's Why People Are Changing Their Facebook Profile Photos to a Red Square." Elite Daily, http://elitedaily.com/news/facebook-profile-photo-red-square/1482528.

Lee, Eunsun, Yeo Jung Kim, and Jungsun Ahn. 2014. "How Do People Use Facebook Features to Manage Social Capital?" *Computers in Human Behavior* 36(C): 440–445.

Lee, Timothy. 2016. "Facebook Is Harming Our Democracy, and Mark Zuckerberg Needs to Do Something About It." Vox.com (November 10).

Lee-Won, Roselyn J., Leo Herzog, and Sung Gwan Park. 2015. "Hooked on Facebook: The Role of Social Anxiety and Need for Social Assurance in Problematic Use of Facebook." *Cyberpsychology, Behavior, and Social Networking* 18(10): 567–574.

Lelkes, Yphtach. 2016. "Mass Polarization: Manifestations and Measurements." *Public Opinion Quarterly* 80(S1): 392–410.

Lelkes, Yphtach, Gaurav Sood, and Shanto Iyengar. 2017. "The Hostile Audience: The Effect of Access to Broadband Internet on Partisan Affect." *American Journal of Political Science* 61(1): 5–20.

Lenhart, Amanda. 2015. "Teens, Social Media, and Technology Overview 2015." Pew Research Center, released on April 9.

Lerman, K., Yan, X., and Wu, X. Z. 2016. "The 'Majority Illusion' in Social Networks." *PLoS ONE* 11(2): e0147617.

Leroy, Car. 1968. "Editorial Cartoons Fail to Reach Many Viewers." *Journalism Quarterly* 45: 533–535.

Levendusky, Matthew S. 2018. "Americans, Not Partisans: Can Priming American National Identity Reduce Affective Polarization?" *Journal of Politics* 80(1): 59–70.
    2013. *How Partisan Media Polarize America*. University of Chicago Press.
    2010. "Clearer Cues, More Consistent Voters: A Benefit of Elite Polarization." *Political Behavior* 32(1): 111–131.
    2009. *The Partisan Sort: How Liberals Became Democrats and Conservatives Became Republicans*. University of Chicago Press.

Levendusky, Matthew S. and Neil Malhotra. 2016a. "(Mis)perceptions of Partisan Polarization in the American Public." *Public Opinion Quarterly* 80(S1): 378–391.
    2016b. "Does Media Coverage of Partisan Polarization Affect Political Attitudes?" *Political Communication* 33(2): 283–301.

Levitan, Lindsey C. and Brad Verhulst. 2016. "Conformity in Groups: The Effects of Others' Views on Expressed Attitudes and Attitude Change." *Political Behavior* 38(2): 277–315.

Leyens, Jacques-Philippe, Vincent Y. Yzerbyt, and Georges Schadron. 1994. *Stereotypes and Social Cognition*. London: Sage Publications.

Lind, Michael. 2016. "This Is What the Future of American Politics Looks Like." *Politico Magazine* (May 22), www.politico.com/magazine/story/2016/05/2016-election-realignment-partisan-political-party-policy-democrats-republicans-politics-213909.

Linville, Patricia W., Gregory W. Fischer, and Peter Salovey. 1989. "Perceived Distributions of the Characteristics of In-Group and Out-Group Members: Empirical Evidence and a Computer Simulation." *Journal of Personality and Social Psychology* 57(2): 165–188.

Lippmann, Walter. 1922. *Public Opinion*. New York: Macmillan.

Lombardini, John. 2013. "Civic Laughter: Aristotle and the Political Virtue of Humor." *Political Theory* 41(2): 203–230.

Ludeke, Steven G. and Colin G. Deyoung. 2014. "Differences in Negativity Bias Probably Underlie Variation in Attitudes toward Change Generally, Not Political Ideology Specifically." *Behavioral and Brain Sciences* 37(3): 319–320.

Lupu, Noam. 2015. "Party Polarization and Mass Partisanship: A Comparative Perspective." *Political Behavior* 37(2): 331–356.

2013. "Party Brands and Partisanship: Theory with Evidence from a Survey Experiment in Argentina." *American Journal of Political Science* 57(1): 49–64.

Makse, Todd and Anand E. Sokhey. 2014. "The Displaying of Yard Signs as a Form of Political Participation." *Political Behavior* 36(1): 189–213.

Mandel, Bethany. 2017. "Facebook Dead at 12, a Victim of 2016." *The Federalist* (February 1).

Manstead, Antony Stephen Reid. 1982. "Perceived Social Support for Opinions: A Test of the Magnitude and Diversity Hypotheses." *British Journal of Social Psychology* 21(1): 35–41.

Markowicz, Karol. 2016. "You're Ruining Facebook (and Friendships) with Political Rants." *New York Post* (October 9).

Marks, Gary and Norman Miller. 1987. "Ten Years of Research on the False-Consensus Effect: An Empirical and Theoretical Review." *Psychological Bulletin* 102(1): 72–90.

Marsden, Peter V. 1987. "Core Discussion Networks of Americans." *American Sociological Review* 52(1): 122–131.

Mason, Lilliana. 2018. *Uncivil Agreement: How Politics Became Our Identity*. University of Chicago Press.

2015. "'I Disrespectfully Agree': The Differential Effects of Partisan Sorting on Social and Issue Polarization." *American Journal of Political Science* 59(1): 128–145.

Mattes, Kyle and David P. Redlawsk. 2014. *The Positive Case for Negative Campaigning*. University of Chicago Press.

Mauri, Maurizio, Pietro Cipresso, Anna Balgera, *et al.* 2011. "Why Is Facebook So Successful? Psychophysiological Measures Describe a Core Flow State While Using Facebook." *Cyberpsychology, Behavior, and Social Networking* 14(12): 723–731.

McCarthy, Justin. 2014. "Trust in Mass Media Returns to All-Time Low." Gallup (September 17).

McCarty, Nolan, Keith T. Poole, and Howard Rosenthal. 2006. *Polarized America: The Dance of Ideology and Unequal Riches*. Cambridge, MA: MIT Press.

McClurg, Scott D. 2006. "Political Disagreement in Context: The Conditional Effect of Neighborhood Context, Disagreement and Political Talk on Electoral Participation." *Political Behavior* 28(4): 349–366.

McCrae, Robert R. 1996. "Social Consequences of Experiential Openness." *Psychological Bulletin* 120(3): 323–337.

McGerr, Michael E. 1986. *The Decline of Popular Politics*. New York: Oxford University Press.

McLeod, Jack M., Dietram A. Scheufele, and Patricia Moy. 1999. "Community, Communication, and Participation: The Role of Mass Media and Interpersonal Discussion in Local Political Participation." *Political Communication* 16(3): 315–336.

McPherson, Miller, Lynn Smith-Lovin, and James M. Cook. 2001. "Birds of a Feather: Homophily in Social Networks." *Annual Review of Sociology* 27(1): 415–444.

McPherson, Miller, Lynn Smith-Lovin, and Matthew E. Brashears. 2006. "Social Isolation in America: Changes in Core Discussion Networks over Two Decades." *American Sociological Review* 71(3): 353–375.

Meffert, Michael F., Sungeun Chung, Amber J. Joiner, *et al.* 2016. "The Effects of Negativity and Motivated Information Processing During a Political Campaign." *Journal of Communication* 56(1): 27–51.

Messing, Solomon. 2013. "Friends that Matter: How Social Transmission of Elite Discourse Shapes Political Knowledge, Attitudes, and Behavior." A dissertation submitted to the Department of Communication and the Committee on Graduate Studies of Stanford University in partial fulfillment of the requirements for the degree of doctor of philosophy.

Messing, Solomon and Sean J. Westwood. 2014. "Selective Exposure in the Age of Social Media: Endorsements Trump Partisan Source Affiliation When Selecting News Online." *Communication Research* 41(8): 1042–1063.

Meyrowitz, Joshua. 1986. *No Sense of Place: The Impact of Electronic Media on Social Behavior*. Oxford University Press.

Miller, P. R. and P. J. Conover. 2015. "Red and Blue States of Mind: Partisan Hostility and Voting in the United States." *Political Research Quarterly* 68(2): 225–239.

Milligan, Susan. 2016. "In 2016 the Culture War Favors the Democrats." U.S. News.

Mitchell, Amy, Jeffrey Gottfried, Jocelyn Kiley, and Katerina Eva Matsa. 2014. "Political Polarization & Media Habits." Pew Research Center, www.journalism.org/2014/10/21/political-polarization-media-habits/.

Mitchell, Amy, Mark Jurkowitz, Jodi Enda, and Kenny Olmstead. 2013. "How Americans Get TV News at Home." Pew Research Center, report released October 11.

Mondak, Jeffery J. 2010. *Personality and the Foundations of Political Behavior*. Cambridge University Press.

Mondak, Jeffery J. and Karen D. Halperin. 2008. "A Framework for the Study of Personality and Political Behaviour." *British Journal of Political Science* 38(2): 335–362.

Mondak, Jeffery J., Matthew V. Hibbing, Damarys Canache, *et al.* 2010. "Personality and Civic Engagement: An Integrative Framework for the Study of Trait Effects on Political Behavior." *American Political Science Review* 104(1): 85–110.

Moreton, Bethany. 2009. *To Serve God and Wal-Mart*. Cambridge, MA: Harvard University Press.

Morrison, Kimberly Rios and Jörg Matthes. 2011. "Socially Motivated Projection: Need to Belong Increases Perceived Opinion Consensus on Important Issues." *European Journal of Social Psychology* 41(6): 707–719.

Mullen, Brian, Jennifer L. Atkins, Debbie S. Champion, *et al.* 1985. "The False Consensus Effect: A Meta-Analysis of 115 Hypothesis Tests." *Journal of Experimental Social Psychology* 21(3): 262–283.

Mullinix, Kevin J., Thomas J. Leeper, James N. Druckman, and Jeremy Freese. 2015. "The Generalizability of Survey Experiments." *Journal of Experimental Political Science* 2(2): 109–138.

Mummolo, Jonathan. 2016. "News from the Other Side: How Topic Relevance Limits the Prevalence of Partisan Selective Exposure." *The Journal of Politics* 78(3): 763–773.

Munger, Kevin, Patrick Egan, Jonathan Nagler, and Joshua Tucker. 2015. "Political Knowledge and Misinformation in the Era of Social Media: Evidence from the 2015 U.K. Election." Paper presented at the APSA Annual Meeting.

Mutz, Diana C. 2008. "Is Deliberative Democracy a Falsifiable Theory?" *Annual Review of Political Science* 11(1): 521–538.

2006a. "How the Mass Media Divide Us," in Pietro S. Nivola and David W. Brady (eds.), *Red and Blue Nation?: Consequences and Correction of America's Polarized Politics*. Baltimore, MD: Brookings Institution Press, vol. 2.

2006b. *Hearing the Other Side: Deliberative Versus Participatory Democracy*. Cambridge University Press.

2002. "The Consequences of Cross-Cutting Networks for Political Participation." *American Journal of Political Science* 46(4): 838–855.

1998. *Impersonal Influence: How Perceptions of Mass Collectives Affect Political Attitudes*. Cambridge University Press.

Newman, M. L., J. W. Pennebaker, D. S. Berry, and J. M. Richards. 2003. "Lying Words: Predicting Deception from Linguistic Style." *Personality and Social Psychology Bulletin* 29: 665–675.

Newport, Frank. 2017. "Democrats Say Their Leaders Should Not Compromise with Trump." Gallup (March 31).

Nicholson, Stephen P. 2012. "Polarizing Cues." *American Journal of Political Science* 56(1): 52–66.

Nicholson, Stephen P., Chelsea M. Coe, and Anna V. Song. 2016. "The Politics of Beauty: The Effects of Partisan Bias on Physical Attractiveness." *Political Behavior* 38(4): 883–898.

Nicholson, Stephen P. and Thomas G. Hansford. 2014. "Partisans in Robes: Party Cues and Public Acceptance of Supreme Court Decisions." *American Journal of Political Science* 58(3): 620–636.

Nisbett, Richard E. and Eugene Borgida. 1975. "Attribution and the Psychology of Prediction." *Journal of Personality and Social Psychology* 32(5): 932.

Noelle-Neumann, Elisabeth. 1974. "The Spiral of Silence: A Theory of Public Opinion." *Journal of Communication* 24(2): 43–51.

Norman, Donald A. 1999. "Affordance, Conventions, and Design." *Interactions* 6(3): 38–43.

Norris, Pippa. 2001. *Digital Divide: Civic Engagement, Information Poverty, and the Internet Worldwide*. Cambridge University Press.

Nyhan, Brendan. 2010. "Why the 'Death Panel' Myth Wouldn't Die: Misinformation in the Health Care Reform Debate." *The Forum* 8(1): 1–5.

2012. "Does the US Media Have a Liberal Bias?" *Perspectives on Politics* 10(3): 767–771.

Nyhan, Brendan and Jason Reifler. 2010. "When Corrections Fail: The Persistence of Political Misperceptions." *Political Behavior* 32(2): 303–330.

Oliver, J. Eric, Thomas Wood, and Alexandra Bass. 2016. "Liberellas Versus Konservatives: Social Status, Ideology, and Birth Names in the United States." *Political Behavior* 38(1): 55–81.

Olson, Parmy. 2013. "The Evolution of Facebook." *Forbes*, www.forbes.com/pictures/edee45edklh/the-evolution-of-facebook-4/#da8boea456dc.

O'Neil, Cathy. 2016. *Weapons of Math Destruction: How Big Data Increases Inequality and Threatens Democracy*. New York: Crown Publishing Group.

Oremus, Will. 2016. "Who Controls Your Facebook Feed?" *Slate*, www.slate.com/articles/technology/cover_story/2016/01/how_facebook_s_news_feed_algorithm_works.html.

O'Shea, Heather. 2016. "New Research: TV Viewers Who Engage on Twitter Have Higher Rates of Ad Recall." Twitter (March 18).

Padgett, Jeremy. 2014. "Predictors of National Broadcast and Cable Television News Coverage of the Members of the US House of Representatives." Doctoral dissertation, Manship School of Mass Communication, Louisiana State University, Baton Rouge, LA.

Park, Bernadette and Charles M. Judd. 1990. "Measures and Models of Perceived Group Variability." *Journal of Personality and Social Psychology* 59(2): 173–191.

Park, Bernadette and Myron Rothbart. 1982. "Perception of Out-Group Homogeneity and Levels of Social Categorization: Memory for the Subordinate Attributes of In-Group and Out-Group Members." *Journal of Personality and Social Psychology* 42(6): 1051–1068.

Park, Bernadette and Reid Hastie. 1987. "Perception of Variability in Category Development: Instance- Versus Abstraction-Based Stereotypes." *Journal of Personality and Social Psychology* 53(4): 621–635.

Park, Chang Sup. 2015. "Pathways to Expressive and Collective Participation: Usage Patterns, Political Efficacy, and Political Participation in Social Networking Sites." *Journal of Broadcasting & Electronic Media* 59(4): 698–716.

Parsons, Bryan M. 2015. "The Social Identity Politics of Peer Networks." *American Politics Research* 43(4): 680–707.

Pelli, Denis G. and Charles Bigelow. 2009. "A Writing Revolution." *Seed Magazine*.

Pennebaker, J. W., C. K. Chung, J. Frazee, *et al.* 2014. "When Small Words Foretell Academic Success: The Case of College Admissions Essays." *PLoS ONE* 9(12): 1–10.

Pennebaker, J. W., R. L. Boyd, K. Jordan, and K. Blackburn. 2015. *The Development and Psychometric Properties of LIWC2015*. University of Texas at Austin.

Perdue, C. W., J. F. Dovidio, and M. B. Gurtman. 1990. "Us and Them: Social Categorization and the Process of Intergroup Bias." *Journal of Personality and Social Psychology* 59(3): 475–486.

Pettigrew, Thomas F. 1998. "Intergroup Contact Theory." *Annual Review of Psychology* 49(1): 65–85.

Pettigrew, Thomas F. and Linda R. Tropp. 2006. "A Meta-Analytic Test of Intergroup Contact Theory." *Journal of Personality and Social Psychology* 90(5): 751–784.

Pettigrew, Thomas F., Linda R. Tropp, Ulrich Wagner, and Oliver Christ. 2011. "Recent Advances in Intergroup Contact Theory." *International Journal of Intercultural Relations* 35(3): 271–280.

Pew Research Center. 2016a. "Partisanship and Political Animosity." Released June 22.

   2016b. "As Election Nears, Voters Divided over Democracy and 'Respect.'" Released October 27.

   2014a. "Political Polarization in the American Public." Released June 12.

   2014b. "Political Polarization and Media Habits." Released October 21.

Poole, Keith T. and Howard Rosenthal. 2001. "D-Nominate after 10 Years: A Comparative Update to Congress: A Political-Economic History of Roll-Call Voting." *Legislative Studies Quarterly* 26(1): 5–29.

   1984. "The Polarization of American Politics." *The Journal of Politics* 46(4): 1061–1079.

Popkin, Samuel L. 1991. *The Reasoning Voter: Communication and Persuasion in Presidential Campaigns*. University of Chicago Press.

Post, Anna. "Avoid Political Pitfalls When Talking, Working and Posting," available at http://emilypost.com/advice/avoid-political-pitfalls/.

Powers, W. 2010. *Hamlet's Blackberry: A Practical Philosophy for Building a Good Life in the Digital Age*. New York: Harper Perennial.

Prior, Markus. 2013. "Media and Political Polarization." *Annual Review of Political Science* 16(1): 101–127.

   2007. *Post-Broadcast Democracy: How Media Choice Increases Inequality in Political Involvement and Polarizes Elections*. Cambridge University Press.

   2003. "Any Good News in Soft News? The Impact of Soft News Preference on Political Knowledge" *Political Communication* 20(2): 149–171.

Prior, Markus, Gaurav Sood, and Kabir Khanna. 2015. "You Cannot Be Serious: The Impact of Accuracy Incentives on Partisan Bias in Reports of Economic Perceptions." *Quarterly Journal of Political Science* 10(4): 489–518.

Prior, Markus and Natalie Jomini Stroud. 2015. "Using Mobilization, Media, and Motivation to Curb Political Polarization," in Nathaniel Persily (ed.), *Solutions to Political Polarization in America*. Cambridge University Press, pp. 178–194.

Quattrone, George A. and Edward E. Jones. 1980. "The Perception of Variability Within In-Groups and Out-Groups: Implications for the Law of Small Numbers." *Journal of Personality and Social Psychology* 38(1): 141–152.

Rainie, Lee. 2012. "Social Media and Voting." Pew Research Center, released November 6.

Rainie, Lee and Aaron Smith. 2012. "Politics on Social Networking Sites." Pew Research Center, released September 4.

Robinson, Robert J., Dacher Keltner, Andrew Ward, and Lee Ross. 1995. "Actual Versus Assumed Differences in Construal: 'Naive Realism' in Intergroup Perception and Conflict." *Journal of Personality and Social Psychology* 68(3): 404–417.

Rogowski, Jon C. and Joseph L. Sutherland. 2016. "How Ideology Fuels Affective Polarization." *Political Behavior* 38(2): 485–508.

Ross, L., Greene, D., and House, P. 1977. "The 'False Consensus Effect': An Egocentric Bias in Social Perception and Attribution Processes." *Journal of Experimental Social Psychology* 13(3): 279–301.

Ross, Lee and Andrew Ward. 1995. "Psychological Barriers to Dispute Resolution." *Advances in Experimental Social Psychology* 27: 255–304.

Rutchick, Abraham M., Joshua M. Smyth, and Sara Konrath. 2009. "Seeing Red (and Blue): Effects of Electoral College Depictions on Political Group Perception." *Analyses of Social Issues and Public Policy* 9(1): 269–282.

Samuelsohn, Darren. 2016. "The Soccer Moms of 2016." *Politico Magazine* (July/ August), www.politico.com/magazine/story/2016/07/2016-election-battleground-swing-states-soccer-moms-nascar-dads-demographics-trump-clinton-214047.

Saunders, Kyle L. and Alan I. Abramowitz. 2004. "Ideological Realignment and Active Partisans in the American Electorate." *American Politics Research* 32(3): 285–309.

Schreiber, Darren. 2007. "Political Cognition as Social Cognition: Are We All Political Sophisticates?" in A. Crigler, M. MacKuen, G. E. Marcus, and W. R. Neuman (eds.), *The Affect Effect: Dynamics of Emotion in Political Thinking and Behavior.* University of Chicago Press.

Schudson, Michael. 1998. *The Good Citizen: A History of American Civic Life.* New York: Free Press.

Sears, David O. and Jonathan L. Freedman. 1967. "Selective Exposure to Information: A Critical Review." *Public Opinion Quarterly* 31(2): 194–213.

Segreti, Giulia. 2016. "Facebook CEO Says Group Will Not Become a Media Company." Reuters (August 29).

Settle, Jaime E. 2018. "Moving Beyond Sentiment Analysis: Social Media and Emotions in Political Communication," in Brooke Foucault-Welles and Sandra Gonzalez Bailon (eds.), *The Oxford Handbook of Networked Communication.* Oxford University Press.

    2012. "Political Competition, Emotions, and Voting: The Moderating Role of Individual Differences." Order No. 3512751, University of California, San Diego, https://proxy.wm.edu/login?url=http://search.proquest.com/docview/1024426440? accountid=15053.

Settle, Jaime E., Robert M. Bond, Lorenzo Coviello, *et al.* 2016. "From Posting to Voting: The Effects of Political Competition on Online Political Engagement." *Political Science Research and Methods* 4(2): 361–378.

Seyle, D. Conor and Matthew L. Newman. 2006. "A House Divided? The Psychology of Red and Blue America." *American Psychologist* 61(6): 571–580.

Shane, Scott. 2017. "From Headline to Photograph, a Fake News Masterpiece." *The New York Times* (January 18).

Sherif, Muzafer and Carolyn W. Sherif. 1953. *Groups in Harmony and Tension: An Integration of Studies of Intergroup Relations.* New York: Harper and Brothers.

Sherif, Muzafer, O. J. Harvey, Jack White, *et al.* 1961. *Intergroup Conflict and Cooperation: The Robbers Cave Experiment.* Norman, OK: University of Oklahoma Book Exchange.

Sherman, David K., Leif D. Nelson, and Lee D. Ross. 2003. "Naïve Realism and Affirmative Action: Adversaries Are More Similar than They Think." *Basic and Applied Social Psychology* 25(4): 275–289.

Sherman, David K., Michael A. Hogg, and Angela T. Maitner. 2009. "Perceived Polarization: Reconciling Ingroup and Intergroup Perceptions under Uncertainty." *Group Processes & Intergroup Relations* 12(1): 95–109.

Shi, Feng, Yongren Shi, Fedor A. Dokshin, *et al.* 2017. "Millions of Online Book Co-Purchases Reveal Partisan Differences in the Consumption of Science." *Nature Human Behaviour* 1(4): 79.

Shin, Youngsoo, Minji Kim, Chaerin Im, and Sang Chul Chong. 2017. "Selfie and Self: The Effect of Selfies on Self-Esteem and Social Sensitivity." *Personality and Individual Differences* 111: 139–145.

Shirky, Clay. 2008. *Here Comes Everybody: The Power of Organizing without Organizations*. New York: Penguin.

Silverman, Craig. 2016. "This Analysis Shows How Viral Fake Election News Stories Outperformed Real News on Facebook." BuzzFeed (November 16).

Sinclair, Betsy. 2012. *The Social Citizen: Peer Networks and Political Behavior*. University of Chicago Press.

Slothuus, Rune and Claes H. De Vreese. 2010. "Political Parties, Motivated Reasoning, and Issue Framing Effects." *The Journal of Politics* 72(3): 630–645.

Smith, Aaron. 2014a. "Cell Phones, Social Media, and Campaign 2014." Pew Research Center (November 3).

2014b. "Six New Facts about Facebook." Pew Research Center's Fact Tank Blog (February 3).

2013. "Civic Engagement in the Digital Age." Pew Research Center, published April 25.

Sokhey, Anand E. and Paul A. Djupe. 2013. "Name Generation in Ego-Centric Network Data: Results from a Series of Experiments." *Social Networks* 36: 147–161.

Standage, Tom. 2013. *Writing on the Wall: Social Media – The First Two Thousand Years*. New York: Bloomsbury.

1998. *The Victorian Internet*. New York: Bloomsbury.

Stanley, Harold. W., William T. Bianco, and Richard G. Niemi. 1986. "Partisanship and Group Support over Time: A Multivariate Analysis." *American Political Science Review* 80(3): 969–976.

Starr, Paul. 2005. *The Creation of the Media: Political Origins of Modern Communications*. Basic Books.

Stewart, James. 2016. "Facebook Has 50 Minutes of Your Time Each Day. It Wants More." *The New York Times* (May 5).

Stinson, Liz. 2016. "Facebook Reactions, the Totally Redesigned Like Button, Is Here." *Wired*, www.wired.com/2016/02/facebook-reactions-totally-redesigned-like-button.

Stonecash, Jeffrey M., Mark D. Brewer, and Mack D. Mariani. 2003. *Diverging Parties: Social Change, Realignment, and Party Polarization*. Boulder, CO: Westview Press.

Stroud, Natalie Jomini. 2011. *Niche News: The Politics of News Choice*. New York: Oxford University Press.

2010. "Polarization and Partisan Selective Exposure." *Journal of Communication* 60(3): 556–576.

2008. "Media Use and Political Predispositions: Revisiting the Concept of Selective Exposure." *Political Behavior* 30(3): 341–366.

Stroud, Natalie Jomini, J. M. Scacco, A. Muddiman, and A. L. Curry. 2015. "Changing Deliberative Norms on News Organizations' Facebook Sites." *Journal of Computer-Mediated Communication* 20(2): 188–203.

Stump, Scott. 2016. "Sheryl Sandberg on Facebook and Fake News: 'We Don't Think It Swayed the Election,'" NBC Today Show (December 8).

Sundar, S. Shyam and Anthony M. Limperos. 2013. "Uses and Grats 2.0: New Gratifications for New Media." *Journal of Broadcasting & Electronic Media* 57(4): 504–525.

Sundquist, James L. 1983. *Dynamics of the Party System*. Washington, DC: Brookings Institute.

Taber, Charles S., Damon Cann, and Simona Kucsova. 2009. "The Motivated Processing of Political Arguments." *Political Behavior* 31(2): 137–155.

Taber, Charles S. and Milton Lodge. 2006. "Motivated Skepticism in the Evaluation of Political Beliefs." *American Journal of Political Science* 50(3): 755–769.

Tajfel, Henri. 1982. "Social Psychology of Intergroup Relations." *Annual Review of Psychology* 33(1): 1–39.

Tajfel, Henri. 1981. *Human Groups and Social Categories: Studies in Social Psychology*. Cambridge University Press.

  1970. "Experiments in Intergroup Discrimination." *Scientific American* 223(5): 96–103.

  1969. "Cognitive Aspects of Prejudice." *Journal of Biosocial Science* 1(S1): 173–191.

  1959. "Quantitative Judgement in Social Perception." *British Journal of Psychology* 50(1): 16–29.

Tajfel, Henri and Alan L. Wilkes. 1963. "Classification and Quantitative Judgement." *British Journal of Psychology* 54(2): 101–114.

Tajfel, Henri and John C. Turner. 1979. "An Integrative Theory of Intergroup Conflict," in W. G. Austin and S. Worchel (eds.), *The Social Psychology of Intergroup Relations*. Monterey, CA: Brooks/Cole, pp. 33–47.

Tajfel, Henri, M. G. Billig, R. P. Bundy, and Claude Flament. 1971. "Social Categorization and Intergroup Behaviour." *European Journal of Social Psychology* 1(2): 149–178.

Tang, Gary and Francis L. F. Lee. 2013. "Facebook Use and Political Participation: The Impact of Exposure to Shared Political Information, Connections with Public Political Actors, and Network Structural Heterogeneity." *Social Science Computer Review* 31(6): 763–773.

Tavernise, Sabrina. 2016. "Young Adolescents as Likely to Die from Suicide as from Traffic Accidents." *The New York Times* (November 3).

Thompson, Dennis F. 2008. "Deliberative Democratic Theory and Empirical Political Science." *Annual Review of Political Science* 11: 497–520.

Thomsen, Danielle M. 2014. "Ideological Moderates Won't Run: How Party Fit Matters for Partisan Polarization in Congress." *The Journal of Politics* 76(3): 786–797.

Thornton, Judd R. 2013. "The Impact of Elite Polarization on Partisan Ambivalence and Indifference." *Political Behavior* 35(2): 409–428.

Tufecki, Zeynup. 2012. "Social Media's Small, Positive Role in Human Relationships." *Atlantic* (April 25).

Turkle, Sherry. 2011. *Alone Together: Why We Expect More from Technology and Less from Ourselves*. New York: Basic Books.

Turner, John C. 1999. "Some Current Issues in Research on Social Identity and Self-Categorization Theories," in Naomi Ellemers, Russell Spears, and Bertjan

Doosje (eds.), *Social Identity: Context, Commitment, Content*. Malden: Blackwell, pp. 6–34.

1981. "The Experimental Social Psychology of Intergroup Behavior," in John C. Turner and Howard Giles (eds.), *Intergroup Behaviour*. Oxford: Blackwell, pp. 66–101.

Turner, John C., Michael A. Hogg, Penelope J. Oakes, *et al.* 1987. *Rediscovering the Social Group: A Self-Categorization Theory*. Oxford and New York: Basil Blackwell.

Tversky, Amos and Daniel Kahneman. 1974. "Judgment under Uncertainty: Heuristics and Biases." *Science* 185(4157): 1124–1131.

Ulbig, Stacy G. and Carolyn L. Funk. 1999. "Conflict Avoidance and Political Participation." *Political Behavior* 21(3): 265–282.

Valenzuela, Sebastián, Yonghwan Kim, and Homero Gil de Zúñiga. 2012. "Social Networks that Matter: Exploring the Role of Political Discussion for Online Political Participation." *International Journal of Public Opinion Research* 24(2): 163–184.

Walsh, Katherine Cramer. 2004. *Talking about Politics: Informal Groups and Social Identity in American Life*. University of Chicago Press.

Weeks, Brian E., Alberto Ardèvol-Abreu, and Homero Gil de Zúñiga. 2017. "Online Influence? Social Media Use, Opinion Leadership, and Political Persuasion." *International Journal of Public Opinion Research* 29(2): 214–239.

Westfall, Jacob, Leaf Van Boven, John R. Chambers, and Charles M. Judd. 2015. "Perceiving Political Polarization in the United States: Party Identity Strength and Attitude Extremity Exacerbate the Perceived Partisan Divide." *Perspectives on Psychological Science* 10(2): 145–158.

Williams, Bruce A. and Michael X. Delli Carpini. 2011. *After Broadcast News: Media Regimes, Democracy and the New Information Environment*. Cambridge University Press.

Wilson, Glenn D., James Ausman, and Thomas R. Mathews. 1973. "Conservatism and Art Preferences." *Journal of Personality and Social Psychology* 25(2): 286–288.

Wojcieszak, Magdalena and Vincent Price. 2009. "What Underlies the False Consensus Effect? How Personal Opinion and Disagreement Affect Perception of Public Opinion." *International Journal of Public Opinion Research* 21(1): 25–46.

Yang, Jung Hwan, Hernando Rojas, Magdalena Wojcieszak, *et al.* 2016. "Why Are "Others" So Polarized? Perceived Political Polarization and Media Use in 10 Countries." *Journal of Computer-Mediated Communication* 21(5): 349–367.

Young, Dannagal. 2006. "Late-Night Comedy and the Salience of the Candidates' Caricatured Traits in the 2000 Election." *Mass Communication & Society* 9(3): 339–366.

Younge, Gary. 2012. "Election 2012: The Return of Culture Wars." *The Guardian*, www.theguardian.com/commentisfree/cifamerica/2012/feb/10/election-2012-return-culture-wars.

Zaller, John. 1992. *The Nature and Origins of Mass Opinion*. Cambridge University Press.

Zschirnt, Simon. 2011. "The Origins & Meaning of Liberal/Conservative Self-Identifications Revisited." *Political Behavior* 33(4): 685–701.

Appendices

The appendix section provides additional information for the studies described in the main text of the book. Appendix A details each of the studies and samples used throughout the book. Appendix B addresses key research design considerations – related to measurement and stimuli selection – that are important for interpreting the results of the studies.

There is considerably more information available in the online appendices. There, the interested reader can find visualizations and details about how the Facebook News Feed operated at the time the book was written. All stimuli and question wording for each of the main studies in the book are also included. Additionally, chapter-by-chapter appendices provide information about the analysis presented throughout the book, including coefficient estimates and model specifications for all regression models and checks. The online appendices are available at www.cambridge.org/Frenemies.

BOOK APPENDICES

Appendix A: Overview of Studies
Appendix B: Measurement Considerations and Research Design

ONLINE APPENDICES

Online Appendix A: The Facebook News Feed Ecosystem
Online Appendix B: Survey Question Wording and Experimental Stimuli
Online Appendix C: Results from Chapters 1–4
Online Appendix D: Results from Chapter 5
Online Appendix E: Results from Chapter 6
Online Appendix F: Results from Chapter 7
Online Appendix G: Results from Chapter 8

Appendix A

Overview of Studies

The main studies in this book are identified in Chapter 1. Here, I include additional details about each study, and then consider the characteristics of the samples used. Information about question wording and experimental stimuli can be found in the online appendices.

Political Discussion Survey

For the purposes of another research project, a survey was fielded by Survey Sampling International (SSI) in early April 2016. The survey was originally contracted for 1,500 respondents, but because of an error on SSI's part in meeting their quotas for a sample that mirrors a nationally representative sample, there were over 3,310 subjects in the sample. The questions that have been used in the analysis in the book are included in online Appendix B. The sample approximates demographic distributions from Census data on gender, age, region, household income, race, and education.

   This study is used in Chapter 1 to demonstrate that there aren't selection effects based on political characteristics structuring who is more likely to have a Facebook account. I included several measures of psychological polarization on this survey that are used in Chapters 7 and 8 to show differences between Facebook users and non-Facebook users on levels of polarization.

END Framework Survey

The respondents to the Political Discussion Survey who indicated that they had Facebook accounts were re-contacted by SSI to answer a second survey about Facebook usage. A total of 1,010 respondents completed the END Framework

Survey between April 13 and 25, 2016. The survey instrument is included in online Appendix B. The sample matches demographic distributions from Census data on gender, age, region, household income, race, and education.

The data from this study appear throughout the book. Descriptive statistics about the incidence and correlates of the independent variables in the book (Facebook usage, political content generation, and exposure to political content on the News Feed) appear in Chapters 1 to 3. Data about respondents' ideological perceptions of media sources appear in Chapter 6. In Chapters 7 and 8, the relationships between various facets of Facebook engagement and psychological polarization are assessed.

Social Connections Battery

One component of the END Framework Survey was a name-generator battery to assess the characteristics and relationships between survey respondents and their three most politically prolific contacts on Facebook. The study was designed to assess people's evaluations of their most politically active social contacts on Facebook. This section of the survey began with a short prompt asking respondents to identify their three social connections on Facebook who generate the most political content. The respondents were first asked to provide a label for each contact "by the nature of your relationship to them, in a way that you will remember who you listed when we ask you more questions about them." The respondents then answered a series of questions about the political behavior of these contacts.

A team of undergraduate research assistants coded the open-ended responses about the nature of the relationship between the respondent and her contacts. Two coders assessed every response; when there was disagreement, I adjudicated between them.

Inference Studies

Status Update Inference Study
The study was fielded on February 18, 2016, to a sample of 150 Mechanical Turk workers. Subjects were randomly assigned to evaluate 10 of 140 stimuli, answering six questions after each. Each stimulus was evaluated by approximately ten subjects. The purpose of this study was to:

(1) test the range of content that subjects would identify as being "about politics" (Chapter 5);
(2) identify the characteristics of individuals most likely to find a wide range of political content (Chapter 5);
(3) test whether people would impute partisanship to the person who posted the content, and how confident people were in their estimations (Chapter 6);
(4) identify the amount of consensus in the perceived partisanship of a poster based on the content (Chapter 6);

(5) assess whether subjects attributed more ideological consistency and extremity to anonymous users whom they perceived were members of the out-party, and how confident people were in their estimations (Chapter 7); and

(6) assess whether subjects were more negative about the knowledge levels of anonymous users whom they perceived were members of the out-party, and how confident people were in their estimations (Chapter 8).

Visual Ledes Inference Study

The study was fielded on March 7, 2016, to a sample of 100 Mechanical Turk workers. Subjects were randomly assigned to evaluate six of thirty-four stimuli, answering six questions after each. Each stimulus was evaluated by approximately fifteen to twenty subjects (there were an unequal number of stimuli assigned to each block). The purpose of this study was to:

(1) test the range of content that subjects would identify as being "about politics" (Chapter 5);

(2) identify the characteristics of individuals most likely to find a wide range of political content (Chapter 5);

(3) test whether people would impute partisanship to the person who posted the content, and how confident people were in their estimations (Chapter 5);

(4) identify the amount of consensus in the perceived partisanship of a poster based on the content (Chapter 5);

(5) assess whether subjects attributed more ideological consistency and extremity to anonymous users whom they perceived were members of the out-party, and how confident people were in their estimations (Chapter 7); and

(6) assess whether subjects were more negative about the knowledge levels of anonymous users whom they perceived were members of the out-party, and how confident people were in their estimations (Chapter 8).

Endorsement and Source Cues

The study was fielded on April 13 and 14, 2016, to a sample of 475 Mechanical Turk workers. Stimuli were selected based on the results of the smaller study (Visual Ledes Study). The key independent variables manipulated in the experiment were (1) the perceived "politicalness" of the stimulus (based on the results from the previous study), (2) the presence or absence of an explicit endorsement of the content, and (3) the presence or absence of a source cue. Subjects were randomly assigned to evaluate six of ninety-six stimuli, answering six questions after each. Each stimulus was evaluated approximately thirty times. The purpose of this study was to:

(1) test whether adding a source cue to content increased the proportion of evaluations that deemed the content to be about politics (Chapter 5);

(2) test whether adding a source cue to News Feed content clarified the signal sent about the political views of the person posting the content (Chapter 6);

(3) assess whether subjects attributed more ideological consistency and extremity to anonymous users whom they perceived were members of the out-party (Chapter 7); and

(4) assess whether subjects were more negative about the knowledge levels of anonymous users whom they perceived were members of the out-party (Chapter 8).

Accuracy Study

The study was fielded in October to November 2016, in advance of the 2016 presidential election. In the first stage of the study, a set of Mechanical Turk workers were asked to write a status update about one of four topics: Black Lives Matter, gun control, Hillary Clinton, or Donald Trump. Some workers were first randomly assigned to read a news article, others were not. Of the examples generated by the Mechanical Turk workers, I picked a set of stimuli that included content (1) written by strong partisans, weak partisans, and independents; (2) written by politically knowledgeable as well as unknowledgeable individuals; (3) written in response to an article and in isolation; and (4) that spanned all four topics. In the second stage of the study, a different sample – a group of students at a small, public university in the Mid-Atlantic region – then evaluated this content in an identical fashion to inference studies described above. The purpose of the study was to:

(1) assess whether Facebook users are able to accurately identify the political views of another Facebook user based solely on a single piece of political content they generate (Chapter 6);

(2) assess whether subjects could recognize politically knowledgeable posters (Chapter 8); and

(3) assess whether subjects would attribute high levels of political knowledge to politically knowledgeable members of the out-party (Chapter 8).

Generation Experiment

The study was fielded in October to November 2016, in advance of the 2016 presidential election. The purpose of the experiment was to test whether receiving social feedback on one's Facebook content reinforces an in-group identity and the estimation of the proportion of one's community that agrees with the views expressed in the Facebook post. The sample was comprised of a group of students at a small, public university in the Mid-Atlantic region.

Subjects were randomly assigned to one of four treatment conditions. The first group was asked to write a status update about their feelings regarding the 2016 presidential candidates. The second group was asked to read a short article and then write a status update in response. Republicans read an article where Donald Trump attacks Hillary Clinton, and Democrats and pure Independents read an article where Hillary Clinton attacked Donald Trump. The third group was exposed to the news article, but not asked to write a status update. The fourth group was a control, and was not asked to do anything before answering the dependent variable questions.

Immediately after exposure to the stimulus, subjects were asked to answer a series of questions about their partisan identity, their perceptions about the number of other subjects and the proportion of Americans who agreed with them, and the distribution of opinion on campus and in the country.

Three to seven days later, subjects came into the lab. Subjects in Treatment Groups 1 and 2 were shown their own words, formatted to look like a status update (if they had only written a status update) or to look like a post accompanying a news lede (if they had read an article). They were randomly assigned into one of two groups: a group that receives high feedback and a group that receives low feedback. After looking at their customized stimulus, they answered the same questions about their identities and the distribution of perceptions. Treatment Group 3 (the subjects who saw an article, but did not write a status update in response) saw the same news articles with high or low levels of aggregated information. The control group was once again just asked the dependent variable questions, in order to establish how much change there was in opinion, absent exposure to any stimuli.

Thanksgiving Study

For the purposes of another research project, we conducted a five-wave cross-sectional survey with two experiments embedded within it on Amazon's Mechanical Turk. The study was fielded in five waves, on five consecutive Monday mornings at the same time of day, in November to December 2014. The results reported here were part of a larger survey containing a battery of questions about respondent demographics, basic political attitudes, their observance of major holidays in the time period, their discussion of politics at these holiday events, and their perceptions of group conflict in the United States.

Data from this survey are analyzed in Chapter 8 to show that Facebook users prefer friendships with co-partisans and perceive that they are more similar.

American National Election Study 2016 Time Series Study (ANES 2016)

As per the information available on the website of the ANES:

In addition to content on electoral participation, voting behavior, and public opinion, the 2016 ANES Time Series Study contains questions in other areas such as media exposure, cognitive style, and values and predispositions. Several items first measured on the 2012 study were asked again including the "Big Five" personality traits using the Ten Item Personality Inventory (TIPI), and skin tone observations made by interviewers in the face-to-face study . . . Data collection for the ANES 2016 Time Series Study began in early September and continued into January, 2017. Pre-election interviews were conducted with study respondents during the two months prior to the 2016 elections and were followed by post-election reinterviewing beginning November 9, 2016. As in 2012, face-to-face interviewing was complemented with data collection on the Internet. Data collection was conducted in the two modes independently, using separate samples but substantially identical questionnaires. Web-administered cases constituted a representative sample separate from the face-to-face.

Data from the 2016 ANES were analyzed in Chapter 8, to show the relationship between measures of Facebook engagement and measures of psychological polarization.

SAMPLE CONSIDERATIONS

Survey Samples

Both of the original surveys, the Political Discussion Survey and the END Framework Survey, use samples of American adults recruited by the survey company Survey Sampling International (SSI). SSI is regularly used for academic studies and recruits individuals to join their panels using opt-in, online recruitment methods. The company then draws from their panelists to create samples that match desired demographic profiles. While these samples are thus non-probability samples, they are more diverse than other kinds of convenience samples. The Political Discussion Survey was intended to mirror the composition of the characteristics of the national population, and the descriptive statistics of the sample are provided later in this appendix.

The END Framework Survey sample was drawn from the sample used for the Political Discussion Survey, based on respondents' answers about whether they had a Facebook account. This second sample was also selected to mirror a nationally representative survey. Although the population of Facebook users is not demographically identical to the American adult population, I chose to mirror a nationally representative sample for two reasons. First, it is difficult to establish the target composition of the Facebook population at any moment in time. For example, while Pew reports data about what percentage of Americans over age 65 have a Facebook account, they do not publish data on what percentage of all American Facebook users are over age 65. Second, the composition of the population of Facebook users has changed dramatically and has become more representative over time. Readers can extrapolate the findings of the study in the future, accounting for whatever selection effects remain in structuring the composition of the Facebook-using population.

Mechanical Turk Samples

Mechanical Turk is a crowdsourcing platform hosted by Amazon. People looking to hire others to complete tasks design what are called Human Intelligence Tasks, or HITs. The platform has become widely adopted in the social sciences (Arceneaux 2012; Berinsky *et al.* 2012; Kriner and Shen 2012; Doherty 2013; Hersh and Schaffner 2013; Huber and Paris 2013; Butler and Powell 2014; Mattes and Redlawsk 2014; Dowling and Wichowsky 2015), where researchers design survey experiments or classification tasks and use the platform for subject recruitment. Mechanical Turk samples are not representative of the adult American population. However, research shows that participants behave in ways similar to the general population (Mullinix *et al.* 2015).

Reliance on Mechanical Turk samples was appropriate given the nature of the studies conducted. By definition, the studies were better suited to be conducted in an online environment, since the tasks were designed to capture the way in which people evaluate and produce content on Facebook. Workers on Mechanical Turk are also incentivized to work quickly, and this replicates the way in which most people use Facebook. When workers were completing the inference tasks, they were providing answers based on their first impressions, analogous to how people process content on the News Feed. When workers were generating content to use as stimuli, they were writing in the way that Facebook users do: rapidly, without editing or proofreading what they've written.

Face-to-Face Samples

The final sample used was that of a student subject pool at a mid-sized public university in the Mid-Atlantic region. This sample faces all of the problems inherent in using "college sophomores" and is obviously unrepresentative of the American population at large.

However, this sacrifice in generalizability was a necessary trade-off for one of the unique advantages of this particular subject pool. Given the size of the university and the number of students in classes in the department, subjects felt connected to each other by the nature of their shared status as students taking courses in the department. Previous studies using this subject pool reveal that the network of subjects is densely connected. Because of the size and characteristics of the university which these students attend, they are very likely to have personal relationships with other people in the subject pool.

This approximation of reality was a key aspect of the research design for this study, where subjects were led to believe that other people were reading the Facebook content they generated and making decisions about how to engage with it. Although this design cannot perfectly replicate the experience of receiving social feedback from one's real network on Facebook, the social ties present among members of the sample enhanced the realism of the study. Although all

TABLE A1 *Demographic Characteristics of the Samples*

	US Census	Political Discussion Study	END Framework Study	Status Update Study	Visual Lede Study	Source Cue Study	Generation Experiment/ Accuracy Study
% Female	50.8%	55%	53.1%	–	–	53.5%	57.6%
% 18–24	9.8%	14.7%	14.6%	–	–	12.1%	–
% 65+	14.9%	8.1%	13.1%	–	–	1.9%	–
High income	37.1%	29.1%	29.5%	–	–	20.3%	80.2%
White	73.6%	66.9%	68.7%	–	–	80.3%	70.5%
College	29.8%	44.9%	44.2%	–	–	55.1%	–
Democrats		50.5%	52.5%	50.7%	44.4%	47.9%	62.5%

1. Census data from the 2015 American Community Survey.
2. High income: $75,000+ in Census, $80,000+ in Internet samples, $90,000+ in student sample.
3. College rate in ACS is among population aged 25+.

TABLE A2 *Overview of the Samples*

Study	N	Unit of Analysis	Study and Sample Description
Political Discussion Study	3,310 subjects	Survey Respondent	Online survey; mirrors a nationally representative sample
END Framework Study (including Social Connections Study)	1,010 subjects	Survey Respondent	Online survey; sample of people who indicated they had a Facebook account; mirrors a nationally representative sample
Status Update Study	150 subjects, 1,500 evaluations	Stimulus Evaluation/ Evaluations Aggregated to Subject Level	Mechanical Turk sample
Visual Lede Study	100 subjects, 600 evaluations	Stimulus Evaluation/ Evaluations Aggregated to Subject Level	Mechanical Turk sample
Source Cue Study	475 subjects, 2,850 evaluations	Stimulus Evaluation/ Evaluations Aggregated to Subject Level	Mechanical Turk sample
Accuracy Study	324 subjects, 3,240 evaluations	Stimulus Evaluation	Student subject pool
Generation Experiment	324 subjects	Subject	Student subject pool

evaluations of generated Facebook content were anonymous, subjects presumably cared about what their fellow students thought about the content they posted.

DESCRIPTIVE STATISTICS

Table A1 provides an overview of the demographic characteristics of the key samples used in the book. Table A2 is a summary of the samples.

Appendix B

Measurement Considerations and Research Design

In this appendix, I explore several of the measurement and research design decisions of the studies presented in the book. Information on the specific question-wording and stimuli used in the studies can be found in the online appendices.

MEASUREMENT CONSIDERATIONS

Unobtrusive Measurement of Independent Variables

Ideally, I would have used an unobtrusively captured measurement of the frequency with which Facebook users access the site, are exposed to political content, and generate political content.

This was infeasible for two main reasons. First and foremost, many institutional review boards have concerns about researchers accessing the Facebook accounts of subjects. The nature of the Facebook platform seamlessly integrates content that the user generates with content that is publicly available with content generated by one's social connections. While the subject can give informed consent for the first two categories of information, she cannot give consent on behalf of the people who posted political content without the knowledge that it would be used by academic researchers unaffiliated with Facebook. This prohibition makes it difficult to collect data from users' accounts in any way that does not anonymize the data as it is gathered.

For this reason, as well as reasons related to the scale of data collection and efficiency of data coding, researchers have turned to automated processes to collect and assess the content associated with a user's account. This can be done maintaining the anonymity of users and their friends. Researchers partnering with Facebook's data scientists can do this quite easily (Bond *et al.* 2012; Settle

2012; Kramer *et al.* 2014; Bakshy *et al.* 2015; Settle *et al.* 2016). Facebook has the capacity to measure the frequency of usage and the frequency of News Feed scrolling, as well as which content is displayed on the News Feed. Absent engagement with content on the feed (clicking it, or providing social feedback), it is difficult to know whether subjects actually read or skimmed the content on the feed. But it is possible to know the pool of content a user could have potentially seen.

Without partnering directly with Facebook, automated processes require explicit consent from the users. Researchers who do not have access to Facebook's data have employed other approaches, including designing their own applications using Facebook's application program interface (API) (Kosinski *et al.* 2013). However, this approach requires sophisticated programming skills, and the data obtained can be incredibly time intensive to process. Thus, the second reason unobtrusive measurement was infeasible is that until standardized automated approaches are developed and more widely adopted for measuring Facebook usage and content engagement, such laborious efforts were beyond the timeline and budget of this project.

Coding Difficulties of Unobtrusive Measurement

Collecting data unobtrusively on users' Facebook behavior is only half the battle (Settle 2018). Once the data are collected, they need to be coded. Hand-coding the content is possible, but it would be time-consuming and again brings up the concerns related to protection of human subjects. My understanding is that this is the approach the ANES is taking to the data they collected from Facebook users' accounts in the 2016 Time Series Study. It is unclear when those data will be released or what they will contain.

Automated techniques can identify the sentiment of Facebook content (Kramer *et al.* 2014), as well as what content is considered political (Settle *et al.* 2016). Others have attempted to measure users' ideology based on their pattern of behavior (Bond and Messing 2015), as well as identify "news" based on the web address (Bakshy *et al.* 2015). It is possible to imagine that eventually we will develop reliable and valid techniques to automatically code political images, memes, and videos as well.

Synthesizing all of this together to develop an automated coding procedure that would reveal what content is politically informative would be a challenging, albeit not impossible, task. However, as the results in Chapter 5 show, it is users' perceptions of content that matters. Thus, any approach that used objective criteria to determine exposure or generation of political content would want to account for variation between individuals in how they perceive content.

Unobtrusive data collection and automated coding of politically informative content remains an important future step in this research agenda.

TABLE B1 *Question Wording for Facebook Usage Variables*

Variable Name	Question Wording
Usage frequency	"How frequently do you spend time on Facebook?" and given a seven-point response set ranging from "a few times a year" to "every day, too many times to count."
News Feed scrolling	Users who indicated that they used the site "most days" or more frequently were then asked, "On a typical day when you use Facebook, how many times a day do you scroll through your News Feed, either on a mobile device (like a phone or tablet) or a computer?" with a four-point response set ranging from "I don't scroll through my News Feed" to "five or more times a day."
Inadvertent exposure	"Think about all the times you access Facebook on your mobile device or computer and scroll through your News Feed. What percent of those times have you seen political news and information, even when you weren't seeking it out?" Subjects were provided a sliding scale from 0 to 100.
Intentional exposure	"Think about all the times you access Facebook on your mobile device or computer and scroll through your News Feed. What percent of those times do you scroll through the News Feed looking specifically for political news and information?" Subjects were provided a sliding scale from 0 to 100.
Content generation	"Think about all the content you interact with on Facebook when you post material yourself, or share, like, or comment on material posted by others. Of all that content, how much of the content that you interact with do you consider to be political?" Users were given six response options, ranging from "none" to "all."

Self-Reported Measurement of Facebook Usage Behavior

As a consequence of the difficulties outlined above, I chose to rely on user self-report to measure the frequency with which people use the site, as well as their engagement with political content. The analysis in this book focuses primarily on five different measures of engagement on Facebook, described in Chapter 3. Table B1 presents the exact wording.

These measures are conceptually distinct, but we anticipate that they will be correlated to one another. For example, users who scroll through their News Feeds more frequently see a larger proportion of all the content their contacts generate than do users who scroll through the feed infrequently. We therefore expect that they should see more political content unintentionally, because the algorithm is showing them content with lower relevancy scores.

The measures are correlated with one another at rates consistent with our theoretical expectations. As a consequence of this, in models assessing the relationship between Facebook engagement and psychological polarization, each variable is typically analyzed in a separate model.

TABLE B2 *Correlations between Facebook Usage Variables*

	Frequency	News Feed Scroll	Inadvertent Exposure	Intentional Exposure	Content Generation
Frequency	1.000	0.623	0.150	0.119	0.115
News Feed scroll	0.623	1.000	0.247	0.166	0.233
Inadvertent exposure	0.150	0.247	1.000	0.490	0.392
Intentional exposure	0.119	0.166	0.490	1.000	0.550
Content generation	0.115	0.233	0.392	0.550	1.000

The END Framework suggests that inadvertent exposure to political content is conceptually distinct from intentional news-seeking behavior. The results presented in the chapters reinforce this finding: the intentional exposure variable is related to the outcome variables in a way very similar to the relationship between political interest and the outcome variables. Inadvertent and intentional exposure are very correlated with one another, as shown in Table B2. However, the distribution of the variables is quite different, as depicted in Figure B1. Approximately one-third of the sample reported that they never intentionally seek political content on the News Feed.

I also included more detailed measures of content generation on the END Framework Survey. These variables assess the extent to which respondents report engaging with eleven different types of political content that circulates on the News Feed (see Tables B3 to B5).

Self-Report Validation: Pew Internet and American Life Project

Because of known problems with self-reported data on behavior, in 2012, the Pew Internet and American Life Project published a report that incorporated both survey measures of Facebook usage and validated usage measures provided by Facebook (Hampton *et al.* 2012). Interested readers are encouraged to consult the report directly, but pertinent findings are included here. Approximately one-third of the respondents in a phone survey agreed to allow Pew and Facebook to match their data from the site from the month-long period (November 2010) when the phone survey was in the field.

The authors report that Facebook users slightly underestimate the number of Facebook friends they have. As for the relationship between self-reported and actual Facebook use, the authors write:

Comparing self-reported survey data to logs of people's actual Facebook activity, we found that survey data is close to actual use. There is a strong positive relationship

TABLE B3 *Distribution of Additional Facebook Content Generation Behavior Variables*

	Min.	Median	Mean	Max.
Content types generated (total)	0	10	8.95	44
Count of content types posted	0	0	1.14	11
Count of content types commented	0	0	1.66	11
Count of content types shared	0	1	2.18	11
Count of content types liked	0	3	3.96	11

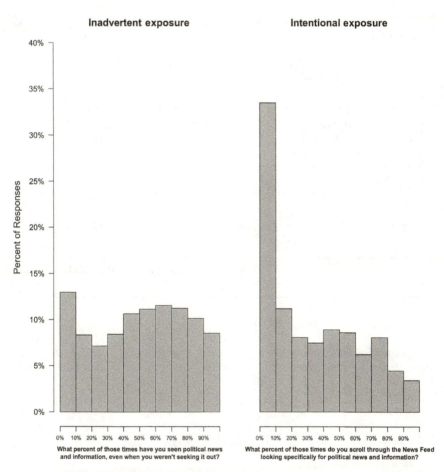

FIGURE B1 Distribution of inadvertent exposure and intentional exposure variables in the END Framework Survey

TABLE B4 *Distribution of Additional Facebook Active Consumption Variables, the Frequency of Content Clicked*

	Rarely/ Never	Occasionally	Frequently	Almost Always
News article about the election, campaign, or politics in general	28.9%	38.8%	23.4%	8.12%
Petition	50.3%	29.6%	13.4%	5.74%
Campaign advertisement	48.7%	29.7%	14.8%	5.64%
Status update (without a link or image)	39.8%	34%	16.7%	8.32%
Political image	36.8%	36.6%	18.7%	6.44%
Political meme	35.9%	33.6%	21.4%	7.92%
Political infographic	42.1%	33.5%	16.8%	6.24%
Video news reports about the election, campaign, or politics in general	33.4%	36.8%	20.4%	8.12%
Video of a candidate speech, press conference, or debate	37%	34.9%	19.6%	7.23%
Humorous or parody videos dealing with political issues	29.4%	34.4%	24.2%	10.79%
Informational videos that explain a political issue	34.7%	35.4%	21%	7.52%

TABLE B5 *Distribution of Additional Facebook Active Consumption Variables, the Frequency of Content Seen*

	Rarely/ Never	Occasionally	Frequently	Almost Always
News article about the election, campaign, or politics in general	15.2%	32.9%	36%	15.25%
Petition	40.4%	38%	15.1%	5.45%
Campaign advertisement	25.3%	37.1%	25.5%	10.89%
Status update (without a link or image)	23.4%	37.2%	26.9%	11.58%
Political image	17.9%	34.8%	34.2%	12.28%
Political meme	22.8%	31%	29.9%	15.45%
Political infographic	29.1%	40.5%	22.4%	6.93%
Video news reports about the election, campaign, or politics in general	22.2%	36.3%	30.5%	9.9%
Video of a candidate speech, press conference, or debate	25.6%	35.1%	28.3%	10%
Humorous or parody videos dealing with political issues	20.6%	32.7%	32.7%	13.17%
Informational videos that explain a political issue	30.4%	39.3%	21.6%	7.52%

TABLE B6 *Proportion of Evaluations Indicating They Would Engage with Facebook Content, by Facebook Usage Frequency*

	Like	Comment	Share
A few times a year	33.3	22.08	16.67
About once or twice a month	25.8	7.63	14.83
About once or twice a week	21.1	11.89	12.39
Most days	23.6	12.06	15.21
Every day, but only once a day	25.6	6.61	7.66
Every day, a few times a day	24.5	11.34	13.73
Every day, too many times a day to count	31.6	15.65	17.68

For example, the bottom row indicates that of all the evaluations made by users who sign on to Facebook multiple times a day, 31.6 percent would have liked the content they saw.

between actual and reported use of the "like" button and for commenting on other users' content. The relationship is slightly more moderate, but still positively correlated for activities that are performed on Facebook less frequently, such as private messaging and status updates or wall posts. Self-report data is generally consistent with actual use, especially for the most popular Facebook activities.

One additional important point is that the least-frequent users of Facebook were the most likely to overstate their usage of the site. It's unclear why this is the case: it could be due to decreased self-awareness of behavior, increased misinterpretation of the survey questions, or social desirability bias (Hampton *et al.* 2012).

If this pattern applies to the survey data analyzed in this book, it should make it harder to detect patterns between Facebook usage frequency and psychological polarization, because the self-report measure of usage frequency will tend to overestimate someone's actual usage of the site and compress the amount of variation between users.

Validating Self-Report Measurement with Study-Based Measurement

There are no direct validation tests in the studies presented in this book between a user's self-reported Facebook usage and their actual Facebook usage. However, the inference studies do permit a test of whether Facebook users who say they more regularly generate political content are more likely to indicate that they would do so (in the form of likes, comments, or shares) in response to the content they see in the study. Because content was randomly assigned to each study participant, there should be no systematic pattern in whether users saw content with which they tended to agree or disagree, or content that on average was more engaging for users.

Consistent with our expectations, Tables B6, B7, and B8 show that there is no relationship between the frequency with which someone uses Facebook and their likelihood of liking, commenting on, or sharing the content they

TABLE B7 *Proportion of Evaluations Indicating They Would Engage with Facebook Content, by Newsfeed Scrolling Frequency*

	Like	Comment	Share
Don't scroll through News Feed	13.8	6.21	4.83
Once a day	24.5	10.28	13.04
2–4 times a day	25.4	12.86	15.21
5+ times a day	31.4	13.31	15.49

For example, the bottom row indicates that of all the evaluations made by users who scroll through the News Feed five or more times a day, 31.4 percent would have liked the content they saw.

TABLE B8 *Proportion of Evaluations Indicating They Would Engage with Facebook Content, by Political Content Generation Frequency*

	Like	Comment	Share
None	13.5	2.87	4.1
Very little	19.6	7.43	8.54
Some	30	14.12	15.66
About half	35.7	20.08	25.89
Most or all	30.7	16.79	22.22

For example, the bottom row indicates that of all the evaluations made by users who report that most or all of their generated content is political, 30.7 percent would have liked the content they saw.

saw in the inference studies. Usage frequency itself does not capture the way in which people use the site, because it is possible that people use other features of the site – such as Messenger, or the group functionalities – that don't provide the same opportunities for content engagement.

There is a relationship between the frequency with which subjects scroll through their News Feeds and how often they engage with content. This makes sense. While it is possible to scroll through the News Feed frequently without engaging with any content, it is uncommon.

Finally, we see an even stronger relationship between the amount of political content respondents say they generate and the rate at which they engaged with content. Users who report that none of the content they generate is political were very unlikely to indicate they would comment or share content, while the opposite is true for high-frequency content generators.

RESEARCH DESIGN CONSIDERATIONS

Here, I provide additional details, rationale, and context for the design decisions in the various studies.

Social Connections Study Name Generator

The design of name generator batteries has been the subject of extensive research in sociology and political science. For a thorough review, see Sokhey and Djupe (2013). In the decades since the landmark work of Huckfeldt and Sprague (1995), most scholars have adopted the same wording. There appears to be very little difference between the classic wording, compared to the slight variant of using an "important matters" prompt (Klofstad *et al.* 2009). Sokhey and Djupe (2014) suggest that the "compound" name generator – one that asks respondents to think about the nature of interaction, topic, and role attributes – provides a valid sample of political networks.

The name generator prompt used in the END Framework Study was:

Think about all the people with whom you are, or have been, connected as friends on Facebook. Now think specifically about the three people who generate (post, share, like or comment) political content most frequently. These may or may not be people with whom you have a relationship outside of Facebook, but rather are the people who seem the most politically engaged on Facebook.

I endeavored to address all three components of the typical compound generator used in political science: the nature of the interaction (Facebook friends), the topic (political content), and the role (connections who are most politically engaged). The goal of this name generator was not to identify those individuals with whom a subject had the most interaction, but rather those individuals who generated the most content.

Second, respondents were asked to identify these individuals in a very particular way:

Please identify them by the nature of your relationship to them, in a way that you will remember who you listed when we ask you more questions about them.

This decision was made for two reasons. First, I was very interested in ascertaining the strength of the relationship that a respondent had with her contact, but I did not want to prime users by asking them to provide a subjective assessment of the strength of the relationship. Future research should further explore this dimension. Second, users have a wide variety of "real-world" relationships with their Facebook friends, ranging from individuals they've never met or only know through friends, to their family and closest friends. A closed-list response set from which subjects could identify the nature of their relationship would have either been exceptionally long or unnecessarily exclusive.

At present, I am unaware of any other studies that use a name generator technique to assess Facebook interaction patterns, although several have asked social media users to identify contacts by the nature of their relationship and then assessed interaction patterns (Jones *et al.* 2013).

Data Quality

Each of the 1,010 respondents in the END Framework Survey were asked to make evaluations about three of their Facebook contacts, so there are 3,030 potential dyads to evaluate. A non-trivial number of evaluations (493) left the name field blank. Although these respondents did not identify their contact with a name or descriptor, most of them filled out the six key questions about the contact. Overall, there are between 152 and 177 missing values for each of the key questions. Most of these accompany dyads for which the respondent left the name blank, indicating that the respondent just skipped this section of the survey.

Coding Process

In the fall of 2016, I had a team of seven student research assistants code the data. Two assistants coded every dyad, and in cases where the students disagreed, I made the final decision. While neither the students nor I were blind to the hypotheses of the study, we coded the data in a separate file from the dataset, including the respondents' evaluations of their contacts. Additional details about the coding process are available upon request.

A substantial portion of the responses did not comply with the instructions and described the contact in a way that made it impossible to evaluate the nature of the relationship (see Table B9). These dyads were excluded from the analysis. The distribution of the dyads is shown in Chapter 5.

Stimulus Creation for Inference Studies

The challenge in designing stimuli for the inference and accuracy studies was to identify examples that were representative of the kind of content that circulates on the News Feed absent any knowledge about the properties of the population of content that I was trying to emulate.

Previous research using experiments to test the consequences of exposure to media have been able to make a clear argument that the stimuli they use is reflective of the kind of content that typically circulates on their medium of choice. For example, Arceneaux and Johnson (2013) explain the methodical approach they used to select news segments for their studies on the effects of cable news exposure. Classic media effects studies typically systematically select stimuli from a known pool of available content.

The situation is considerably more complex when thinking about how to choose stimuli that are reflective of the kind of information that circulates on the News Feed. First and foremost, every user's News Feed is personally customized, so there is no universal set of content which could be sampled. Relatedly, there is no census of third-party "content producers" on Facebook that could be sampled or selected from in a deliberate and representative manner.

TABLE B9 *Coding Scheme for Social Connections Battery*

	Tie Code	Problem Type
Strong Ties		
Family		
Spouse or partner	1	
Parent or siblings	2	
In-law	3	
Child or grandchild	4	
Other relative	5	
Close friend	6	
Weak Ties		
Co-worker	7	
Acquaintance	8	
Past friend/acquaintance	9	
Neighbor	10	
Employer/employee	11	
Used word "friend"	12	
Unidentifiable		
First or last name		101
Initials		102
Number		103
Adjective		104
Blank		105
Incoherent		106
"None," "None of the Above," N/A		107
Not disclosing/not saying		108
Celebrity or political persona		109

I leave systematic consideration of which characteristics of content are most potentially polarizing to future work, and here, include as diverse a set of content as possible. The effects shown in the inference studies therefore represent an average across all stimuli in a given category. Detection of these average effects is only a first step, and there are almost certainly heterogeneous effects based on characteristics of the content that are not theorized here. Future work should strive to typologize and differentiate Facebook politically informative content to better understand which kinds of content tend to have the largest effects.

Status Update Study

To assess the kind of written text that people judge to be political, I selected from content that is structurally similar to status updates, but is much more readily available: tweets from Twitter. I gathered ten publicly available tweets on each of fourteen different topics (see online Appendix B, Table 5.1), posted in early 2016. Seven of these topics were hypothesized to be explicitly political, using keywords associated with key policy debates. Seven were not explicitly tied to a contemporary political debate, but potentially carried a political signal based on findings from pilot data, media characterizations, or previous research (Moreton 2009). The tweets were selected quasi randomly, selecting the first ten intelligible tweets returned from a query to Twitter's API.

The choice to use the low bar of "intelligibility" was intentional. Most people do not carefully proofread their status updates, and many users post them from their phones, leading to a high rate of typos and non-standard punctuation. I wanted to replicate the features of content that actually circulates on Facebook as closely as possible. As a result, however, some of the stimuli are quite brief and decontextualized, presumably making it difficult for other social media users to draw inference. Given the context in which people encounter News Feed content organically, this choice seemed appropriate.

On the nights of January 31, 2016 and February 4, 2016, the tweets were collected using the Twitter REST API's search function. While Twitter does not specify exactly how their search tool works, their documentation states "Twitter filters search results for quality Tweets and accounts." A Python script was written to utilize the API to save the tweets as a text file. The tweets were unfiltered, with the exception of removing any tweets that contained any links (initial testing showed that including links produced a significant amount of spam). Additionally, after collection, tweets that were either not in English, or extremely similar in content to a previously collected tweet, were removed.

Using Adobe Photoshop, I then formatted these tweets to appear as though they were status updates, blurring out any aspects of the message that in a real status update would reveal the poster's identity. All formatting aspects of the status updates were identical. Figure 5.5 in Chapter 5 depicts an example, and the full set of tweets can be found in online Appendix B.

Memes, Cartoons, and Visual Ledes Inference Study

I scoured the Facebook pages of a variety of different media and other sources to identify news stories or memes that had been disseminated on Facebook in the weeks before the study launched. The full set of stimuli are available in online Appendix B, but in brief, they can be categorized into one of three types. First, *political memes and cartoons* are visual depictions of political humor. Example topics include taxes, government regulation, economic policies, environmental policies, and voter identification laws. Second, *politicized or policy news* stimuli are visual Facebook ledes for news stories pertaining to politically relevant news, such as immigration, gas prices, and health-care policies. Finally, *culture news* stimuli are visual Facebook ledes for news stories that do not explicitly pertain to politics. Example topics include arts and culture events. All the stimuli were edited in Adobe Photoshop to remove any identifying information about the original source or the person who posted it.

Accuracy Study

Although political interaction on Facebook increases in the months leading up to an election (Settle *et al.* 2016), most of the time the interactions that users have with one another that are politically relevant are not about candidates. Thus, I included four news articles in this study: two about the 2016 presidential candidates, one about a perennially salient policy debate (gun control), and one about a topic that had been in the news frequently in 2016 (the Black Lives Matter movement). Half of subjects read an article and wrote a status update in response to it; the other half wrote a status update without reading an article. The resulting eight prompts therefore led to a variety of generated content, reflecting a mix of status updates and content posted with expression cues.

Generation Experiment

Because this study was fielded in conjunction with the evaluations made of the content created in the Accuracy Study, I used the same two candidate prompts. This way, after subjects generated their own status updates about the presidential candidates, they were evaluating content that could plausibly have been written by other subjects in the same study.

Question Ordering in Inference Studies

Respondents evaluated between six and ten stimuli in each study. After every stimulus, they were asked, "Sometimes our first impressions of people are quite accurate. We are interested in your first impressions of the person who posted the following status update on Facebook." Below the image appeared a series of six questions: whether the post was about politics, to identify the knowledge level of the poster, the partisanship, the poster's ideological position on five issues, the respondent's confidence in their estimates, and whether the respondent would engage with the content if posted by one of their friends on Facebook.

The ordering of the questions intentionally put the knowledge judgment question first and the partisanship inference question later. The judgment question therefore assesses the subjects' instincts before being primed to think about partisan identity. This is premised on the idea that people become aware of their intuition of a poster's partisanship based on the content of the stimulus. Thus, the knowledge judgment reflects their recognition of the poster as a member of the in-group or out-group, but the subject has not yet been asked to think intentionally about this recognition.

Historical Availability of Survey Measures

As noted in Chapter 8, the studies presented in this book do not demonstrate that, over time, individuals who use social media more frequently have become more psychologically polarized.

What would the critical test be to demonstrate this? Randomly assigning people to use Facebook could give us the best leverage for causal inference, but given the high penetrance of Facebook in our society at present, it is difficult to locate individuals who would be willing to participate in a randomized, controlled trial of Facebook use. Short of this, well-designed observational study could also give us some leverage.

Ideally, in 2003 (before the creation of Facebook), we would have begun a panel study of Americans' use of media, following the same set of individuals over a fifteen-year period to observe what happened as they created Facebook accounts – at various points in time – and began to integrate Facebook into their daily lives. Given the evolution of the functionalities of the Facebook site, such as the introduction of the News Feed, we could track precisely when and how regularly they utilize particular features. In addition to precisely measuring their social media habits, we would also measure their exposure to the other factors known to be polarizing, such as exposure to cable news, campaign advertising, and face-to-face discussions. We would have had the foresight to intensely study measures of affective polarization of our attitudes of our fellow citizens, not just opinion polarization or attitudes toward elites or the parties. And because this is an idealistic vision, let's assume that Facebook was willing to work with academic researchers and match data from the company's servers to the participants in our study.

Of course, in 2003, it was impossible to predict the emergence and growth of the Facebook site. Even as late as 2007 or 2008, it might have been difficult to forecast how the changes to the functionalities of Facebook would make it so conducive to polarizing political communication. Similarly, the concept of affective polarization had not yet been widely recognized. According to Google Trends, the first reported usage of the term "affective polarization" was not until March 2008; the concept wasn't officially introduced into the political science literature until 2010 (Iyengar *et al.* 2012). Isolated scholars were cognizant of the concept, but the phenomenon hadn't been systematically studied or discussed. The cost and logistical complications of panel studies would have been challenges even if someone had been prescient enough to forecast a relationship between social media use and polarization. And while Facebook was initially quite receptive to academic partnerships, it has retreated from that position considerably since the company went public.

Absent a panel study with validated Facebook data, cross-sectional surveys conducted at regular intervals could be analyzed to assess whether Facebook usage has become associated with psychological polarization over time. Because of the rapid growth of the Facebook user base, as well as the rapid evolution of the site itself, it is not necessarily clear that using Facebook should have had a polarizing effect on individuals in its early days, before the creation of the News Feed, before the adoption of politicians and media to the site, and before the proliferation of sites dedicated solely to creating content to circulate on social media. Presumably, at some point after the introduction of the News Feed in September 2006 and the "like" button in February 2009, the norms of the site crystallized sufficiently that the dynamics described in this book could have begun to impact the attitudes that Americans hold about each other.

Questions collected on one of the well-established, long-running cross-sectional surveys – such as the American National Election Study, the General Social Survey, or the Cooperative Congressional Election Study – that asked both about general social media usage and questions related to polarization, could establish the strength of the relationship between social media usage and psychological polarization over time. The plethora of political variables available in the ANES could also help rule out confounding factors that might explain a statistically significant relationship between the variables.

Unfortunately, the datasets from the years 2009 to 2015 didn't ask the kinds of questions we would need to make these inferences. The questions measuring aspects of psychological polarization are inconsistent across time and survey sponsor, and do not capture Americans' attitudes about each other, only about the abstract notions of the parties. Furthermore, while not all of these surveys include questions about social media, the surveys that do only ask about explicitly political social media behaviors – like following a candidate's page or encouraging other people to vote – not the general usage patterns that the evidence in this book suggests should be relevant for the majority of Facebook users.

The Pew Research Center's Internet and American Life Project, referenced throughout this book, provides an invaluable source of data for snapshots about changing social media behavior over time. While they provide excellent data for assessing the explanatory variable, we are missing data about what we hope to explain: psychological polarization. Other Pew projects have measured facets of polarization – such as polarized media usage, ideological extremity, or the growth in values differences – but these surveys were conducted on a different set of respondents than were the surveys assessing social media behavior.

Index

Index

abortion, 170, 174, 180, 288

abstraction-based stereotyping, 80, 165–166, 170

accentuation principle, 162, 164

Accuracy Study, 17, 190, 207, 287–288
  analysis of, 207
  data generation for, 307
  introduction of, 17
  sample used for, 291
  subject participation in, 190

active exposure, 115

affective polarization, 5, 7, 77–78, 86, 89–90, 148, 164, 197, 217, 227–228, 232–233
  behavioral consequences of, 233
  definition of, 5, 78
  elite cues and, 90
  END interactions facilitating, 77
  evidence for in ANES data, 228
  measurement of, 86, 232
  previous evidence for, 6
  recognition of political identity and, 148
  social identity theory and, 164, 197, 217
  social networks and, 89

affordances, 8–10, 15, 19, 21, 23–25, 29, 50, 56, 61, 69, 80, 97, 237–239, 243–244, 247–255
  active perspective taking and, 255
  changes to, 19, 24, 243–244, 246–254
  convergence of on Facebook, 9–10, 15, 21, 25, 29, 50, 56, 69, 97
  definition of, 8, 23
  mapping to outcomes, 237–239
  news production and, 61

social distancing behaviors and, 80

aggregated information, 41–42, 186, 289

Ahler, Douglas J., 169

Allport, Gordon, 211

Amazon's Mechanical Turk, 54, 151, 288, 291

American National Election Study 1997 pilot study, 169

American National Election Study (ANES), 6, 85, 163, 226–227, 289–290, 296, 307

American Trends Panel 2014, 184

anchoring effects, 186

Anspach, Nicolas, 40, 64, 190

apolitical content, 126

Arab Spring, 236

Arceneaux, Vin, xv, 13, 64, 91, 94, 224

asynchronicity, 25

authoritarianism, 81

Barbera, Pablo, 234, 242

Berelson, Bernard R., 85

biased reasoning, 63

Black Lives Matter, 151, 288, 307

broadcast news, 20, 24, 59, 64, 244

bumper stickers, 58, 195

by-product learning, 64

cable news, 7, 13–14, 62, 91, 94, 119, 166, 224, 228

Campbell, Angus, 85

captive audience, 59, 64

Carlson, Taylor, 250

categorization, 94–98

category-based expectancies, 166